Welcome to our neighborhood..

As a residential builder or developer, you will find in this catalogue the answers to many of the m lems you may face in the day-to-day business of new home development.

This **Special Edition** will serve as an introduction to Nelson Design Group, LLC, Residential Planners - Designers, a national full-service design firm that specializes in an uncompromising commitment to total customer service, regardless of the size of the client.

At NDG, it's not just a home...It's a neighborhood. We don't just sell home plans - we sell beautifully functional neighborhoods, a lifestyle, a theme for living spaces. We offer marketing expertise and materials to make your planned community from concept to a 'brick and mortar' reality.

We are a nationally known design firm with plans published by *Garlinghouse, Home Design Alternatives, Builder Magazine, Home Planners, Better Homes & Gardens*, and many more. During our move into the national marketplace in the 1990's, it quickly became apparent that residential builders and developers were not receiving the type of prompt service routinely offered by NDG, nor were they being offered the marketing materials necessary to successfully sell their homes during the raw construction stages - a sales period absolutely crucial to the builder's success.

Filling the void in customer service is top priority for NDG. Serving our customers and providing prompt answers to your questions - is just routine business for us. This commitment is not just empty words; we have numerous customers who will testify to our continued response to critical issues and our old-style Southern hospitality.

Our more than 15 years of experience in both the residential design and real estate markets have allowed us to see the need for professional marketing materials and services to be readily available and affordable for builders and developers. We offer a complete marketing package of materials for presentation in model homes including full color feature sheets, matted color renderings and other items for display.

The lack of diversity in planned community designs has allowed us to bring fresh and exciting ideas into developments around the country. NDG's community designs incorporate a neighborhood continuity and ease of lifestyle that is in such great demand among today's homebuyer.

In the pages of this catalogue you will find home collections that are designed to become warm and inviting, yet remarkably functional. And all of our plans can be easily and inexpensively modified to meet your customers' individual needs. The satisfaction of living in a Nelson Design Group home - a home that was built under your company name - will translate into a goodwill message from your homebuyer to others that no amount of money could ever produce.

We believe that, in Nelson Design Group, you have found not only a source for all of your home plan needs, but also a partner upon whom you can fully rely.

With Nelson Design Group, it's not just a home...It's a neighborhood.

Best Regards,

Michael E. Nelson
President

About Our Plans

Our goal is to provide our clients with a design that perpetuates a constant feeling of pride. Each home owner should step into their dream home each day knowing they made the best possible decision, not only with their home design, but with their surroundings. Our experienced staff offers creativity and efficiency, and can modify any of our plans to suit your needs, saving time and guaranteeing customer satisfaction.

Table of Contents

Charted Neighborhoods
page 6

Nelson Design Group Collections
page 10

Nelson Design Group Stock Plans
page 145

Marketing Your Home
page 274

Tru-Cost Estimating
page 278

About Our Plans
page 282

Order Form
page 285

Products
page 287

Nelson Design Group Collections

Village at WINDSTONE

Windstone Collection I
page 10

Windstone Collection II
page 21

Windstone Collection III
page 33

page 58

page 93

page 106

The Urban Collection
page 44

page 73

page 118

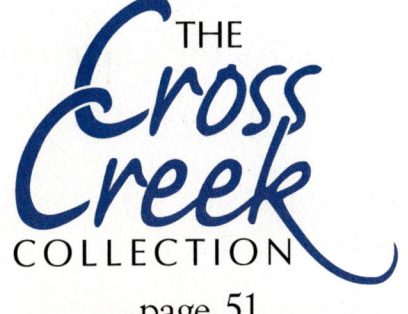

page 51

page 86

page 134

"Solutions for Master Planned Communities"
Planning - Design - Marketing

A "Charted Neighborhood" is Nelson Design Group's approach for design *"plus"* marketing services making your job easier when developing "Master Planned Communities". As the name implies, a Charted Neighborhood represents a distinctive new direction and concept in residential design and marketing – an approach that is unique to Nelson Design Group.

To view plans visit www.84lumber.com/ndgplans - 800.359.8484

*T*oday, a public awakening now highly values its heritage of great neighborhoods. Updated interiors of the homes many of us grew up in are now incorporated into Neo-Traditional, or Traditional Neighborhood Design. Hence, the pursuit of the American Dream has taken an indirect path, away from suburban sprawl and back to a renewed appreciation of development patterns of our predecessors. Some of these planning and design principals date back to the late 1800's.

*I*n more recent years, New Urbanism has caused a revival among historic towns, cities and villages, where the home-buying public want more than just a place to sleep after work. A new appreciation for a richer social and civic life is integral to today's Master Planned Communities, in which families can get to know their neighbors by relaxing on spacious front porches and walking along tree covered streets and sidewalks.

*T*o supply to the demand of Traditional Neighborhood Designs and Neighborhoods, today's building professional is looking for a design firm that can be much more than just a vendor of stock plans. Until now, builders and developers have indicated that a true "total resource" for planning, design, cost-analysis and value-added marketing services, is almost unheard of. Most builders need a home plan source that essentially functions as his very own "in-house, one-stop source" for new home design and associated services. Nelson Design Group is a firm that concentrates on true personal service, and one that will modify plans as necessary, always delivering much more.

To view plans visit www.84lumber.com/ndgplans - 800.359.8484

No longer will you need different firms to provide plans or modifications, and still be on your own to market the project afterwards. Regardless of your Company's size and volume, whether builder or developer, we want to be your "personal design and promotional partner." We are happy to consult with you on individual plans or small in-fill projects, and yet we are large enough to work with you on the design of new large-scale Charted Neighborhood communities. Quite simply, we do it all - always with a personal touch and at a reasonable fee.

Because builders and developers across the country already rely on us to provide their plans and marketing resources, we cater daily to a diverse marketplace with a broad mix of consumers, real estate professionals and home builders. We know what buyers want, how builders 'build,' and how to design and market homes that sell quickly.

Each Nelson Design Group plan offers stunning elevations and fresh interior floor plans with unique features such as kids nooks, hearth rooms, and grilling porches to attract homeowner interests and promote a carefree lifestyle. Our designs are supported with our wide array of economical customized marketing materials to promote your project during construction, and then facilitate a quick sale-often at premium appraisal values.

To view plans visit www.84lumber.com/ndgplans - 800.359.8484

*I*n the following pages, you will find individual designs and also several different groups of plans such as our new *Wellington, Renaissance and Florida Collections*. Our designs have complementary themes that work together to build a single home, a neighborhood, or a full-scale development. There is almost certainly something you can immediately incorporate into your building program.

*W*hen online, point your browser to our comprehensive website, nelsondesigngroup.com. Our site features a handy "search" option where you can select from hundreds of plans to simplify locating designs that accommodate your lot dimensions and preferred architectural style. Give us a call or send us an E-mail. Above all, please let us know if you have any questions or special requirements. We are always interested in hearing about your projects and how we might serve you now, and in the future.

*A*s we say, "Welcome to our Neighborhood." On behalf of Michael E. Nelson and our entire staff of friendly designers, marketing specialists, cost-analysts and customer service team, we are pleased to introduce Nelson Design Group, LLC, America's fastest growing design, planning, and marketing firm.

To view plans visit www.84lumber.com/ndgplans - 800.359.8484

Village at WINDSTONE

When you choose a Nelson Design Group collection, you not only create beautiful homes, you achieve ideal master planned communities. The Village at Windstone Collection features living spaces of 1,800 to 2,800 square feet replicating historical Southern style designs. Each of these plans complement the other, resulting in an effective Traditional Neighborhood Design theme — making development easy for you. All plans are designed to fit lots of 50 feet to 80 feet. Nelson Design Group also offers complementary collections with the same traditional appeal and quality as our Village at Windstone Collection.

Nelson Design Group LLC

RESIDENTIAL PLANNERS · DESIGNERS

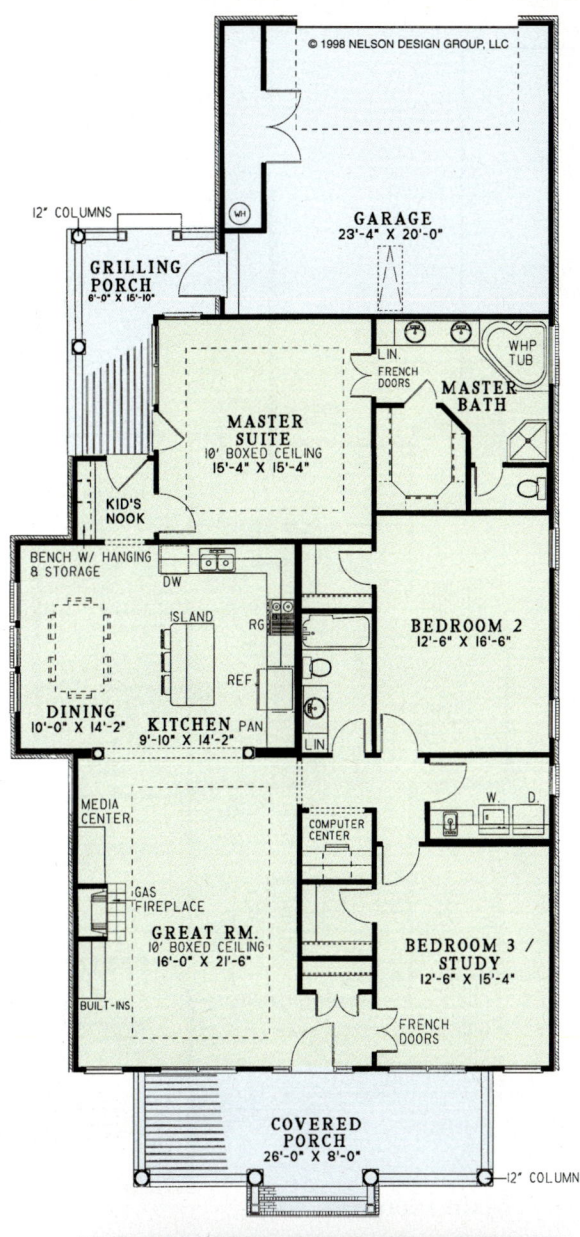

Check This Plan Mike

312 Windstone Place

Windstone Collection I

A beautifully-designed eight foot covered porch with 12 inch columns is just one of the elements that makes this Nelson Design Group home such a treasure. Southern charm surrounds the formal foyer leading to an impressive great room with gas fireplace and built-in shelves and media center. Beyond the great room is the kitchen and dining area. Enjoy hours of privacy in your secluded master suite with access to a rear covered grilling porch. The porch also leads to the dining and kitchen areas, providing hours of hassle-free entertainment.

Width:	39'	Main Ceiling:	9 ft.
Depth:	81'	Bedrooms:	3
Total Living:	1,832 sq. ft.	Baths:	2
Price Tier:	B	Foundation:	Crawl, Slab

To view similar plans visit www.84lumber.com/ndgplans - 800.359.8484

321 Windstone Place
Windstone Collection I

An eight foot wrap-around entry porch with classic southern columns allows you to enjoy an exquisite view from every direction of this Nelson Design Group home. Take advantage of hours of quality family time in a marvelous great room with an open stairway leading to the upper level. A double bedroom area with connecting full bath is ideal for kids of all ages. A bright breakfast area with access to a spacious kitchen and rear grilling porch conveniently provides entertaining and relaxing family dinners. Traveling to the upper level, find a huge bonus area for use as a game room or even another private suite.

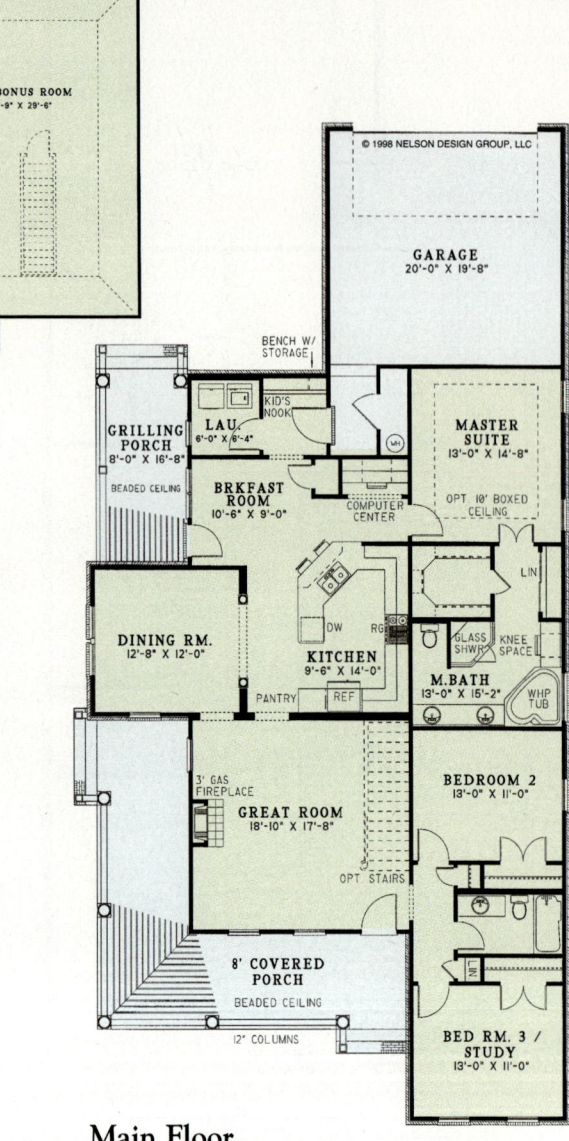

Upper Floor

Main Floor

Width: 41' 4"
Depth: 83' 8"
Total Living: 1,825 sq. ft.*
*Optional Bonus: 1,191 sq. ft.
Price Tier: B

Main Ceiling: 9 ft.
Bedrooms: 3
Baths: 2
Foundation: Crawl, Slab, Opt. Basement, Opt. Daylight Basement

To view similar plans visit www.84lumber.com/ndgplans - 800.359.8484

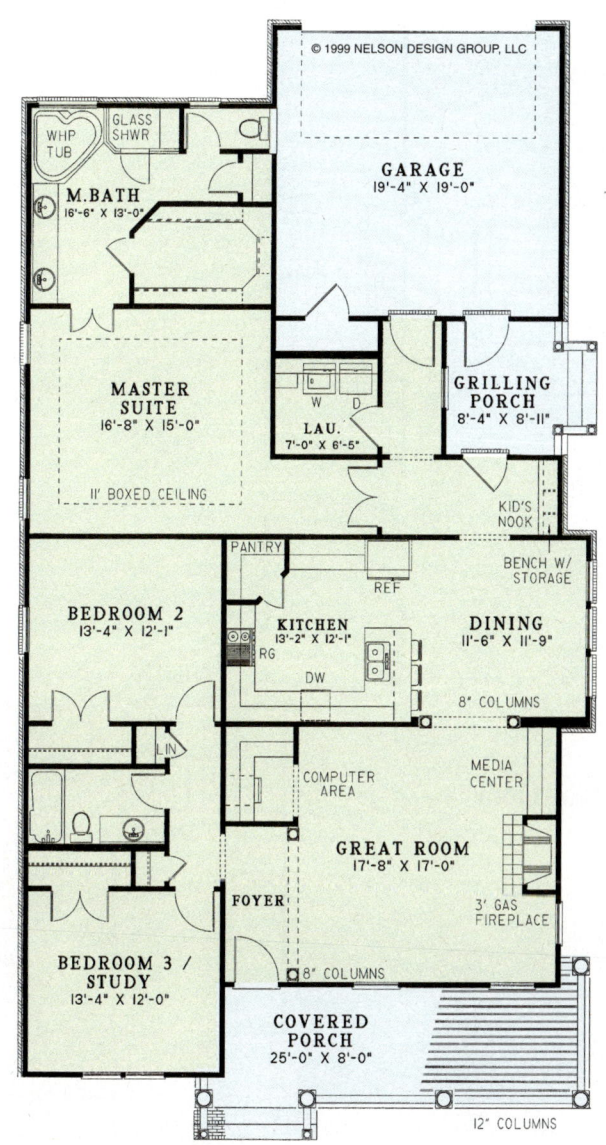

317 Windstone Place
Windstone Collection I

This master-planned Nelson Design Group home is designed to capture the classic style and splendor of historical Southern architecture. Let summer days slip away on a traditional eight foot covered front porch. An elegant foyer leads directly to a marvelous great room complete with a built-in media center, computer nook and efficient gas fireplace. Pass through remarkable wooden columns into a formal dining area — perfect for elegant dinner parties and conveniently located with fluid access to the kitchen. Invite friends over for a cookout using the side covered grilling porch. Intricate french doors lead to a grand master suite and adjoining full master bath with all the amenities you've come to expect.

Width: 39'
Depth: 72'
Total Living: 1,915 sq. ft,
Main Ceiling: 10 ft.
Price Tier: B

Bedrooms: 3
Baths: 2
Foundation: Crawl, Slab

316 Windstone Place

Windstone Collection I

Forget the fast-paced hustle and bustle and embrace quiet times of yesterday when you enjoy the view from a spacious covered front porch on a warm spring day in this Nelson Design Group home. An extraordinary great room with gas fireplace, accented with open stairs leading to the upper floor, will certainly provide countless hours of entertainment for the entire family. Attached to the great room is a formal dining area – perfect for elegant dinner parties and enhanced by beautifully-crafted wood columns. Past the stairway, and accessible only through privacy french doors, is the master suite and bath. The upper floor is a perfect haven for children of all ages, complete with a built-in computer desk and balcony.

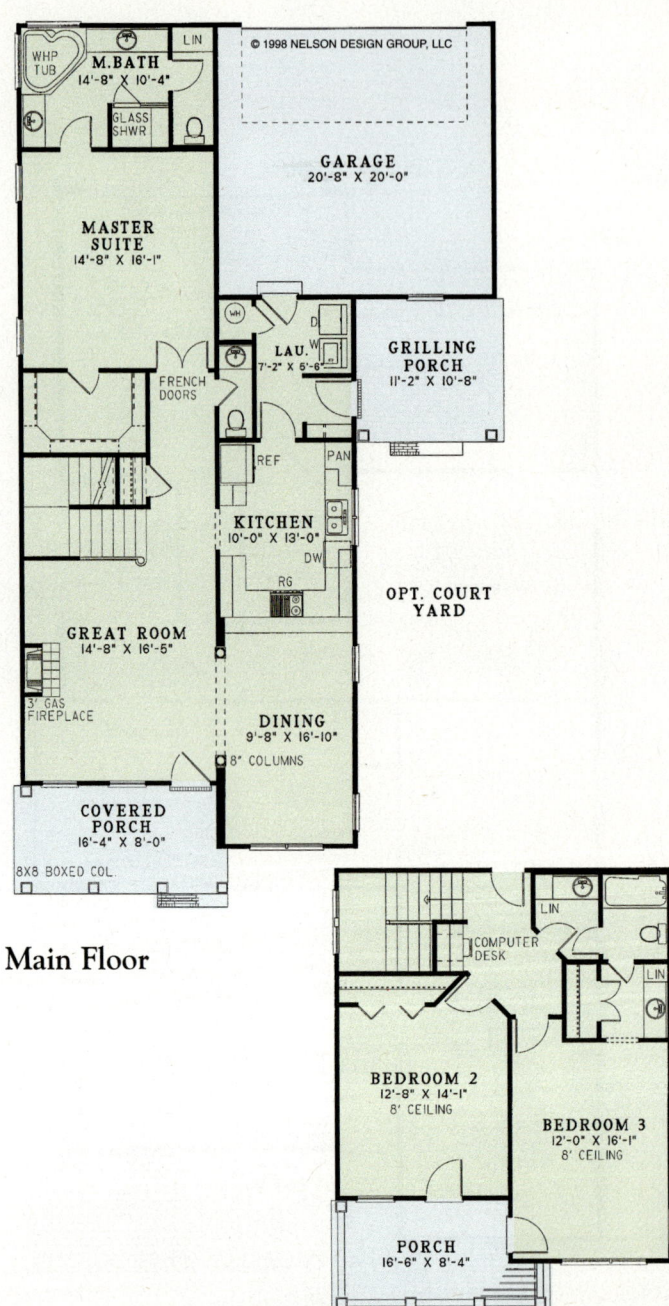

Main Floor

Upper Floor

Width: 36' 4"	Main Ceiling: 9 ft.
Depth: 64' 10"	Upper Ceiling: 8 ft.
Main Floor: 1,298 sq. ft.	Bedrooms: 3
Upper Floor: 624 sq. ft.	Baths: 2 1/2
Total Living: 1,922 sq. ft.	Foundation: Crawl, Slab, Opt. Basement, Opt. Daylight Basement
Price Tier: B	

To view similar plans visit www.84lumber.com/ndgplans - 800.359.8484

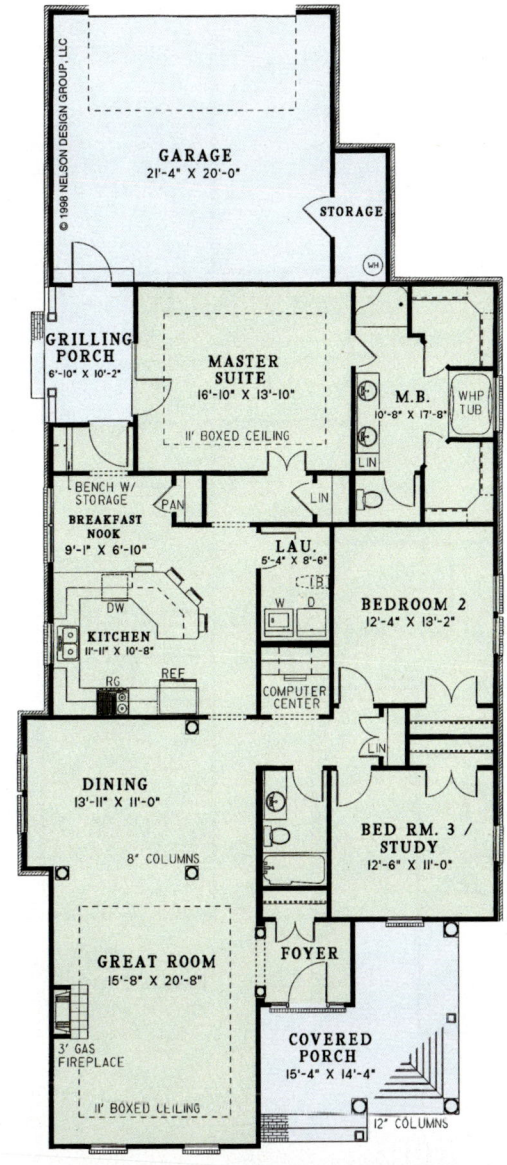

314 Windstone Place
Windstone Collection I

Step back in time as you journey onto the eight foot covered porch of this Nelson Design Group home. Historical southern style accents the traditional foyer as you enter the large great room accented by an eleven foot boxed ceiling and dining area divided by majestic eight inch wooden columns. Off the dining area, you'll find a bright kitchen area with breakfast nook— perfect for lazy Sunday mornings and an eat-in bar perfect for weekday meals on the run. A rear grilling porch with access to the master suite and kitchen makes entertaining a breeze.

Width: 36' 8"	Bedrooms: 3
Depth: 85'	Baths: 2
Total Living: 1,934 sq. ft.	Foundation: Crawl, Slab
Main Ceiling: 10 ft.	
Price Tier: B	

To view similar plans visit www.84lumber.com/ndgplans - 800.359.8484

310 Windstone Place
Windstone Collection I

Reminiscent of traditional Southern Charleston style, this Nelson Design Group home takes you to a time when conversation with friends and neighbors on your covered front porch was all that mattered. Time stands still as you enter from the porch into the formal foyer leading you to a spacious great room — perfect for entertaining and relaxing. Delight your friends with an evening cookout on your covered grilling porch located just off the kitchen and dining area. A secluded master suite and master bath, complete with whirlpool tub, will offer plenty of privacy. As you travel to the upper floor, you'll find a full bath and three spacious bedrooms or convert one to a game room for the kids. An eight foot balcony beautifully completes this home.

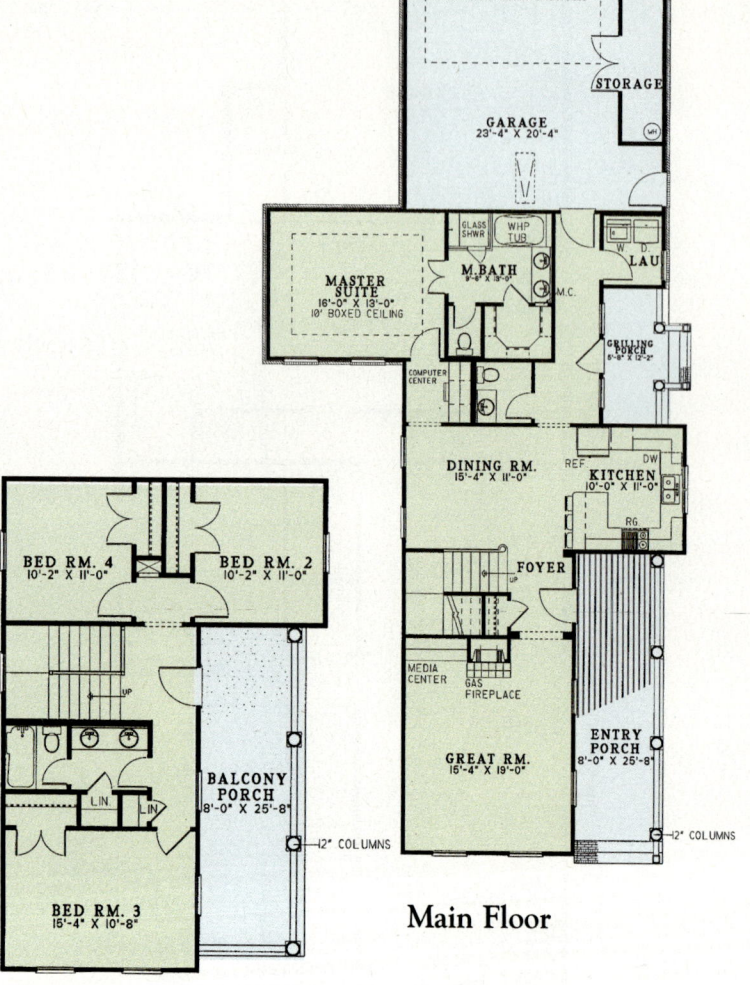

Upper Floor

Main Floor

Width: 38' 6"
Depth: 78' 6"
Main Floor: 1,295 sq. ft.
Upper Floor: 664 sq. ft.
Total Living: 1,959 sq. ft.
Price Tier: B

Main Ceiling: 9 ft.
Upper Ceiling: 9 ft.
Bedrooms: 4
Baths: 2 1/2
Foundation: Crawl, Slab, Opt. Basement, Opt. Daylight Basement

To view similar plans visit www.84lumber.com/ndgplans - 800.359.8484

Upper Floor

Main Floor

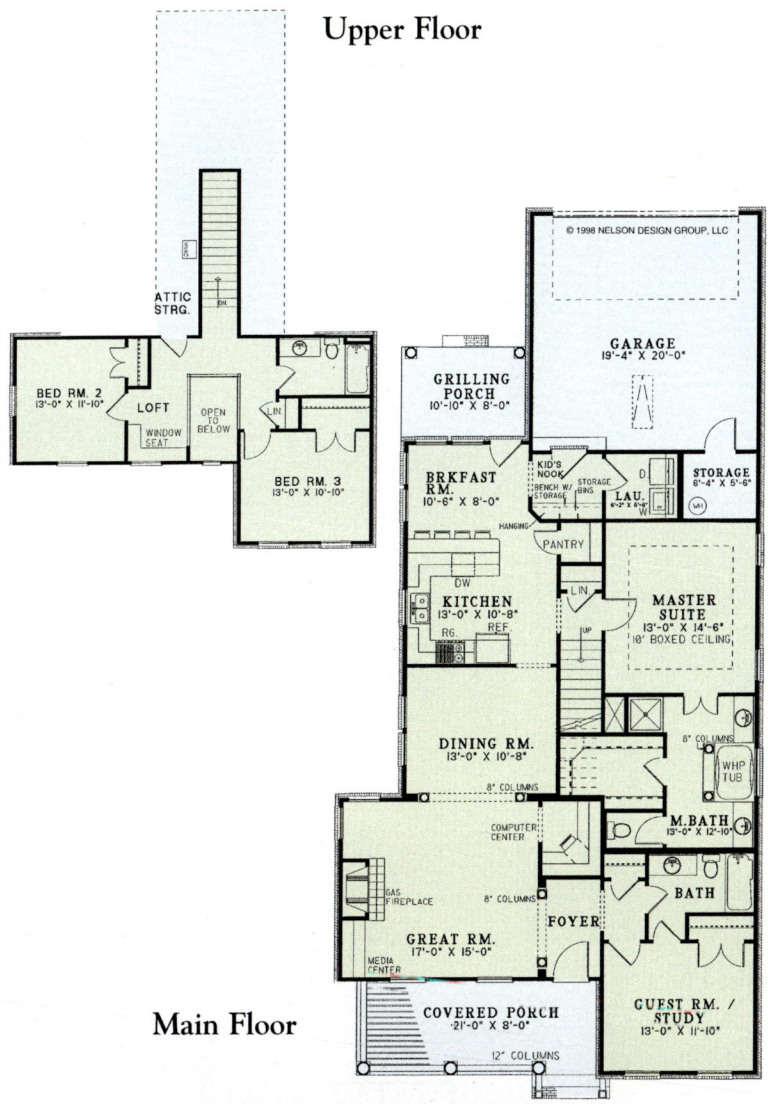

309 Windstone Place
Windstone Collection I

This traditional Nelson Design Group home is enhanced by historical southern style. After enjoying hours of relaxation on your covered front porch, retreat to the great room with its romantic gas fireplace and built-in media center. Attached is the formal dining area with elegant eight inch wood columns, perfect for lovely dinner parties or quiet romantic evenings. A spacious kitchen and breakfast area opens to a rear covered grilling porch and kid's nook complete with built-in storage bench, storage bins and hanging space. Traveling upstairs you'll find two spacious bedrooms accented by an open loft with a view of the foyer below.

Width:	36' 4"	Main Ceiling:	9 ft.
Depth:	73' 6"	Upper Ceiling:	8 ft.
Main Floor:	1,558 sq. ft.	Bedrooms:	4
Upper Floor:	429 sq. ft.	Baths:	3
Total Living:	1,987 sq. ft.	Foundation:	Crawl, Slab, Opt. Basement, Opt. Daylight Basement
Price Tier:	B		

To view similar plans visit www.84lumber.com/ndgplans - 800.359.8484

318 Windstone Place
Windstone Collection I

Pamper yourself with Southern charm when you select this Nelson Design Group home. Become instantly immersed in tradition as you step into an elegant foyer designed with an open entrance to the formal dining room. Brilliant french doors open to a private study for late night work or quiet time with your favorite book. Enjoy romantic nights in front of a roaring fire while you sip drinks from the built-in wet bar in the great room. Plan a fun cookout and show off your famous barbeque skills while utilizing the side grilling porch. A spacious upper level with a bonus room – perfect for a game or study area – allows plenty of space for the kids to be kids.

Width: 35' 4"
Depth: 71' 6"
Main Floor: 1,698 sq. ft.
Upper Floor: 533 sq. ft.
Total Living: 2,231 sq. ft.*
*Optional Bonus: 394 sq. ft.
Price Tier: C

Main Ceiling: 9 ft.
Upper Ceiling: 8 ft.
Bedrooms: 3
Baths: 2 1/2
Foundation: Crawl, Slab, Basement, Daylight Basement

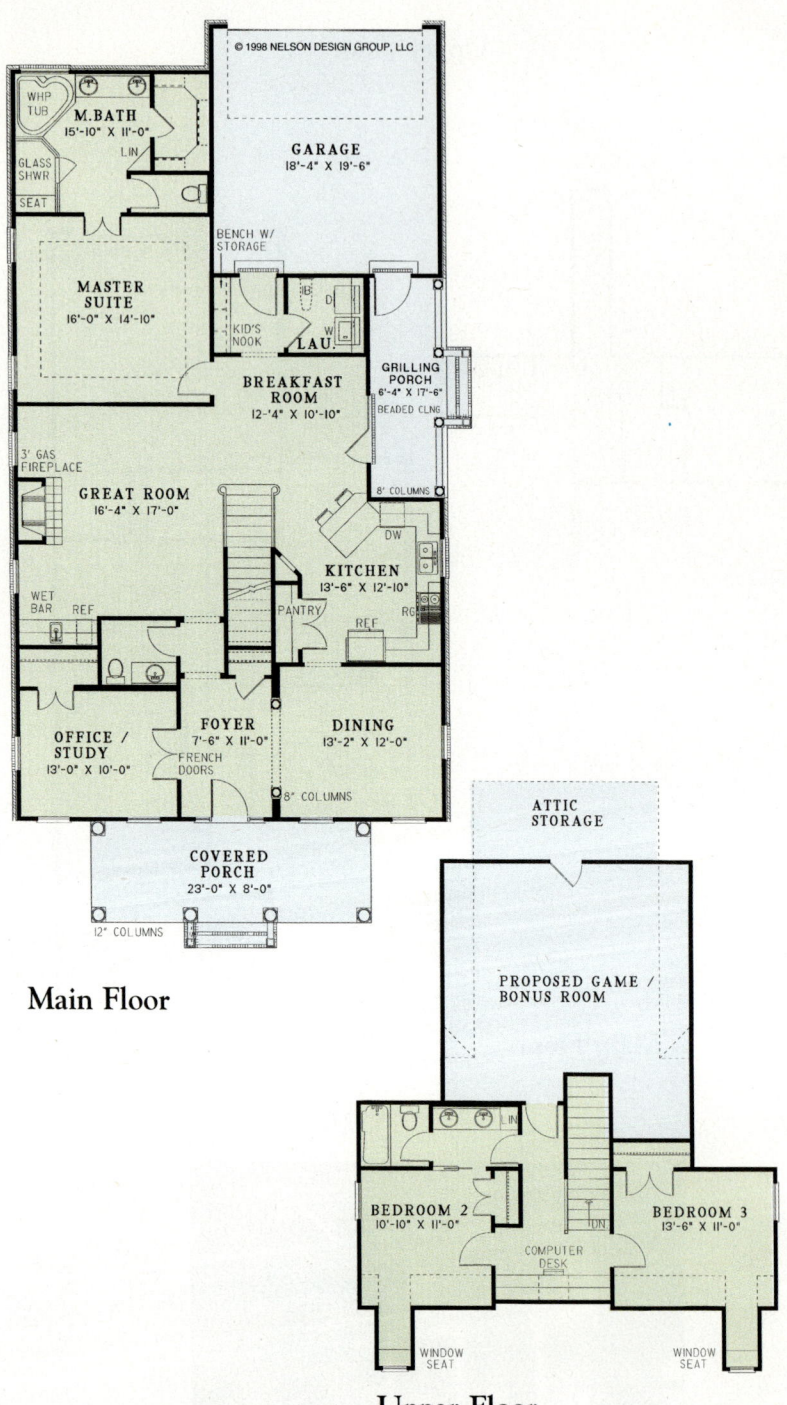

Main Floor

Upper Floor

To view similar plans visit www.84lumber.com/ndgplans - 800.359.8484

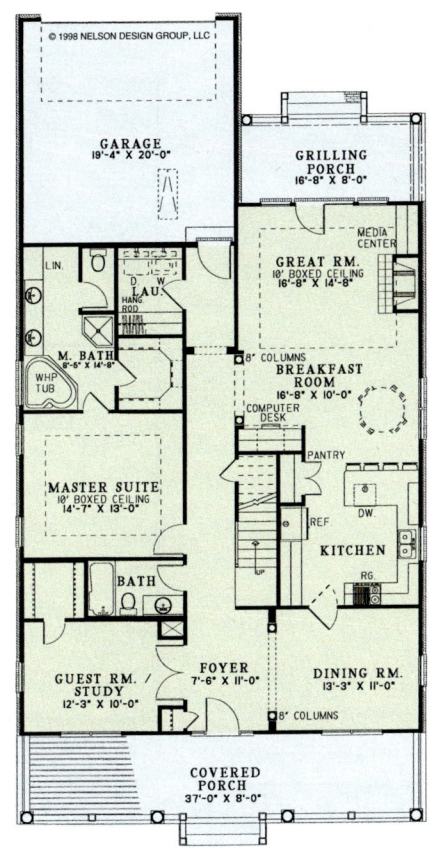

Main Floor

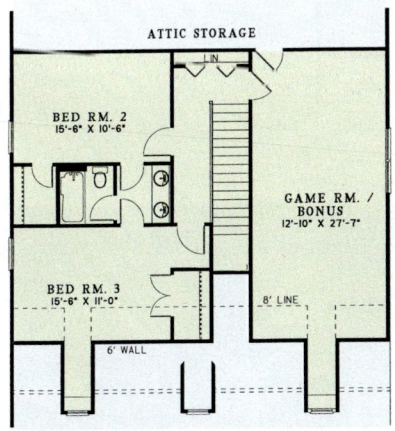

Upper Floor

307 Windstone Place

Windstone Collection I

This Nelson Design Group home is full of all the amenities of true southern style. Lazy summer afternoons slip by as you sit and visit with friends and family on the traditional eight foot covered entry porch. A formal foyer with eight inch wood columns leads you through to an elegant dining area. A master suite and bath will pamper you as you enjoy the luxury of a corner whirlpool tub with privacy glass block windows, large walk-in closet, corner glass shower and double 'his and hers' vanities with linen cabinet. The rear grilling porch with atrium doors leads to the great room – perfect for entertaining any time of year. The upper floor creates a wonderful area for kids of all ages with two spacious bedrooms with walk-through bath and a large game room.

Width: 37'	Main Ceiling: 9 ft.
Depth: 73'	Upper Ceiling: 8 ft.
Main Floor: 1,713 sq. ft.	Bedrooms: 3
Upper Floor: 610 sq. ft.	Baths: 3
Total Living: 2,323 sq. ft.*	Foundation: Crawl, Slab, Opt. Basement, Opt. Daylight Basement
*Optional Bonus: 384 sq. ft.	
Price Tier: C	

To view similar plans visit www.84lumber.com/ndgplans - 800.359.8484

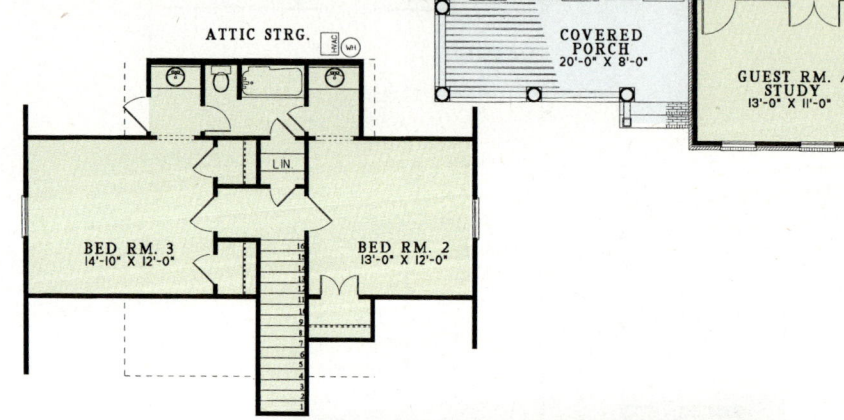

Main Floor

Upper Floor

308 Windstone Place
Windstone Collection I

This Nelson Design Group home is a perfect traditional southern family retreat. An eight foot covered entry porch welcomes you to days gone by. Here, you can entertain friends with lemonade and conversation or move to the rear grilling porch for an afternoon cookout, enhanced by convenient entry to the breakfast room and kitchen. A great room offers plenty of rainy day entertainment with gas fireplace and built-in media center. Attached is a formal dining area enhanced by eight inch wood columns. Open stairs from the foyer lead you up to the second floor. Eight foot ceilings create a pleasant openness in the upper two bedrooms, complete with walk-through bath.

Width: 36'	Main Ceiling: 9 ft.
Depth: 69'	Upper Ceiling: 8 ft.
Main Floor: 1,694 sq. ft.	Bedrooms: 4
Upper Floor: 558 sq. ft.	Baths: 3
Total Living: 2,252 sq. ft.	Foundation: Crawl, Slab, Opt. Basement, Opt. Daylight Basement
Price Tier: C	

To view similar plans visit www.84lumber.com/ndgplans - 800.359.8484

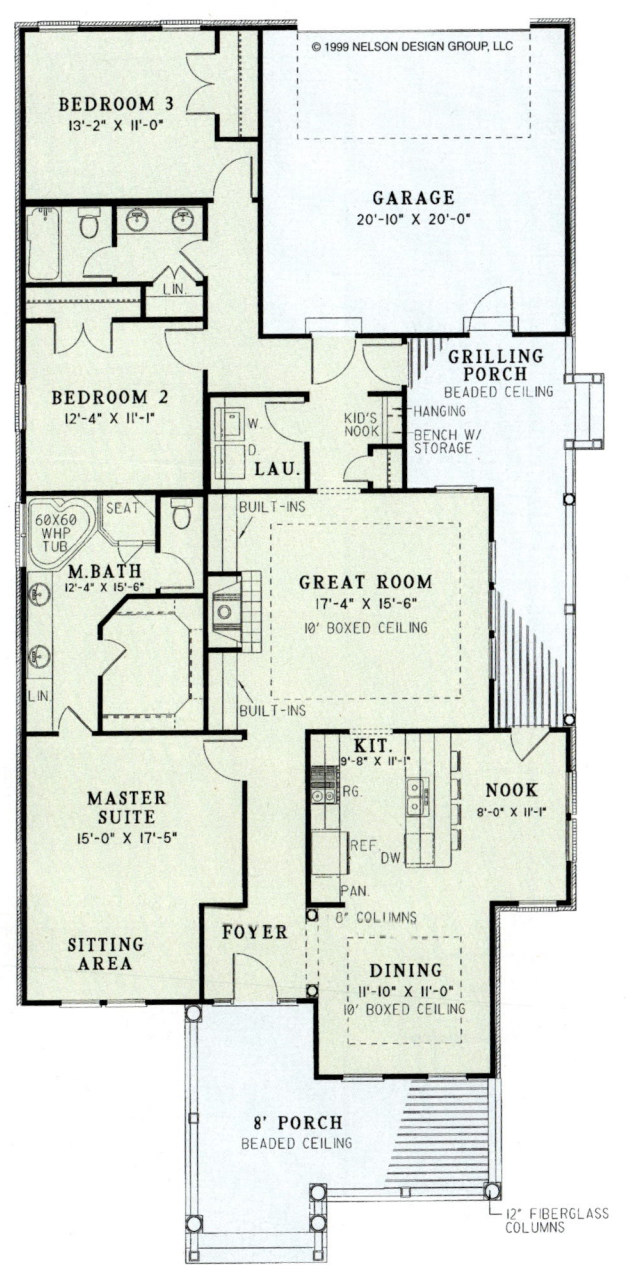

338 Windstone Place
Windstone Collection II

Step inside this traditional Nelson Design Group home and leave the world behind. Enjoy comfortable evenings relaxing in your spacious great room, complete with gas fireplace and built-in shelving. Dinner parties are a breeze in the comfort of your formal dining area enhanced by eight inch wood columns. For more casual gatherings, invite friends over for a delicious cookout on your grilling porch, accessible from sitting nook and garage. Finally, relish in the privacy of your large master suite and relax in the corner whirlpool tub of the master bath.

Width:	38'	Main Ceiling:	9 ft.
Depth:	79' 6"	Bedrooms:	3
Total Living:	1,848 sq. ft.	Baths:	2
Price Tier:	B	Foundation:	Crawl, Slab

355 Windstone Place
Windstone Collection II

Imagine yourself in this Nelson Design Group home. Each day is a dream come true as you enjoy quiet summer evenings over iced tea and conversation on your covered front porch. Become the perfect host or hostess of charming dinners in your dining room easily and conveniently accessible to the kitchen and breakfast room. A side grilling porch just off the breakfast room provides ample space for entertaining as well. After dining, adjourn to the great room for coffee in front of a gas fireplace. Then retreat to a wonderful master suite complete with master bath including a whirlpool tub and double vanity. But don't worry about the kids, they'll have plenty of space to play in the proposed upper level bonus area with nine foot ceilings.

Width: 39'
Depth: 82' 4"
Total Living: 1,927 sq. ft.
Price Tier: B

Main Ceiling: 10 ft.
Bedrooms: 3
Baths: 2
Foundation: Crawl, Slab, Basement, Daylight Basement

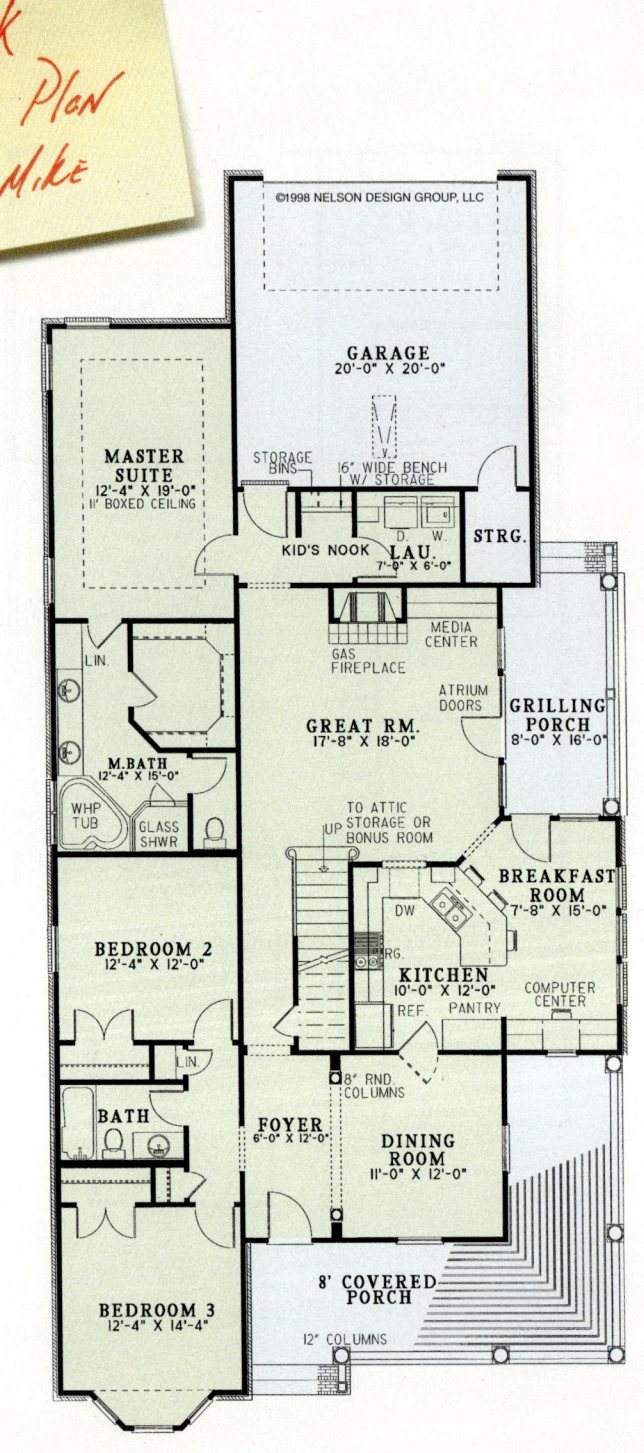

To view similar plans visit www.84lumber.com/ndgplans - 800.359.8484

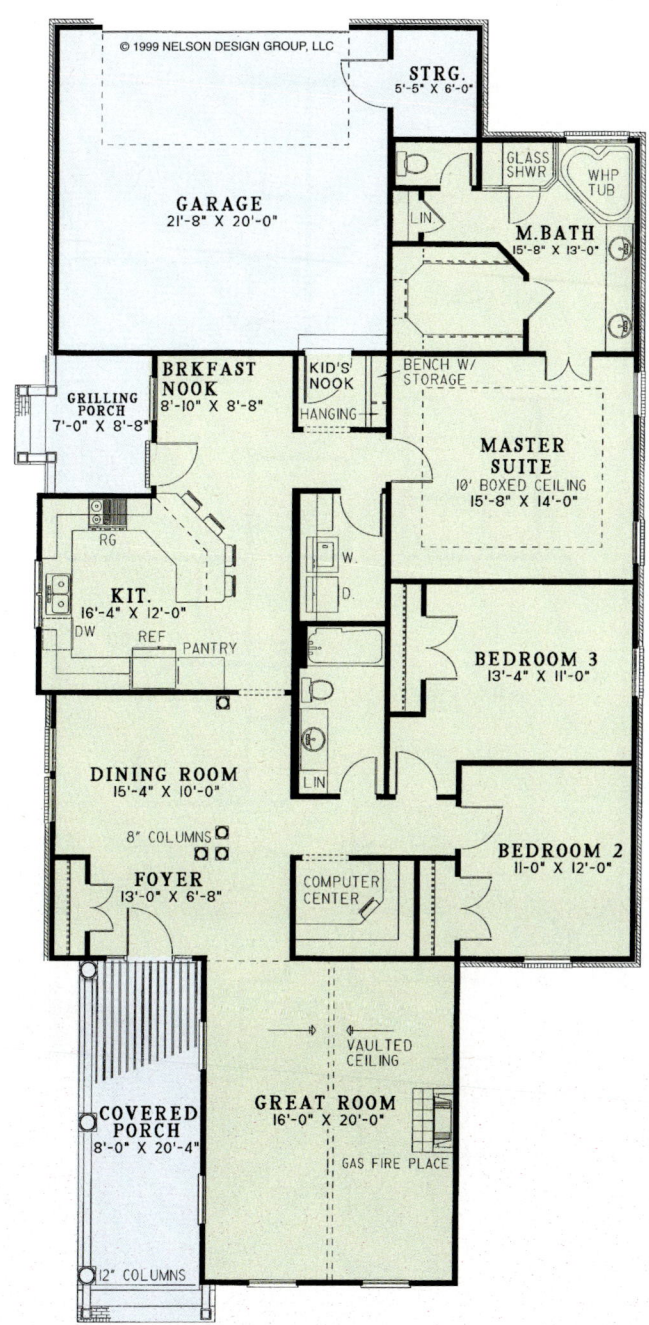

353 Windstone Place
Windstone Collection II

Forget the stress of the corporate world and slip into the Southern comfort of this Nelson Design Group home. A historical covered porch welcomes guests into an open foyer and spacious great room with a vaulted ceiling and romantic gas fireplace. Enjoy the open dining room enhanced by eight inch round columns. A spacious and functional kitchen adjoins the bright breakfast nook accessible to a side grilling porch — perfect for entertaining. A secluded master suite with a ten foot boxed ceiling and master bath provides just the right amount of privacy from the kids. Two bedrooms and a full bath are located next to a central computer nook.

Width: 38'	Main Ceiling: 9 ft.
Depth: 79'	Bedrooms: 3
Total Living: 1,965 sq. ft.	Baths: 2
Price Tier: B	Foundation: Crawl, Slab, Opt. Basement, Opt. Daylight Basement

To view similar plans visit www.84lumber.com/ndgplans - 800.359.8484

350 Windstone Place
Windstone Collection II

This Nelson Design Group home has the amenities of a Traditional Neighborhood Design, all with a southern flair. A well-crafted and spacious covered porch leads you to a beautiful foyer adjoining an elegant dining room enhanced by eight inch columns and ten foot boxed ceiling. Traveling down the hall, enter an incredibly spacious great room with fluid entry to the kitchen and breakfast nook. A rear side grilling porch is accessible to the great room as well. Three large bedrooms, including a private master suite, complete the design.

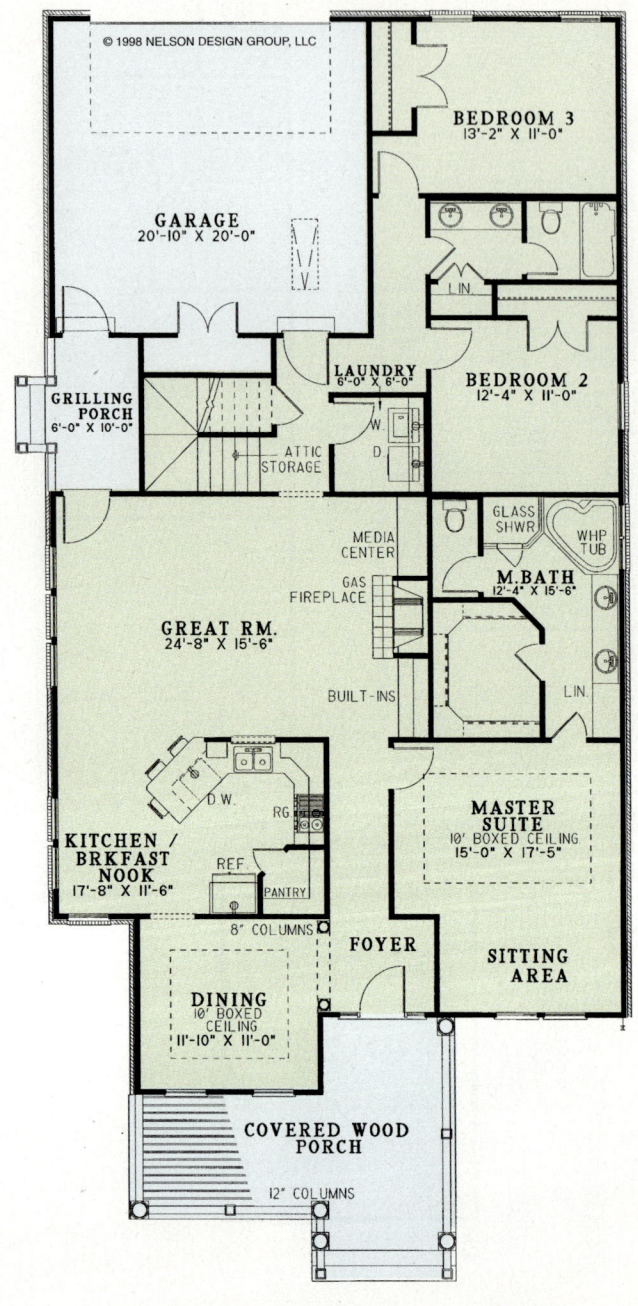

Width: 38' 0"
Depth: 79' 6"
Total Living: 1,966 sq. ft.
Price Tier: B

Main Ceiling: 9 ft.
Bedrooms: 3
Baths: 2
Foundation: Crawl, Slab, Opt. Basement, Opt. Daylight Basement

To view similar plans visit www.84lumber.com/ndgplans - 800.359.8484

Main Floor

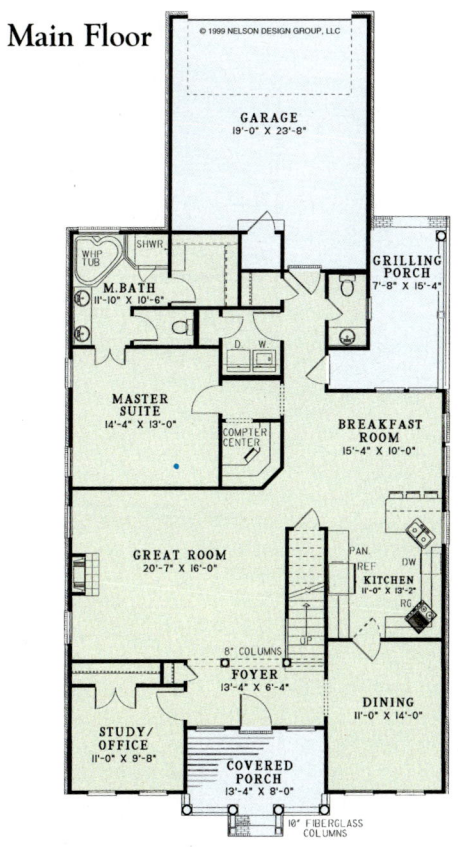

Upper Floor

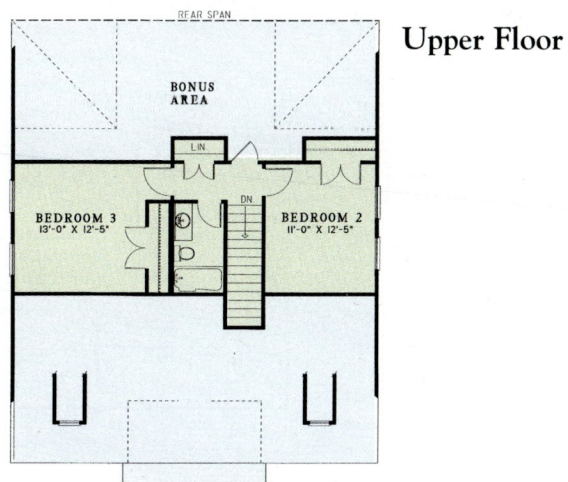

337 Windstone Place
Windstone Collection II

Stepping onto the covered entry porch and through the main floor of this Nelson Design Group home, you'll instantly feel the grandeur of traditional southern style. Enjoy hours of family entertainment in your huge great room adjacent to a formal dining room — perfect for elegant parties or casual gatherings. A convenient swinging door allows access from the dining room to a wonderful kitchen area, providing ultimate ease in the preparation and presentation of your favorite meals. After a long day, retreat to a secluded master suite, while the kids enjoy two spacious bedrooms on the upper floor. An upstairs bonus area can be easily converted to an extraordinary game room or quiet study space.

Width: 36' 8"	Main Ceiling: 9 ft.
Depth: 75' 6"	Upper Ceiling: 8 ft.
Main Floor: 1,690 sq. ft.	Bedrooms: 3
Upper Floor: 450 sq. ft.	Baths: 2 1/2
Total Living: 2,140 sq. ft.	Foundation: Crawl, Slab, Opt. Basement, Opt. Daylight Basement
Price Tier: C	

To view similar plans visit www.84lumber.com/ndgplans - 800.359.8484

Main Floor

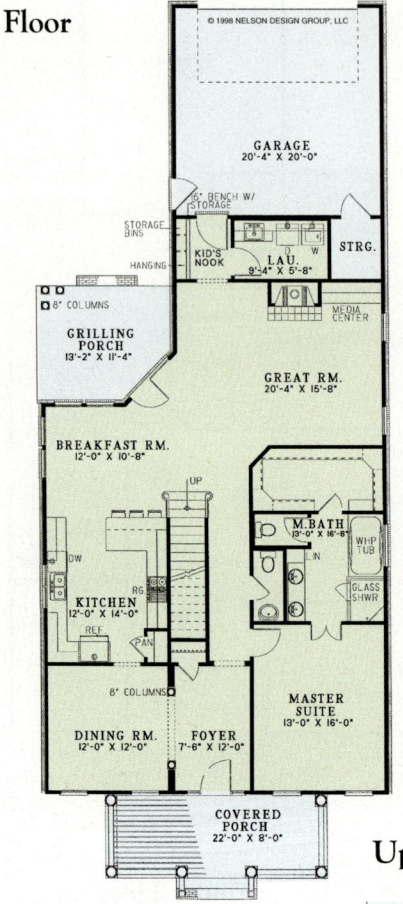

Upper Floor

357 Windstone Place
Windstone Collection II

Images of traditional values come to mind with this quaint southern Nelson Design Group home. A delightful covered porch connects to a beautiful foyer leading you to a spacious dining area. The modern and efficient kitchen opens to a breakfast room, adjoined to a great room with gas fireplace and built-in media center. Accessible to both areas is a grilling porch providing the perfect atmosphere for entertaining. Up the stairs, you'll find two bedrooms with eight foot ceilings that share a computer center. This home also features a proposed bonus room designed as a convenient future recreation room.

Width:	34' 2"	Main Ceiling:	9 ft.
Depth:	84' 2"	Upper Ceiling:	8 ft.
Main Floor:	1,644 sq. ft.	Bedrooms:	3
Upper Floor:	573 sq. ft.	Baths:	2 1/2
Total Living:	2,217 sq. ft.	Foundation:	Crawl, Slab, Opt. Basement, Opt. Daylight Basement
Price Tier:	C		

To view similar plans visit www.84lumber.com/ndgplans - 800.359.8484

Main Floor

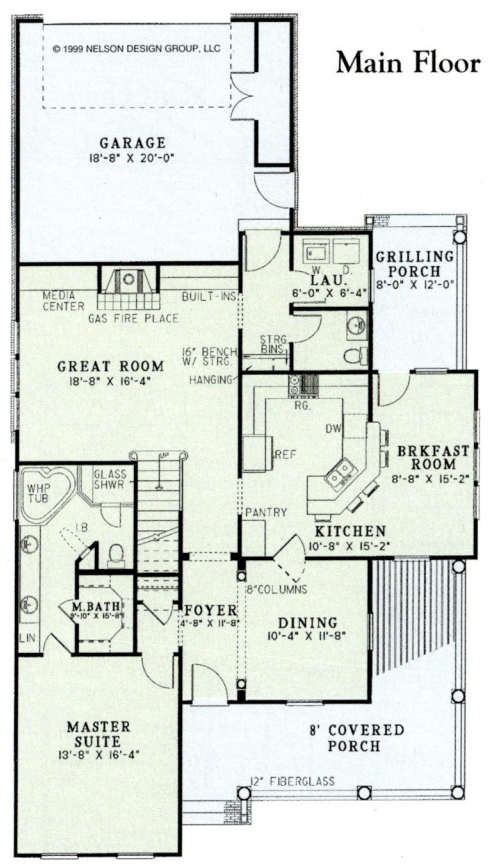

Upper Floor

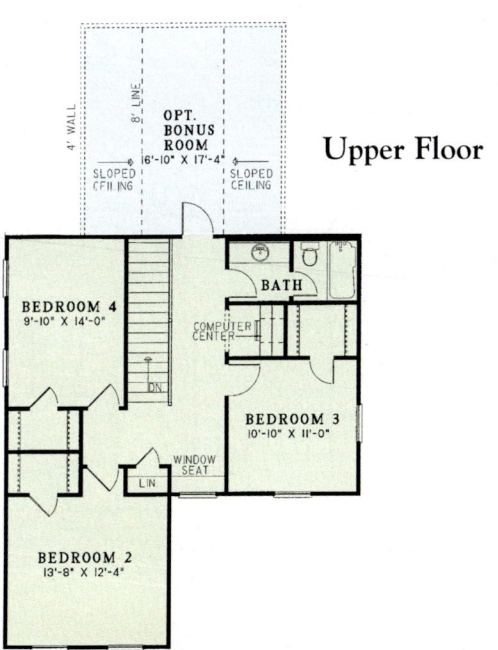

351 Windstone Place
Windstone Collection II

Do you ever long for the quiet, peaceful days of yesterday? This Nelson Design Group home makes the dream a reality. Forget the hustle and bustle with a traditional wrap around porch designed with 12 inch columns. As the sun begins to fade, travel to the dining room, conveniently accessible to a spacious kitchen by clever swinging doors. Sip hot chocolate in front of a romantic fire or retreat to a private master suite complete with double vanity, corner whirlpool tub and corner glass shower. Adjacent to a bright breakfast nook just off the kitchen is a marvelous grilling porch — perfect for an aspiring grill master.

Width: 39'4"	Main Ceiling: 9 ft.
Depth: 70'	Upper Ceiling: 9 ft.
Main Floor: 1,419 sq. ft.	Bedrooms: 4
Upper Floor: 841 sq. ft.	Baths: 2 1/2
Total Living: 2,260 sq. ft.*	Foundation: Crawl, Slab, Basement, Daylight Basement
*Optional Bonus: 309 sq. ft.	
Price Tier: C	

358 Windstone Place
Windstone Collection II

Old-fashioned charm and southern flair are at the heart of this Nelson Design Group home. The focal point of the design is a spacious and warm great room. Get-togethers of all occasions are perfect here, as well as quiet family nights in front of the gas fireplace. A bright breakfast room has access to your fabulous grilling porch. Swinging doors lead you directly into the dining area. All characteristics perfect for entertaining any time. The upper level provides plenty of space for the kids or guests with two bedrooms and large bonus room.

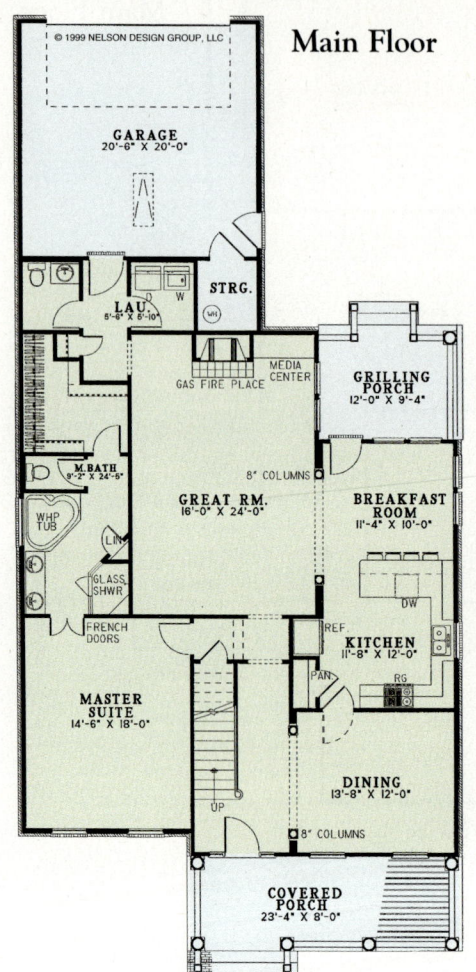

Main Floor

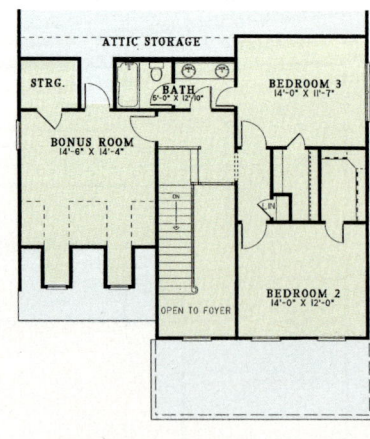

Upper Floor

Width: 38' 2"	Main Ceiling: 9 ft.
Depth: 79' 8"	Upper Ceiling: 9 ft.
Main Floor: 1,675 sq. ft.	Bedrooms: 3
Upper Floor: 604 sq. ft.	Baths: 2 1/2
Total Living: 2,279 sq. ft.*	Foundation: Crawl, Slab, Opt. Basement, Opt. Daylight Basement
*Optional Bonus: 285 sq. ft.	
Price Tier: C	

To view similar plans visit www.84lumber.com/ndgplans - 800.359.8484

Main Floor

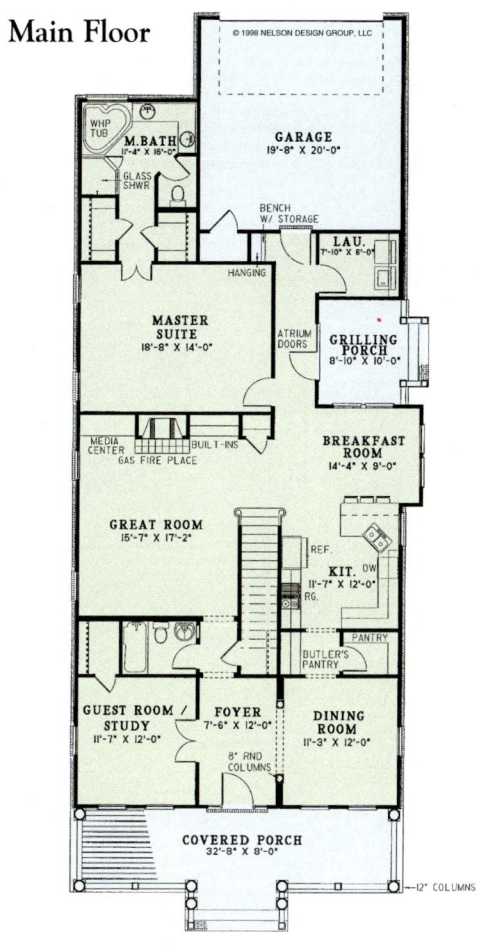

Upper Floor

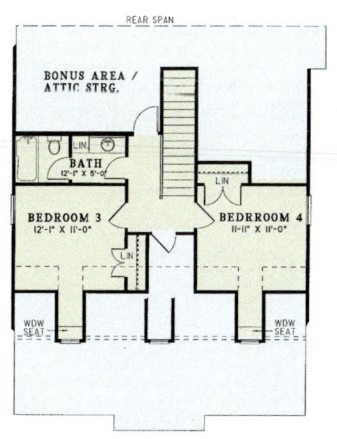

343 Windstone Place
Windstone Collection II

Upon entering this Nelson Design Group home notice the elegant dining room, adjoined to a butler pantry, creating fluid entry to a marvelously spacious kitchen. The great room, complete with a romantic gas fireplace and built-in media center, is at the heart of the design with an open entry to a breakfast room. Enjoy countless possibilities entertaining on your convenient grilling porch. Stairs with left and right hand volutes take you to the spacious upper level. Two bedrooms with window seats, a full bath and bonus area with attic storage provide plenty of room for the kids.

Width: 32'	Main Ceiling: 9 ft.
Depth: 83' 4"	Upper Ceiling: 8 ft.
Main Floor: 1,831 sq. ft.	Bedrooms: 4
Upper Floor: 455 sq. ft.	Baths: 3
Total Living: 2,286 sq. ft.	Foundation: Crawl, Slab, Basement, Daylight Basement
Price Tier: C	

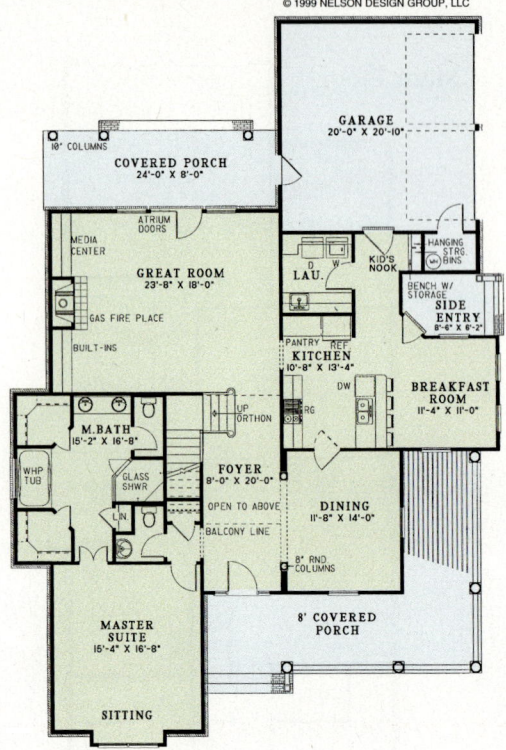

Main Floor

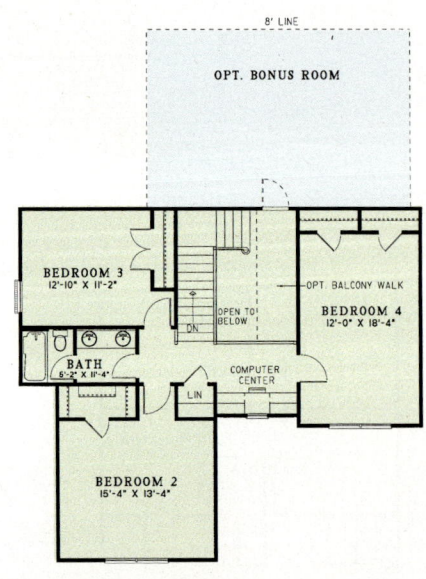

Upper Floor

356 Windstone Place
Windstone Collection II

This spacious, four bedroom, two and a half bath Nelson Design Group home is the definition of grand southern style. A traditional wrap-around covered porch welcomes you inside a gorgeous foyer with open ceiling to the upper floor. Continuing, you'll enter the heart of the design — the great room. Here, enjoy countless hours of excitement and relaxation with family and friends. Convenient atrium doors open from the great room to a rear covered porch with ten inch columns for romantic nights under the stars. A secluded master suite and bath, enhanced by an elegant sitting room, provides all the privacy you need. Traveling up an open stairway you'll find ample bedroom space for the kids, a perfect guest quarters or playroom complete with computer center and balcony walk opening over the foyer below.

Width: 50' 4"	Main Ceiling: 9 ft.
Depth: 73'	Upper Ceiling: 8 ft.
Main Floor: 1,797 sq. ft.	Bedrooms: 4
Upper Floor: 879 sq. ft.	Baths: 2 1/2
Total Living: 2,676 sq. ft.	Foundation: Crawl, Slab, Basement,
Price Tier: D	Daylight Basement

To view similar plans visit www.84lumber.com/ndgplans - 800.359.8484

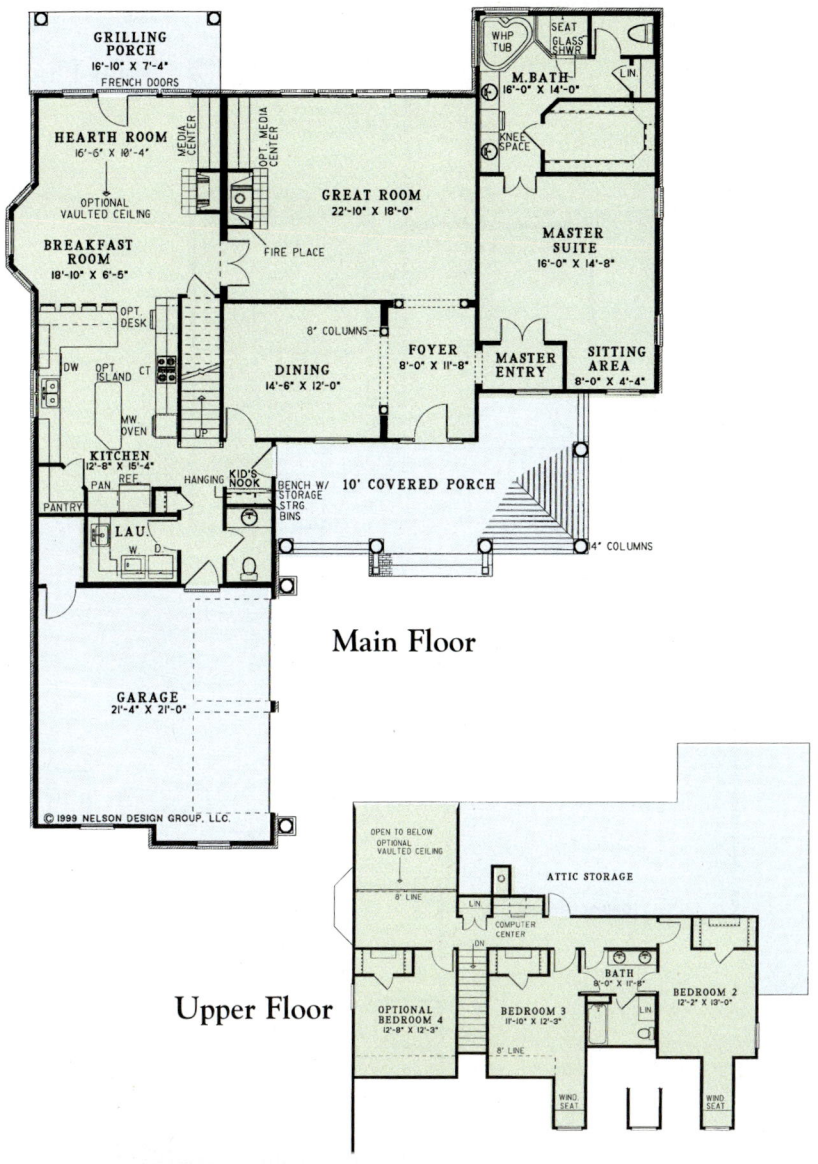

Main Floor

Upper Floor

354 Windstone Place

Windstone Collection II

This grand one and a half story Nelson Design Group home combines historic southern charm with modern technology and design. A spacious two-car garage and engaging covered front porch with 14 inch columns allow optimum convenience. A marvelous foyer leads directly to an elegant dining room and comfortable great room — perfect for family fun. A separate entrance opens to a sitting area joined to the master suite, providing ample privacy and comfort. The family will love cookouts on your grilling porch — accessible to both a hearth room and breakfast nook by way of French doors. Traveling to the upper level you'll find ample bedrooms for the kids — complete with a computer area.

Width: 59' 4"	Main Ceiling: 9 ft.
Depth: 74' 2"	Upper Ceiling: 8 ft.
Main Floor: 2,082 sq. ft.	Bedrooms: 4
Upper Floor: 695 sq. ft.	Baths: 2
Total Living: 2,777 sq. ft.*	Foundation: Crawl, Slab, Opt. Basement, Opt. Daylight Basement
*Optional Bonus: 310 sq. ft.	
Price Tier: D	

To view similar plans visit www.84lumber.com/ndgplans - 800.359.8484

360 Windstone Place
Windstone Collection II

This Nelson Design Group home purely defines true southern charm and beauty. Space abounds with nine foot ceilings throughout the home. Begin family traditions with game night in the great room. Or retreat to your secluded master suite, with a gas fireplace and access to the backyard — a perfect setting for a romantic evening in front of the fire. A unique hearth room is located just off the kitchen and connected to a grilling porch — perfect for entertaining guests. When out-of-towners arrive, they will enjoy a night in the guest room with private entrance from the front porch. Traveling to the upper level, you'll find the perfect haven for the kids — two bedrooms, a game room with a window seat and plenty of storage.

Width: 56'	Main Ceiling: 9 ft.
Depth: 85' 7"	Upper Ceiling: 8 ft.
Main Floor: 2,257 sq. ft.	Bedrooms: 4
Upper Floor: 949 sq. ft.	Baths: 3
Total Living: 3,206 sq. ft.	Foundation: Crawl, Slab, Opt. Basement, Opt. Daylight Basement
Price Tier: E	

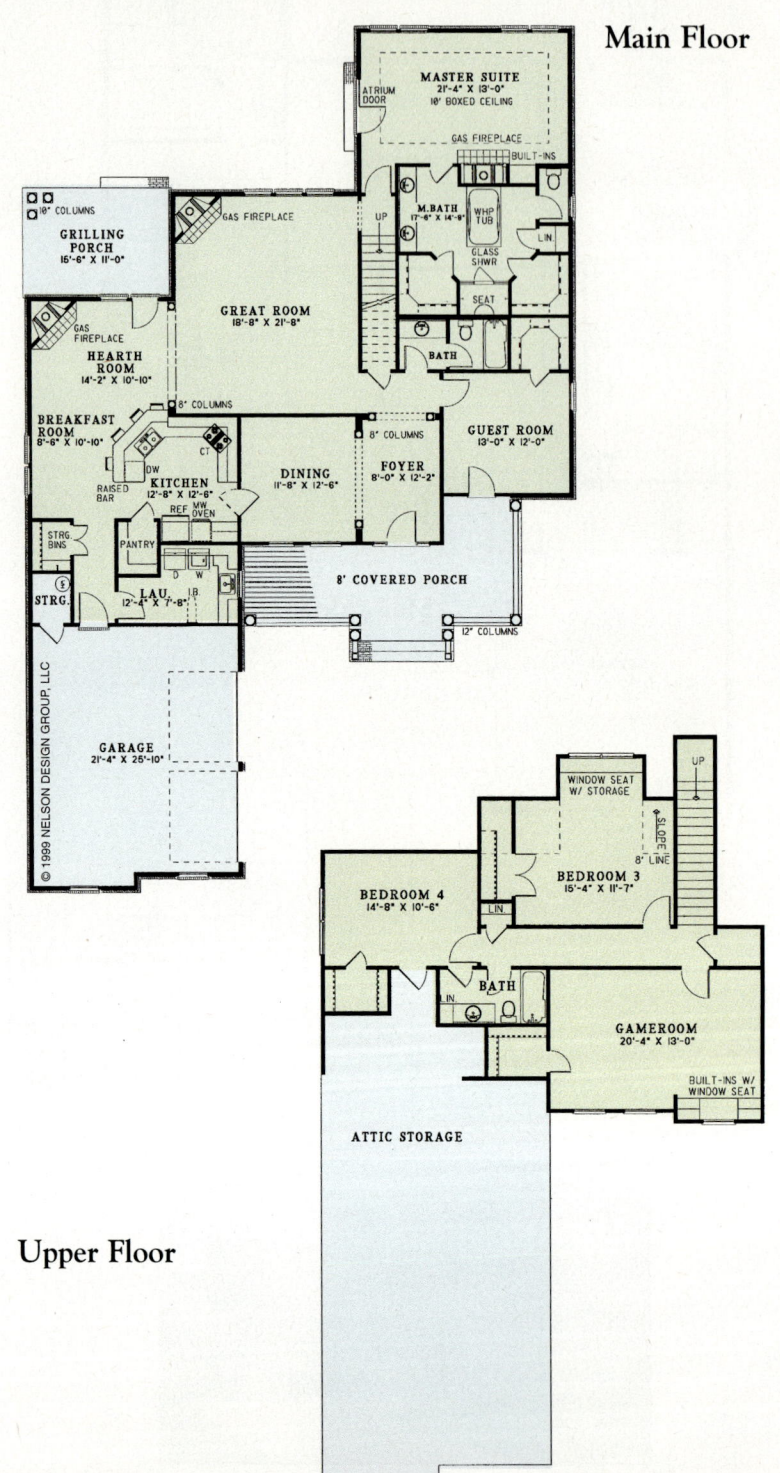

Main Floor

Upper Floor

To view similar plans visit www.84lumber.com/ndgplans - 800.359.8484

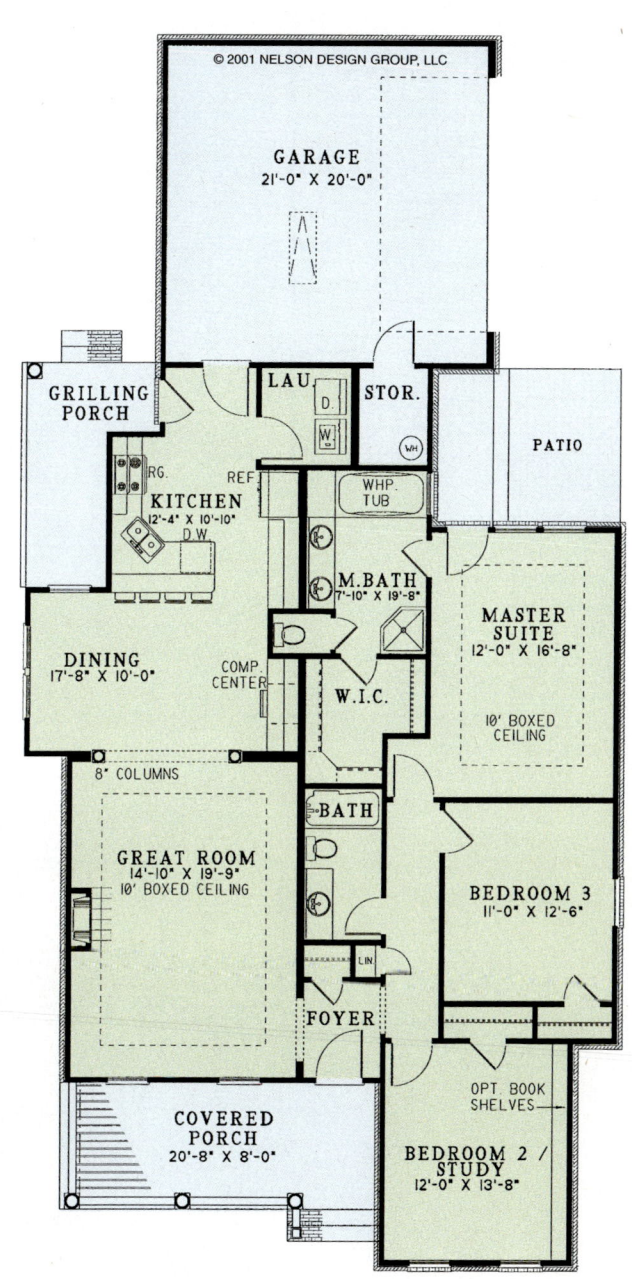

504 Windstone Place
Windstone Collection III

Wonderful street appeal and a lovely-covered porch. This traditional Nelson Design Group home has the utmost in amenities. Privacy is an added feature as the foyer totally separates the bedrooms from the living quarters. Boxed ceilings in the great room and master suite add elegance as do the 8" columns that frame the formal dining room opening. A built-in computer center is centrally located for family to enjoy while the kitchen has a direct view of the entire living areas and access to a rear grilling porch. The master bathroom has a whirlpool tub, double vanity, shower and a private toilet room. Also, a large walk-in closet in the master bathroom keeps a clutter-free bedroom. The master suite also has private access to a rear patio and rear entry garage.

Width: 39'	Main Ceiling: 9 ft.
Depth: 77' 2"	Bedrooms: 3
Total Living: 1,601 sq. ft.	Baths: 2
Price Tier: B	Foundation: Crawl, Slab

To view similar plans visit www.84lumber.com/ndgplans - 800.359.8484

444 Windstone Place
Windstone Collection III

A historically inspired home with a covered porch and balcony make this Nelson Design Group plan a perfect Traditional Neighborhood design. The wooden porch leads your guests into the foyer which separates Great room from the dining room and leads to an upstairs. The great room has a fireplace and media center for the electronic buff. Back to the dining room, entertaining is a must with the kitchen and grilling porch access. And of course, the master suite is enhanced with a ten foot boxed ceiling and double french door entry into the master bathroom for added luxury. The bathroom amenities include a large walk-in closet, glass shower, private toilet room and whirlpool tub. Upstairs, three bedrooms and a full bathroom with plenty of linen closets make for a clutter free downstairs!

Width: 25' 0"	Main Ceiling: 9 ft.
Depth: 54' 10"	Upper Ceiling: 9 ft.
Main Floor: 1,095 sq. ft.	Bedrooms: 4
Upper Floor: 606 sq. ft.	Baths: 2 1/2
Total Living: 1,701 sq. ft.	Foundation: Crawl, Slab, Opt. Basement, Opt. Daylight Basement
Price Tier: B	

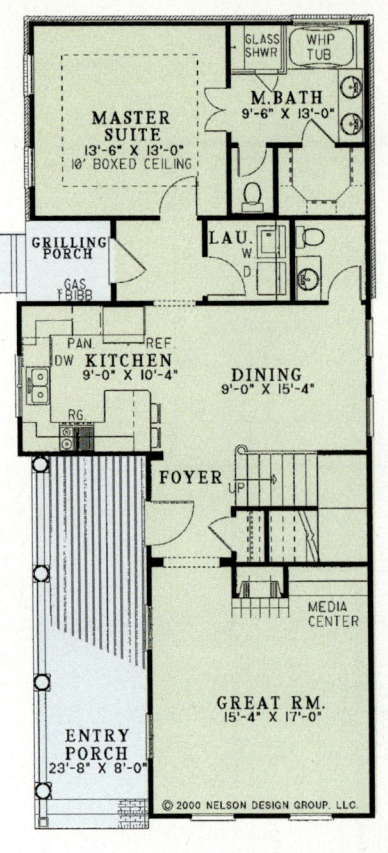

Main Floor

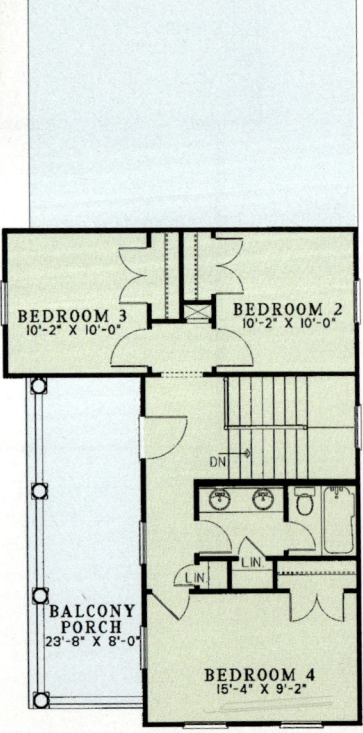

Upper Floor

To view similar plans visit www.84lumber.com/ndgplans - 800.359.8484

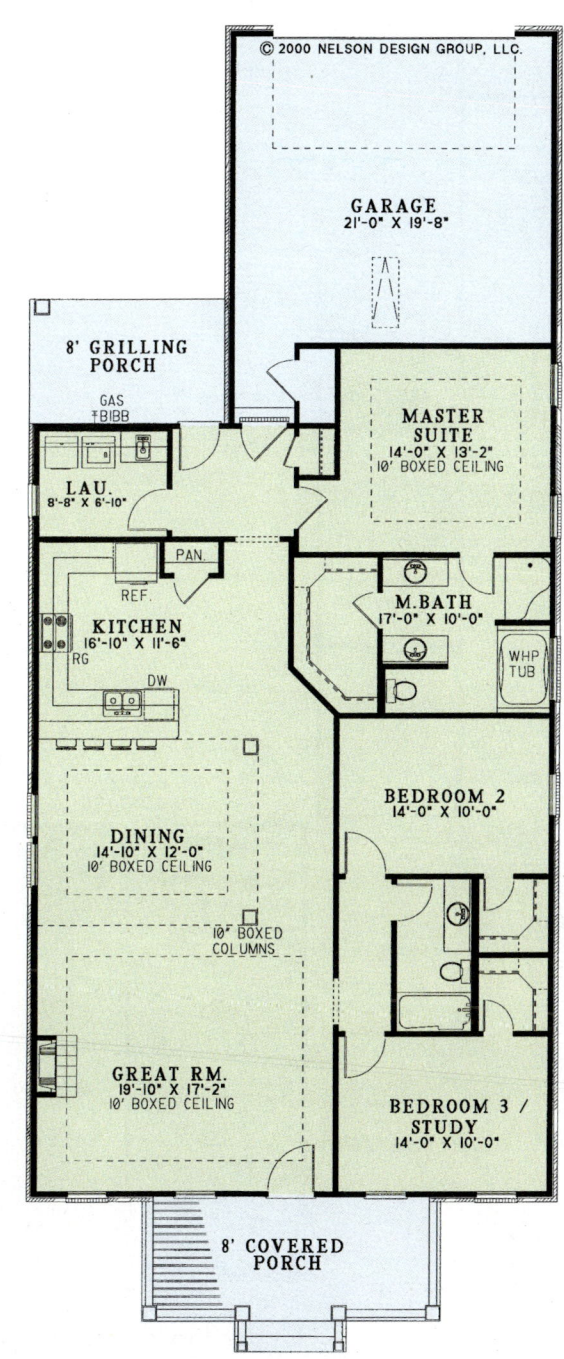

495 Windstone Place
Windstone Collection III

This Nelson Design Group home is historically inspired with modern amenities and utilizes space most efficiently. Upon entering the front door, enjoy an open view of the great room and formal dining area both enhanced with 10 foot boxed ceilings. For holidays, use the eat-at bar as a buffet while having direct access to the kitchen. Afterwards, retire to your Master suite enjoying a warm soak in your whirlpool tub. The master bathroom also has a large walk-in closet, two opposite vanities and a separate shower. This lovely southern traditional style design has all the amenities to enjoy comfortable living, so sit on your porch swing and enjoy an afternoon breeze.

Width: 34' 10"	Main Ceiling: 9 ft.
Depth: 83' 0"	Bedrooms: 3
Total Floor: 1,811 sq. ft.	Baths: 2
Price Tier: B	Foundation: Crawl, Slab

521 Windstone Place
Windstone Collection III

History repeats itself in this beautiful Nelson Design Group design. This Traditional Neighborhood Design is perfect for a narrow lot and is packed with amenities. A covered porch with a balcony above and grilling porch on the side is wonderful for afternoon relaxation. The Great room has a corner fireplace and opens to a column enhanced dining room. The kitchen is efficiently arranged and adjoins a roomy breakfast room. French doors lead you into the Master Bedroom Suite where privacy awaits. The master bathroom is loaded with a whirlpool tub, glass shower and double lavatories. This split bedroom plan has a full bathroom and two additional bedrooms that both access the balcony. A computer desk is centrally located above the stairs.

Width: 36' 4"
Depth: 64' 10"
Main Floor: 1,298 sq. ft.
Upper Floor: 624 sq. ft.
Total Living: 1,922 sq. ft.
Price Tier: B

Main Ceiling: 9 ft.
Upper Ceiling: 8 ft.
Bedrooms: 3
Baths: 2 1/2
Foundation: Crawl, Slab, Opt. Basement, Opt. Daylight Basement

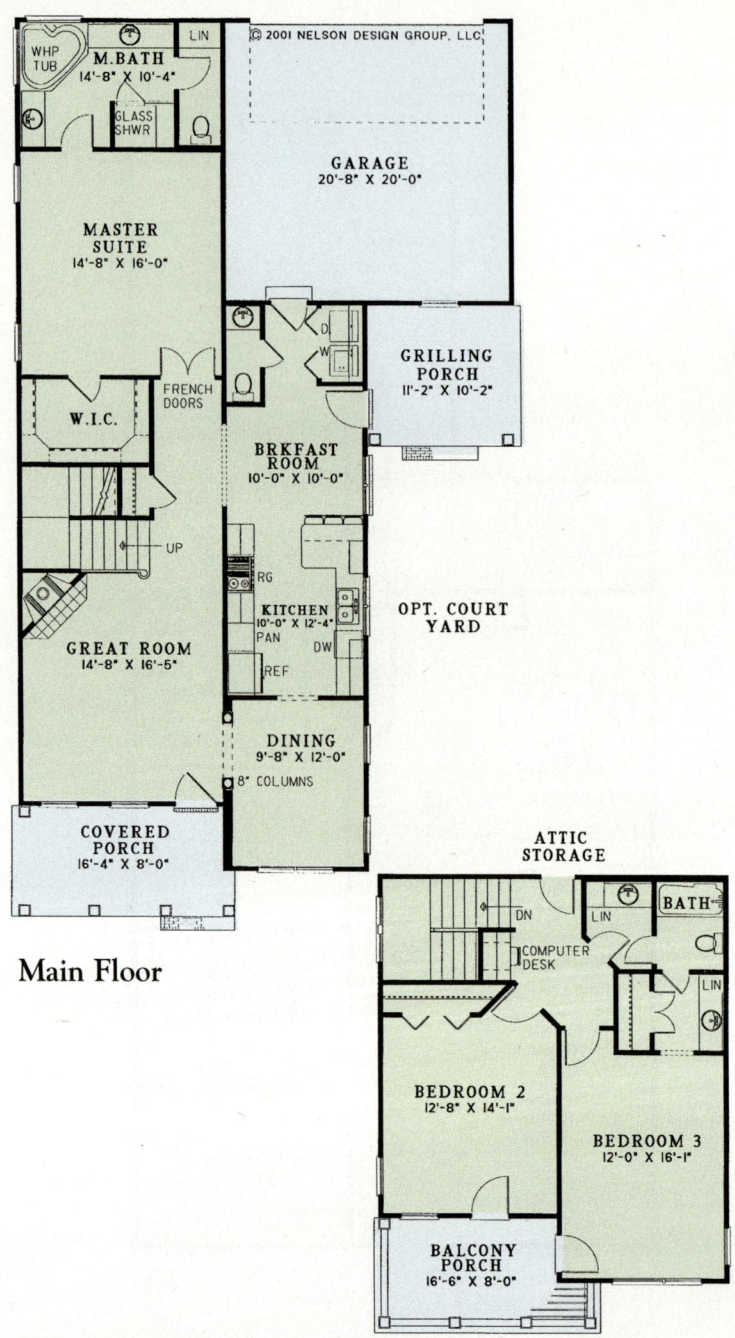

Main Floor

Upper Floor

To view similar plans visit www.84lumber.com/ndgplans - 800.359.8484

Main Floor

Upper Floor

529 Windstone Place
Windstone Collection III

This Nelson Design Group design offers the utmost living environment. Enter the front door and begin a journey of truly inspired family areas. The breakfast nook, a room of its own, adjoins the kitchen complete with extra bar seating and an open view of the great room. For a central location, the computer desk is conveniently placed in a hall nook outside of the great room. The master suite located on the main floor, has a ten foot boxed ceiling a bathroom filled with amenities and a large walk-in closet. This split bedroom plan has two bedrooms upstairs, each with a private access vanity and share a tub/toilet room. An optional media/TV room is available as is a huge bonus room located above the garage.

Width: 35' 6"	Main Ceiling: 9 ft.
Depth: 74' 8"	Upper Ceiling: 8 ft.
Main Floor: 1,485 sq. ft.	Bedrooms: 3
Upper Floor: 531 sq. ft.	Baths: 2 1/2
Total Living: 2,016 sq. ft.*	Foundation: Crawl, Slab, Opt. Basement, Opt. Daylight Basement
*Optional Bonus: 426 sq. ft.	
Price Tier: C	

To view similar plans visit www.84lumber.com/ndgplans - 800.359.8484

503 Windstone Place
Windstone Collection III

This is historically representative of a home that our parents grew up in. Nelson Design Group has recreated a traditional design with modern amenities. The covered porch welcomes visitors like outreached open arms. Upon entering the foyer, a formal dining room is on your left and accesses a breakfast nook through to the kitchen. An angled bar area opens into a great room with media center and built-ins. The large master bathroom has a walk-in closet, corner whirlpool tub, separate shower and separates the Master suite from the other bedrooms for added privacy. A sitting area in the master bedroom can be used as a study area. A kid's nook is creatively added to help organize a busy lifestyle and accesses a garage which is recessed for added street appeal.

Width: 58'
Depth: 79' 6"
Total Living: 2,026 sq. ft.
Price Tier: C

Main Ceiling: 9 ft.
Bedrooms: 3
Baths: 2
Foundation: Crawl, Slab, Opt. Basement, Opt. Daylight Basement

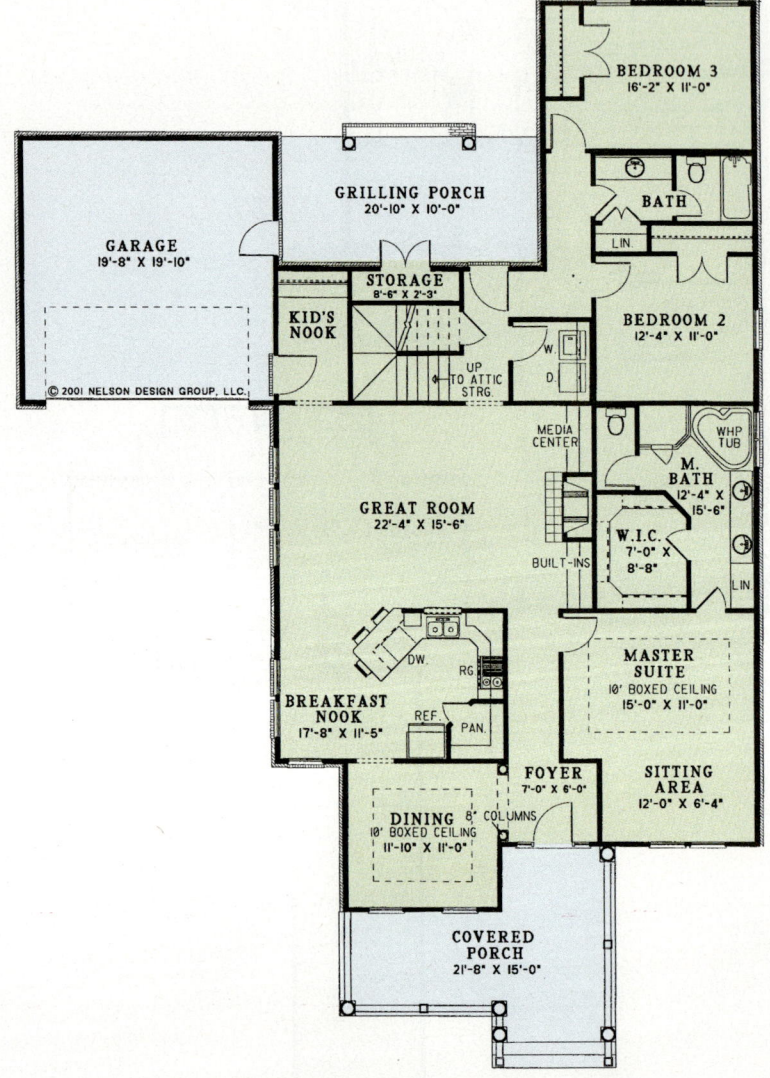

To view similar plans visit www.84lumber.com/ndgplans - 800.359.8484

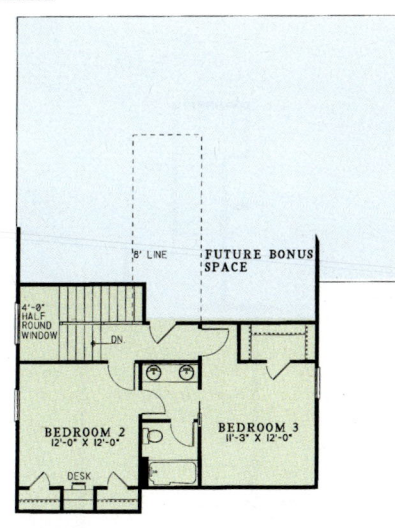

Main Floor

Upper Floor

391 Windstone Place
Windstone Collection III

Welcome your friends and family to this traditional Nelson Design Group home. Leading your guests into the foyer, they'll notice all the beautiful columns surrounding all entrances from the foyer to the adjoining rooms. Your spacious great room has a warm fireplace for those cold mornings. The gorgeous courtyard can be viewed by accessing the side covered patio from either the great room or master suite. The optional fireplace in the breakfast room will create a cozy environment for family breakfasts. Upstairs, you'll find two more bedrooms with walk-thru access to the bath.

Width:	38' 10"	Main Ceiling:	9 ft.
Depth:	70' 4"	Upper Ceiling:	8 ft.
Main Floor:	1,654 sq. ft.	Bedrooms:	3
Upper Floor:	492 sq. ft.	Baths:	2 1/2
Total Living:	2,146 sq. ft.	Foundation:	Crawl, Slab, Opt. Basement, Opt. Daylight Basement
Price Tier:	C		

To view similar plans visit www.84lumber.com/ndgplans - 800.359.8484

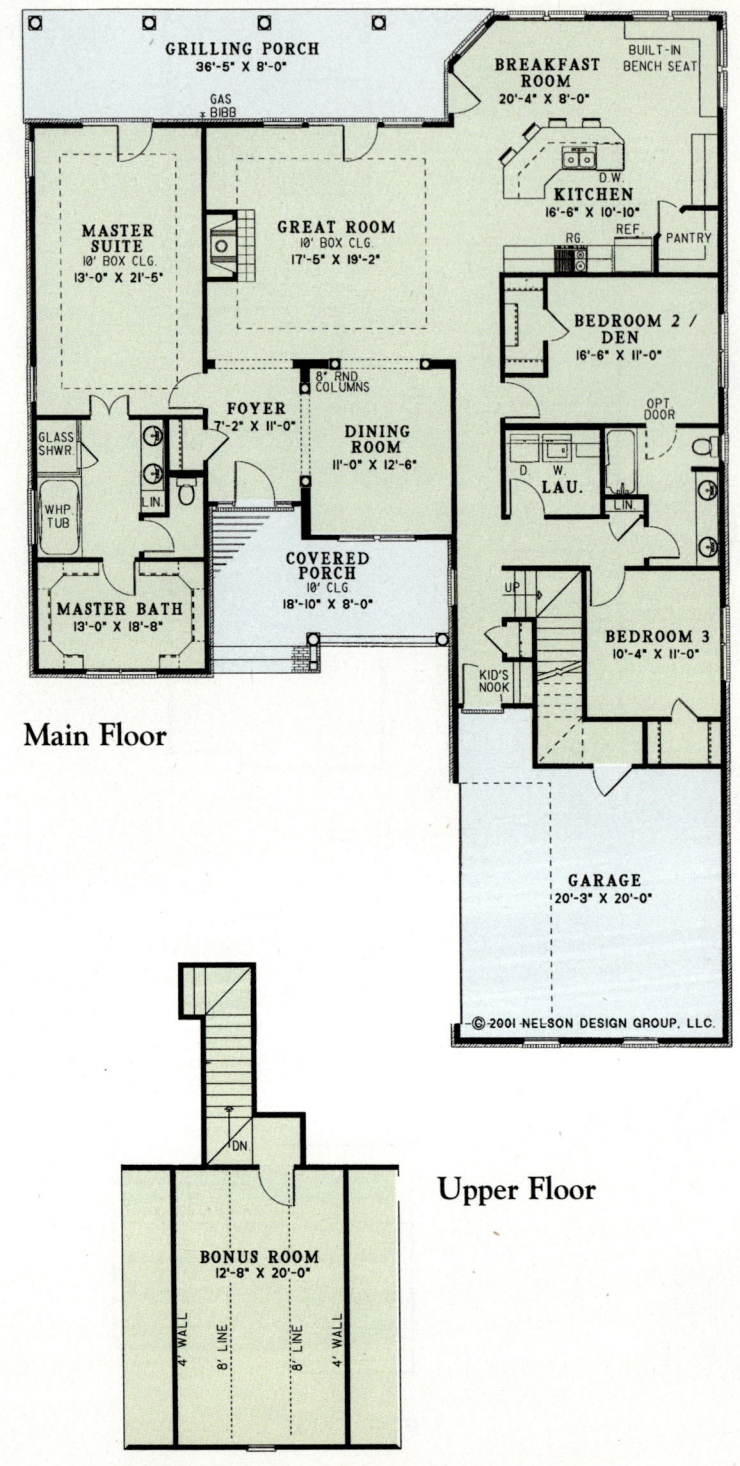

Main Floor

Upper Floor

537 Windstone Place
Windstone Collection III

A courtyard entry garage for privacy and a deep covered porch adorn this Nelson Design Group design. One of our Traditional Neighborhood designs perfect for narrow lot incorporating ten foot boxed ceilings and eight inch round columns. The dining room is centrally located and looks through to the great room which accesses a rear grilling porch. This split bedroom plan gives you the ultimate in privacy for the master suite complete with large walk-in closet and bathroom amenities galore. At the other end of the house is the kitchen breakfast room combo with island seating and a built-in bench seat and walk-in pantry. Down the hall is a den or extra bedroom with private access to the full bathroom making it great for guests. Upstairs allows for a bonus room if needed.

Width: 54' 0"
Depth: 76' 10"
Total Living: 2,211 sq. ft.*
*Optional Bonus: 278 sq. ft.
Price Tier: C

Main Ceiling: 9 ft.
Upper Ceiling: 8 ft.
Bedrooms: 3
Baths: 2
Foundation: Crawl, Slab

To view similar plans visit www.84lumber.com/ndgplans - 800.359.8484

Main Floor

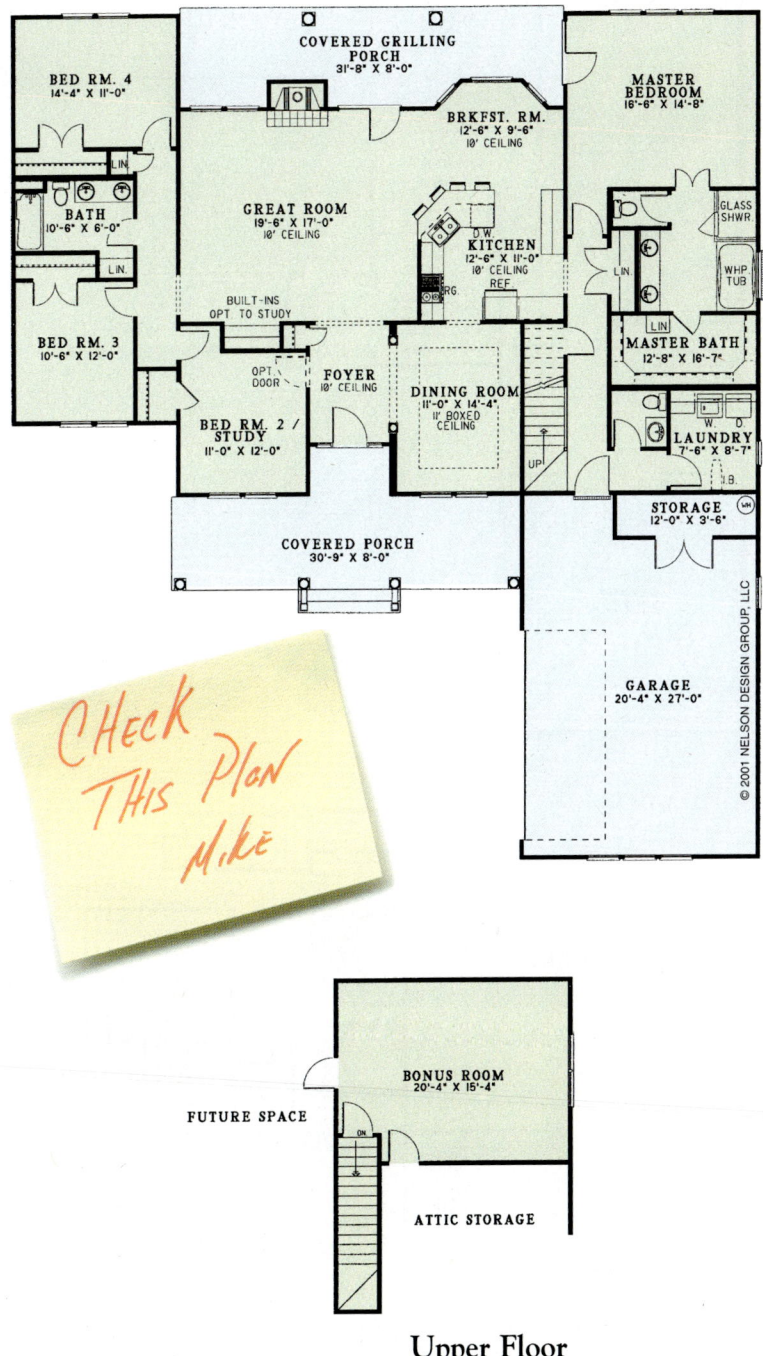

528 Windstone Place
Windstone Collection III

Cedar shake and a cozy porch with round columns introduce this split bedroom plan. Our Nelson Design Group home is elegant enough for the elite and conservative at the same time. Once inside the foyer, a ten foot ceiling continues through to the great room for a grand effect. The dining room has a column entry and opening to the kitchen enhanced with an eleven foot boxed ceiling and open bar seating. The kitchen and breakfast room both with ten foot ceilings, enjoy an outside view looking through a large covered grilling porch. An elegant master suite includes a large walk-in closet, whirlpool tub, shower and separate toilet room. A large laundry room and half bathroom lead to a courtyard entry garage. An upstairs bonus room is available if desired.

Width: 66' 0"	Bedrooms: 4
Depth: 72' 7"	Baths: 2 1/2
Total Living: 2,354 sq. ft.	Foundation: Crawl, Slab, Opt. Basement, Opt. Daylight Basement
Main Ceiling: 9 ft.	
Upper Ceiling: 8 ft.	
Price Tier: C	

Upper Floor

To view similar plans visit www.84lumber.com/ndgplans - 800.359.8484

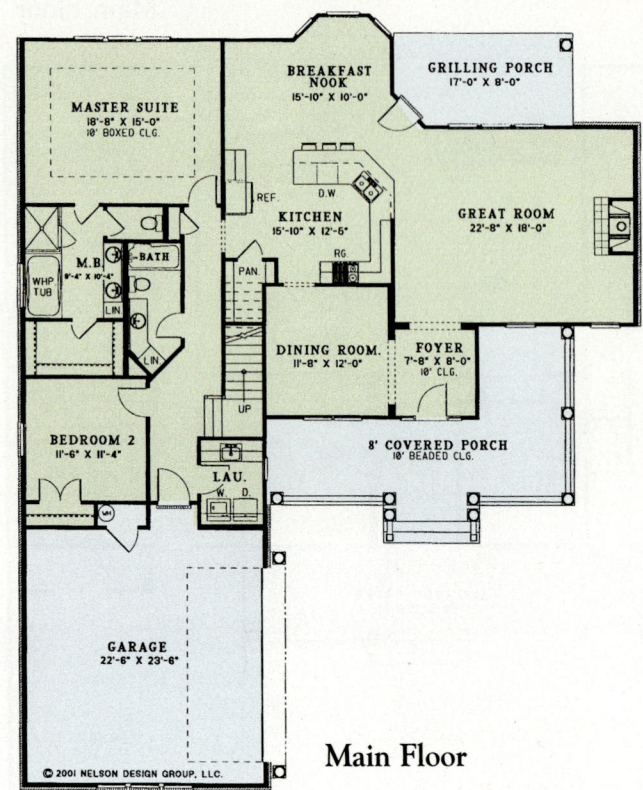

Main Floor

538 Windstone Place
Windstone Collection III

A wrap around porch with a ten foot beaded ceiling, round columns and gentle arches welcome you into this Nelson Design Group home. The foyer also carries a ten foot ceiling and leads into a great room with fireplace and a view overlooking the grilling porch. A wide walkway leads you into a breakfast bay adjoining the kitchen and through to the formal dining room. Entertaining will be enjoyable for both you and guests with this easy flowing floor plan. The master suite adorned with a boxed ceiling, as well as one bedroom and full bath are on the main floor. Upstairs has two additional bedrooms, a full bath and large bonus room located over the garage.

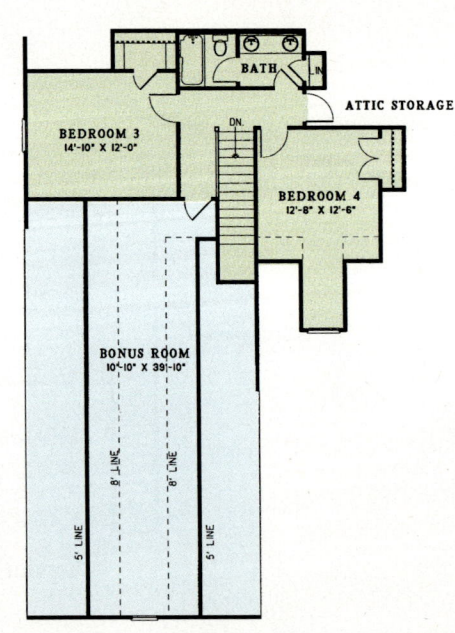

Upper Floor

Width: 58' 6"
Depth: 71' 10"
Main Floor: 1,992 sq. ft.
Upper Floor: 643 sq. ft.
Total Living: 2,635 sq. ft.*
*Optional Bonus: 468 sq. ft.
Price Tier: D

Main Ceiling: 9 ft.
Upper Ceiling: 9 ft.
Bedrooms: 4
Baths: 3
Foundation: Crawl, Slab, Opt. Basement, Opt. Daylight Basement

To view similar plans visit www.84lumber.com/ndgplans - 800.359.8484

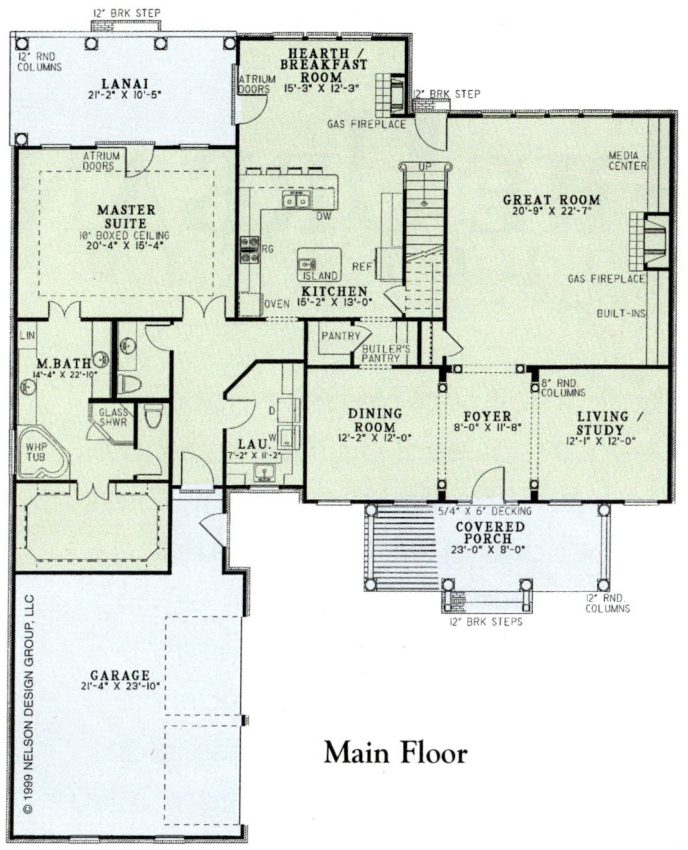

Main Floor

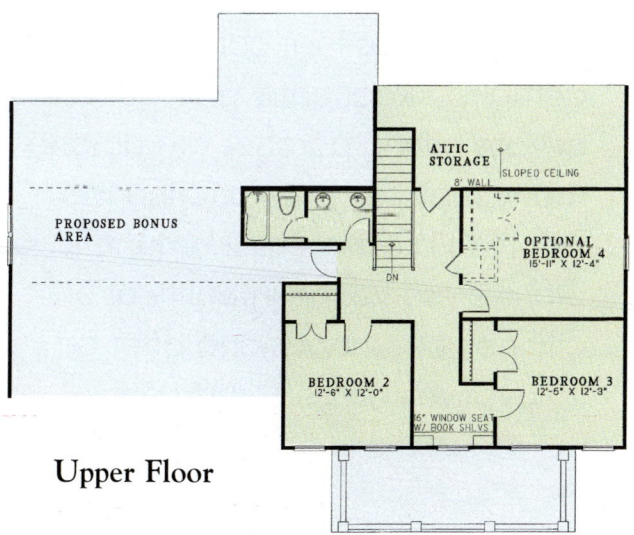

Upper Floor

363 Windstone Place
Windstone Collection III

This southern traditional Nelson Design Group home has nine foot ceilings throughout the main floor. Breakfast tradition begins in the Hearth room including a gas fireplace and atrium doors which lead to a rear Lanai with 12 inch columns. Enjoy romantic evenings in your secluded master suite with private access to the Lanai. The master bath includes a whirlpool tub and a large walk-in closet. Making your way upstairs, the kids will have all the privacy they need with two bedrooms, an optional fourth bedroom, proposed bonus/game room, and plenty of storage.

Width: 61' 5"
Depth: 73' 3"
Main Floor: 2,196 sq. ft.
Upper Floor: 647 sq. ft.
Total Living: 2,843 sq. ft.*
*Optional Bonus: 215 sq. ft.
Price Tier: D

Main Ceiling: 9 ft.
Upper Ceiling: 9 ft.
Bedrooms: 4
Baths: 2 1/2
Foundation: Crawl, Slab, Opt. Basement, Opt. Daylight Basement

THE URBAN
COLLECTION

These Traditional Neighborhood Designs represent a growing trend in the New Urbanism movement. Cities are becoming stronger by building historically inspired homes in existing neighborhoods thus preserving communities of 50 to 100 years old. Our Urban Collection offers six plans ranging in square footage from 1,200 to 1,500 with modern living spaces and amenities that consumers demand. Rear entry garages and private grilling porches are among the many features while offering the safety of a close environment. These plans preserve the integrity of our city neighborhoods and offer an innovative living environment.

Nelson Design Group LLC

RESIDENTIAL PLANNERS - DESIGNERS

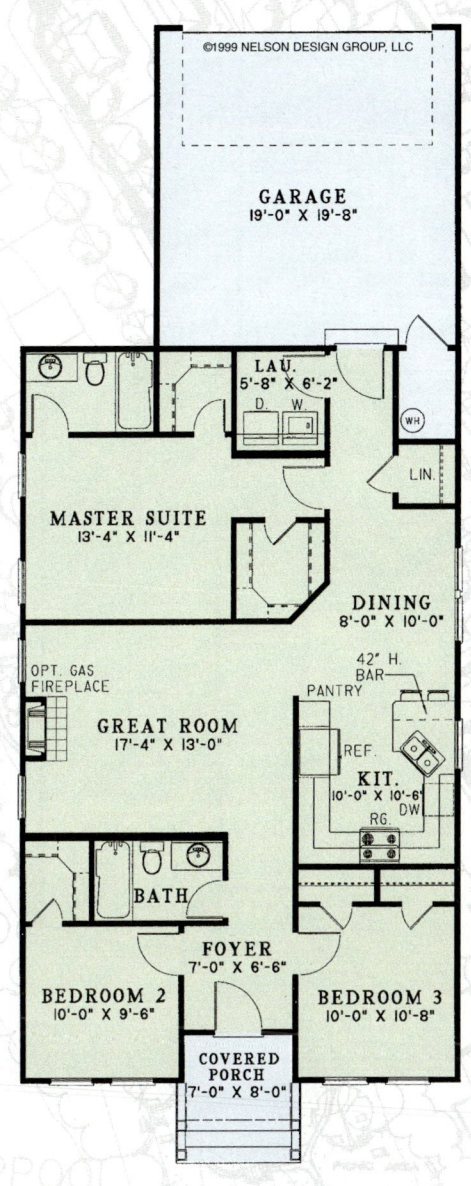

398 Urban Lane

Picture yourself greeting your family and friends on the covered entry porch of this Nelson Design Group home. The warmth of this split bedroom design will enchant you and your guests as they enter the foyer. The attractive great room offers you the perfect place to relax and enjoy the company of loved ones in front of the fireplace. Dinner will be delicious and convenient with easy access to the kitchen from the dining room. As evening falls and the guests leave you will find seclusion in the master suite complete with spacious 'his and her' walk-in closets and private bath. This southern traditional style design has all the amenities you've come to expect.

Width: 28' 4"
Depth: 66' 0"
Total Living: 1,260 sq. ft.
Main Ceiling: 9 ft.
Price Tier: A

Bedrooms: 3
Baths: 2
Foundation: Crawl, Slab

To view similar plans visit www.84lumber.com/ndgplans - 800.359.8484

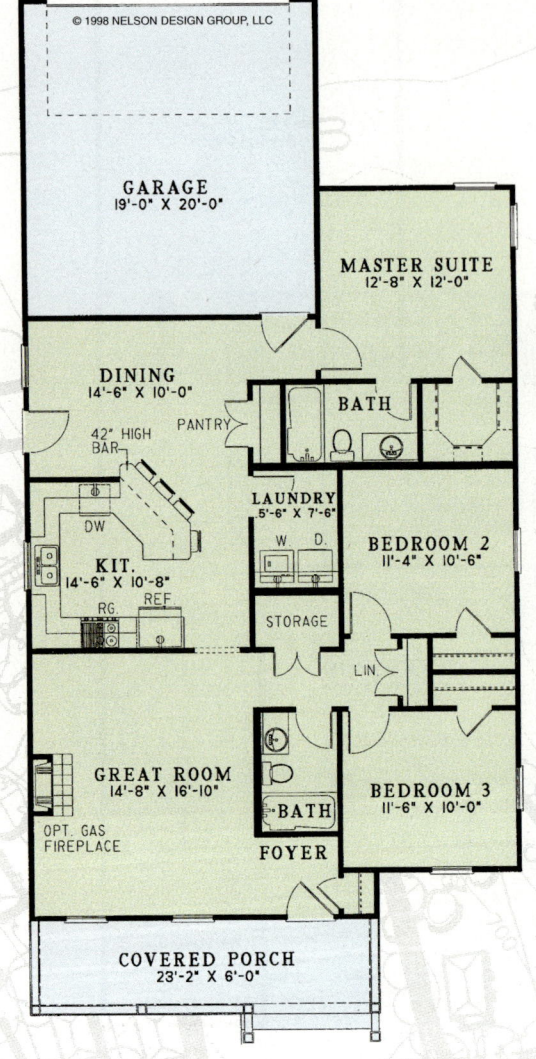

400 Urban Lane

Imagine yourself coming home to this southern traditional Nelson Design Group home. Upon entering the foyer, you can relax away the day in your charming great room with optional fireplace. You will have ample room in the kitchen and dining room to spend some quality time with your family. Helping the kids with their homework or finishing that report for work can be easy with an optional study. As the evening sets in, you will be able to relax in the privacy of the master suite with private bath and spacious walk in closet. This delightful neighborhood design has all the pleasantries you're looking for in your future home.

Width: 32' 8"
Depth: 64' 10"
Total Living: 1,342 sq. ft.
Main Ceiling: 9 ft.
Price Tier: A

Bedrooms: 3
Baths: 2
Foundation: Crawl, Slab, Opt. Basement, Opt Daylight Basement

To view similar plans visit www.84lumber.com/ndgplans - 800.359.8484

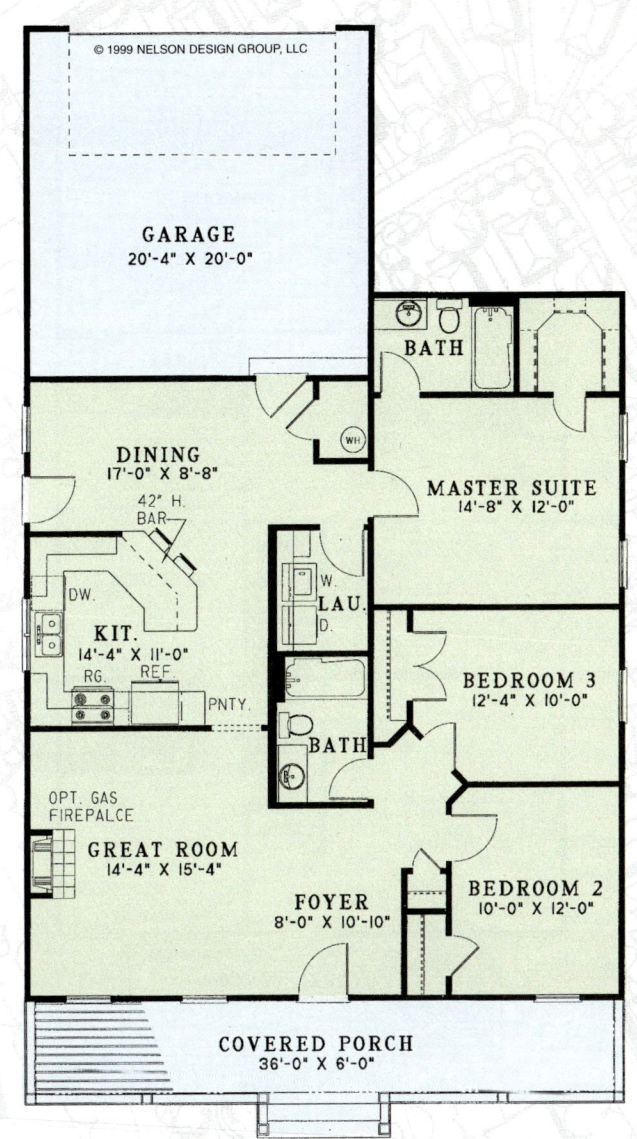

397 Urban Lane

Sit back and breathe deeply on the covered porch of this traditional southern style Nelson Design Group home. The great room, with fireplace is the perfect place to converse with your loved ones and friends. Easy access from the dining room to the kitchen makes serving your family a delight on those warm Sunday afternoons. This traditional neighborhood design offers a double bedroom area with full bath that is ideal for the kids or overnight guests. After a full day of activity you can seclude yourself in the master suite with private bath and huge walk-in closet.

Width: 36' 0"
Depth: 62' 4"
Total Living: 1,381 sq. ft.
Main Ceiling: 9 ft.
Price Tier: A

Bedrooms: 3
Baths: 2
Foundation: Crawl, Slab, Opt. Basement, Opt Daylight Basement

To view similar plans visit www.84lumber.com/ndgplans - 800.359.8484

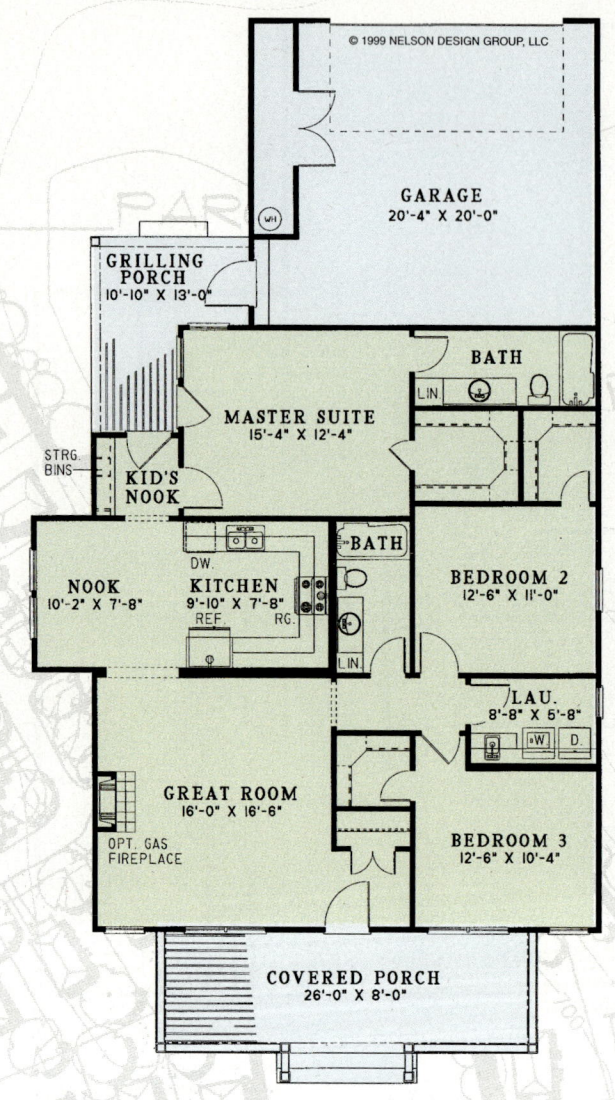

401 Urban Lane

This Nelson Design Group home has classic southern traditional charm. Picture yourself gazing in the distance on the front covered porch of your new home as the sun sets. Traveling inside you'll feel right at home in the spacious great room with optional fireplace. You'll start family traditions in the cozy breakfast nook with access to the kid's nook which includes built in storage bins. The rear side grilling porch, with access to the master suite will make entertaining a breeze on those warm summer weekends. As night falls you'll find peace in your master suite with private bath and large walk-in closet. Two bedrooms with large walk-in closets complete the design.

Width: 39' 0"	Bedrooms: 3
Depth: 70' 6"	Baths: 2
Total Living: 1,401 sq. ft.	Foundation: Crawl, Slab
Main Ceiling: 9 ft.	Price Tier: A

To view similar plans visit www.84lumber.com/ndgplans - 800.359.8484

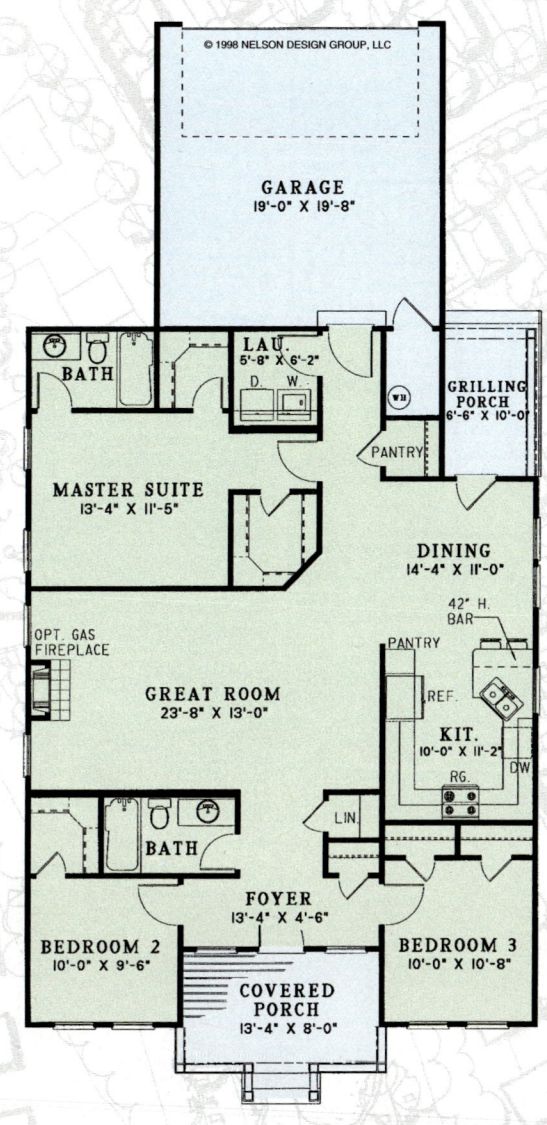

402 Urban Lane

This adorable Nelson Design Group home is the perfect starter home for you and your new family. Imagine coming home after a long day and basking in the afternoon sun on the cozy covered porch, while watching the kids play. After entering the charming foyer, you'll travel into the spacious great room, which will serve as the heart of your home. Spending time in front of the fireplace will warm the hearts of family and friends. Dining will be fun for the whole family with easy access to the grilling porch. After the kids are in bed, you'll be able to find solitude in your master suite with private bath and 'his and her' closets. This split bedroom traditional style design has all the amenities you'll need to call it home.

Width: 34' 8"
Depth: 71' 0"
Total Living: 1,442 sq. ft.
Main Ceiling: 9 ft.
Price Tier: A

Bedrooms: 3
Baths: 2
Foundation: Crawl, Slab

To view similar plans visit www.84lumber.com/ndgplans - 800.359.8484

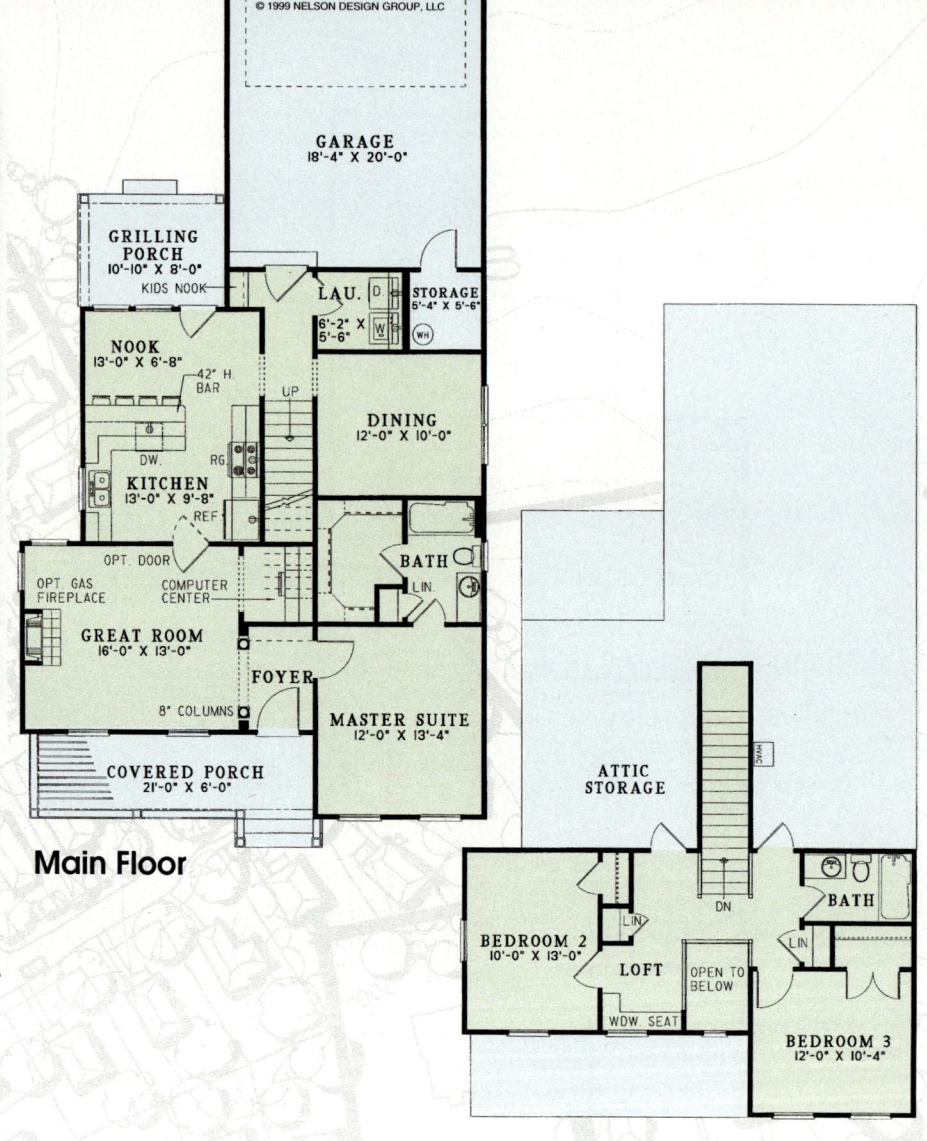

Main Floor

Upper Floor

399 Urban Lane

The simple elegance of this Nelson Design Group home will capture your imagination. As you enter the foyer, you'll admire the graceful appeal of the eight inch columns that invite you into the spacious great room. The warmth of this room will provide the perfect place to create lasting memories with family and friends. Starting the day will be fun for everyone in the charming breakfast nook with access to the rear grilling porch. After everyone is off to work or play, you'll be able to relax upstairs, maybe reading your favorite book on the window seat, or retreating to the master suite with private bath complete with a huge walk in closet. This home also features two large bedrooms, loft area, and has ample storage space to suit your needs.

Width: 34' 4"	Main Ceiling: 9 ft.
Depth: 61' 6"	Upper Ceiling: 8 ft.
Main Floor: 1,063 sq. ft.	Bedrooms: 3
Upper Floor: 496 sq. ft.	Baths: 2
Total Living: 1,559 sq. ft.	Foundation: Crawl, Slab, Opt. Basement, Opt Daylight Basement
Price Tier: B	

To view similar plans visit www.84lumber.com/ndgplans - 800.359.8484

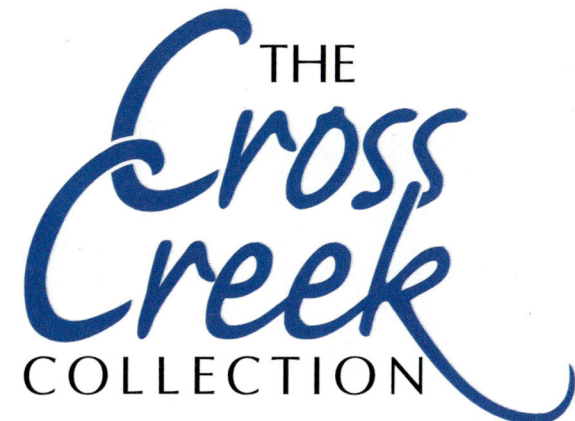

THE *Cross Creek* COLLECTION

When you choose a Nelson Design Group collection, you not only create beautiful homes, you achieve ideal master planned communities. The Cross Creek Collection features living spaces of 1,300 to 1,700 square feet and front loading garages gently tiered for street appeal. Each of the six plans complement each other, resulting in an effective Traditional European design theme and a complete neighborhood – making development easy for you. All plans are designed to fit a narrow lot of 50 feet to 60 feet. Nelson Design Group also offers complementary collections with the same traditional appeal and quality as our Cross Creek Collection.

NDG Nelson Design Group LLC

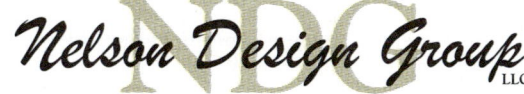

RESIDENTIAL PLANNERS - DESIGNERS

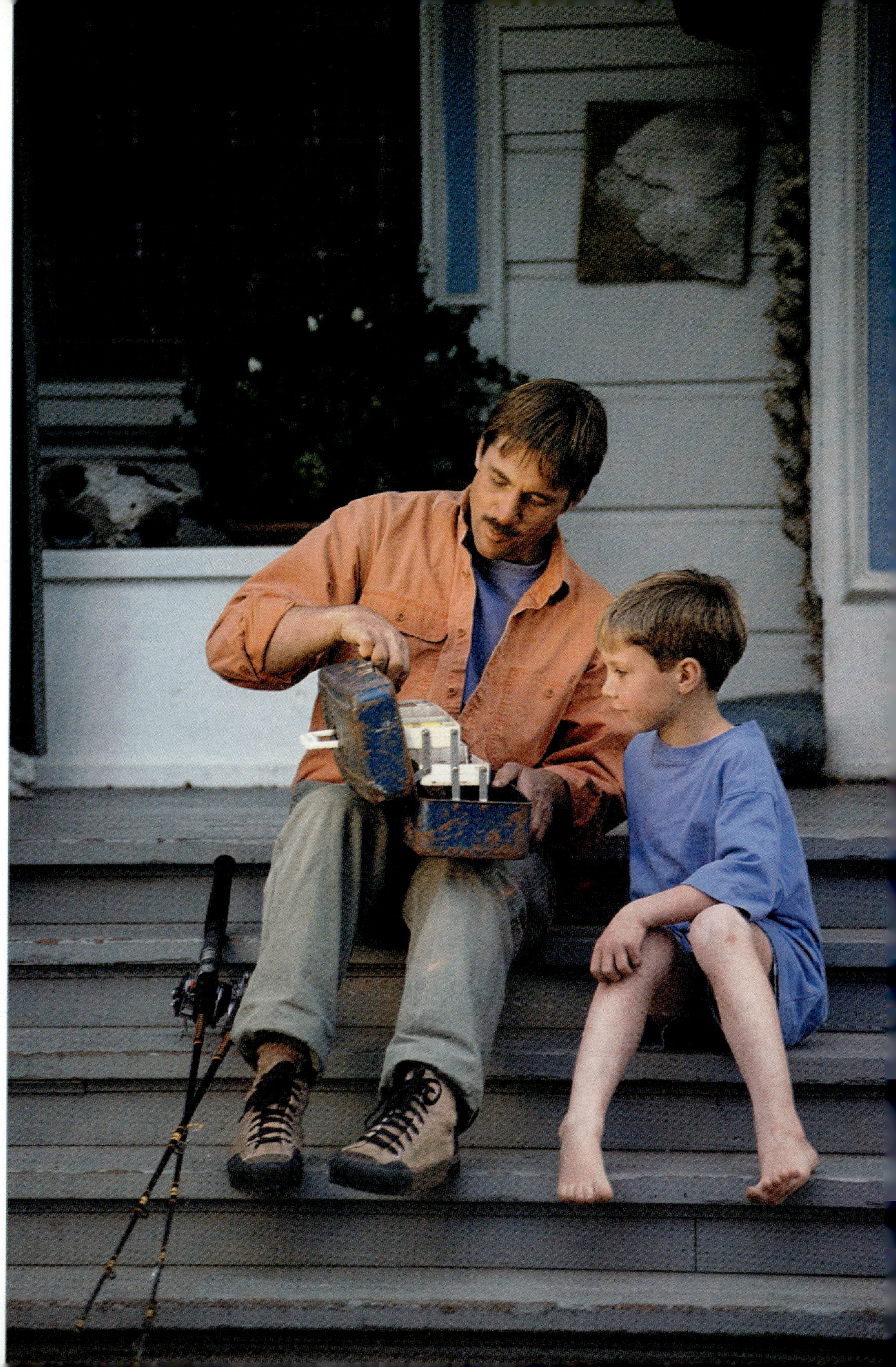

Elevation A

Elevation B

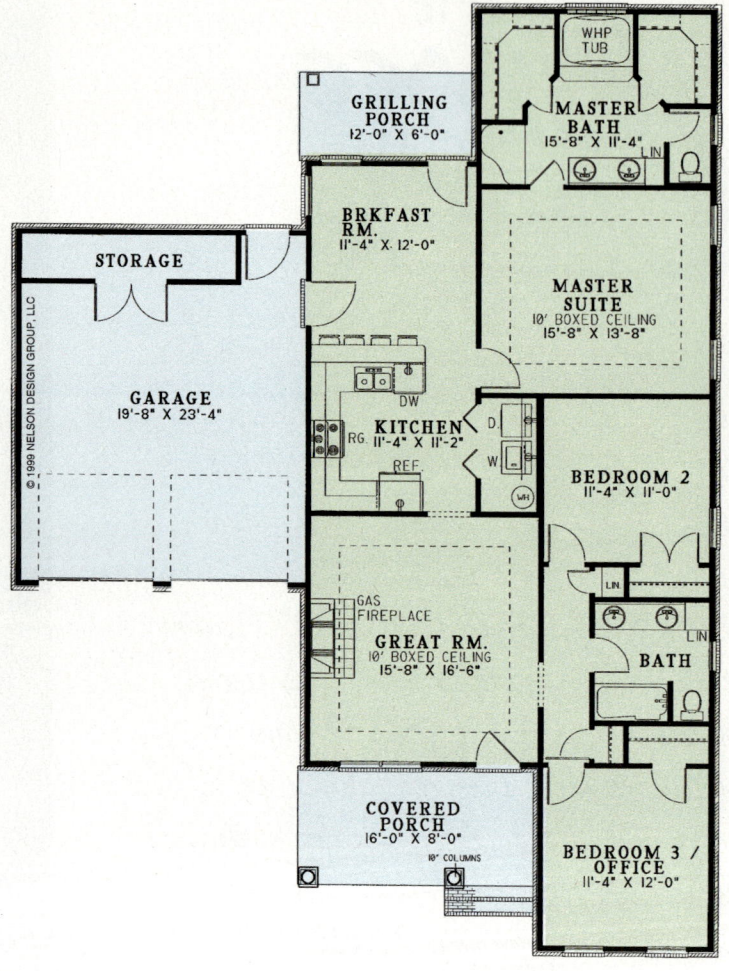

299 Cross Creek

If you can picture yourself hosting an elegant dinner party surrounded by friends and family, then step into this Nelson Design Group home. After greeting guests on the covered porch, guide them into the spacious great room. Here, mingling can begin and maybe drinks around the romantic gas fireplace. Conveniently accessible to the kitchen, you can slip away to check on the excellent cuisine you are preparing. A connecting breakfast room can serve as more space for guests or a quiet place just for you. A door opening to a grilling porch allows you to even prepare grilled meats with ease. When all the excitement is over, enjoy the privacy of the master suite or relax in a whirlpool bath.

Width: 48'	**Bedrooms:** 3
Depth: 63' 4"	**Baths:** 2
Total Living: 1,452 sq. ft.	**Foundation:** Crawl, Slab
Main Ceiling: 9 ft.	**Price Tier:** A

To view similar plans visit www.84lumber.com/ndgplans - 800.359.8484

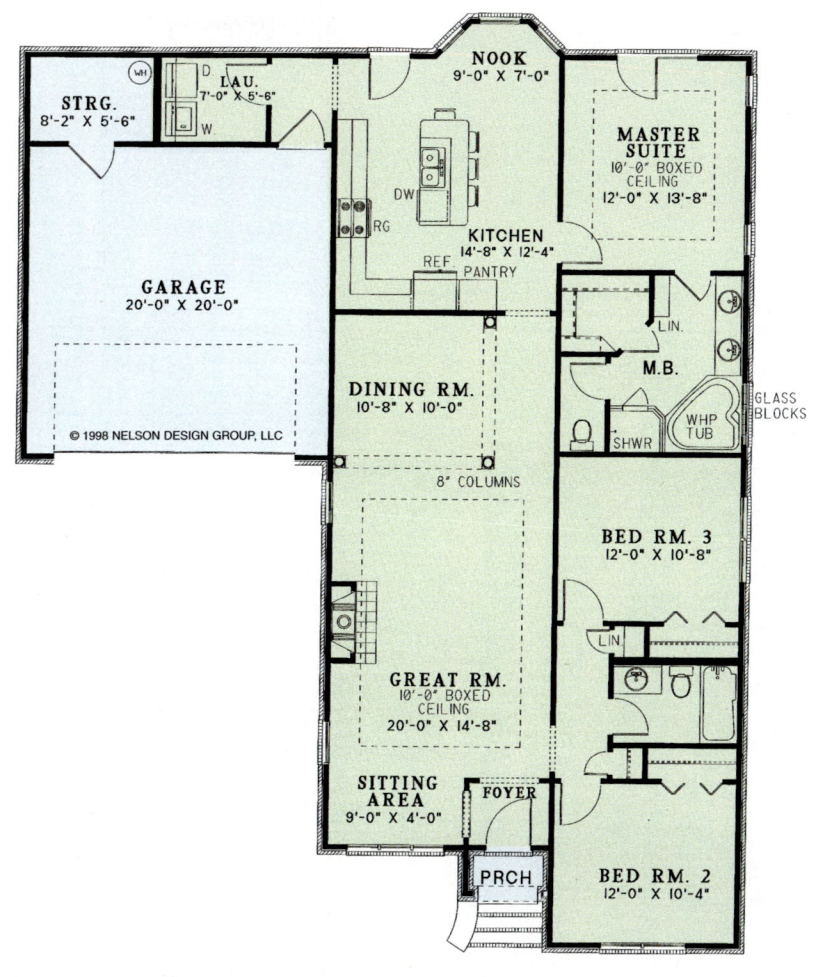

Elevation A

Elevation B

298 Cross Creek

Elegance radiates through this Nelson Design Group home. Through a traditional foyer, enter a tasteful sitting area — perfect for greeting guests before continuing into the great room with intricate ten foot boxed ceiling. Set off by magnificently crafted wooden columns, the dining room area provides an excellent atmosphere for graceful dinner parties — business or pleasure. A wonderfully open kitchen with island and bright bay window nook will ensure you have all the tools you need.

Width: 48'	Bedrooms: 3
Depth: 60' 4"	Baths: 2
Total Living: 1,598 sq. ft.	Foundation: Crawl, Slab
Main Ceiling: 9 ft.	Price Tier: B

To view similar plans visit www.84lumber.com/ndgplans - 800.359.8484

Elevation A

Elevation B

302 Cross Creek

Entering through majestic columns into the traditional foyer, you instantly feel the grandeur of this Nelson Design Group home. Imagine an evening of exquisite cuisine as you entertain your close friends and colleagues in the elegant dining room enhanced by ten foot ceilings and beautifully crafted columns. A grilling porch, located off the spacious kitchen and breakfast room, provides the ease needed to serve your favorite recipes. Following the festivities, retreat to a private master suite and relax in your whirlpool tub.

Width: 52' 8" **Bedrooms:** 3
Depth: 60' 6" **Baths:** 2
Total Living: 1,627 sq. ft. **Foundation:** Crawl, Slab
Main Ceiling: 9 ft. **Price Tier:** B

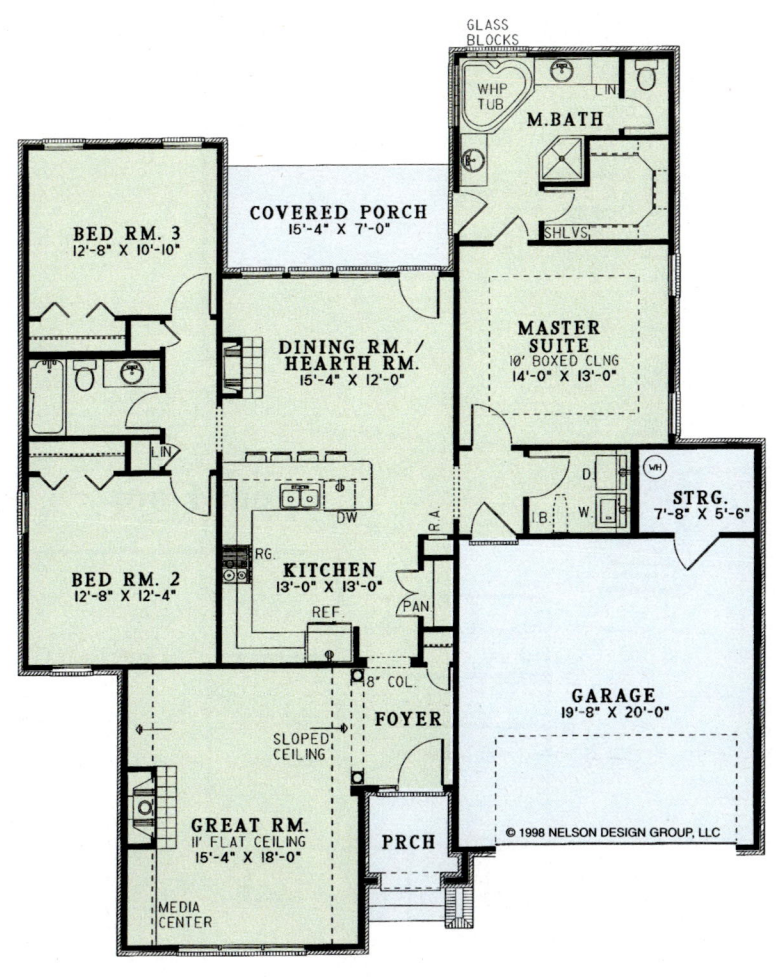

Elevation A

Elevation B

301 Cross Creek

A covered entry porch sets the stage for elegance in this Nelson Design Group home. Travel through the foyer and enter a spacious great room with unique sloped ceilings, complete with built-in media center, for hours of family entertainment. Take advantage of the distinguished dining and hearth room with a lovely fireplace. Continue entertaining on your covered rear porch over conversation and a breath-taking view.

Width: 49'	**Bedrooms:** 3
Depth: 58' 6"	**Baths:** 2
Total Living: 1,654 sq. ft.	**Foundation:** Crawl, Slab, Basement, Daylight Basement
Main Ceiling: 9 ft.	
Price Tier: B	

Elevation A

Elevation B

Main Floor

Upper Floor

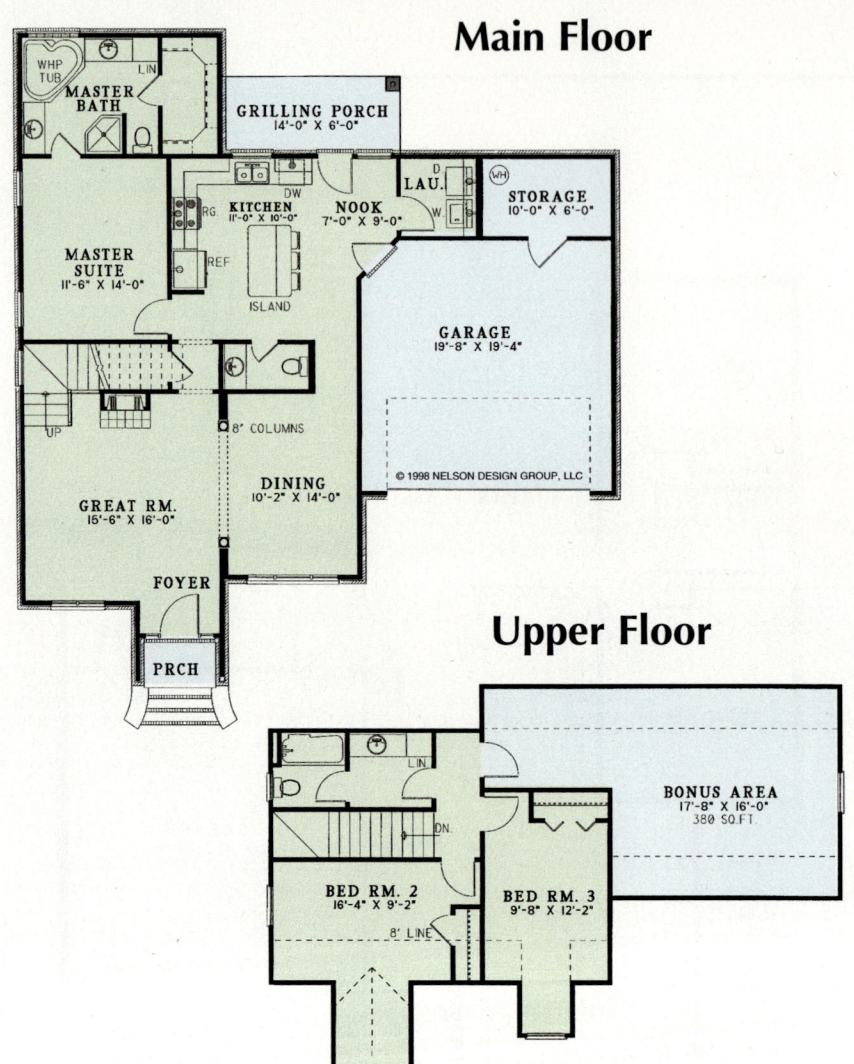

300 Cross Creek

Become enchanted by European beauty as you enter this Nelson Design Group home. Nine foot ceilings create a marvelous openness throughout the entire plan especially in the great room. Spend hours entertaining friends and family, before journeying to the elegant dining room for a spectacular meal followed by conversation over coffee. A clever grilling porch just off the kitchen area provides ample room and convenience to prepare the cuisine. After the party ends, retreat to your private master suite or relax in the whirlpool tub of your master bath. A large bonus room and two bedrooms, with adjoining bath on the upper level, make an excellent children's suite.

Width: 47'	Main Ceiling: 9 ft.
Depth: 50'	Upper Ceiling: 8 ft.
Main Floor: 1,155 sq. ft.	Bedrooms: 3
Upper Floor: 529 sq. ft.	Baths: 2 1/2
Total Living: 1,684 sq. ft.*	Foundation: Crawl, Slab, Opt. Basement, Opt. Daylight Basement
*Bonus: 380 additional sq. ft.	
Price Tier: B	

To view similar plans visit www.84lumber.com/ndgplans - 800.359.8484

Main Floor

Upper Floor

Elevation A

Elevation B

Check This Plan Mike

303 Cross Creek

Width: 48'
Depth: 43'
Main Floor: 1,356 sq. ft.
Upper Floor: 441 sq. ft.
Total Living: 1,797 sq. ft.
Price Tier: B

Main Ceiling: 9 ft.
Upper Ceiling: 8 ft.
Bedrooms: 3
Baths: 2 1/2
Foundation: Crawl, Slab, Basement, Daylight Basement

The lovely covered entry porch of this Nelson Design Group home leads you into a traditional foyer — perfect for greeting guests before an elegant dinner party. Through graceful wooden columns, enter the dining area with ten foot ceiling, creating the perfect dining ambiance. Following dinner, retreat with guests to a spacious great room for conversation over coffee and dessert. After a full night of entertaining, retreat to the comfort and privacy of a secluded master suite. The children will be fast asleep on the upper level in the two bedrooms with walk-through bath.

To view similar plans visit www.84lumber.com/ndgplans - 800.359.8484

The Village at Wellington

This collection has been put together to ease in the selection of a home plan with minimal yet efficient space. Enjoy charming traditional front porches and gently recessed garages for better street appeal. All of these fourteen plans range between 1,000 to 1,500 square feet and are perfect for narrow lots and Traditional Designed Neighborhoods. Take a moment and stroll through our Village at Wellington for a beautifully designed plan to suit your needs.

Nelson Design Group LLC

RESIDENTIAL PLANNERS - DESIGNERS

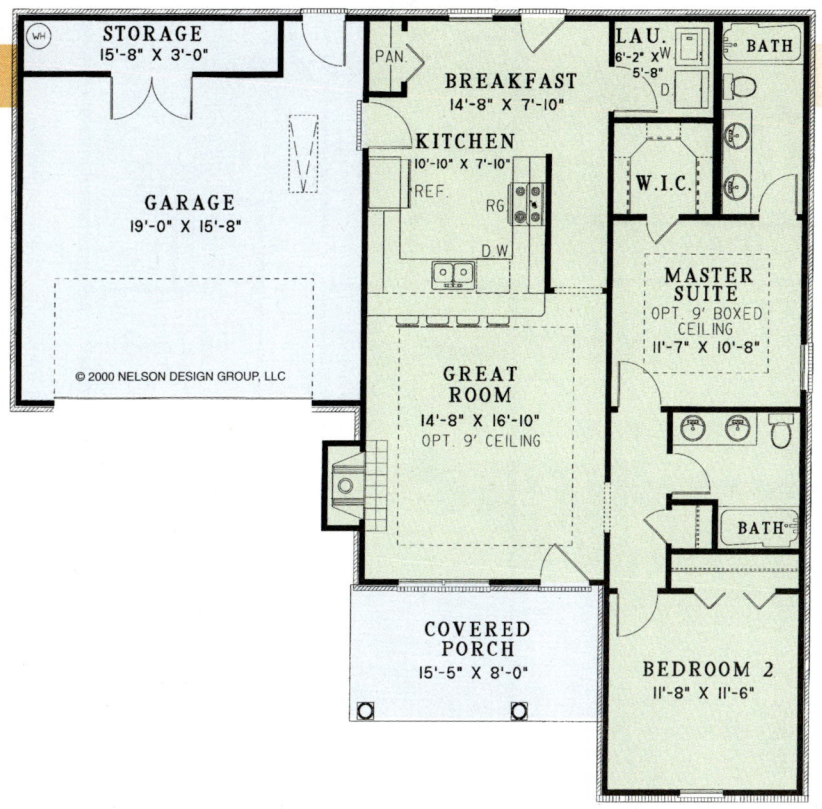

524 Wellington Lane

This stately Nelson Design Group home has all the amenities you're looking for in a home. The covered front porch is accented by ten inch round columns and a beaded ceiling. As you enter the expansive great room with optional nine foot ceiling, you'll enjoy the openness created by the eat at snack bar open to the kitchen. Starting your day will be fun and easy in the convenient kitchen with breakfast room. After a full day of activity you'll breathe easy in the privacy of the master suite, with full bath and huge walk-in closet. The second bedroom would make a lovely nursery for the family just starting out, or the perfect spare bedroom for overnight guests.

Width: 48' 8"
Depth: 45' 10"
Total Living: 1,067 sq. ft.
Main Ceiling: 8 ft.

Bedrooms: 2
Baths: 2
Foundation: Crawl, Slab
Price Tier: A

To view similar plans visit www.84lumber.com/ndgplans - 800.359.8484

531 Wellington Lane

Enjoy warm summer evenings under the stars on the front porch of this Nelson Design Group home. Traveling inside you'll feel the ambiance created by the intricate ten foot boxed ceiling in the living room and the elegance of the boxed columns leading to the dining room. The convenient kitchen with eat at snack bar is adjacent to the second bedroom or study. The master suite offers you a world of it's own with spacious nine foot boxed ceiling, a large master bath complete with 'his and her' vanities and ample closet space. This Traditional Country design will make your dreams come true.

Width: 48' 4"
Depth: 53' 0"
Total Living: 1,169 sq. ft.
Main Ceiling: 8 ft.
Price Tier: A

Bedrooms: 2
Baths: 2
Foundation: Crawl, Slab

To view similar plans visit www.84lumber.com/ndgplans - 800.359.8484

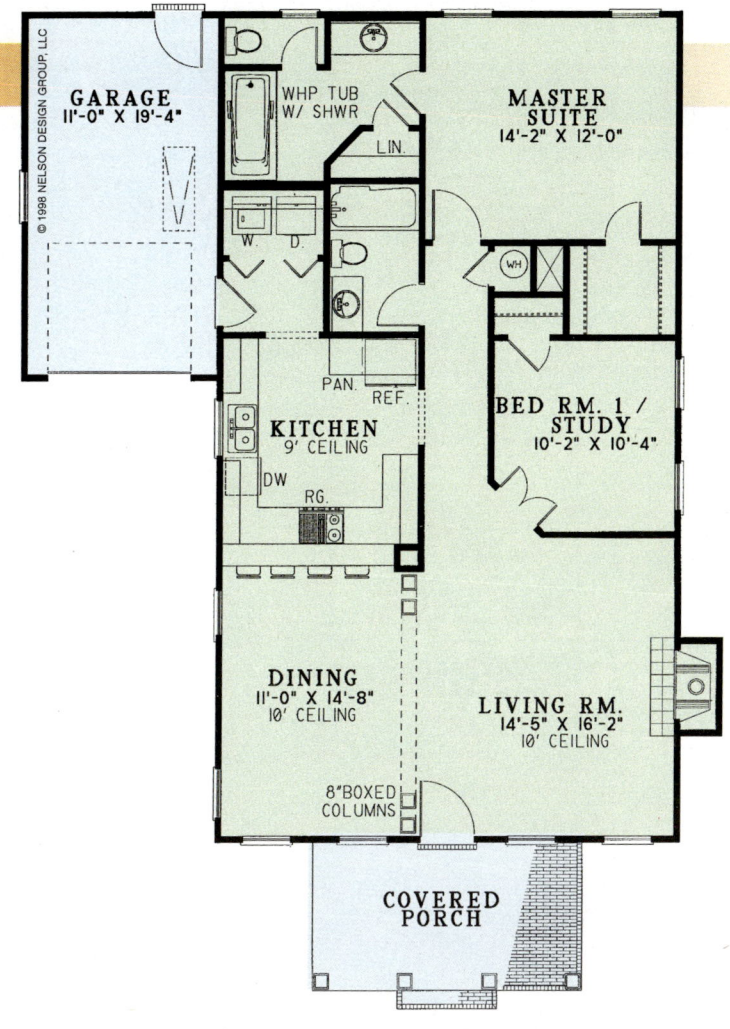

270 Wellington Lane

Charming columns welcome you onto the front porch of this Nelson Design Group home. Inside you'll feel the warmth of the fireplace and an openness created by ten foot ceilings in both the living room and formal dining room, also enhanced with eight inch boxed columns. You'll have extra dinner seating or a buffet line by utilizing the bar area that ties the kitchen to the dining room making entertaining a breeze. A roomy kitchen with a pantry and nine foot ceiling make cooking a joy. The second bedroom can serve as a spare room for overnight guests or easily converted into a study if you have the luxury of working at home. The master suite with a large walk-in closet and whirlpool tub with shower complete the design.

Width: 37' 0"
Depth: 53' 0"
Total Living: 1,172 sq. ft.
Main Ceiling: 9 ft.
Price Tier: A

Bedrooms: 2
Baths: 2
Foundation: Crawl, Slab

To view similar plans visit www.84lumber.com/ndgplans - 800.359.8484

525 Wellington Lane

Imagine coming home to this enchanting Nelson Design Group home. Friends and family will feel welcomed onto the charming front porch of this traditional neighborhood design. On those cold wintery evenings, you and your family will create lasting memories in front of the fireplace in the great room. Start family traditions in the morning by eating breakfast with your loved ones in the breakfast nook open to the kitchen and eat at bar. After the kids are in their own beds separated by a full bath, you can retreat to the privacy of the master suite complete with nine foot boxed ceiling, walk-in closet, and master bath with 'his and her' vanities.

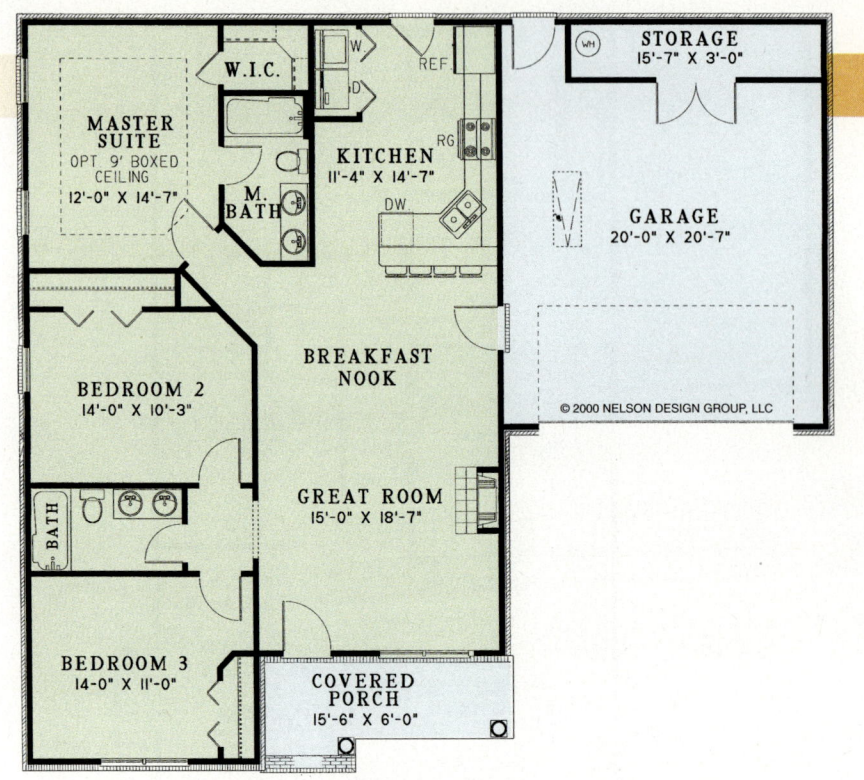

Width: 50' 4"
Depth: 45' 0"
Total Living: 1,250 sq. ft.
Main Ceiling: 8 ft.
Price Tier: A

Bedrooms: 3
Baths: 2
Foundation: Crawl, Slab, Opt Basement, Opt. Daylight Basement

To view similar plans visit www.84lumber.com/ndgplans - 800.359.8484

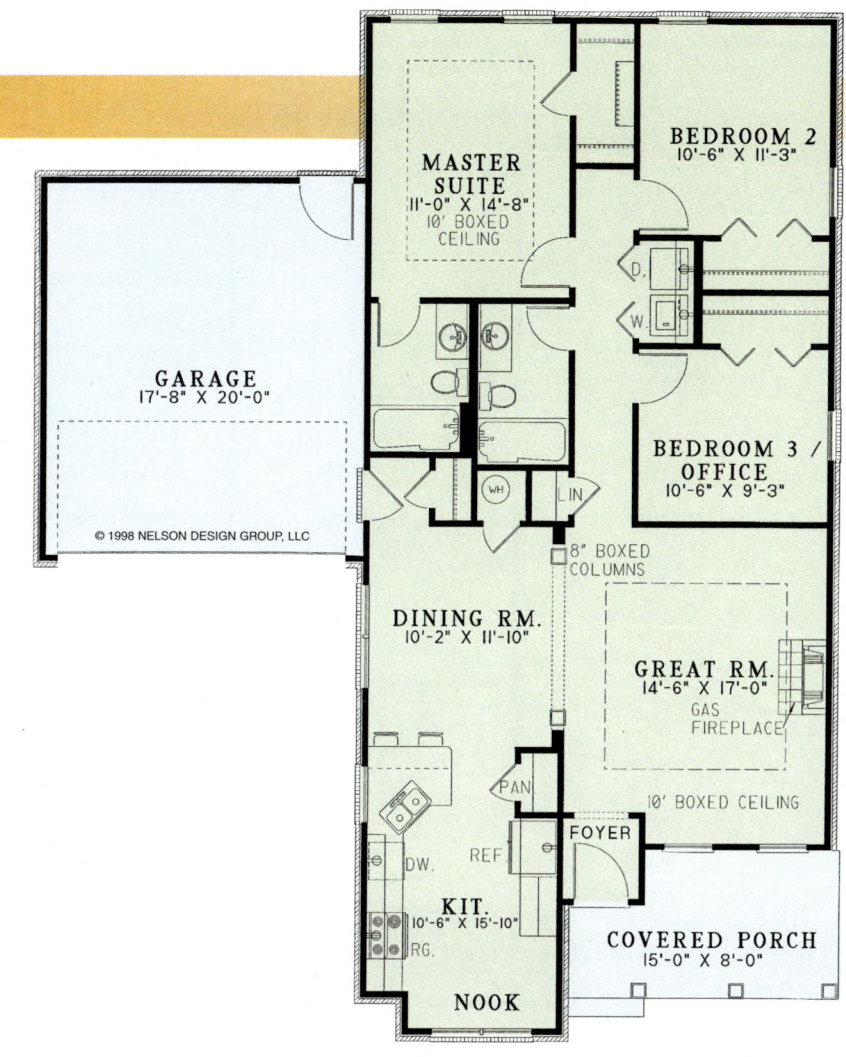

289 Wellington Lane

Impressive boxed columns surround the covered porch of this Nelson Design Group home. As you enter the foyer, you notice a spacious great room with fireplace that will be a wonderful gathering place for family and friends to begin an evening of entertainment. Serve your elegant cuisine in the dining room detailed with eight inch boxed columns with a view to the kitchen with a quaint breakfast nook. After your guests leave, you can retire to your master suite with ample room in the large walk-in closet.

Width: 44' 0"
Depth: 54' 8"
Total Living: 1,281 sq. ft.
Main Ceiling: 9 ft.
Price Tier: A

Bedrooms: 3
Baths: 2
Foundation: Crawl, Slab

To view similar plans visit www.84lumber.com/ndgplans - 800.359.8484

292 Wellington Lane

This traditional neighborhood Nelson Design Group home has a quaint covered porch to welcome friends and family for an afternoon of visiting. Entering through the foyer, your guests will enjoy gathering in the great room with a fireplace to warm themselves from the frigid temperatures that winter brings. During the summer, entertain on your rear grilling porch. When entertaining, you will enjoy quiet time in your master suite, with a large walk-in closet and private bath. Two additional bedrooms complete this design.

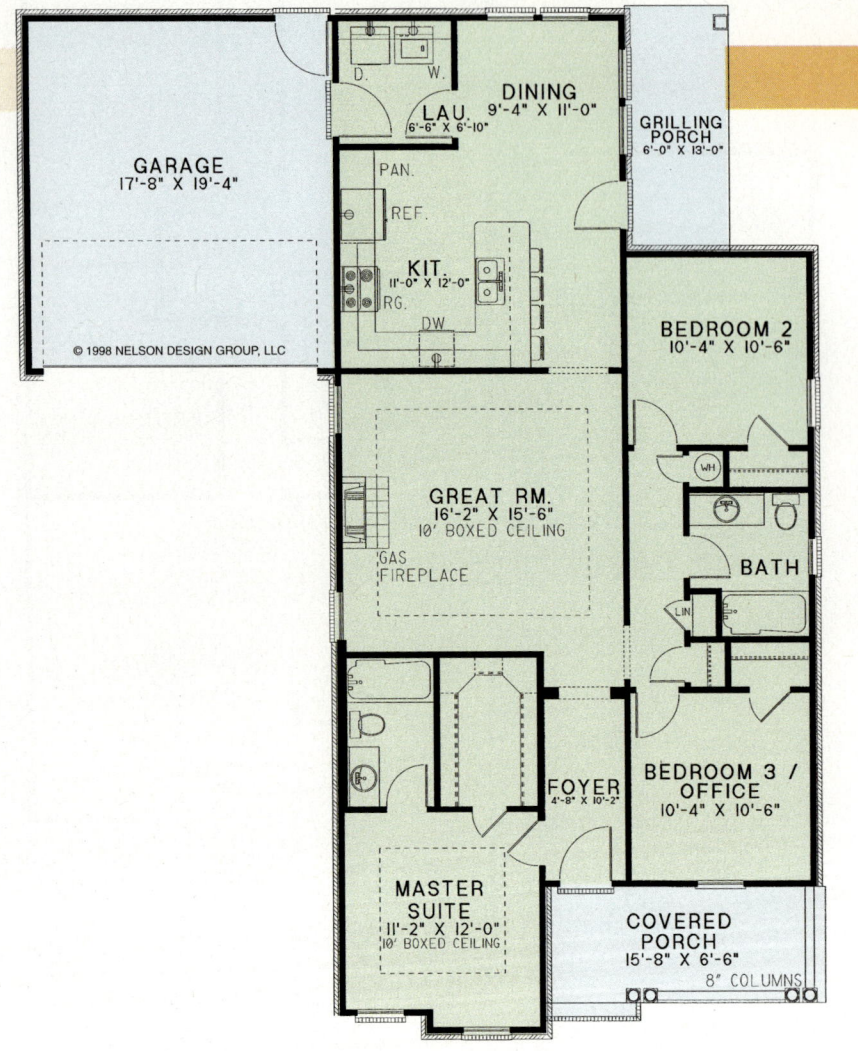

Width: 45' 6"
Depth: 56' 10"
Total Living: 1,289 sq. ft.
Main Ceiling: 9 ft.
Price Tier: A

Bedrooms: 3
Baths: 2
Foundation: Crawl, Slab

To view similar plans visit www.84lumber.com/ndgplans - 800.359.8484

530 Wellington Lane

Beautiful ferns and boxed columns embellish the front porch of this Nelson Design Group home. Upon entering the foyer, you'll be welcomed into the great room with a cozy fireplace and nine foot boxed ceiling. Across and through a column cased opening is the formal dining directly accessing the kitchen for ease in entertaining. Down the hall is the master suite also enhanced by a nine foot ceiling, large walk-in closet with built-ins and a full bathroom with double vanity. The second and third bedrooms or study share a full bathroom located in the hall. This Traditional Country design offers you and your family an array of amenities you've come to look for in your future home.

Width: 46' 0"
Depth: 54' 8"
Total Living: 1,294 sq. ft.
Main Ceiling: 8 ft.
Price Tier: A

Bedrooms: 3
Baths: 2
Foundation: Crawl, Slab

To view similar plans visit www.84lumber.com/ndgplans - 800.359.8484

291 Wellington Lane

This split bedroom Nelson Design Group home will turn your dreams into reality. Imagine greeting your family and friends on the front porch adorned with ten inch columns. Upon entering the home you'll notice the expansive great room with fireplace, open to the dining room and kitchen. This will make entertaining guests a cinch. The Master suite will be your haven with it's spacious ten foot boxed ceiling and full bath. The second and third bedrooms offer the kids their own part of the home with a full bath complete with 'his and her' vanities, as well as ample closet space.

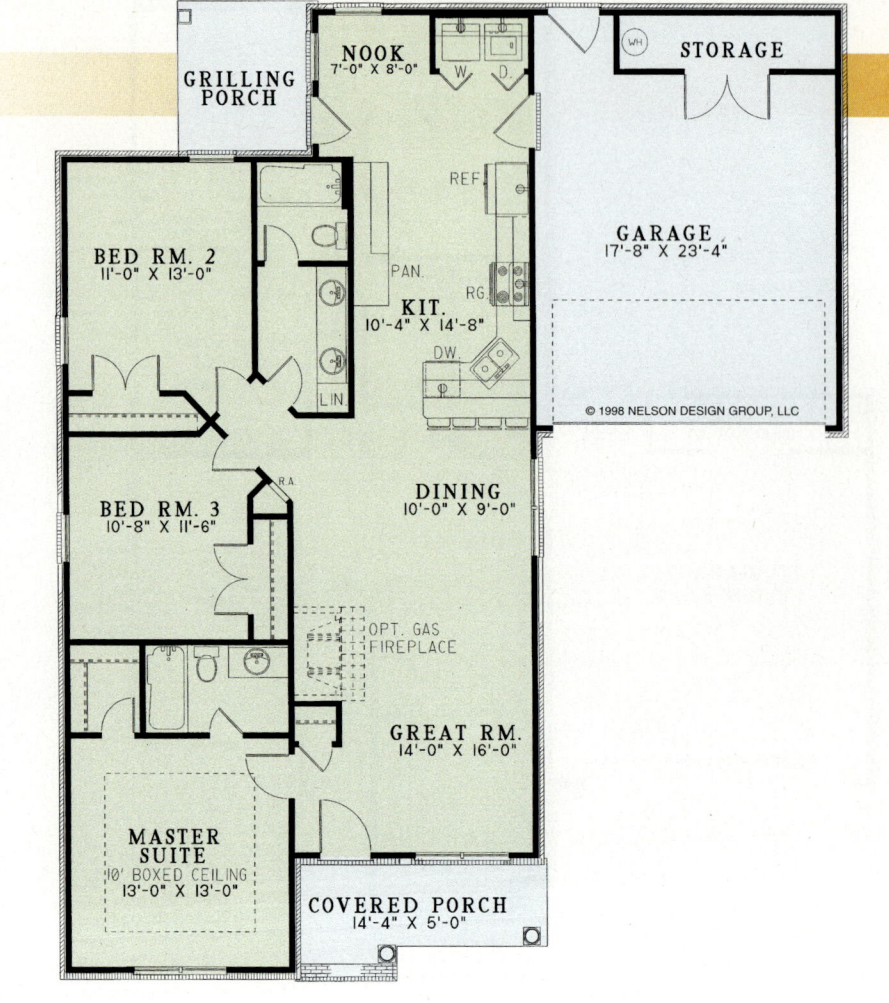

Width: 46' 0"
Depth: 54' 10"
Total Living: 1,317 sq. ft.
Main Ceiling: 9 ft.
Price Tier: A

Bedrooms: 3
Baths: 2
Foundation: Crawl, Slab, Basement, Daylight Basement

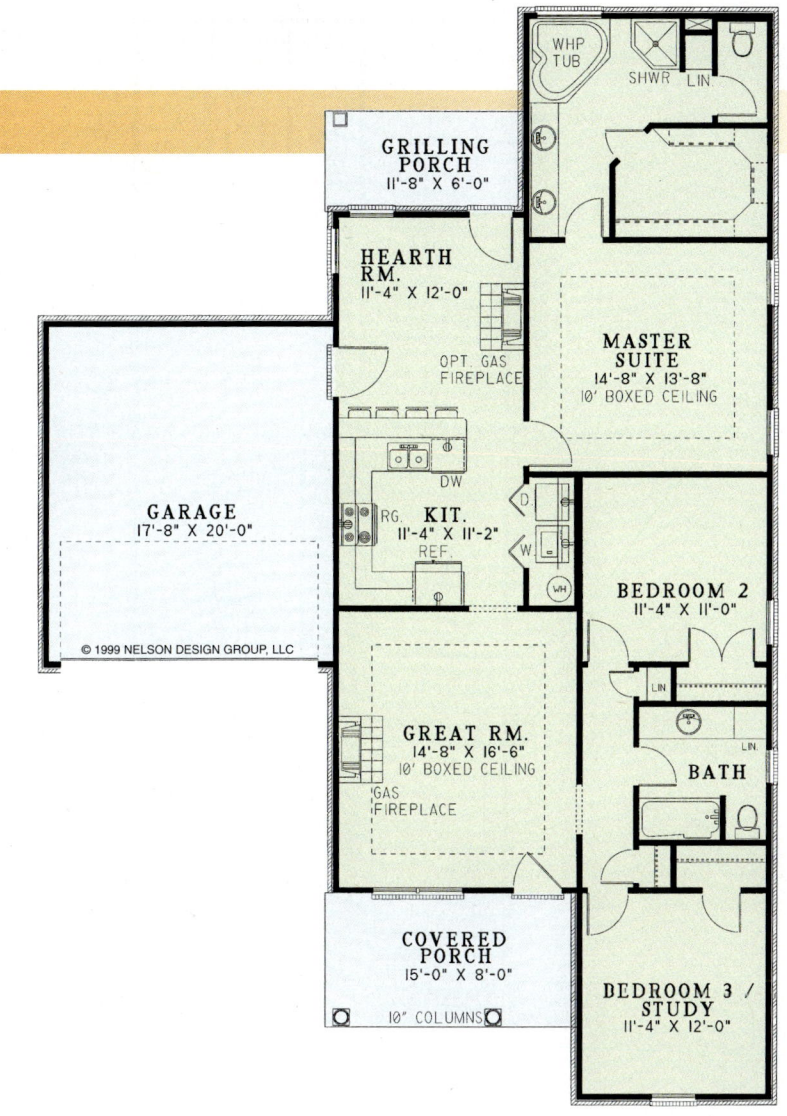

290 Wellington Lane

Enjoy peaceful fall evenings watching the sun set in this Nelson Design Group home. When it gets too cold, you can warm yourself in the comfortable great room, complete with fireplace. Begin each day with coffee and the morning paper in the hearth room with fluid access to the kitchen. The family chef will love displaying his or her skills during an afternoon cookout on the rear grilling porch. After the day has come to a close, you will find it most relaxing to soothe those aches away in the privacy of your master bath.

Width: 45' 0"
Depth: 64' 10"
Total Living: 1,425 sq. ft.
Main Ceiling: 9 ft.
Price Tier: A

Bedrooms: 3
Baths: 2
Foundation: Crawl, Slab

To view similar plans visit www.84lumber.com/ndgplans - 800.359.8484

69

297 Wellington Lane

This split bedroom Nelson Design Group home offers all the amenities you're looking for in a home. Once inside you'll feel an openness created by the spacious great room with fireplace and elaborate ten foot boxed ceiling. The third bedroom or study, with elegant eight inch columns, is open to the great room creating a spacious feel throughout the design. Spending quality time with the family will be a delight in the breakfast room with access to the grilling porch. You'll find solitude in the master suite complete with a heavenly whirlpool tub and huge walk-in closet. A full bath separates bedroom two from the study completing the design.

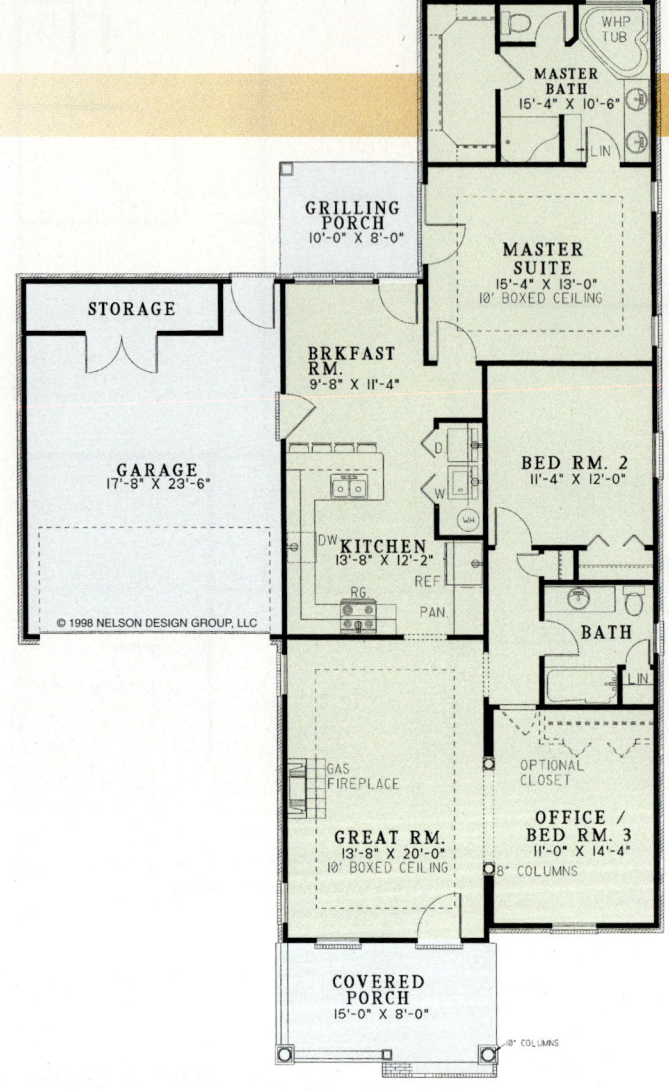

Width: 44' 0"
Depth: 71' 2"
Total Living: 1,449 sq. ft.
Main Ceiling: 9 ft.
Price Tier: A

Bedrooms: 3
Baths: 2
Foundation: Crawl, Slab

To view similar plans visit www.84lumber.com/ndgplans - 800.359.8484

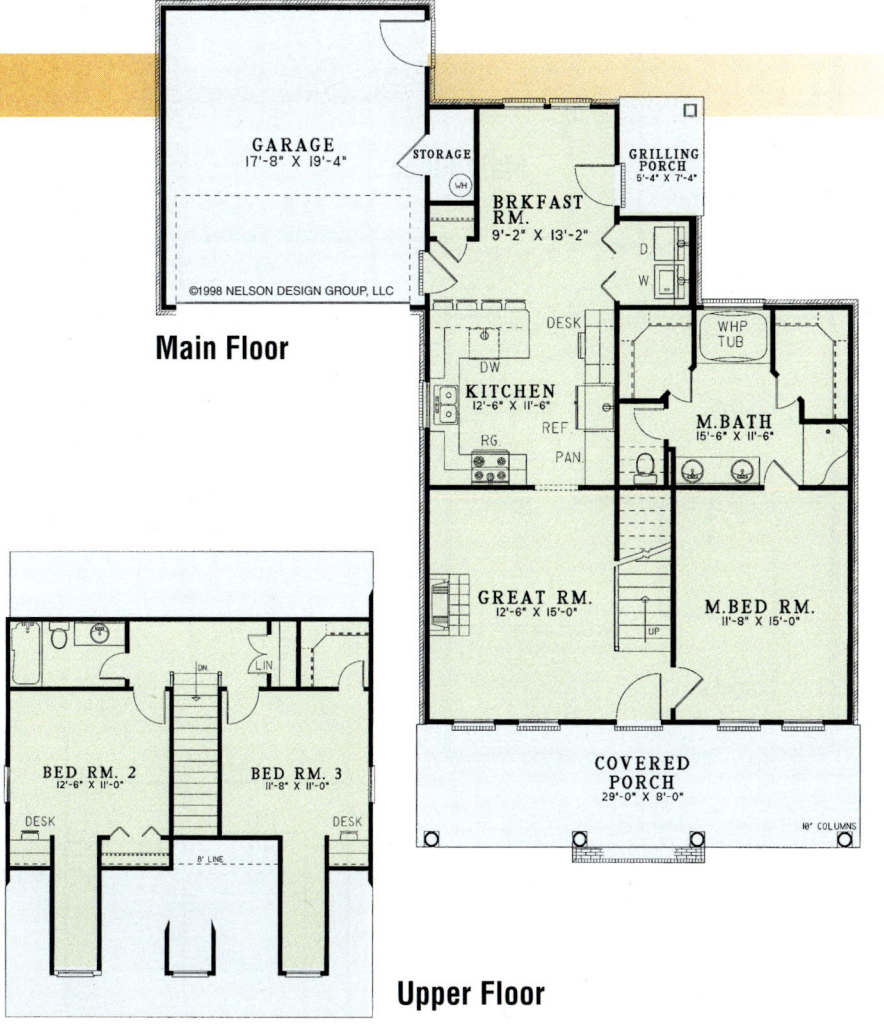

Main Floor

Upper Floor

293 Wellington Lane

A charming front porch attracts everyone in this traditional Nelson Design Group home. Entertaining will be easy on your convenient grilling porch which allows you to prepare dinner with ease. After dinner, your guests can gather in the spacious great room for games and laughter. After the guests leave, you can retire to your private master suite and bath which features an enticing whirlpool bath as well as 'his and her' walk-in closets. Upstairs, the children will be tucked away in their own bedrooms.

Width: 47' 0"
Depth: 55' 2"
Main Floor: 980 sq. ft.
Upper Floor: 561 sq. ft.
Total Living: 1,541 sq. ft.
Price Tier: B

Main Ceiling: 9 ft.
Upper Ceiling: 8 ft.
Bedrooms: 3
Baths: 2
Foundation: Crawl, Slab, Basement, Daylight Basement

To view similar plans visit www.84lumber.com/ndgplans - 800.359.8484

296 Wellington Lane

This quaint Nelson Design Group home provides the traditional family all the privacy they need. Beautiful columns welcome you into the great room with a built-in media center and gas fireplace. The grill master of the family can try their luck on the rear grilling porch for those friends who tend to drop by. A spacious kitchen allows you to prepare quick meals with ease. When night falls, travel to your master suite where you'll relax with a corner whirlpool bath, double vanities and separate corner glass shower. Upstairs you'll find two more bedrooms, just right for the kids.

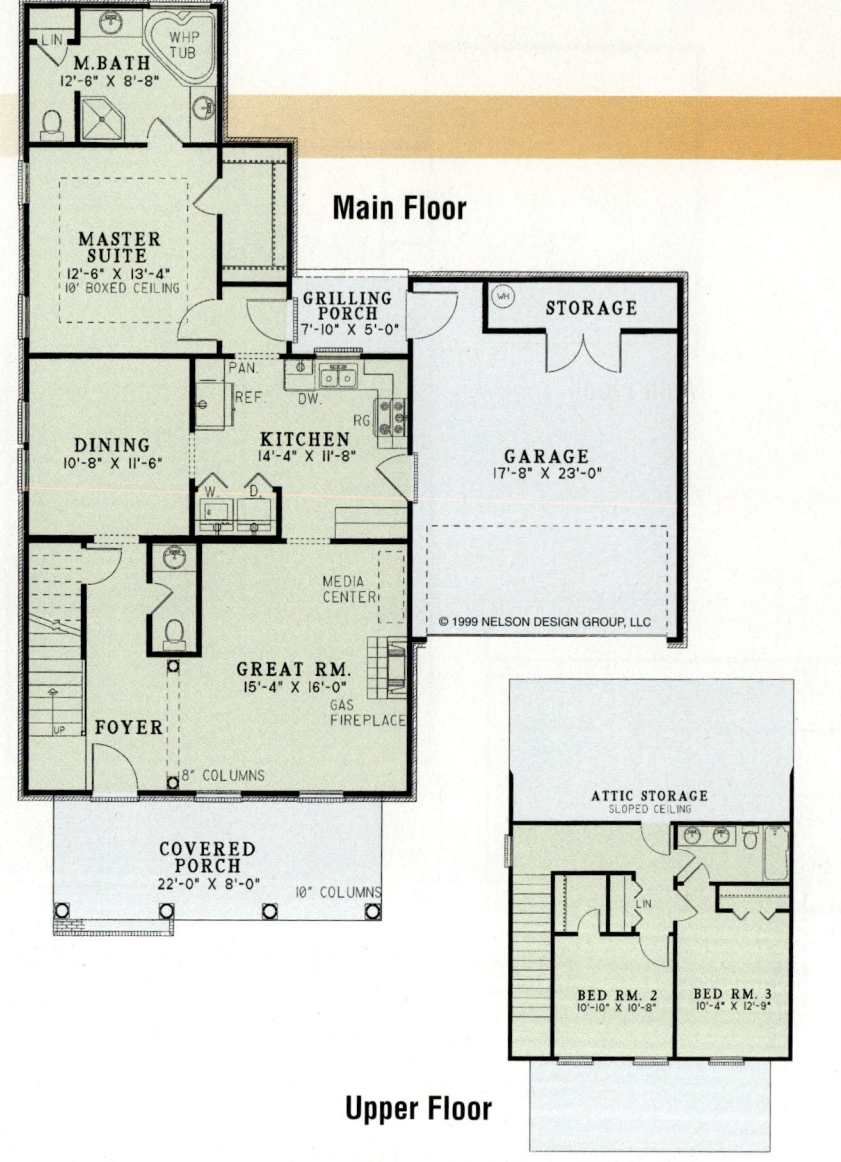

Main Floor

Upper Floor

Width: 44' 0"
Depth: 59' 4"
Main Floor: 1,112 sq. ft.
Upper Floor: 483 sq. ft.
Total Living: 1,595 sq. ft.
Price Tier: B

Main Ceiling: 9 ft.
Upper Ceiling: 8 ft.
Bedrooms: 3
Baths: 2 1/2
Foundation: Crawl, Slab, Basement, Daylight Basement

To view similar plans visit www.84lumber.com/ndgplans - 800.359.8484

Sage Meadows
COLLECTION

When you choose a Nelson Design Group collection, you not only create beautiful homes, you achieve ideal master planned communities. The Sage Meadows Collection of French Country designs feature living spaces of 1,100 to 1,600 square feet — advantageous for rear access and open views for lake or golf course settings. Each of the twelve plans complement each other, resulting in an effective overall design theme and a complete neighborhood — making development easy for you. All plans are designed to fit a narrow lot of 50 feet to 60 feet. Nelson Design Group also offers complementary collections with the same traditional appeal and quality as our Sage Meadows Collection.

Nelson Design Group LLC

RESIDENTIAL PLANNERS - DESIGNERS

288 Sage Meadows

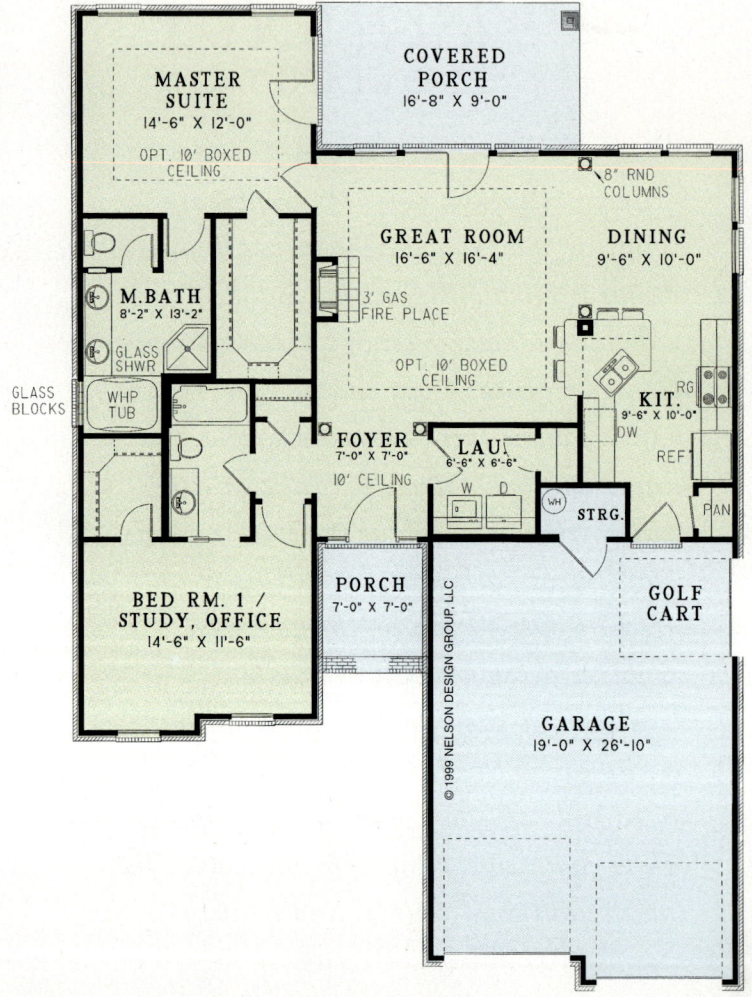

Imagine the luxury of waking to a warm spring morning, walking out an atrium door from your master suite onto a rear covered porch overlooking a beautiful lake or golf course. With this Nelson Design Group home, the dream is a reality. The covered porch makes entertaining friends easy with convenient access to the great room — complete with gas fireplace and ten-foot boxed ceilings.

Width: 41' 10"
Depth: 59' 8"
Total Living: 1,287 sq. ft.
Main Ceiling: 9 ft.
Price Tier: A

Bedrooms: 2
Baths: 2
Foundation: Crawl, Slab, Basement, Daylight Basement

To view similar plans visit www.84lumber.com/ndgplans - 800.359.8484

279 Sage Meadows

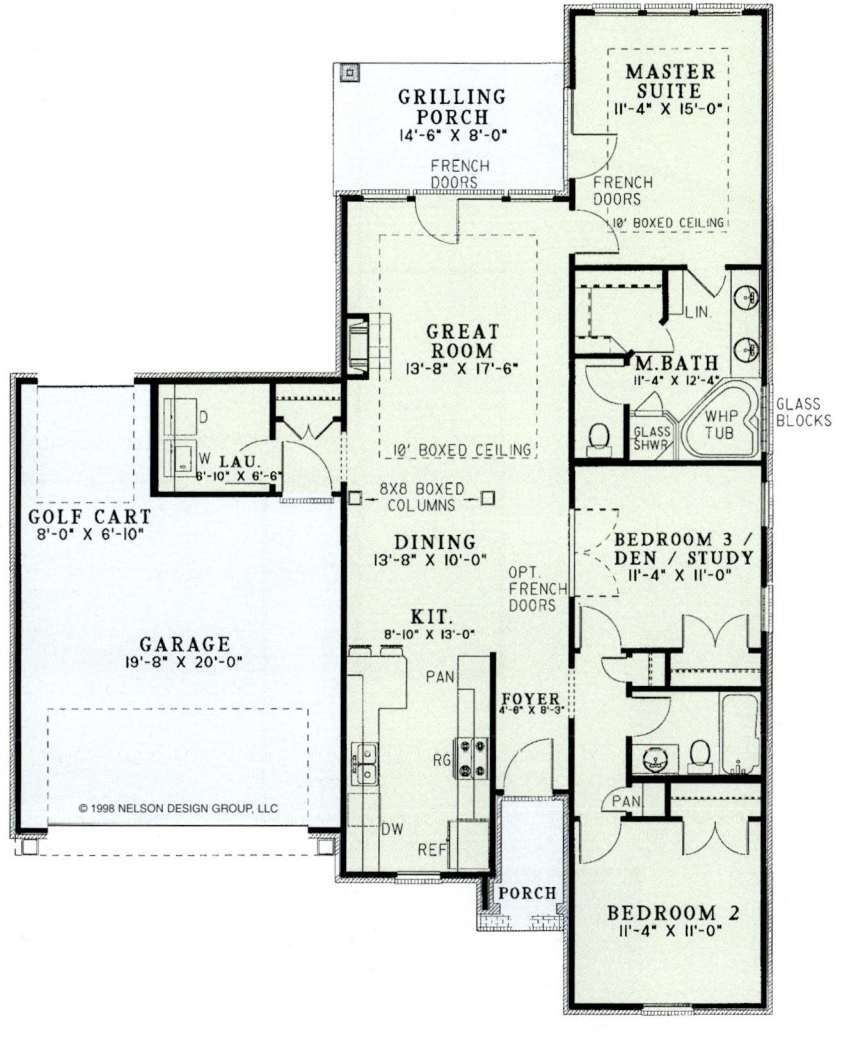

Throughout this Nelson Design Group home, you'll feel the openness achieved by the grandeur of 9' ceilings. A covered rear porch makes entertaining friends and family a breeze, and perfect for a delicious summer barbecue. Elegant french doors lead you back inside where you'll enjoy conversation in your spacious great room, conveniently accessible to the dining area and kitchen. An additional third bedroom can be converted to a den or study to accommodate everyone.

Width: 46'	Bedrooms: 3
Depth: 60' 4"	Baths: 2
Total Living: 1,359 sq. ft.	Foundation: Crawl, Slab
Main Ceiling: 9 ft.	
Price Tier: A	

282 Sage Meadows

Enter this French Country Nelson Design Group home and find a traditional covered entry porch with marvelous ten foot ceilings. Following through the foyer, you're led into a spacious great room where you can spend cold winter nights in front of a warm fire. In addition, convenient access from the master suite to the covered rear porch provides the atmosphere for private romantic summer evenings.

Width: 38' 4"
Depth: 68' 6"
Total Living: 1,379 sq. ft.
Main Ceiling: 9 ft.
Price Tier: A

Bedrooms: 3
Baths: 2
Foundation: Crawl, Slab

To view similar plans visit www.84lumber.com/ndgplans - 800.359.8484

281 Sage Meadows

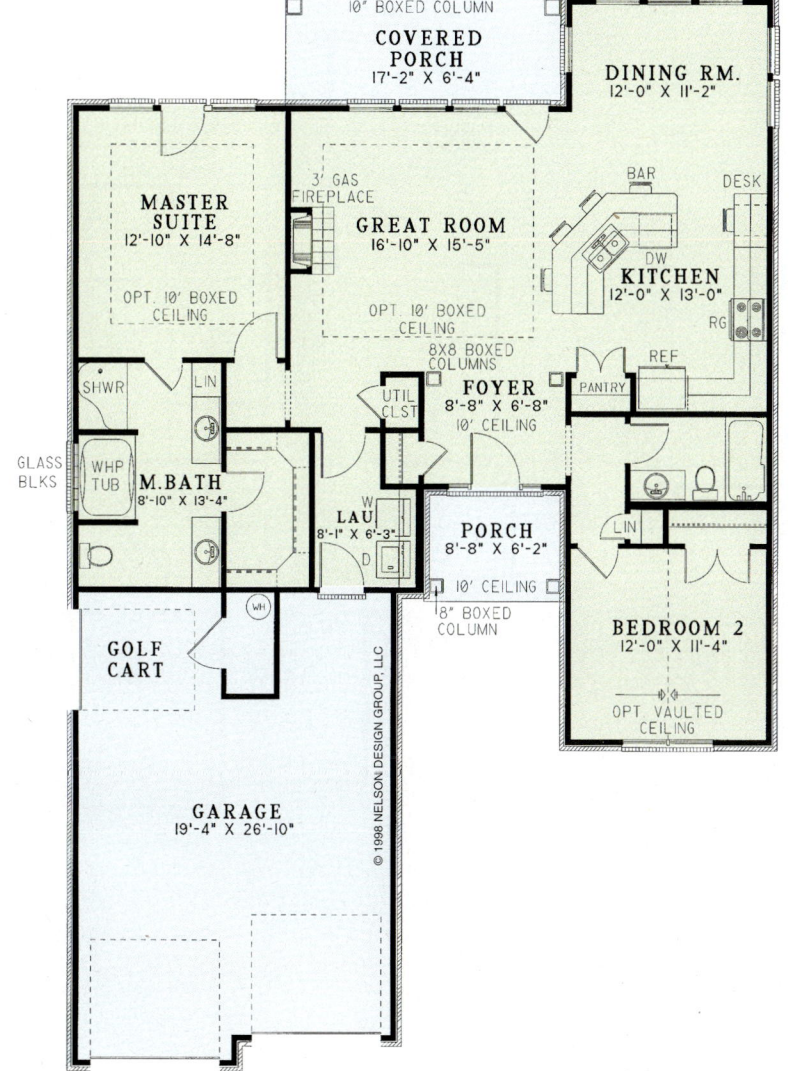

After a great game, drive your golf cart right off the course and up to your spacious two-car garage with side golf cart entry in this French Country Nelson Design Group home. Or come up the front walk and enter a beautiful porch with ten foot ceiling and boxed columns leading to an open foyer and great room where you'll enjoy hours of relaxation and entertainment. Share conversation or sit in silent awe as you watch the calming lake from your rear covered porch.

Width: 43'	Bedrooms: 2
Depth: 63' 6"	Baths: 2
Total Living: 1,387 sq. ft.	Foundation: Crawl, Slab, Opt. Basement, Opt. Daylight Basement
Main Ceiling: 9 ft.	
Price Tier: A	

To view similar plans visit www.84lumber.com/ndgplans - 800.359.8484

285 Sage Meadows

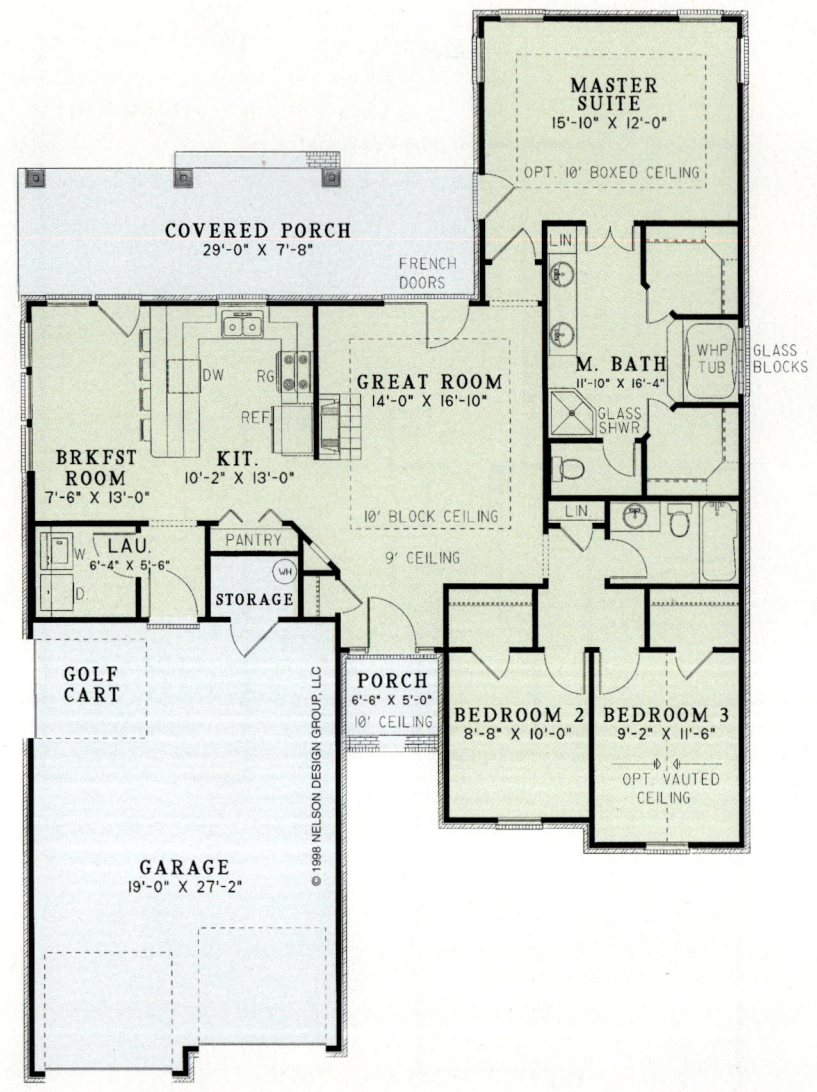

Begin each day in comfort in this Nelson Design Group home. A spacious breakfast area, with the warmth of a sun room, allows early morning sunshine to peek through wonderful windows. French doors lead onto a spacious rear covered porch, perfect for entertaining or relaxing, which features a private entry to the master suite. French doors from the porch bring you back into the center of the home – the great room. Here, spend hours of quality time with your family playing games or reading a good book before retreating to your private master suite.

Width: 45'
Depth: 64' 2"
Total Living: 1,395 sq. ft.
Main Ceiling: 9 ft.
Price Tier: A

Bedrooms: 3
Baths: 2
Foundation: Crawl, Slab

286 Sage Meadows

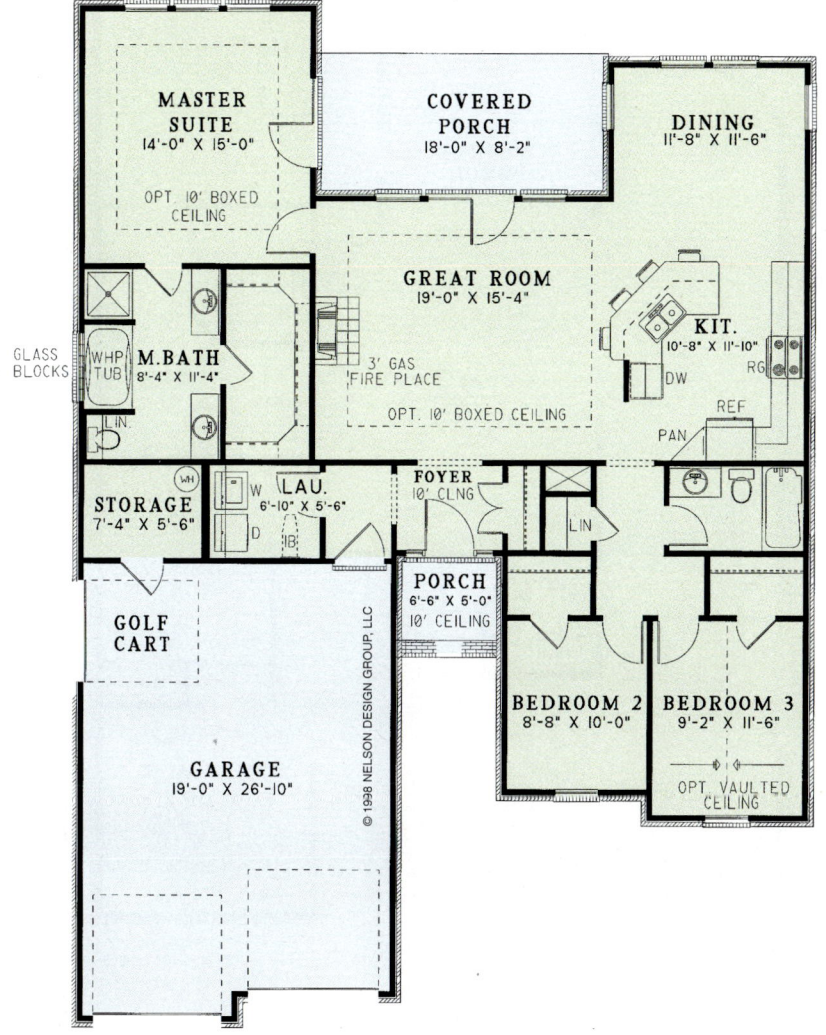

Whether entering through the traditional covered porch with ten foot ceiling or the wonderful two-car garage with offset doors and side golf cart storage, this French Country Nelson Design Group home has plenty to offer. Passing through the foyer, you'll find an expansive great room complete with a gas fireplace and atrium doors leading to a rear covered porch, the ideal setting for grilling and entertaining. Enjoy the convenience of preparing meals in a spacious kitchen with angular island and eat-at bar. After a long day of work or play, relax in your private master suite with a beautiful view and access to the rear porch.

Width: 45'	**Bedrooms:** 3
Depth: 60' 4"	**Baths:** 2
Total Living: 1,472 sq. ft.	**Foundation:** Crawl, Slab
Main Ceiling: 9 ft.	
Price Tier: A	

To view similar plans visit www.84lumber.com/ndgplans - 800.359.8484

283 Sage Meadows

At the heart of this Nelson Design Group home is an impressive great room with ten foot ceilings and peninsula fireplace. Off the great room, your family will enjoy meals together any time of day in the expansive kitchen. With an island, eat-at open bar, and breakfast nook complete with bay windows, you won't hear any excuses for not finding time to eat. A secluded private entrance with french doors from the master suite to a rear covered porch allows you the opportunity to "get away" from it all.

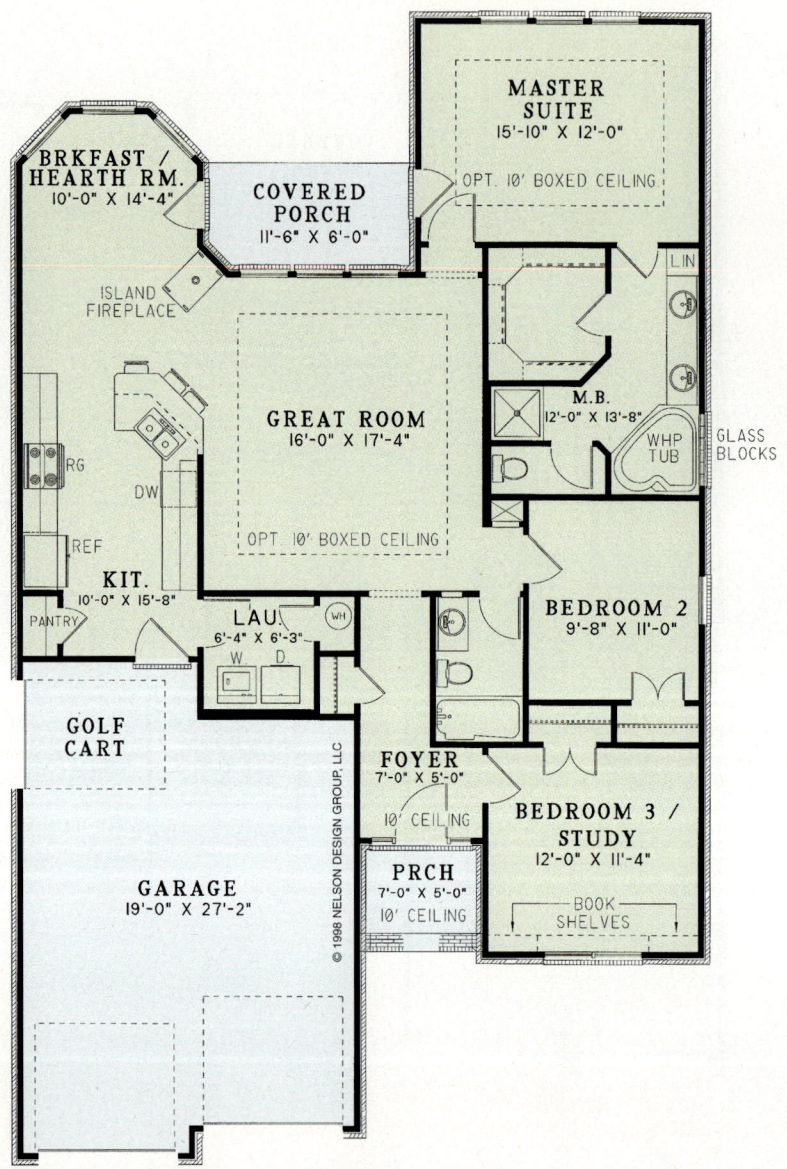

Width: 39' 4"
Depth: 63' 2"
Total Living: 1,480 sq. ft.
Main Ceiling: 9 ft.
Price Tier: A

Bedrooms: 3
Baths: 2
Foundation: Crawl, Slab

To view similar plans visit www.84lumber.com/ndgplans - 800.359.8484

278 Sage Meadows

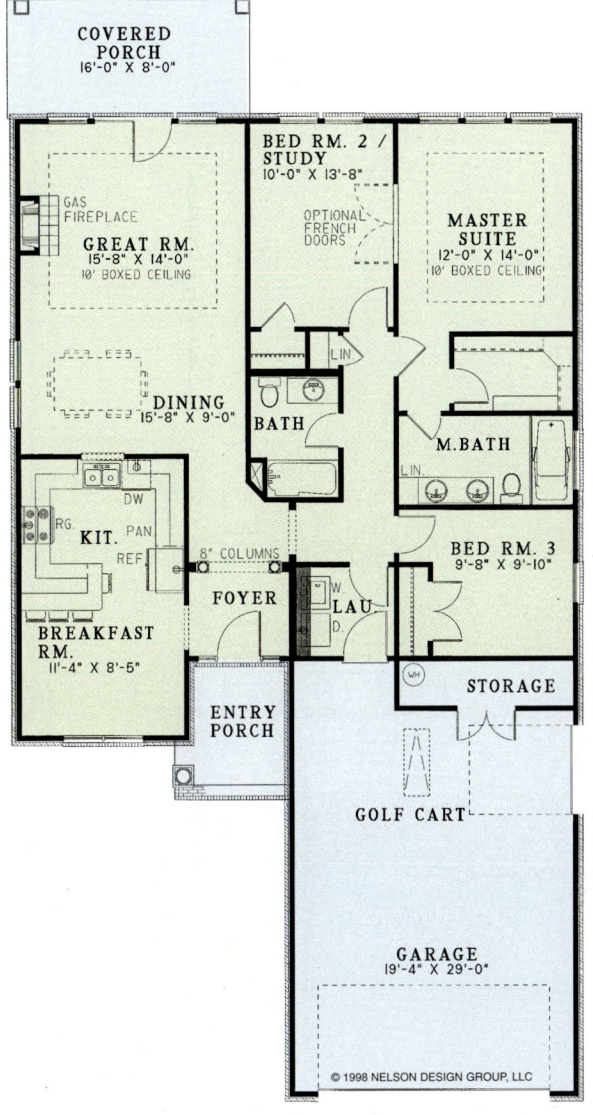

Feel the French Country flair as you step onto the covered entry porch of this Nelson Design Group home complete with traditional columns and fluid entry into a formal foyer. Enjoy cozy nights at home in your spacious great room or entertain friends on warm summer evenings on your covered back porch. Early morning breakfasts are a delight with an eat-at kitchen bar opening to a quiet breakfast nook.

Width:	39'	**Bedrooms:**	3
Depth:	73' 10"	**Baths:**	2
Total Living:	1,487 sq. ft.	**Foundation:**	Crawl, Slab, Opt. Basement, Opt. Daylight Basement
Main Ceiling:	9 ft.		
Price Tier:	A		

To view similar plans visit www.84lumber.com/ndgplans - 800.359.8484

284 Sage Meadows

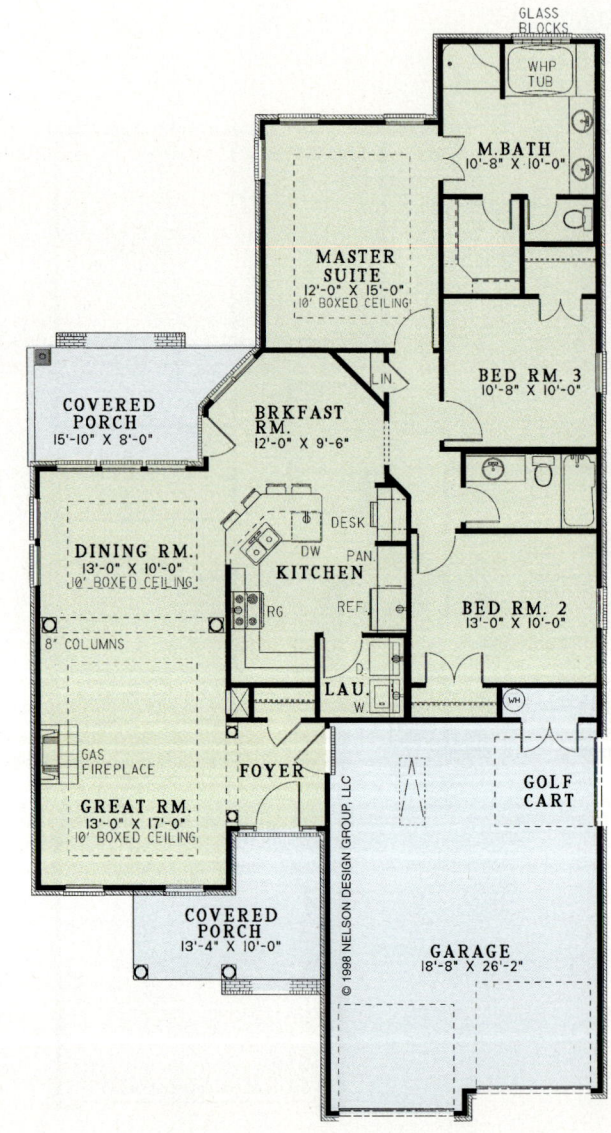

As you enter this Nelson Design Group home, you are welcomed onto a lovely covered porch with ten foot ceilings and led directly into the traditional foyer. From there you'll enjoy a combination great room and dining area divided only by magnificent wooden columns. An easily accessible kitchen is accented by a breakfast nook complete with bay windows and entry to a rear covered grilling porch. Spend hours delighting friends and family with your grilling expertise.

Width: 39' 6"
Depth: 72' 5"
Total Living: 1,504 sq. ft.
Main Ceiling: 9 ft.
Price Tier: B

Bedrooms: 3
Baths: 2
Foundation: Crawl, Slab, Opt. Basement, Opt. Daylight Basement

To view similar plans visit www.84lumber.com/ndgplans - 800.359.8484

287 Sage Meadows

Main Floor

Upper Floor

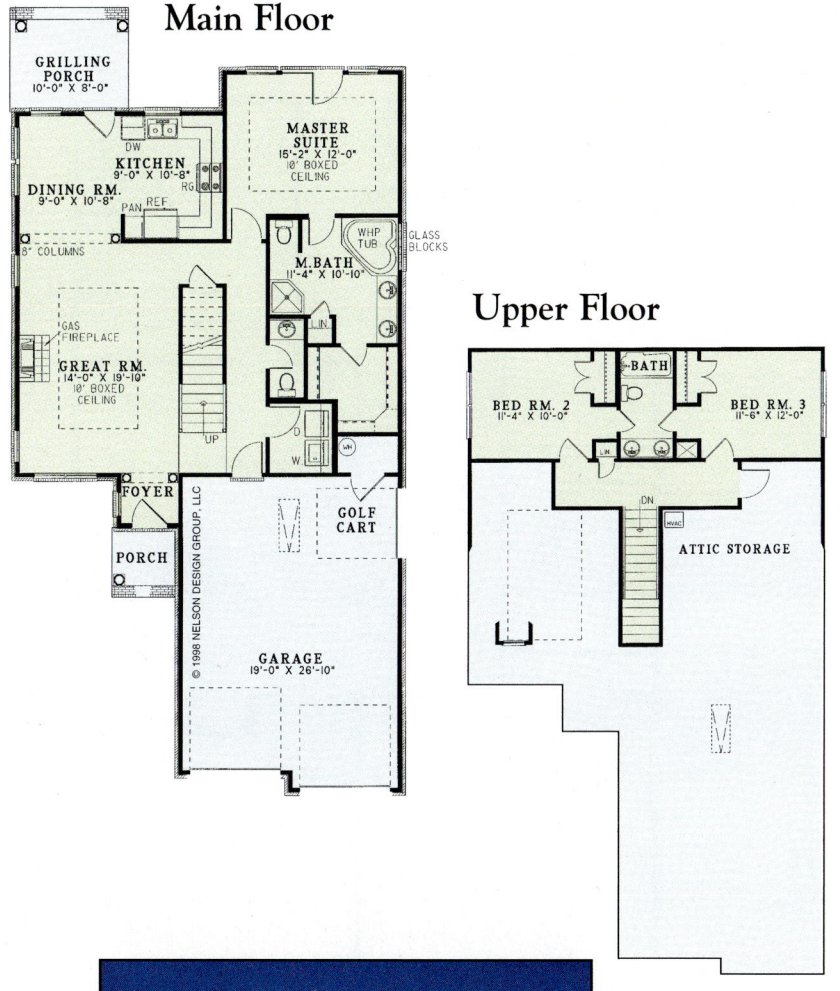

Entering this French Country Nelson Design Group home, you are led through a traditional foyer enhanced by wooden columns and into a spacious great room – perfect for family get-togethers. Enjoy the privacy of your master suite complete with atrium doors and windows opening onto the rear yard. Delight your friends with your famous hamburgers any time of year on your convenient grilling porch located right off the kitchen. As you travel upstairs, you'll find two spacious bedrooms with a walk-through bath – a wonderful solution for the kids.

Width:	34'	**Main Ceiling:**	9 ft.
Depth:	66' 8"	**Upper Ceiling:**	8 ft.
Main Floor:	1,131 sq. ft.	**Bedrooms:**	3
Upper Floor:	443 sq. ft.	**Baths:**	2 1/2
Total Living:	1,574 sq. ft.	**Foundation:**	Crawl, Slab, Opt. Basement, Opt. Daylight Basement
Price Tier:	B		

To view similar plans visit www.84lumber.com/ndgplans - 800.359.8484

280 Sage Meadows

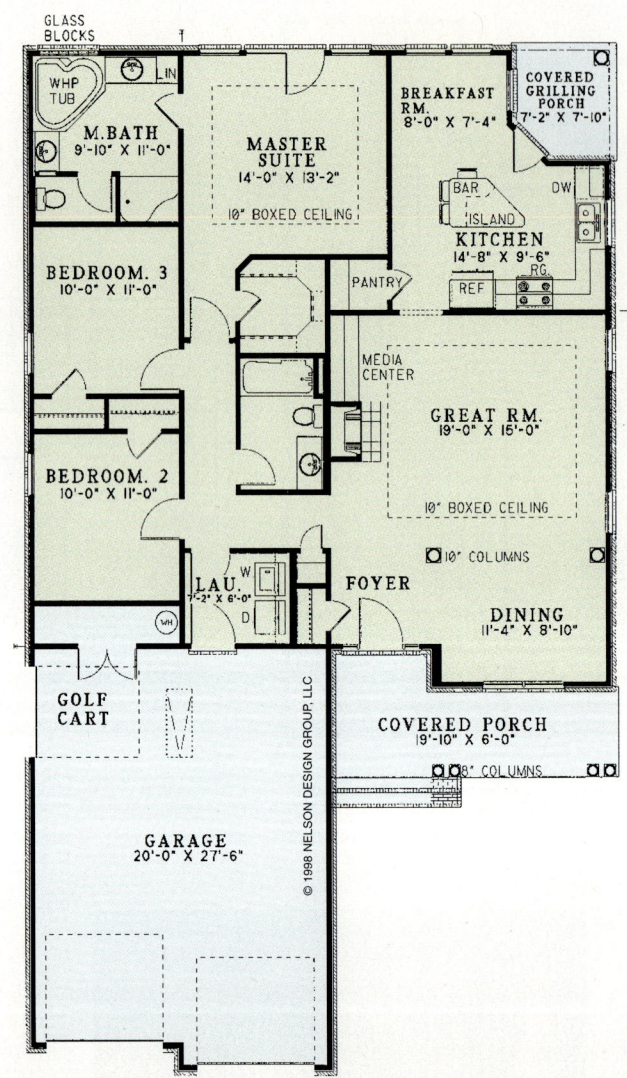

Entering this French Country Nelson Design Group home, you come upon a long covered porch enhanced by beautifully crafted columns. A quaint foyer leads you to a marvelous dining area with wooden columns and the great room with a ten foot boxed ceiling. Enjoy many hours of food and laughter with friends and family year-round when utilizing the convenience of your covered grilling porch.

Width: 40'
Depth: 67' 4"
Total Living: 1,535 sq. ft.
Price Tier: B

Main Ceiling: 9 ft.
Bedrooms: 3
Baths: 2
Foundation: Crawl, Slab

277 Sage Meadows

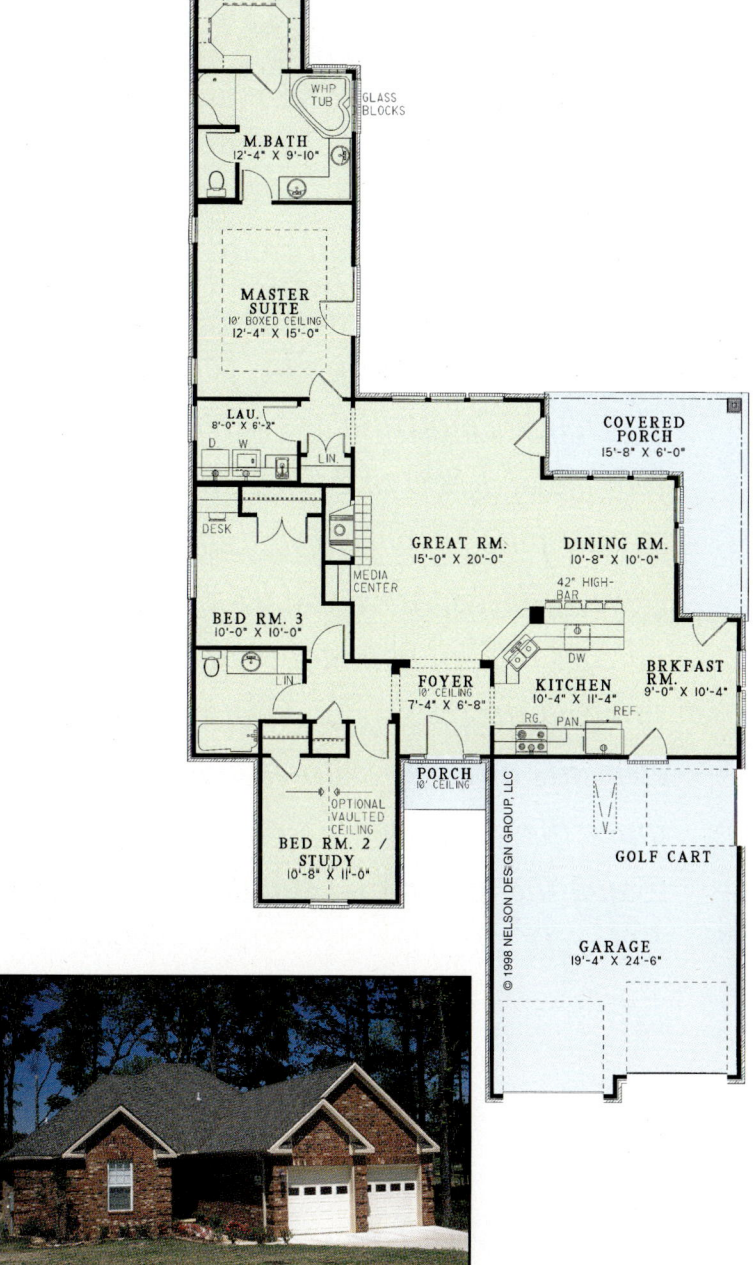

Step inside this Nelson Design Group home and enter a beautiful formal foyer with a ten foot ceiling. The foyer opens into a wonderfully spacious family area, perfect for special quality time. Visit with family or entertain friends on the timeless covered porch overlooking a calming lake or rolling golf course. Accessibility to both the great room and a cozy breakfast nook makes this porch both relaxing and convenient. Finally, enjoy your secluded master suite and bath complete with corner whirlpool tub and privacy corner glass block windows.

Width:	44'	Main Ceiling:	9 ft.
Depth:	86' 2"	Bedrooms:	3
Total Living:	1,601 sq. ft.	Baths:	2
Price Tier:	B	Foundation:	Crawl, Slab

To view similar plans visit www.84lumber.com/ndgplans - 800.359.8484

Renaissance
A FRENCH COUNTRY NEIGHBORHOOD

A "rebirth" of the small country cottage and stone house combining grace, comfort and warmth. This collection of French Country plans range in square footage of 1,800 to 2,200. Country living entails pure enjoyment and love for the countryside, so we've added grilling porches and an abundance of windows to bring the outside in. Distinctive elements of boxed ceilings and columns grace these six French Country designs. Enjoy the return of a simple yet elegant life style.

Nelson Design Group LLC
RESIDENTIAL PLANNERS - DESIGNERS

Main Floor

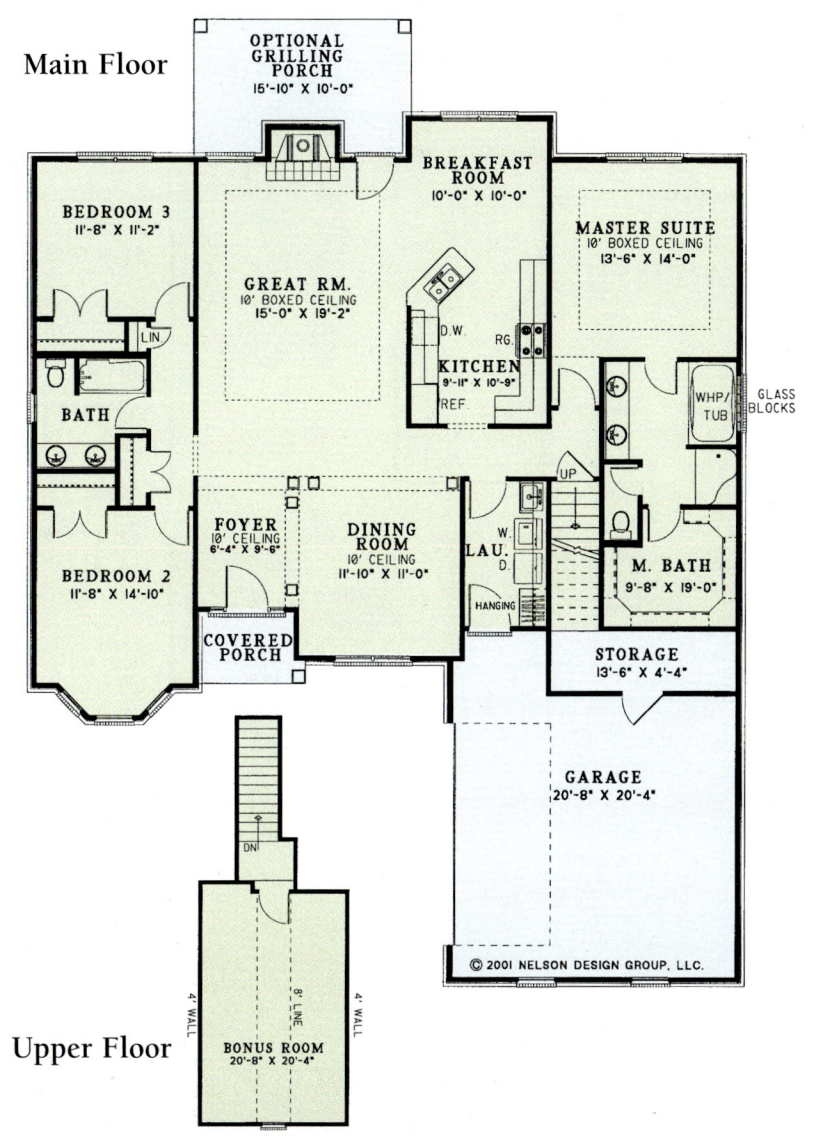

Upper Floor

545 Calais Drive

Width: 52' 0"
Depth: 69' 6"
Total Living: 1,869 sq. ft.*
*Optional Bonus: 288 sq. ft.
Price Tier: B

Main Ceiling: 9 ft.
Bonus Ceiling: 8 ft.
Bedrooms: 3
Baths: 2
Foundation: Crawl, Slab, Opt. Basement, Opt. Daylight Basement

Beautiful stone and siding give warmth to this French Country design. Elegance is achieved in our Nelson Design Group home by using boxed columns and ten foot ceilings. The foyer and dining rooms are lined with columns and adjoin the great room, all with high ceilings. The kitchen and breakfast room are great for entertaining and have access to the grilling porch. This split bedroom plan has a master suite with large walk-in closet, whirlpool tub, shower and private area. A bonus room above the garage, is available with stair access near the master suite. Two bedrooms and a large bathroom are located on the other side of the great room giving privacy to the entire family.

To view similar plans visit www.84lumber.com/ndgplans - 800.359.8484

523 Fontenay Drive

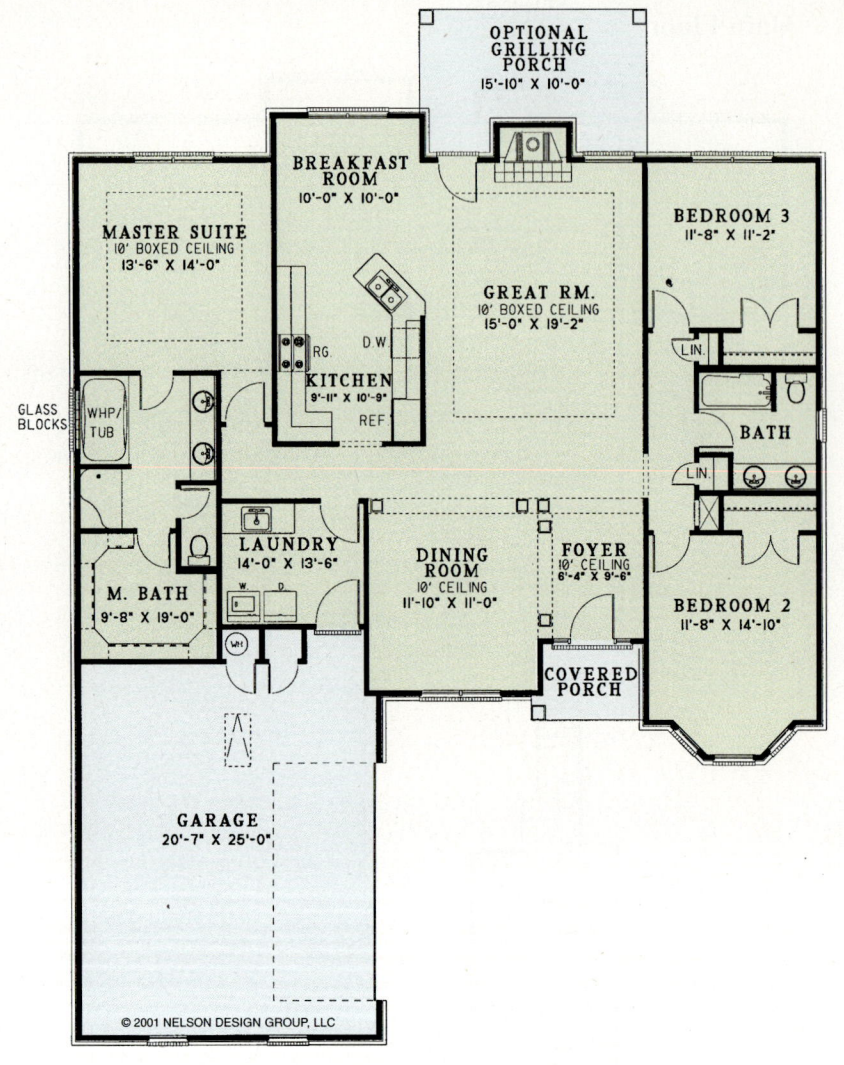

Upon entering the foyer of this Nelson Design Group home, you'll notice the magnificent boxed columns surrounding the Dining room. Ten foot ceilings enhance the foyer, dining and great rooms giving this split bedroom plan a very open effect. Entertaining becomes simple for the grill master on the grilling porch accessible to the great room. As night falls, retreat to your master bath by relaxing in your whirlpool tub. The courtyard entry garage enhances the street appeal of this beautiful French country home.

Width: 52' 0"
Depth: 69' 6"
Total Living: 1,882 sq. ft.
Main Ceiling: 9 ft.
Price Tier: B

Bedrooms: 3
Baths: 2
Foundation: Crawl, Slab, Opt. Basement, Opt. Daylight Basement

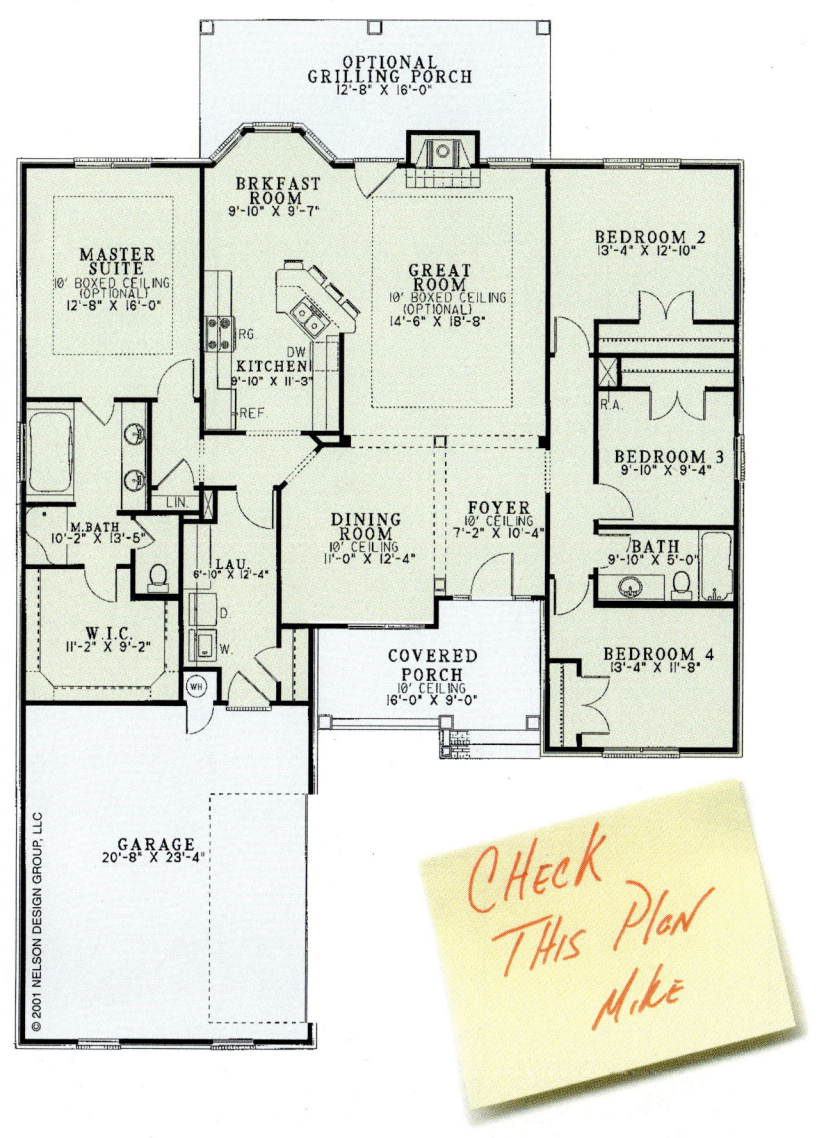

522 Calais Drive

This enchanting Nelson Design Group home incorporates the best in floor planning all in one level. The great room - which is convenient for those family gatherings that need extra room, is highlighted by a fireplace and a nine foot boxed ceiling. Easy access from the kitchen to the dining room makes hosting a dinner party more convenient. Entertain friends and family during the summer out on the rear grilling porch. As evening approaches, retreat to your master bath complete with large walk-in closet, double vanities and corner whirlpool bath.

Width: 52' 0"
Depth: 71' 6"
Total Living: 1,930 sq. ft.
Main Ceiling: 9 ft.
Price Tier: B

Bedrooms: 4
Baths: 2
Foundation: Crawl, Slab, Opt. Basement, Opt. Daylight Basement

519 Chantilly Circle

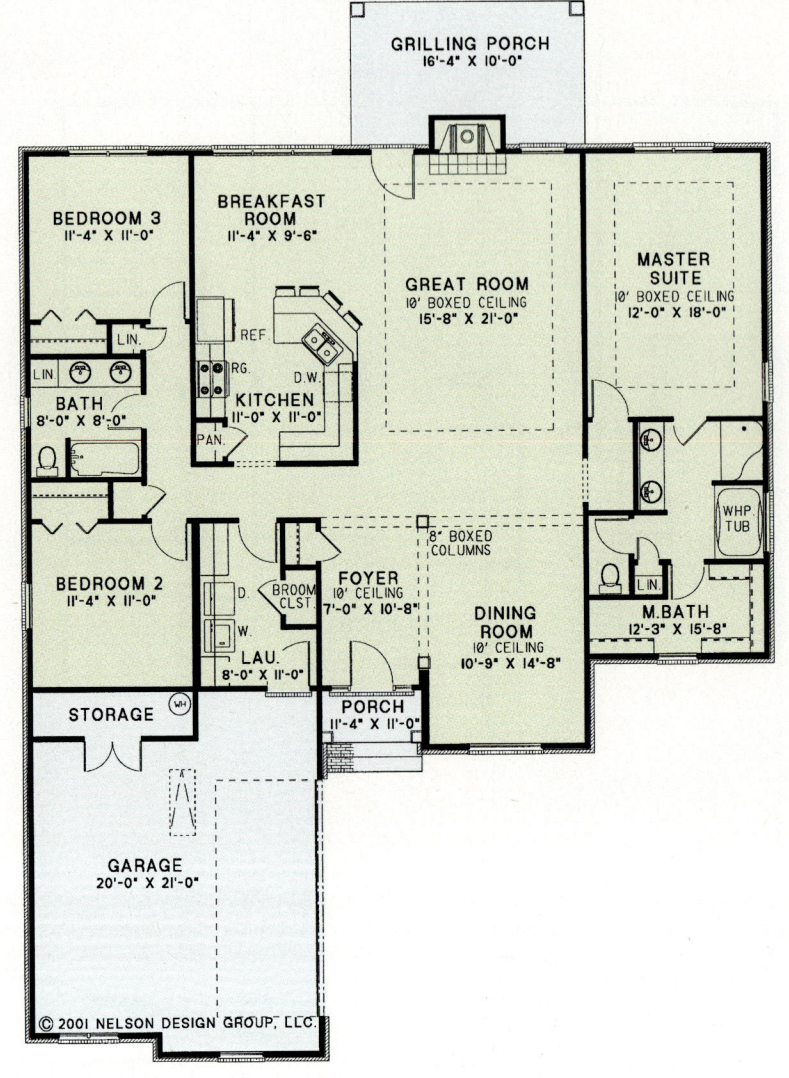

Welcome your dinner guests into this elegant Nelson Design Group home enhanced by ten foot ceilings and an open floor plan. Once in the foyer, notice the boxed columns separating the dining room and great room. The great room has a fireplace and door accessing the rear grilling porch which makes for entertaining ease. Two bedrooms and a full bath are located on one side of the house, allowing the master suite total privacy. This large master bedroom has plenty of wall space for large furniture and a master bathroom with whirlpool tub, double vanity, separate shower with seat, toilet room and a walk-in closet. Enjoy this beautiful home with plenty of room for your family.

Width: 52' 0"
Depth: 71' 2"
Total Living: 1,973 sq. ft.
Main Ceiling: 9 ft.
Price Tier: B

Bedrooms: 3
Baths: 2
Foundation: Crawl, Slab, Opt. Basement, Opt. Daylight Basement

To view similar plans visit www.84lumber.com/ndgplans - 800.359.8484

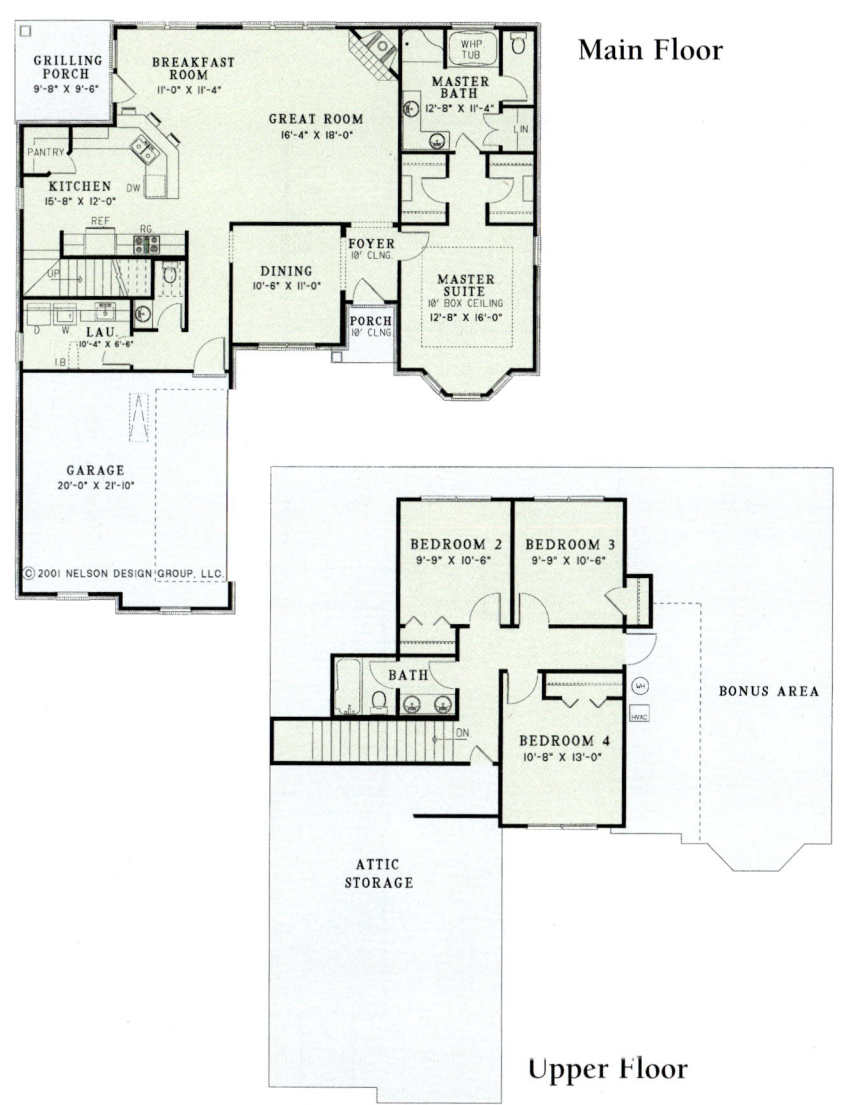

Main Floor

Upper Floor

520 Fontenay Drive

Drive into a courtyard entry garage and retreat to your French Country home. Nelson Design Group has designed a beautiful floor plan that is very family oriented beginning with a porch and foyer with ten foot ceilings. Enter the foyer and travel into a massive great room adjoining the breakfast room with access to a grilling porch. The kitchen bar area makes grilling easy and gives extra seating for large family gatherings. The master suite enhanced by a ten foot ceiling, is located on the main level and has his' and her' closets leading to the master bathroom full of amenities. As you travel upstairs, you'll find three bedrooms and a full bath with optional bonus area.

Width: 50' 6"	Main Ceiling: 9 ft.
Depth: 54' 8"	Upper Ceiling: 8 ft.
Main Floor: 1,495 sq. ft.	Bedrooms: 4
Upper Floor: 546 sq. ft.	Baths: 2 1/2
Total Living: 2,041 sq. ft.	Foundation: Crawl, Slab, Opt. Basement, Opt. Daylight Basement
Price Tier: C	

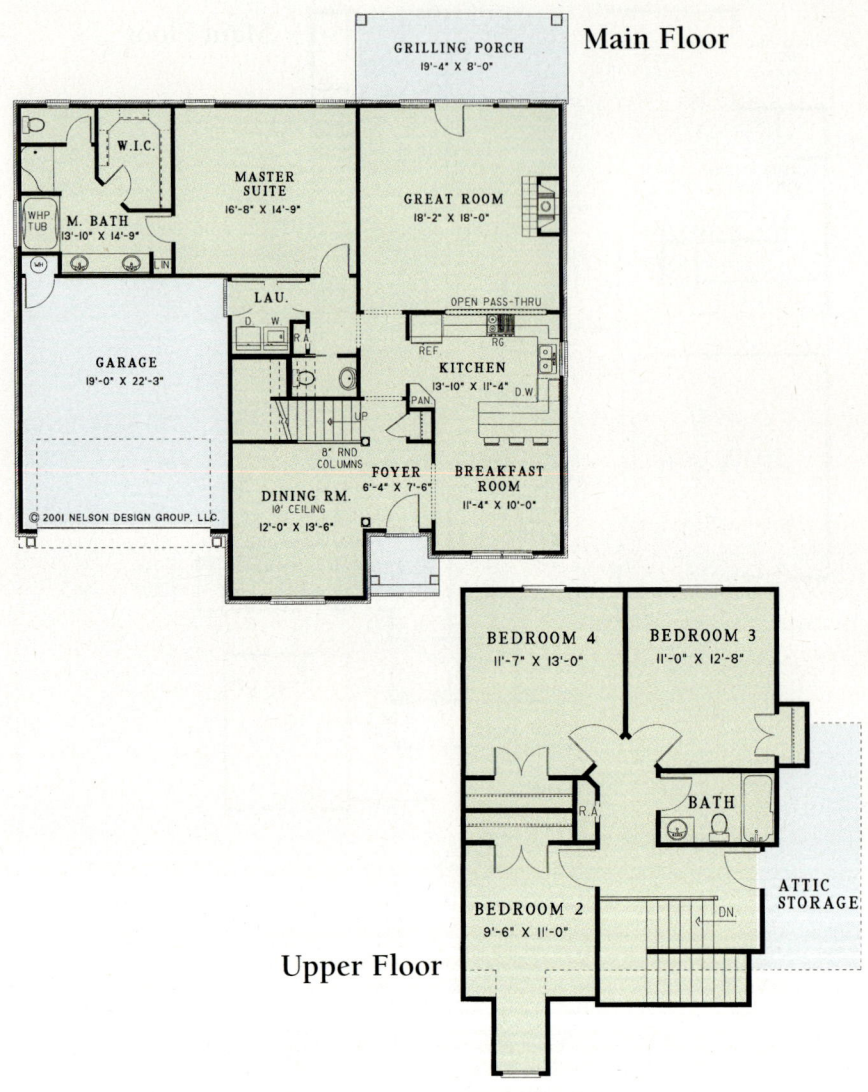

Main Floor

Upper Floor

536 Chantilly Circle

The focal point of this French Country plan is a large stone wrapped window extending a feeling of warmth in the neighborhood. This lovely Nelson Design Group home has a great room with fireplace and access to a rear grilling porch. The kitchen has a pass thru to the great room and adjoins a large breakfast room with a bar counter. The master suite is on the main floor and has a large bathroom with walk-in closet and all the amenities. Travel upstairs and find three bedrooms and a full bathroom. Attic storage is easily accessed for seasonal usage.

Width: 50' 2"	Main Ceiling: 9 ft.
Depth: 52' 0"	Upper Ceiling: 8 ft.
Main Floor: 1,563 sq. ft.	Bedrooms: 4
Upper Floor: 727 sq. ft.	Baths: 2 1/2
Total Living: 2,290 sq. ft.	Foundation: Crawl, Slab
Price Tier: C	

THE *Florida* COLLECTION

An oasis of amenities in twelve designs created for a warm climate. These designs range between 1,800 to 3,600 square feet and include open spacious living areas, luxurious master suites and lanais perfect for entertaining. High ceilings and columns are used throughout giving a grand effect while arched openings and a plenitude of windows allow natural light to flow throughout.

Nelson Design Group LLC

RESIDENTIAL PLANNERS - DESIGNERS

The Windsor

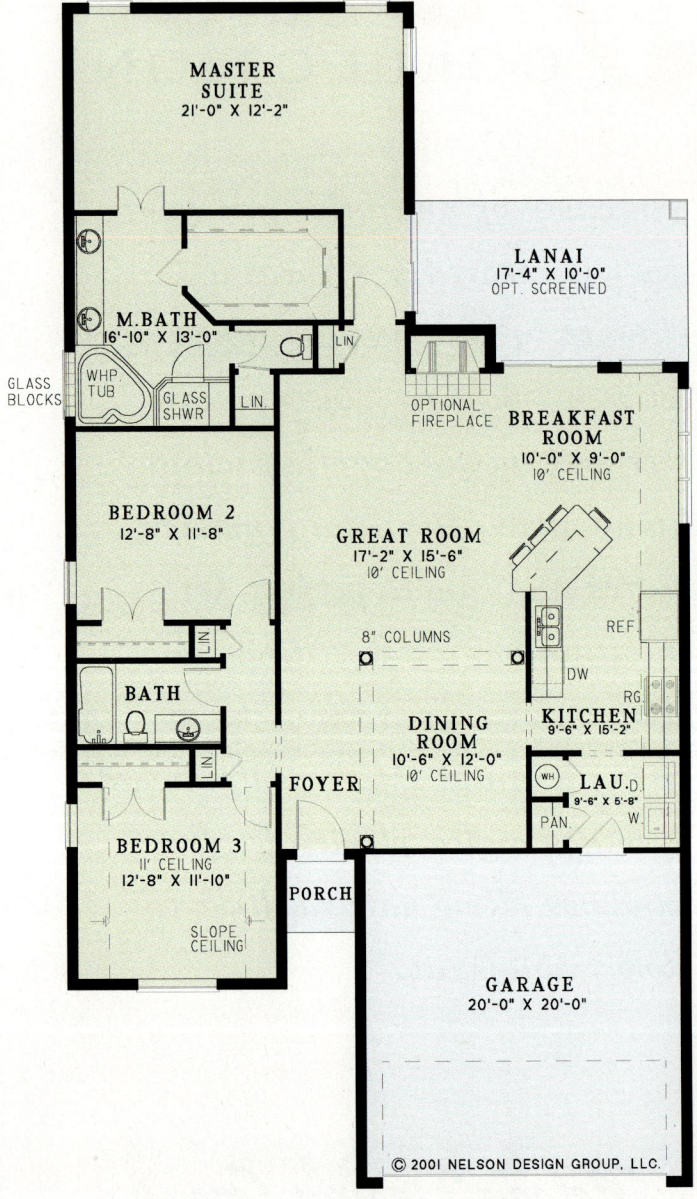

A sheltered porch protects visitors from the elements in this efficient plan from Nelson Design Group. The open foyer blends into the formal dining room offset by three stylish columns. The spacious walk-through kitchen features an angled snack bar and joins a window-filled breakfast room. The optional fireplace brightens the vast great room. The master suite boasts a private sliding door entrance to the lanai and a corner whirlpool tub backed with stylish glass blocks.

Width: 39' 8"
Depth: 73' 4"
Total Living: 1,818 sq. ft.
Main Ceiling: 9' 4" ft.

Bedrooms: 3
Baths: 2
Foundation: Slab
Price Tier: B

To view similar plans visit www.84lumber.com/ndgplans - 800.359.8484

The Clarion

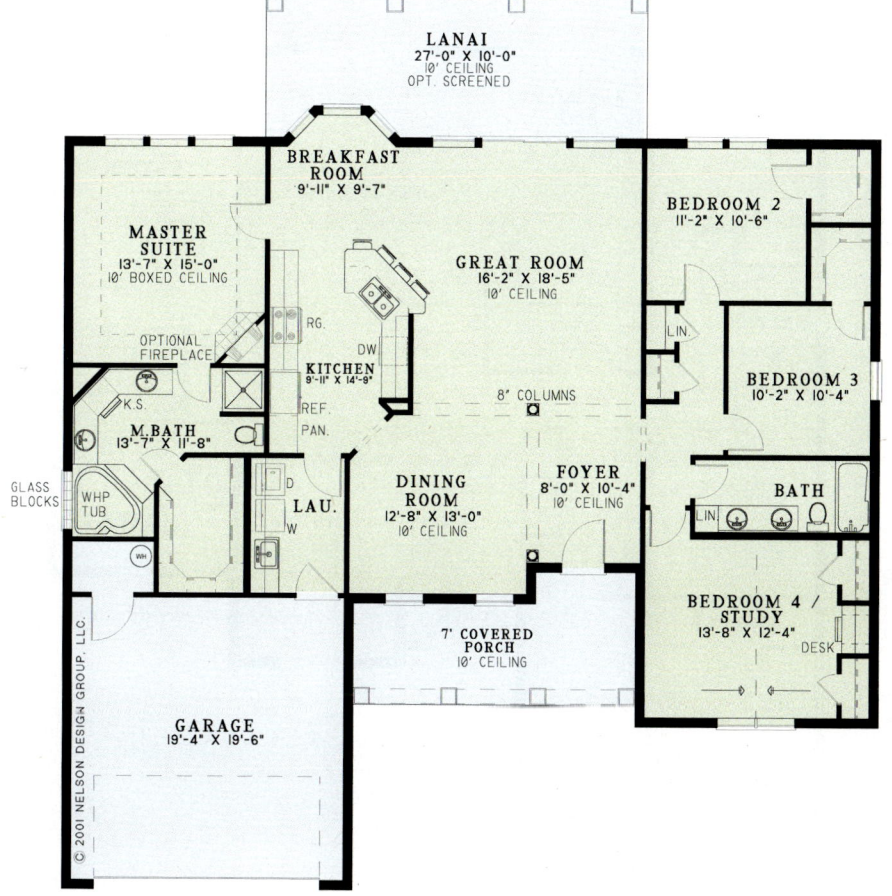

This exciting combination of functional floor plan and stunning detail make this split-bedroom Nelson Design Group home a popular choice. The open design of the formal dining room and spacious great room promotes a smooth transition from mealtime to casual conversation. The bay-windowed breakfast room and angled eat-at bar offer optional casual dining locales. The fourth bedroom can double as a study with its built-in desk. A romantic corner fireplace warms the elaborate master suite.

Width: 58' 0"	Bedrooms: 4
Depth: 61' 10"	Baths: 2
Total Living: 1,976 sq. ft.	Foundation: Slab
Main Ceiling: 9' 4" ft.	Price Tier: B

To view similar plans visit www.84lumber.com/ndgplans - 800.359.8484

The Devon

An open layout makes entertaining in this charming Nelson Design Group split-bedroom home both easy and enjoyable. The large great room flows smoothly into the formal dining room and breakfast room. The walk-through kitchen with angled bar promotes quick serving access to all living areas. An optional screened lanai provides an excellent place to enjoy the outdoors during inclement weather conditions. The master bath wing features a dual-sink vanity, separate whirlpool tub and shower, along with a large walk-in closet.

Width: 54' 0"
Depth: 74' 0"
Total Living: 2,056 sq. ft.
Main Ceiling: 9' 4" ft.

Bedrooms: 3
Baths: 2
Foundation: Slab
Price Tier: C

To view similar plans visit www.84lumber.com/ndgplans - 800.359.8484

The Avalon

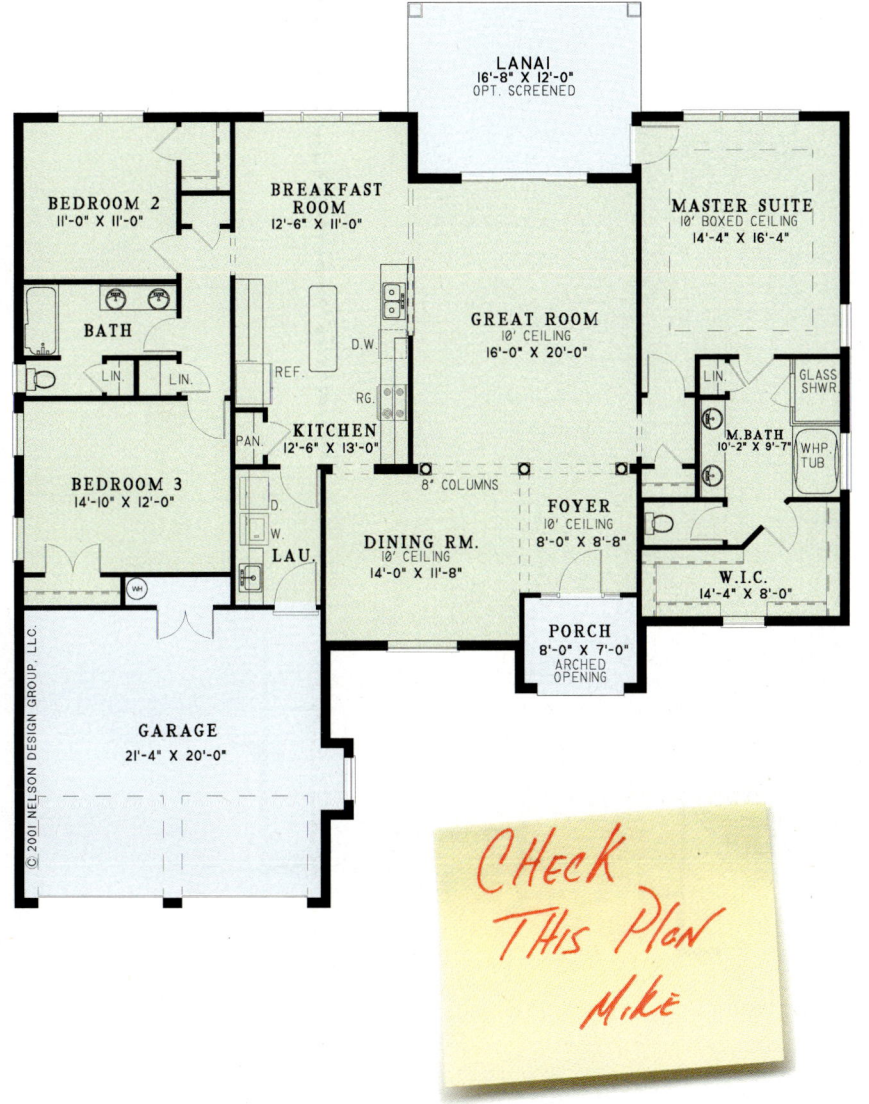

*A*n elegant, open foyer, offset by stylish columns, provide a dazzling entrance to this split bedroom Nelson Design Group offering. The convenient great room allows unimpeded access to all areas of the house, including sliding glass doors to the screened lanai. The gourmet kitchen utilizes a large, functional island and easily serves the adjacent breakfast room and formal dining room. The elaborate master bath includes a private entrance to the lanai and separate whirlpool tub and glass shower.

Width: 60' 0"	Bedrooms: 3
Depth: 63' 4"	Baths: 2
Total Living: 2,059 sq. ft.	Foundation: Slab
Main Ceiling: 9' 4" ft.	Price Tier: C

To view similar plans visit www.84lumber.com/ndgplans - 800.359.8484

The Downing

A convenient private office with French door entry and built-ins adjoining the extravagant master suite highlights this Nelson Design Group home. The expansive great room features sliding glass doors leading to the lanai. A functional eat-at bar helps the kitchen provide quick service to the convenient breakfast room and formal dining room. The generous master bath showcases a raised corner whirlpool tub with columned-entry.

Width: 67' 2"	Bedrooms: 3
Depth: 64' 8"	Baths: 2
Total Living: 2,121 sq. ft.	Foundation: Slab
Main Ceiling: 9' 4" ft.	Price Tier: C

To view similar plans visit www.84lumber.com/ndgplans - 800.359.8484

The Armhurst

*L*ots of open space capable of both formal and casual entertaining characterize this lovely split-bedroom home from Nelson Design Group. The extensive great room allows unencumbered transitions to the formal dining room, kitchen and enormous breakfast room. The kitchen enjoys a walk-in pantry and an angled eat-at bar. The secluded master suite offers a private entrance to the screened lanai, 10' boxed ceiling, and a substantial walk-in closet.

Width: 60' 2"	Bedrooms: 3
Depth: 64' 8"	Baths: 2
Total Living: 2,237 sq. ft.	Foundation: Slab
Main Ceiling: 9' 4" ft.	Price Tier: C

The Anniston

Striking front and rear arches adorn this attractive four-bedroom plan from Nelson Design Group. Inside, a spacious foyer opens to an elaborate formal dining room, column-lined gallery and expansive great room all sharing 12 foot ceilings. The fourth bedroom can do double-duty as an office and includes a private entrance to the screened lanai. French doors enhance the transition from the master bedroom to the bath that showcases a dual-sink vanity and oversized whirlpool tub backed by glass blocks.

Width: 58' 8"
Depth: 73' 10"
Total Living: 2,287 sq. ft.
Main Ceiling: 9' 4" ft.

Bedrooms: 4
Baths: 2
Foundation: Slab
Price Tier: C

To view similar plans visit www.84lumber.com/ndgplans - 800.359.8484

The Austin

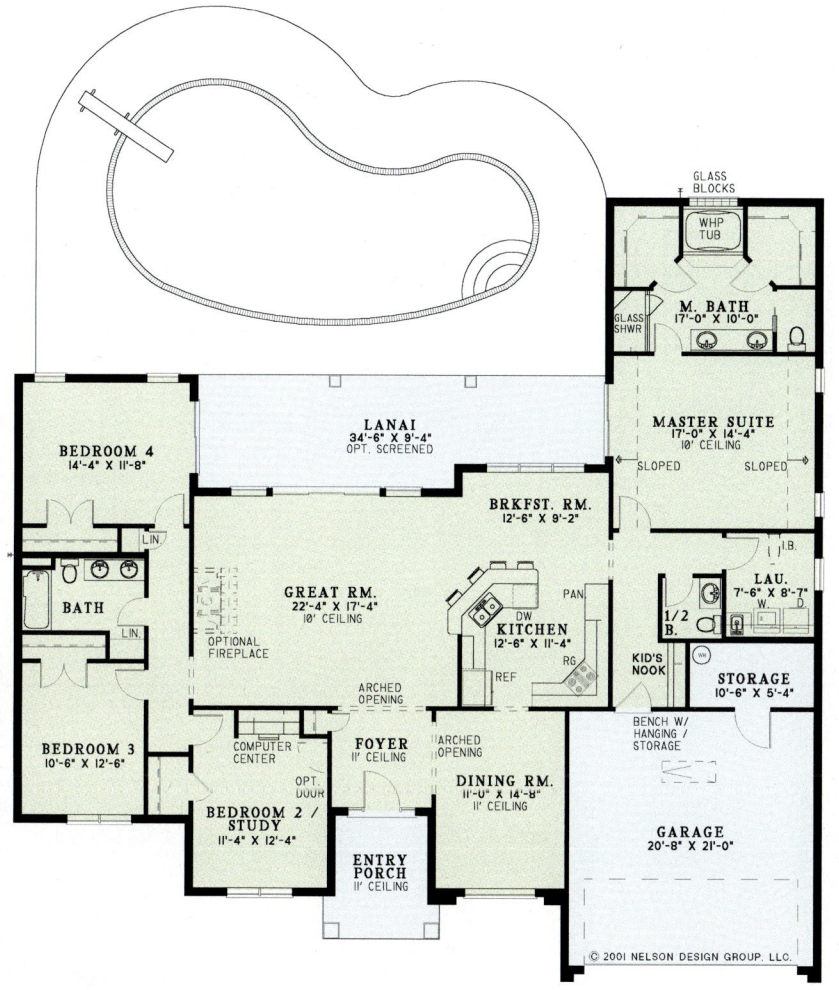

*G*ather around the great room's cozy fireplace to ward off winter's chill in this roomy and efficient four bedroom home from Nelson Design Group. Arched openings from the foyer escort you to the expansive great room and formal dining room. The culinary enthusiast will thrive in the walk-through kitchen's ample space while onlookers enjoy the convenience of the eat-at bar and nearby breakfast room. The second bedroom easily converts to a study with the aid of a built-in computer center and optional door to the foyer.

Width: 68' 6"	Bedrooms: 4
Depth: 64' 8"	Baths: 2 1/2
Total Living: 2,388 sq. ft.	Foundation: Slab
Main Ceiling: 9' 4" ft.	Price Tier: C

The St. August

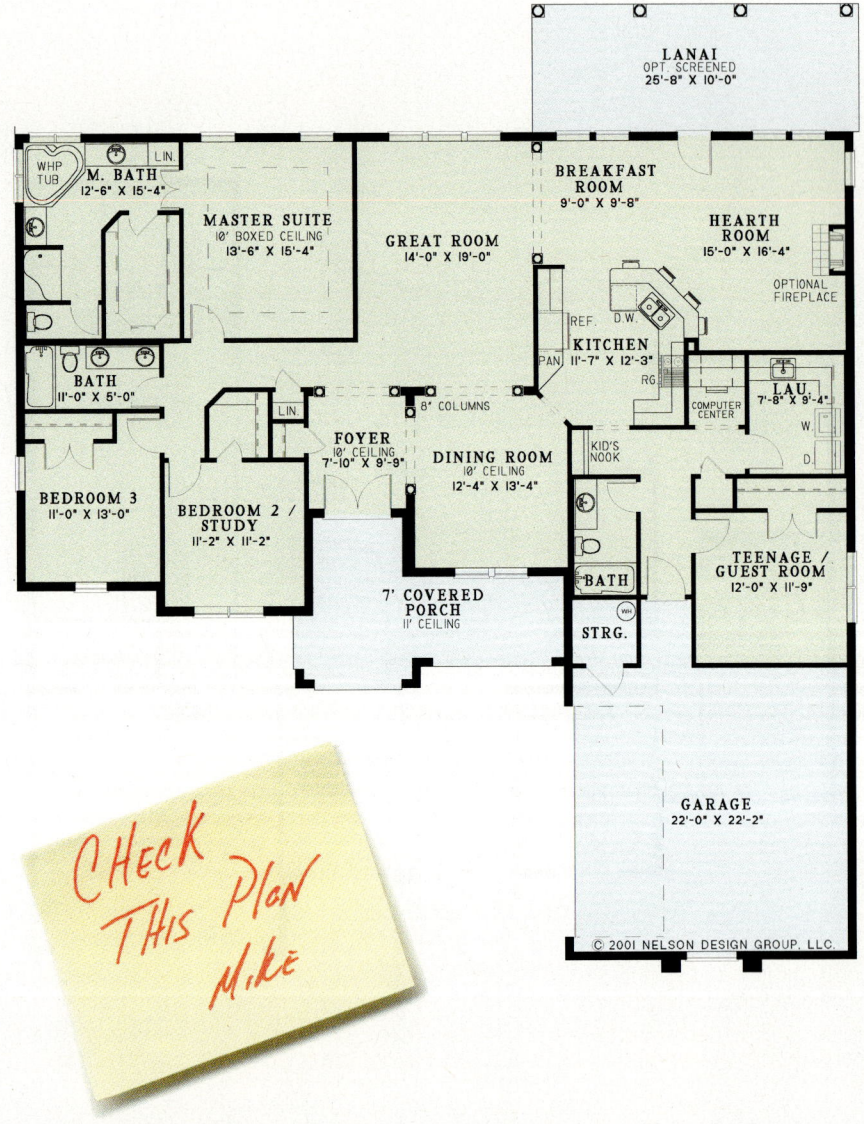

You're sure to appreciate the courtyard entry garage on this exquisite four-bedroom home from Nelson Design Group. The kid's nook helps keep backpacks and coats from getting misplaced. The centrally located kitchen enjoys a convenient snack bar and overlooks the radiant hearth room anchored by a cheery fireplace with access to the screened lanai. A teenager or overnight guest will enjoy the privacy offered by the isolated fourth bedroom. The splendid master suite showcases a beautiful corner whirlpool tub.

Width: 67' 4"
Depth: 74' 8"
Total Living: 2,501 sq. ft.
Main Ceiling: 9' 4" ft.

Bedrooms: 4
Baths: 3
Foundation: Slab
Price Tier: D

The Evandale

This sprawling four-bedroom plan from Nelson Design group centers on an ultra-functional kitchen accessing all living areas with ease. A handy eat-at bar and island help make this kitchen any gourmet's dream. Separate living and great rooms each flaunt gas fireplaces and lots of open space. All three secondary bedrooms feature private bath entrances. The exquisite master suite presents a radiant fireplace, large sitting area, private entrance to the lanai and a massive bath that includes his and her walk-in closets and an oversized whirlpool tub.

Width: 74' 2"	Bedrooms: 4
Depth: 81' 2"	Baths: 3
Total Living: 3,021 sq. ft.	Foundation: Slab
Main Ceiling: 9' 4" ft.	Price Tier: E

The Mansor

A family home if ever there was one, this Nelson Design Group house achieves it all in one single level plan. Columns and pan ceilings accent the main living areas, which access the kitchen through arched cased openings. A large gathering room at the back of the house features a fireplace and entry to the covered porch. The split-bedroom plan gives each secondary bedroom its own bath, while the master bedroom dominates the right wing of the house. Twin walk-around-in closets, a huge master bath and an adjoining nursery or study round out the suite.

Width: 70' 0"	Bedrooms: 4
Depth: 88' 6"	Baths: 3 1/2
Total Living: 3,167 sq. ft.	Foundation: Slab
Main Ceiling: 9' 4" ft.	Price Tier: E

To view similar plans visit www.84lumber.com/ndgplans - 800.359.8484

The Arlington

Designed for abundant living, this outstanding offering from Nelson Design Group has everything. The three bedrooms are split for privacy, with an enormous bay-windowed master suite accessed beneath an arched opening off the foyer, just beyond the library. Arches also frame the formal dining room, which opens to the great room with its 12-foot ceiling. The kitchen, breakfast room and den with fireplace all look out on the lanai with beaded ceiling and columns. A three-car attached garage completes the package.

Width: 81' 7"
Depth: 97' 2"
Total Living: 3,654 sq. ft.
Main Ceiling: 10 ft.

Bedrooms: 3
Baths: 3
Foundation: Slab
Price Tier: F

To view similar plans visit www.84lumber.com/ndgplans - 800.359.8484

105

The Waterfront Collection

Eleven beautiful designs that give focus to the rear view of the plan. Enjoy a waterfront or lake view through large windows while vaulted ceilings draw in natural lighting. These plans range between 1,200 to 6,500 square feet and include beautiful fireplaces, loft areas and massive decks, perfect for entertaining. These designs are family oriented and luxurious while allowing full enjoyment of your natural setting.

Nelson Design Group LLC

RESIDENTIAL PLANNERS - DESIGNERS

Main Floor

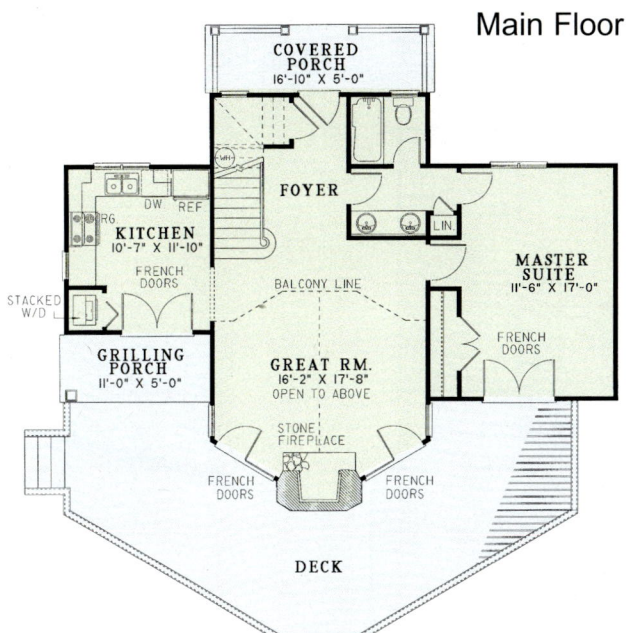

Upper Floor

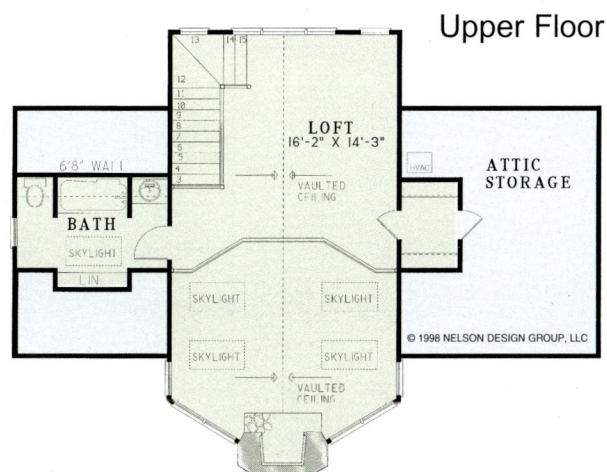

Front Elevation

Rear Elevation

174 Waterfront Cove

This charming romantic Nelson Design Group home has the master suite on the main floor with french door access to the rear deck, perfect for overlooking a calming lake. Lead your guests through the foyer and entertain in the spacious great room with skylights and stone fireplace - perfect after a day on the lake. Mornings can begin in your kitchen with french door access to the rear deck for morning coffee. After a long day, retreat to the master suite with full master bath. The upstairs loft features vaulted ceilings and large closet accessing attic storage. A full bath with skylight completes this plan.

Width: 42' 0"	Main Ceiling: 9 ft.
Depth: 36' 2"	Upper Ceiling: 8 ft.
Main Floor: 862 sq. ft.	Bedrooms: 2
Upper Floor: 332 sq. ft.	Baths: 2
Total Living: 1,194 sq. ft.	Foundation: Crawl, Slab, Basement, Daylight Basement
Price Tier: A	

Front Elevation

Main Floor

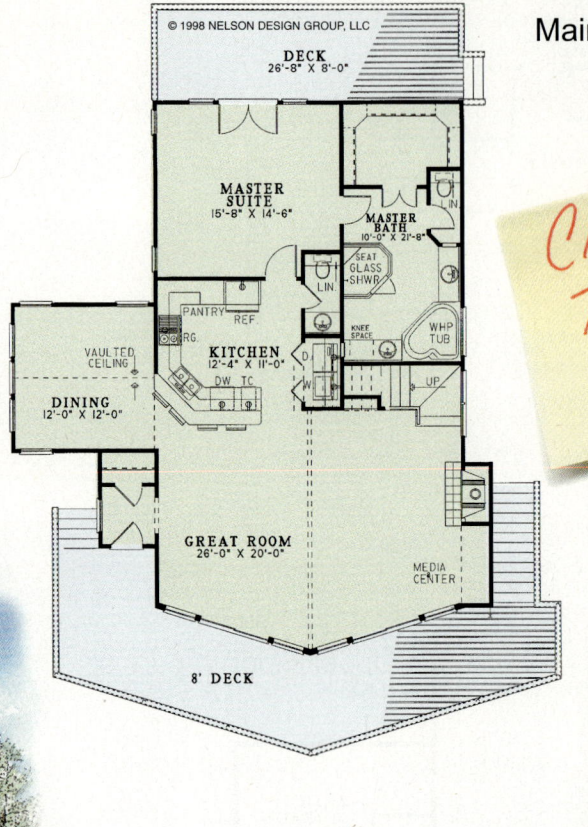

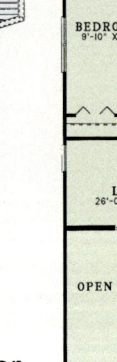

Rear Elevation

Upper Floor

231 Waterfront Cove

Vacation throughout the year in this Nelson Design Group home. You will be delighted with the open great room with vaulted ceiling and full window view of the lake or mountains. A media center and fireplace add efficiency as well as enjoyment. Enjoy cozy evenings locked away in your secluded master suite and bath which include double vanities, glass shower and large whirlpool tub. The loft area features two bedrooms which share a full bath. This home is heavenly for a family and weekend guests.

Width: 47' 0"	Main Ceiling: 8 ft.
Depth: 63' 0"	Upper Ceiling: 8 ft.
Main Floor: 1,413 sq. ft.	Bedrooms: 3
Upper Floor: 641 sq. ft.	Baths: 2 1/2
Total Living: 2,054 sq. ft.	Foundation: Crawl, Slab, Basement, Daylight Basement
Price Tier: C	

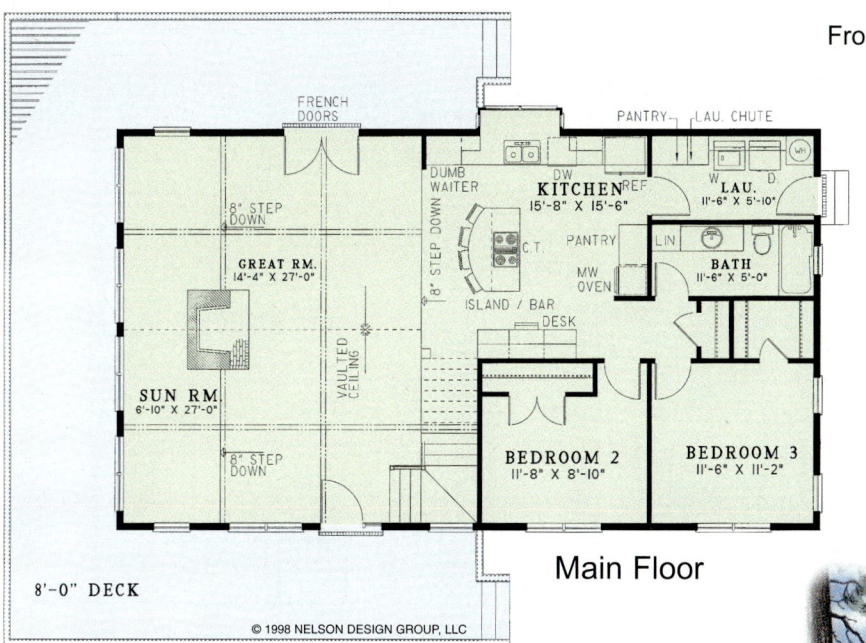

Front Elevation

Main Floor

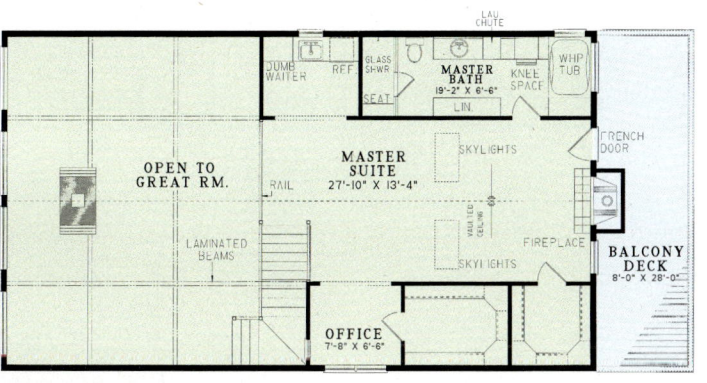

Upper Floor

Rear Elevation

173 Waterfront Cove

A vacation home with the master suite upstairs makes this Nelson Design Group home desirable. The eight foot wrap around deck with access to both sides of the great room is perfect for entertaining weekend guests. Breakfast is made easy with an island bar, ideal for those big breakfasts outdoorsmen enjoy. The master suite comes complete with skylights, vaulted ceilings and a fireplace, just right for those romantic evenings for the two of you. You also have a private access to the rear balcony deck through French doors.

Width: 50' 0"	Main Ceiling: 8 ft.
Depth: 28' 0"	Upper Ceiling: 8 ft.
Main Floor: 1,400 sq. ft.	Bedrooms: 3
Upper Floor: 743 sq. ft.	Baths: 2
Total Living: 2,143 sq. ft.	Foundation: Crawl, Slab, Opt. Basement, Opt. Daylight Basement
Price Tier: C	

To view similar plans visit www.84lumber.com/ndgplans - 800.359.8484

Front Elevation

Main Floor

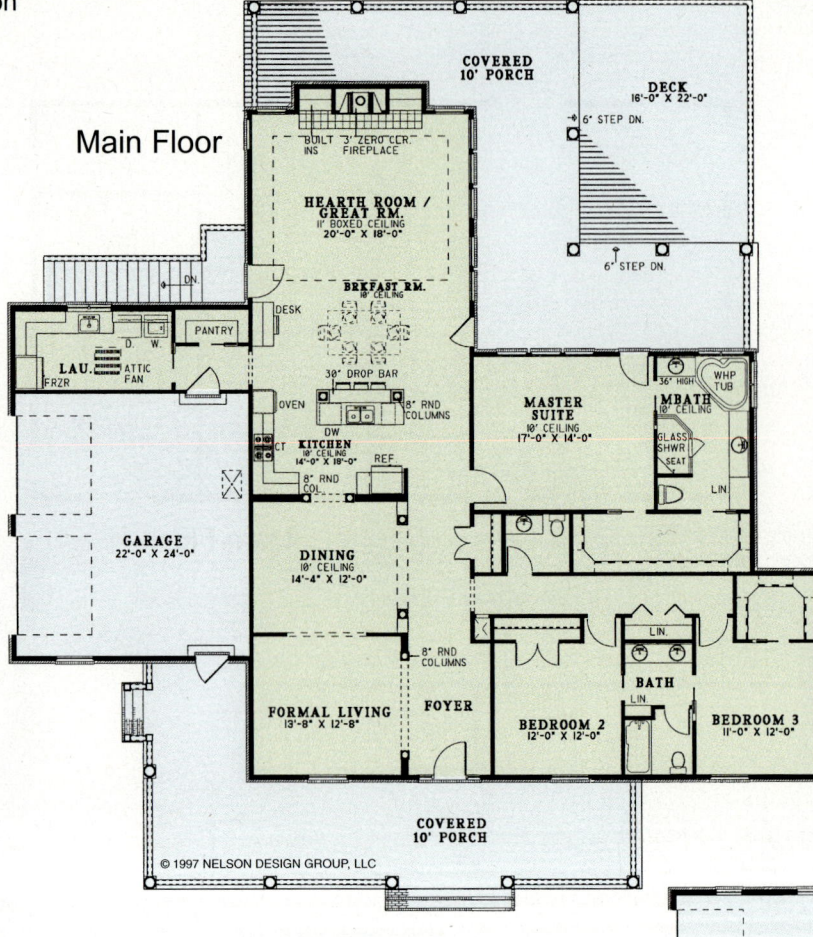

Rear Elevation

Lower Floor

225 Waterfront Cove

Your friends and neighbors will enjoy all the comforts in this Nelson Design Group lake home. Entertaining is easy with the formal living and dining areas which provide ample room for your guests. As you prepare your meal in the spacious kitchen with island bar, friends can relax in the great room/hearth room with fireplace. Try your hand at grilling on the rear deck with convenient access to the breakfast room. Evenings are more enjoyable relaxing in your master suite and bath with double vanities, glass shower and corner whirlpool bath.

Width: 75' 4"	Bedrooms: 3
Depth: 81' 0"	Baths: 2 1/2
Total Living: 2,607 sq. ft.	Foundation: Crawl, Slab, Opt.
Main Ceiling: 9 ft.	Basement, Opt.
Lower Ceiling: 8 ft.	Daylight Basement
Price Tier: D	

To view similar plans visit www.84lumber.com/ndgplans - 800.359.8484

Main Floor

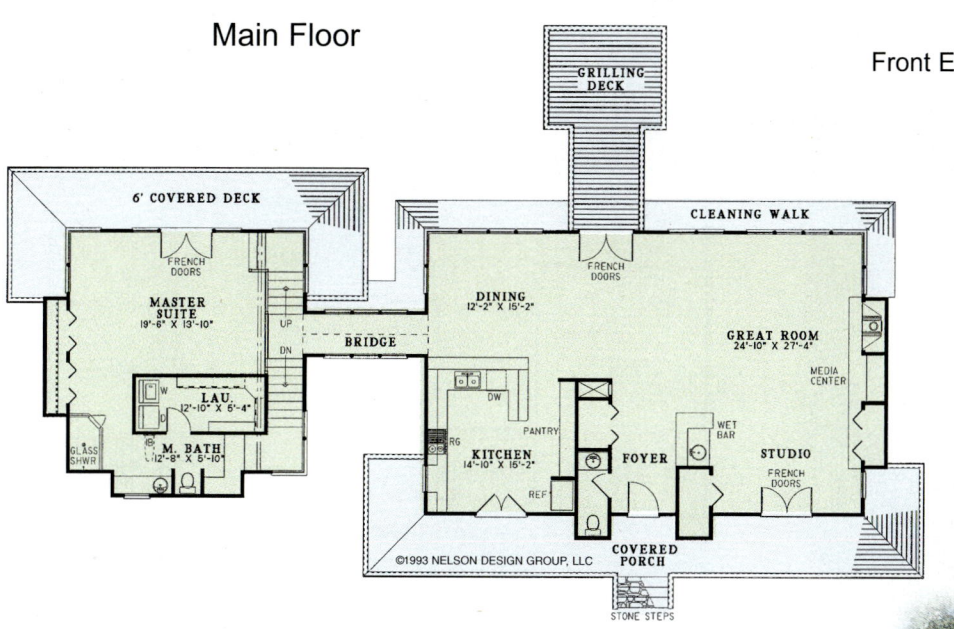

Front Elevation

Rear Elevation

Lower Floor

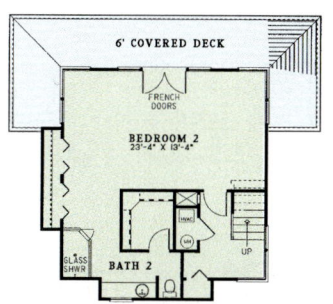

311 Waterfront Cove

Stone steps and a covered porch welcome you to this Nelson Design Group treehouse style home. French doors open to the studio with a wet bar providing relaxation while enjoying the great room fireplace. Your guests will enjoy the openness of the dining room and kitchen created by the vaulted ceilings above. A peninsula grilling deck allows you to prepare your meals with ease. Separated from the living areas by a bridge, your master suite includes corner glass shower and walk-in closet with a convenient laundry area. The lower level has an identical bedroom suite with French door access to the rear deck.

Width: 91' 10"	Main Ceiling: Vaulted
Depth: 54' 0"	Lower Ceiling: 10 ft.
Main Floor: 1,976 sq. ft.	Bedrooms: 2
Lower Floor: 634 sq. ft.	Baths: 2 1/2
Total Living: 2,610 sq. ft.	Foundation: Crawl, Basement, Daylight Basement
Price Tier: D	

To view similar plans visit www.84lumber.com/ndgplans - 800.359.8484

332 Waterfront Cove

This premier Nelson Design Group vacation home is perfect for entertaining out-of-town guests. Your friends will enjoy remembering old times in the vaulted great room which includes wet bar, media center, built-ins and access to the rear deck through a sliding door. Start the next morning with a big breakfast in your kitchen and breakfast room before heading to the lake. Evenings can begin with an elegant cuisine in the formal dining room, before making your way upstairs to the game room for a round of pool. Next, relax and unwind in the outdoor hot tub.

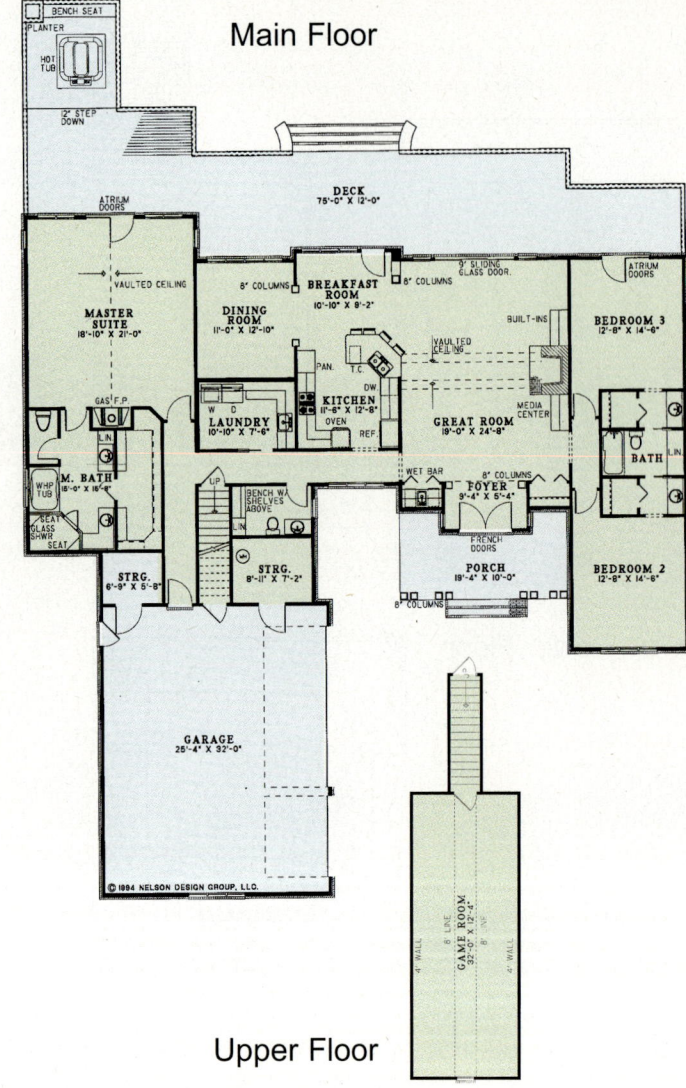

Main Floor

Upper Floor

Width: 75' 0"	Main Ceiling: 9 ft.
Depth: 100' 0"	Upper Ceiling: 8 ft.
Total Living: 2,611 sq. ft.*	Bedrooms: 3
*Optional Bonus: 424 sq. ft.	Baths: 2 1/2
Price Tier: D	Foundation: Crawl, Slab, Basement, Daylight Basement

To view similar plans visit www.84lumber.com/ndgplans - 800.359.8484

Main Floor

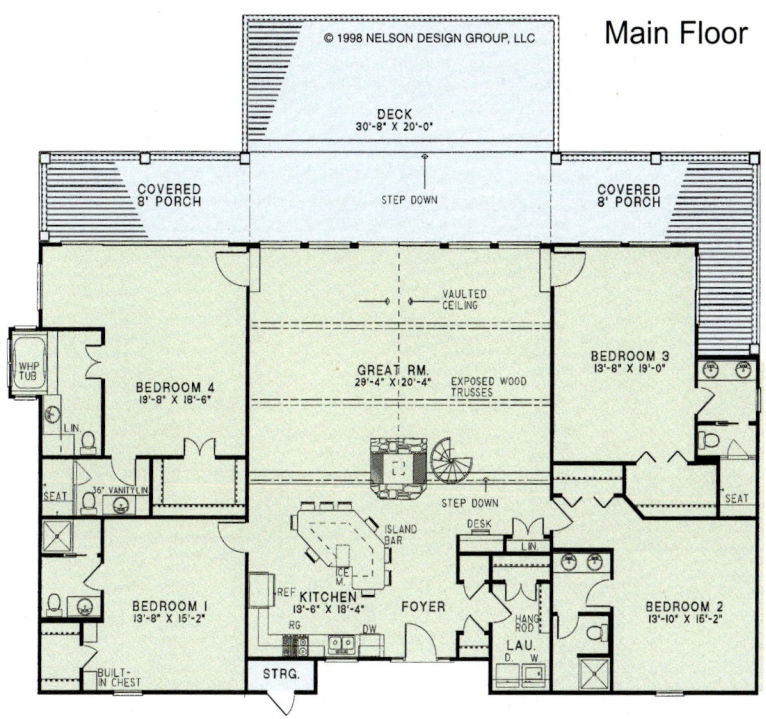

Upper Floor

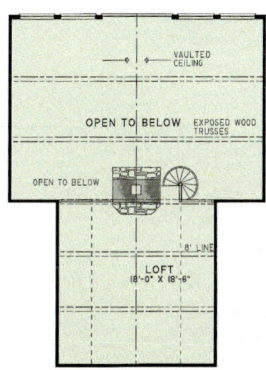

Front Elevation

Rear Elevation

226 Waterfront Cove

This Nelson Design Group plan is a vacation dream home come true. As you enter the foyer, you are exposed to the spacious great room with large rock fireplace - perfect for entertaining family and friends. If more room is needed for the party, lead them into your kitchen with large island bar. Your guests will enjoy climbing the spiral staircase to the loft above with a great view of the lake. You'll find plenty of space and privacy in all of your bedrooms, complete with their own baths. The fourth bedroom and bath includes a whirlpool bath and glass shower for relaxing comfort.

Width: 73' 0"	Main Ceiling: 8 ft.
Depth: 69' 4"	Upper Ceiling: 8 ft.
Main Floor: 2,687 sq. ft.	Bedrooms: 4
Upper Floor: 342 sq. ft.	Baths: 5
Total Living: 3,029 sq. ft.	Foundation: Crawl, Slab, Opt. Basement, Opt. Daylight Basement
Price Tier: E	

To view similar plans visit www.84lumber.com/ndgplans - 800.359.8484

Front Elevation

Rear Elevation

Main Floor

Lower Floor

224 Waterfront Cove

A traditional Nelson Design Group home with two front porches and boxed columns - perfect for lazy afternoons. This split bedroom plan offers mom and dad just enough privacy. The master suite is complete with built-ins, boxed ceilings and access to the rear covered porch for romantic evenings. Entertaining is easy in your spacious great room with soothing fireplace. A hobby room off the garage is useful for the kids and adults. Downstairs, you'll find an optional bedroom with a great view of the lake. The massive deck and covered porch give this plan a five star rating.

Width:	79' 0"	**Main Ceiling:**	9 ft.
Depth:	77' 8"	**Lower Ceiling:**	8 ft.
Main Floor:	2,650 sq. ft.	**Bedrooms:**	4
Upper Floor:	409 sq. ft.	**Baths:**	4
Total Living:	3,059 sq. ft.	**Foundation:**	Crawl, Slab, Basement, Daylight Basement
Price Tier:	E		

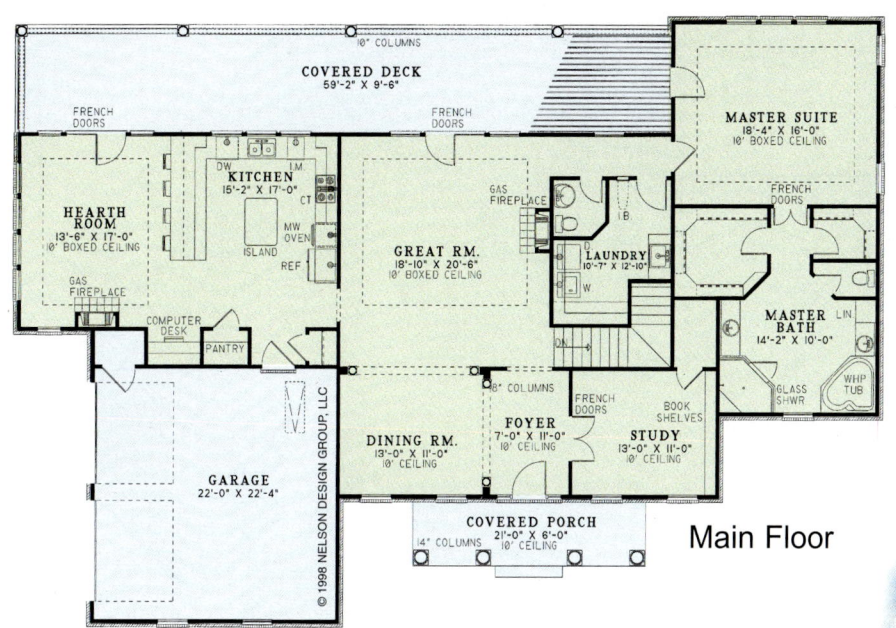

Main Floor

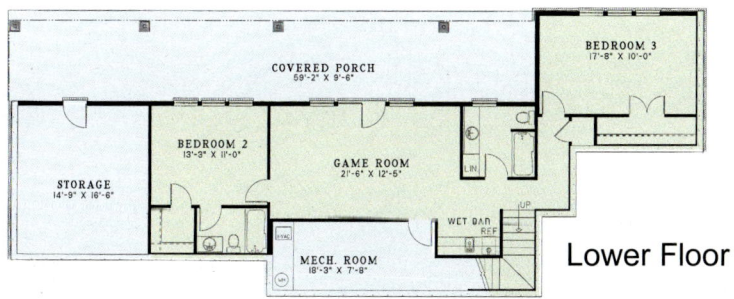

Lower Floor

Front Elevation

Rear Elevation

232 Waterfront Cove

This traditional style Nelson Design Group home is the best of both worlds. Your guests will be amazed at the large columns and ten foot entry porch when they arrive. Entering the foyer, French doors open to the study and the formal dining room. The great room provides an awesome view of the lake and has French door access to the rear covered deck - perfect for those wanting to watch the sun set. Preparing the meal is easy in your spacious kitchen with island. When it's all over, retreat to your master bath with corner whirlpool tub.

Width: 78' 2"	**Main Ceiling:** 9 ft.
Depth: 53' 8"	**Lower Ceiling:** 9 ft.
Main Floor: 2,235 sq. ft.	**Bedrooms:** 3
Lower Floor: 1,250 sq. ft.	**Baths:** 3 1/2
Total Living: 3,485 sq. ft.	**Foundation:** Crawl, Slab, Opt. Basement, Opt. Daylight Basement
Price Tier: E	

To view similar plans visit www.84lumber.com/ndgplans - 800.359.8484

Front Elevation

Rear Elevation

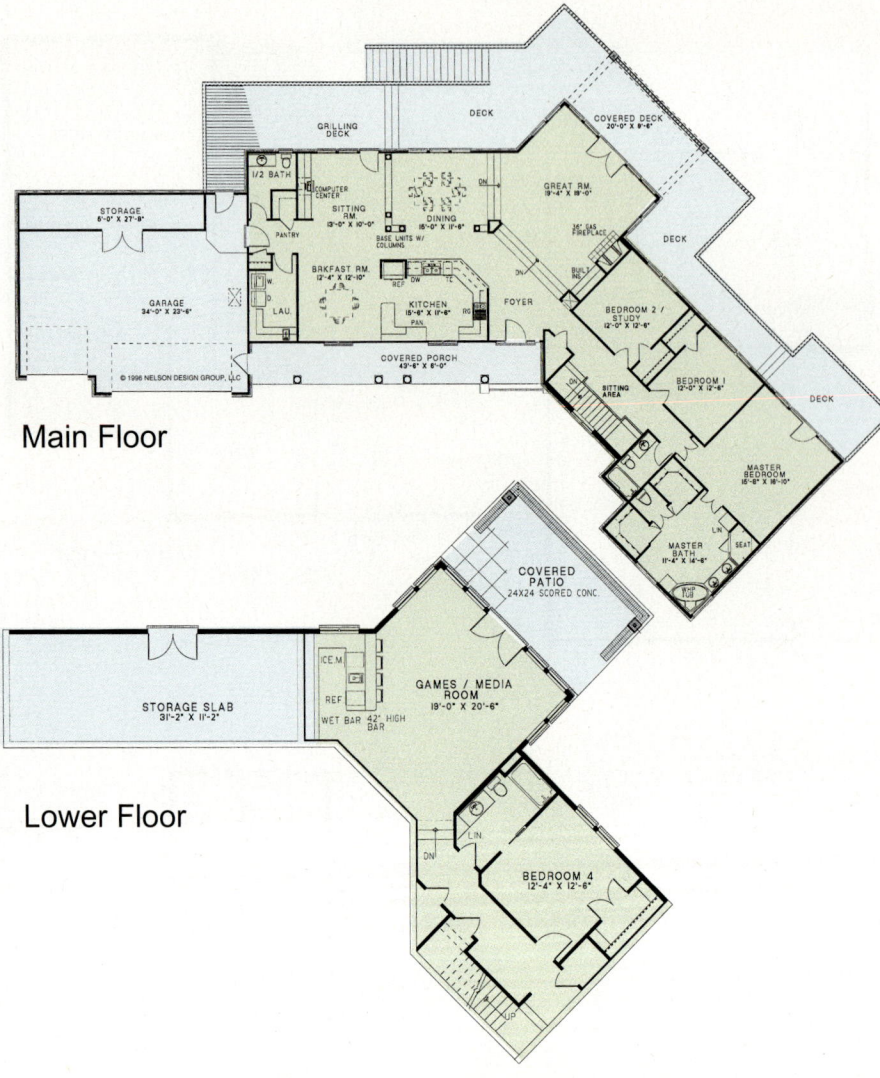

Main Floor

Lower Floor

144 Waterfront Cove

This Nelson Design Group home is perfect for entertaining guests and has a great lake view from all the main rooms. Step down into the great room and out onto the covered deck. This deck runs the entire length of the home and is perfect for grilling. The main level also features a sitting area and breakfast room. The large master bedroom features a corner whirlpool bath and 'his and her' walk-in closets. The kids will enjoy the computer center which is centrally located for easy monitoring. The downstairs features a game room, wet bar and guest room with full bath.

Width: 122' 10"	**Main Ceiling:** 9 ft.
Depth: 75' 5"	**Lower Ceiling:** 8 ft.
Main Floor: 2,711 sq. ft.	**Bedrooms:** 4
Lower Floor: 948 sq. ft.	**Baths:** 3 1/2
Total Living: 3,659 sq. ft.	**Foundation:** Basement, Daylight Basement
Price Tier: F	

412 Hidden Hill Cove

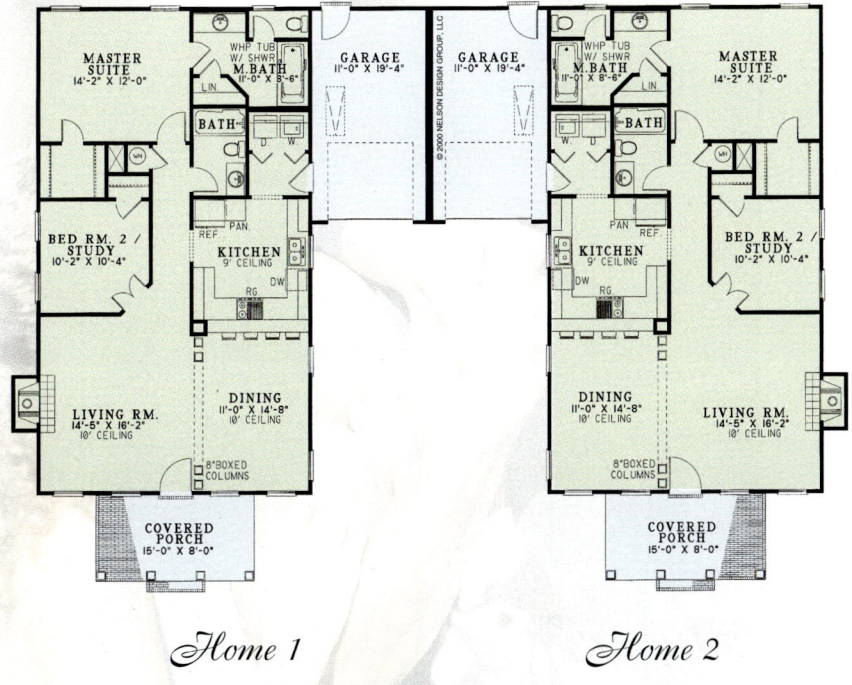

Home 1   Home 2

Picture yourself coming home to this southern traditional Nelson Design Group duplex home. Sit back and watch the sun set from the lovely covered porch of this traditional neighborhood design. Traveling inside you'll feel the openness and elegance created by the ten foot ceilings and intricate boxed columns which lead into the formal dining room. Entertaining will be a success with the convenient kitchen with eat-at bar open to the dining room. End your busy day by retiring to the Master suite with whirlpool tub and shower. The second bedroom or optional study completes this design.

Width: 78' 8"	Bedrooms: 4
Depth: 53'	Baths: 4
Total Living: 2,344 sq. ft.	Foundation: Crawl, Slab
Main Ceiling: 9 ft.	Price Tier: C

457 Wilshire Circle

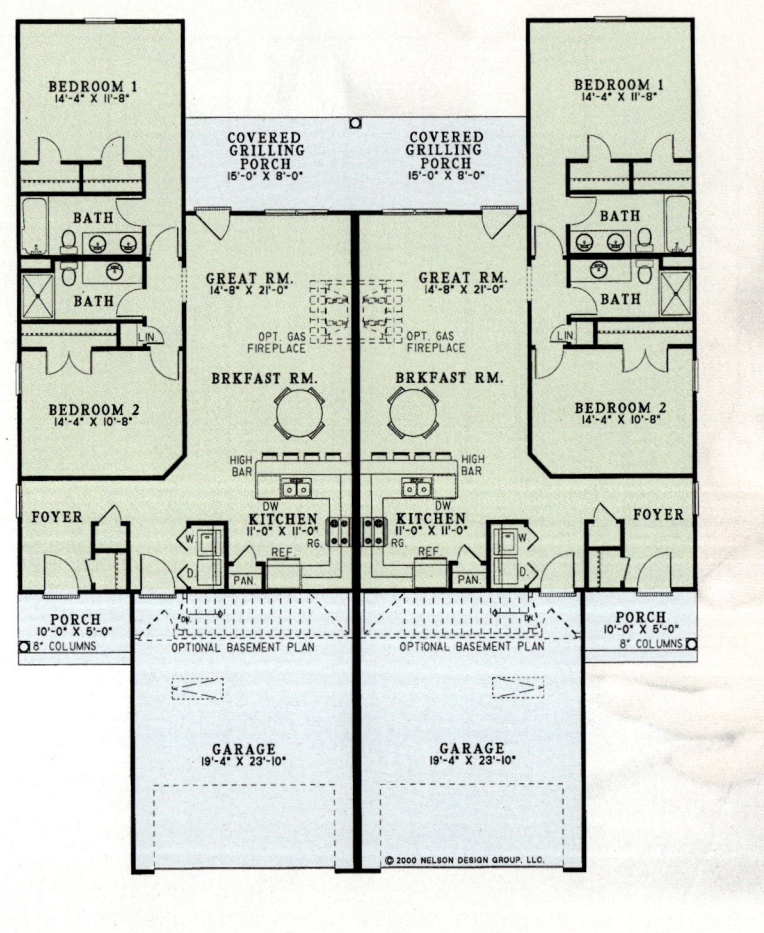

Nelson Design Group has created a beautiful traditional country design duplex. The covered entry porch with ten inch columns will welcome you and your guests. Upon entering the foyer you'll feel the openness created by the convenient kitchen with breakfast room open to the great room. This will serve as the heart of the home, and it will be a great place for serving your guests their after dinner drinks. For that summertime barbeque, the rear grilling porch will be a success. The two bedrooms have ample closet space as well as their own baths, one is complete with 'his and her' vanities and tub.

Width: 60'
Depth: 72' 8"
Total Living: 2,478 sq. ft.
Main Ceiling: 9 ft.
Price Tier: C

Bedrooms: 4
Baths: 4
Foundation: Crawl, Slab, Basement, Daylight Basement

To view similar plans visit www.84lumber.com/ndgplans - 800.359.8484

413 Brookshire

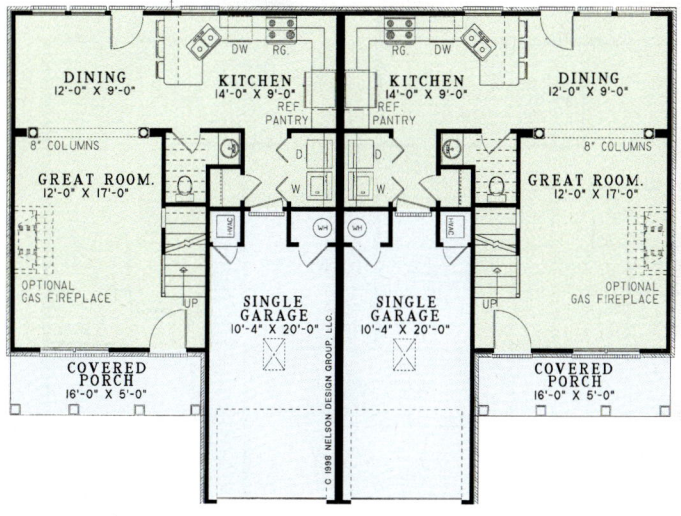

Home 1　　　Home 2

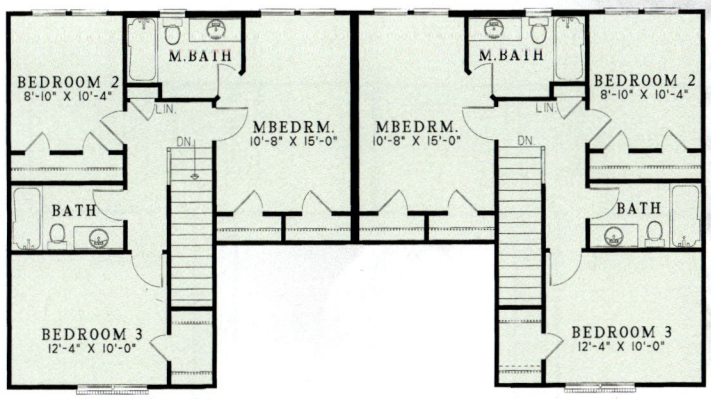

This charming Nelson Design Group duplex awaits you and your family. The quaint covered porch with boxed columns is perfect for greeting family and guests. Traveling inside you'll feel at home in the spacious great room complete with fireplace and eight inch columns leading into the dining room. On the upper floor you'll find the secluded master suite with full bath and ample closet space. The children will have all the space they will need in their own rooms and connecting bath. This traditional design has all the amenities you want in a home.

Width: 54'	Main Ceiling: 9 ft.
Depth: 39'	Upper Ceiling: 9 ft.
Main Floor: 1,218 sq. ft.	Bedrooms: 6
Upper Floor: 1,284 sq. ft.	Baths: 4, 2-1/2
Total Living: 2,502 sq. ft.	Foundation: Crawl, Slab
	Price Tier: D

To view similar plans visit www.84lumber.com/ndgplans - 800.359.8484

394 Wilshire Circle

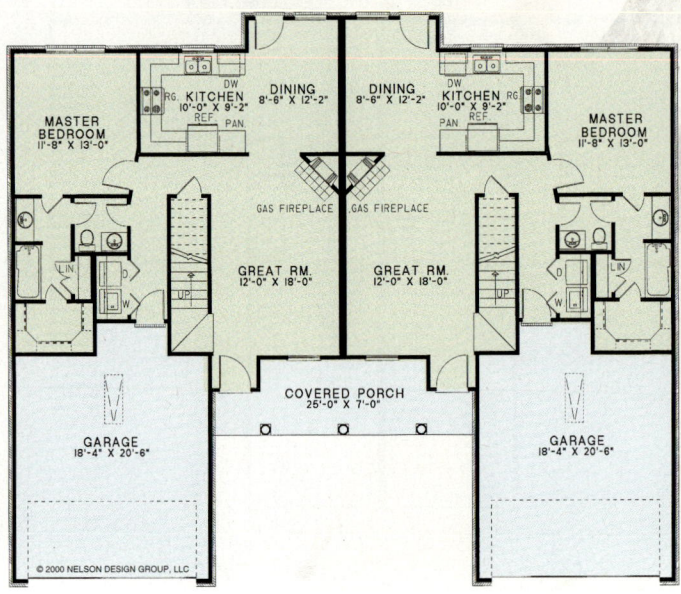

Home 1   *Home 2*

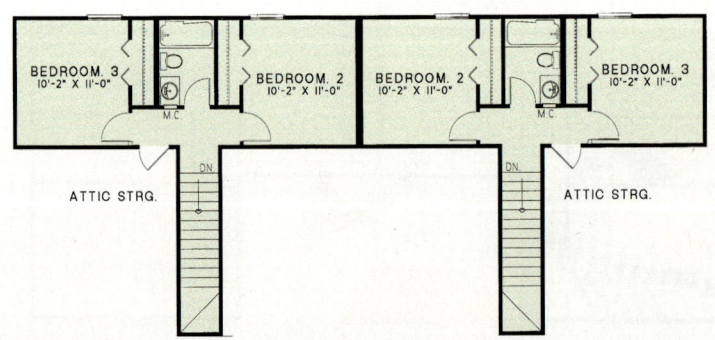

You'll enjoy all the comforts of home in this Nelson Design Group design. Upon entering this southern traditional design, you'll feel warmth in the spacious great room with an angled fireplace. The kitchen is open to a spacious dining room both enjoying windows and a door accessing the back yard. You'll find ultimate seclusion in the master suite with a full bath and huge walk-in closet. The kids will be in a world of their own, upstairs complete with two bedrooms and a full bath.

Width: 63'	Main Ceiling: 8 ft.
Depth: 52'	Upper Ceiling: 8 ft.
Main Floor: 1,822 sq. ft.	Bedrooms: 6
Upper Floor: 748 sq. ft.	Baths: 4
Total Living: 2,570 sq. ft.	Foundation: Crawl, Slab
	Price Tier: D

To view similar plans visit www.84lumber.com/ndgplans - 800.359.8484

430 Rosewood

Home 1 Home 2

Enjoy peaceful fall evenings watching the sun set in this Nelson Design Group home. When it gets too cold, you can warm yourself in the comfortable great room, complete with fireplace. Begin each day with coffee and the morning paper in the hearth room with fluid access to the kitchen. The family chef will love displaying his or her skills during an afternoon cookout on the rear grilling porch. After the day has come to a close, you will find it most relaxing to soothe those aches away in the privacy of your master bath.

Width: 76'
Depth: 64' 10"
Total Living: 2,854 sq. ft.
Main Ceiling: 9 ft.

Bedrooms: 6
Baths: 4
Foundation: Crawl, Slab
Price Tier: D

408-1 Heather Ridge

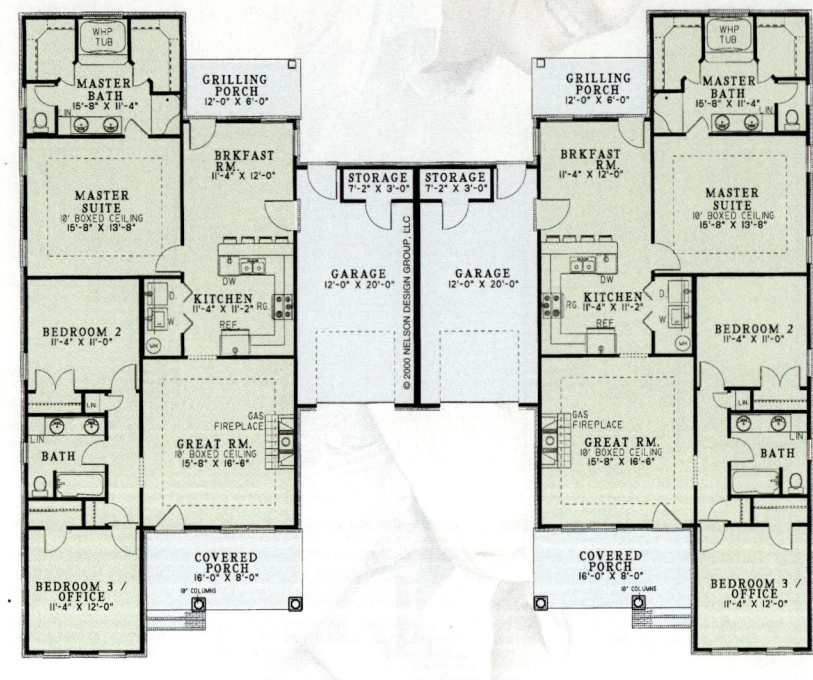

Home 1   *Home 2*

'Picture yourself hosting a dinner party surrounded by family in this Nelson Design Group Traditional Neighborhood home. After greeting guests on the covered porch, guide them into the spacious great room. Here, mingling can begin and maybe drinks around the romantic gas fireplace. Conveniently accessible to the kitchen, you can slip away to check on the excellent cuisine you are preparing. A connecting breakfast room can serve as more space for guests or a quiet place just for you. A door opening to a grilling porch allows you to prepare grilled meats with ease. When all the excitement is over, enjoy the privacy of the master suite or relax in the whirlpool bath.

Width: 80' 8"	Bedrooms: 6
Depth: 63' 4"	Baths: 4
Total Living: 2,910 sq. ft.	Foundation: Crawl, Slab
Main Ceiling: 9 ft.	Price Tier: D

To view similar plans visit www.84lumber.com/ndgplans - 800.359.8484

448 Ivy Green

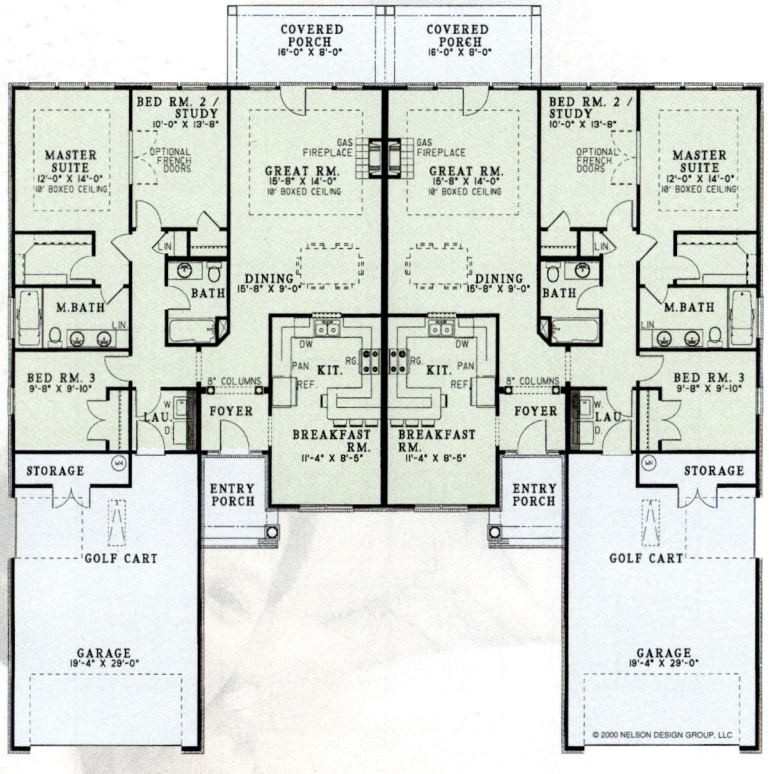

Home 1   Home 2

Feel the French Country flair as you step onto the covered entry porch of this Nelson Design Group French Country home complete with traditional columns and fluid entry into a formal foyer. Enjoy cozy nights at home in your spacious great room or entertain friends on warm summer evenings on your covered back porch. Early morning breakfasts are a delight with an eat-at kitchen bar opening to a quiet breakfast nook.

Width: 78'	Bedrooms: 6
Depth: 73' 10"	Baths: 4
Total Living: 2,974 sq. ft.	Foundation: Crawl, Slab
Main Ceiling: 9 ft.	Price Tier: D

427 Carriage Hill

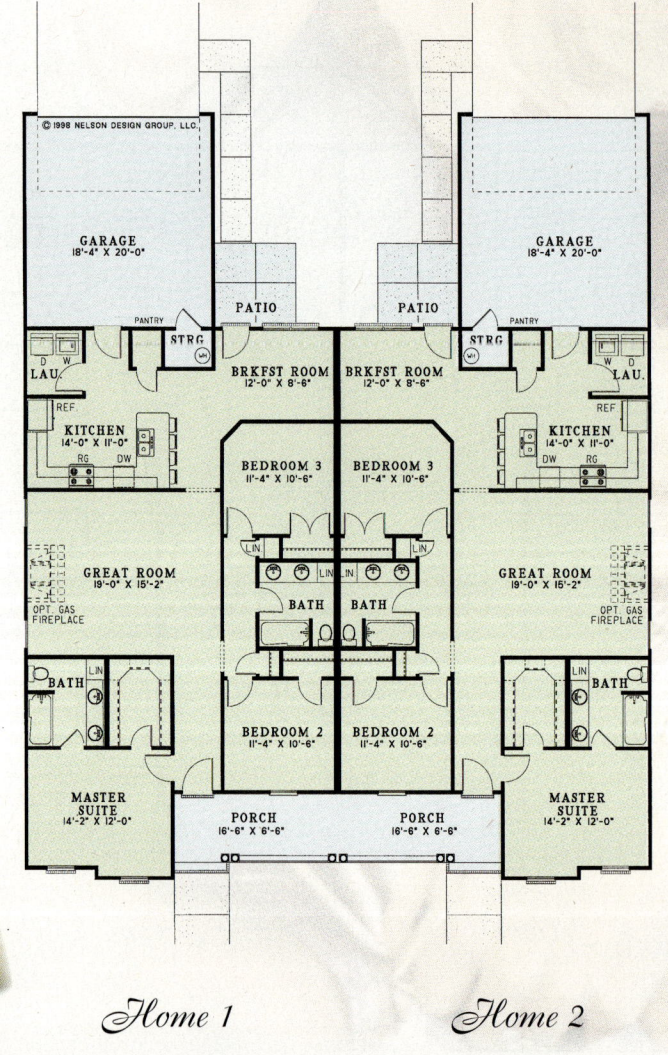

Home 1   Home 2

This traditional neighborhood Nelson Design Group home has a quaint covered porch to welcome friends and family for an afternoon of visiting. Entering through the foyer, your guests will enjoy gathering in the great room with a fireplace to warm themselves from the frigid temperatures that winter brings. During the summer, entertain on your rear grilling porch. After entertaining, you will enjoy quiet time in your master suite, with a large walk-in closet and private bath. Two additional bedrooms complete this design.

Width: 62' 4"
Depth: 72' 10"
Total Living: 3,026 sq. ft.
Main Ceiling: 9 ft.

Bedrooms: 6
Baths: 4
Foundation: Crawl, Slab
Price Tier: E

Check This Plan Mike

To view similar plans visit www.84lumber.com/ndgplans - 800.359.8484

407-1 Auburn Place

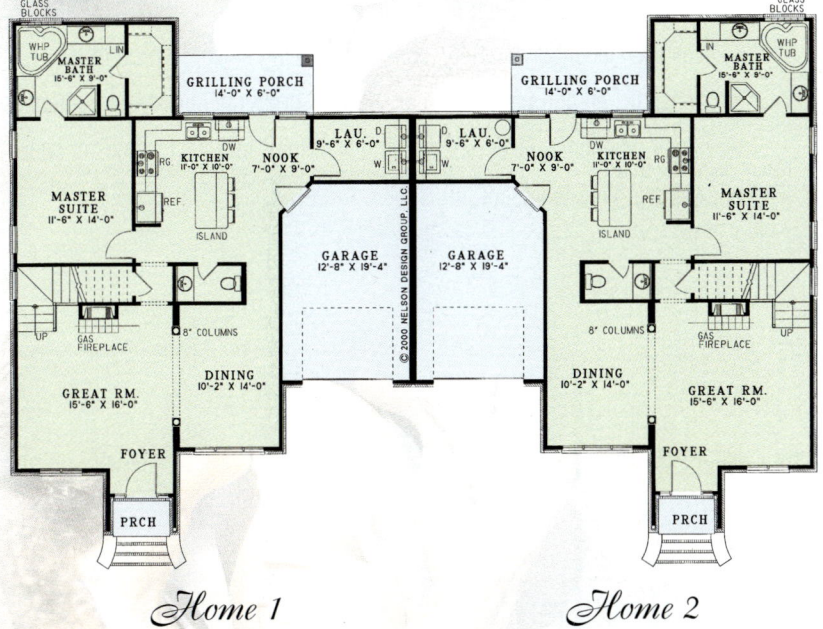

Home 1   Home 2

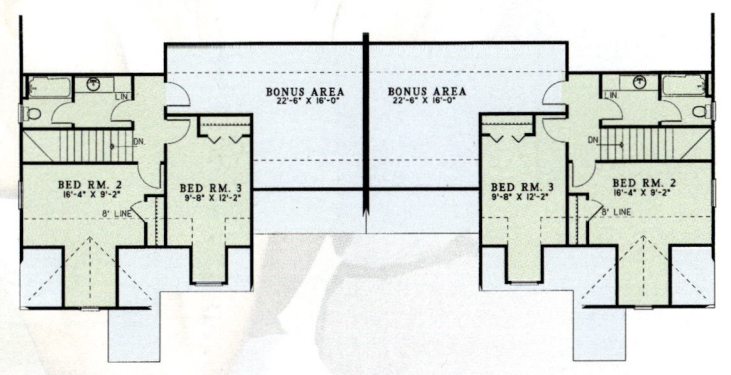

This traditional Nelson Design Group duplex will enchant you as you enter through the covered porch into the spacious great room with gas fireplace. The nine foot ceilings and eight inch wooden columns create a warm ambiance for you and guests. Spend hours of quality time with loved ones in the convenient kitchen with bar and access to the rear grilling porch. The upper floor with unique ceilings and two bedrooms with full bath is perfect for a children's suite. You'll be able to relax away the day in your private master suite complete with master bath, 'his and her' vanities, whirlpool tub with glass blocks and large walk-in closet.

Width: 80'	Main Ceiling: 9 ft.
Depth: 50'	Upper Ceiling: 8 ft.
Main Floor: 2,308 sq. ft.	Bedrooms: 6
Upper Floor: 1,058 sq. ft.	Baths: 4, 2-1/2
Total Living: 3,366 sq. ft.*	Foundation: Basement, Daylight Basement
*Optional Bonus: 530 sq. ft.	
Price Tier: E	

405 Carriage Hill

Entering through majestic columns into the traditional foyer, you instantly feel the grandeur of this Nelson Design Group Traditional Neighborhood home. Imagine an evening of exquisite cuisine as you entertain your close friends and neighbors in the elegant dining room enhanced by ten foot ceilings and beautifully crafted columns. A grilling porch, located off the spacious kitchen and breakfast room, allows occasional backyard barbeques with your neighbors. After long workdays, retreat to a private master suite and relax in your whirlpool tub.

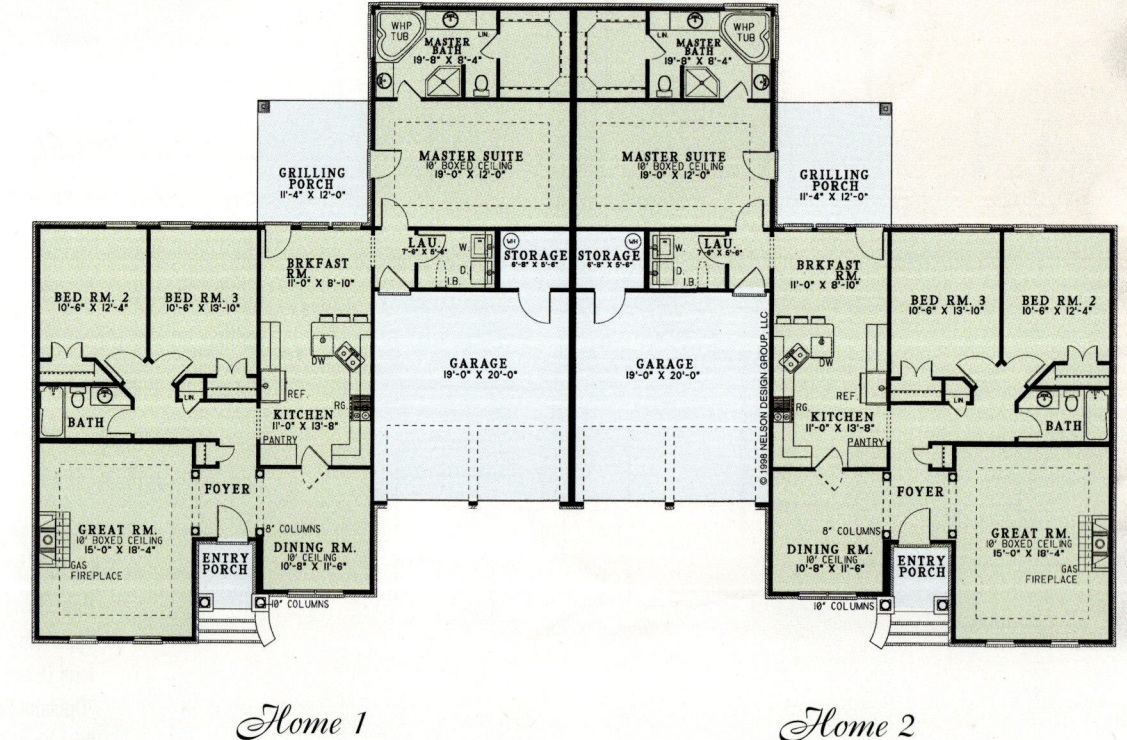

Width: 105' 4"
Depth: 60' 6"
Total Living: 3,396 sq. ft.
Main Ceiling: 9 ft.
Bedrooms: 6
Baths: 4
Foundation: Crawl, Slab
Price Tier: E

Home 1   *Home 2*

To view similar plans visit www.84lumber.com/ndgplans - 800.359.8484

405-1 Centre Grove Circle

This traditional neighborhood design duplex blends elegance with grandeur as it's ten inch columns on the entry porch welcome you into to this Nelson Design Group home. The exquisite foyer will make you feel right at home as you travel into the great room complete with intricate eight inch columns, boxed ceilings, and fireplace. Entertaining will be a breeze with the formal dining room with swinging door access to the kitchen complete with breakfast room. For those summer gatherings, the rear grilling porch will make barbequing with guests a cinch. This spit bedroom plan is perfect for tucking kids in their own side of the home complete with full bath. After your full day, retreat to the master suite and relax in style in your corner whirlpool tub with glass blocks.

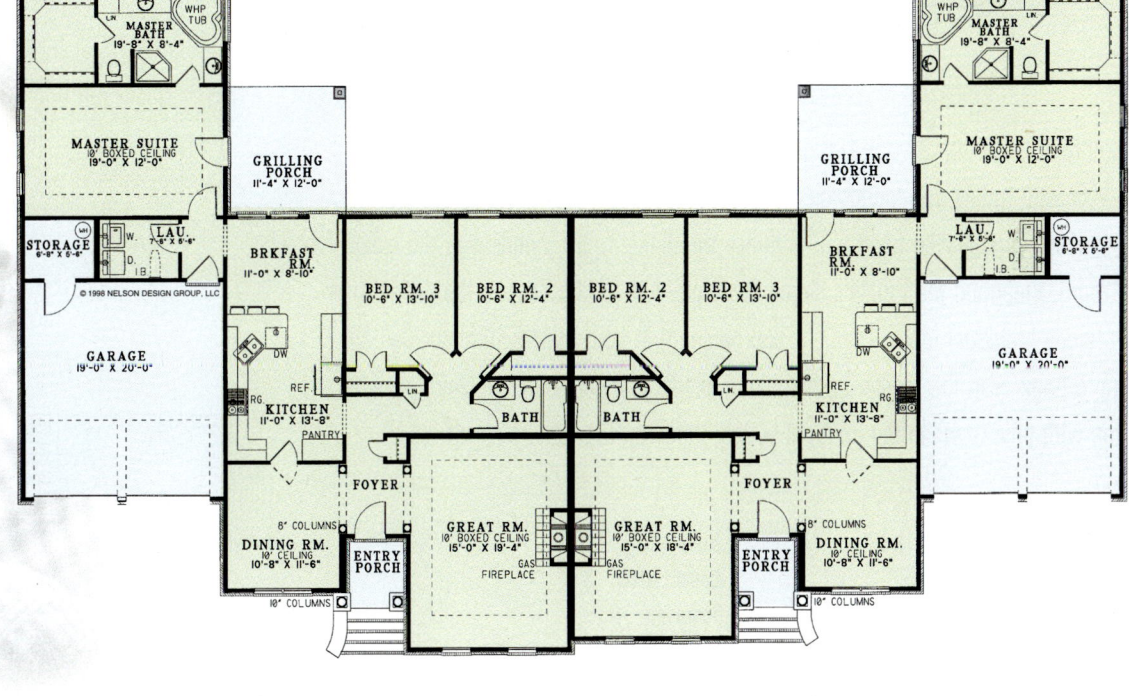

Width: 105' 4"
Depth: 61' 6"
Total Living: 3,419 sq. ft.
Main Ceilings: 9 ft.

Bedrooms: 6
Baths: 4
Foundation: Crawl, Slab
Price Tier: E

Home 1 *Home 2*

To view similar plans visit www.84lumber.com/ndgplans - 800.359.8484

443 Centre Grove Circle

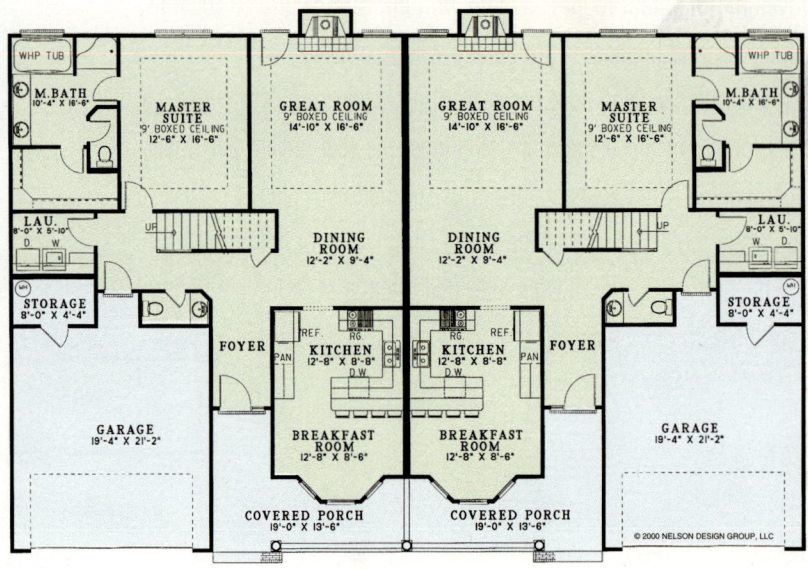

Home 1 *Home 2*

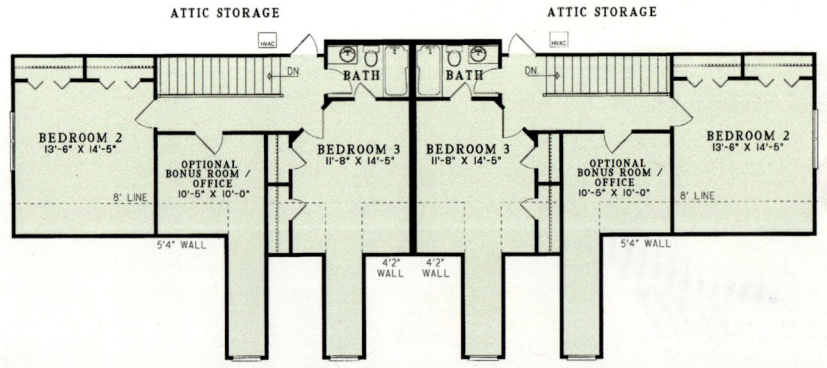

This southern traditional Nelson Design Group home is designed with a split bedroom plan. Visit with family and friends on the front porch as the children play in the front yard. Walking through the foyer, you'll notice the dining room, opening to the expansive great room. Preparing the family's dinner is simple with fluid access to the dining room and a handy breakfast room. Evenings can be spent in your master suite cuddled up reading a book or in the master bath soaking in the whirlpool bath. Upstairs provides children with privacy while the optional bonus room can function as an office.

Width: 78'	Main Ceiling: 8 ft.
Depth: 52'	Upper Ceiling: 8 ft.
Main Floor: 2,598 sq. ft.	Bedrooms: 6
Upper Floor: 1,196 sq. ft.	Baths: 4, 2-1/2
Total Living: 3,794 sq. ft.*	Foundation: Crawl, Slab
*Optional Bonus: 290 sq. ft.	Price Tier: F

To view similar plans visit www.84lumber.com/ndgplans - 800.359.8484

440 Cambridge Court

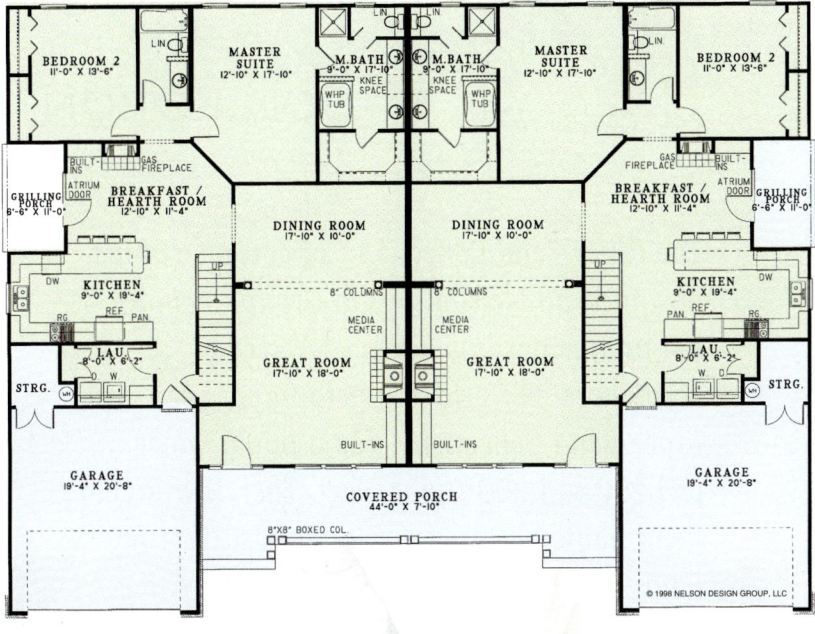

Home 1   *Home 2*

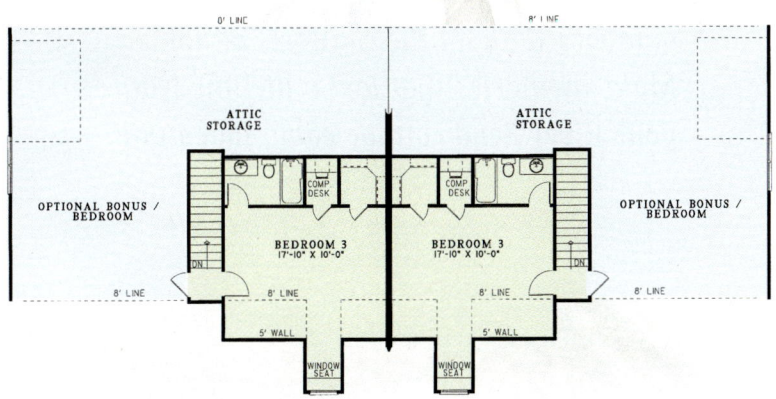

Picture staring into the warm orange sunset from the covered porch of this Nelson Design Group home. On those cool autumn evenings you will be able to sip your cocoa in front of the built-in fireplace in the spacious great room. Entertaining will be a breeze with the exquisite dining room with eight inch columns. Spending quality time with your family will be heart felt in the convenient kitchen, and hearth room with fireplace and atrium door leading to the grilling porch. After the kids are tucked in, you'll find peace in the master suite, or relax in the whirlpool tub. Upstairs, you'll have your choice of a third bedroom or maybe a game room with it's own bath and built-in computer desk.

Width: 84'	Main Ceilings: 9 ft.
Depth: 62' 4"	Upper Ceiling: 8 ft.
Main Floor: 3,536 sq. ft.	Bedrooms: 6
Upper Floor: 828 sq. ft.	Baths: 6
Total Living: 4,364 sq. ft.	Foundation: Crawl, Slab
	Price Tier: G

THE RiverBend™ COLLECTION

The River Bend Collection™ of cottage cabins, designed by Nelson Design Group, includes ten unique designs perfect for second residences and relaxing getaways. Each River Bend Collection™ has a living space of 1,200 to 1,500 square feet. There's a River Bend home perfect for your favorite setting. Enjoy fly fishing for rainbows, casting for lunker bass, a deer hunt or a secluded weekend. Our spacious, feature-filled designs allow you to enjoy the great outdoors with all the comforts of home. Make memories that last a lifetime from your River Bend cottage cabin hideaway.

Nelson Design Group LLC

RESIDENTIAL PLANNERS · DESIGNERS

River View

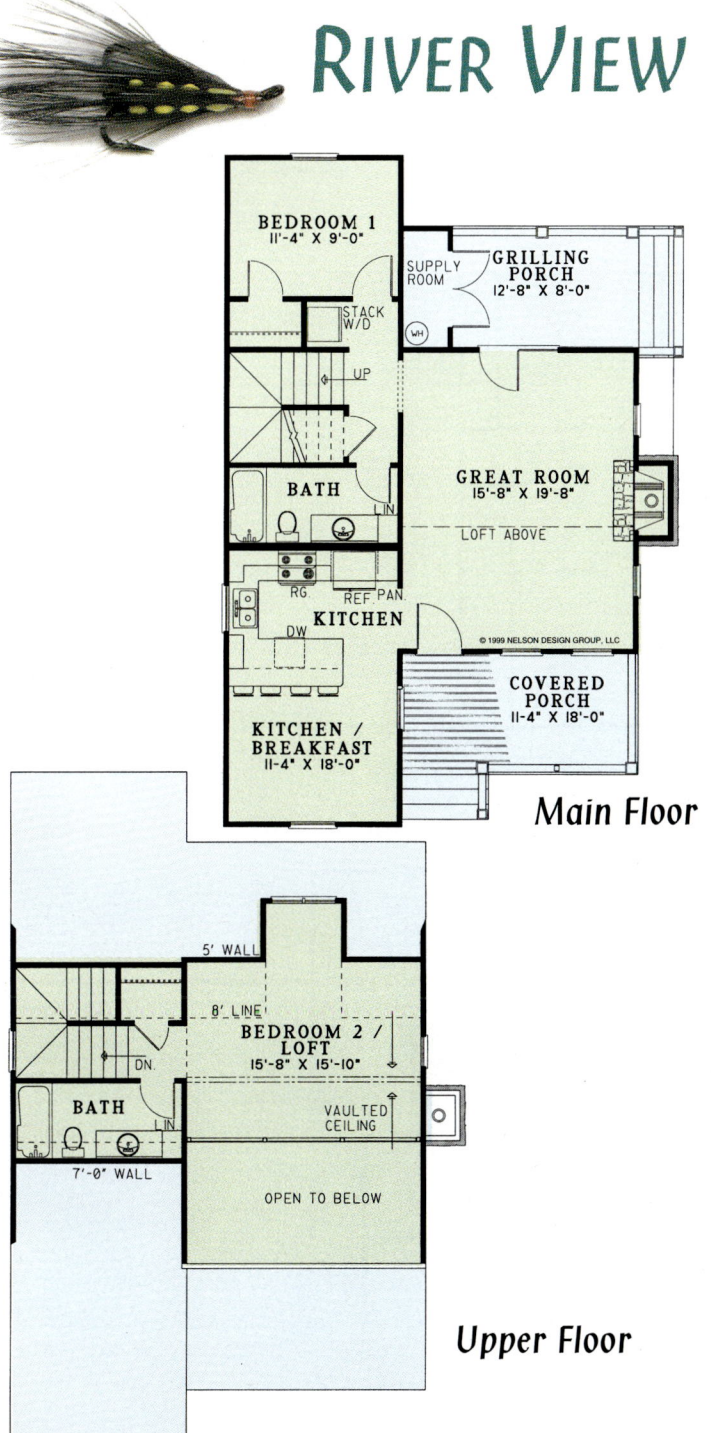

Main Floor

Upper Floor

Width: 30' 4"
Depth: 44' 6"
Main Floor: 859 sq. ft.
Upper Floor: 319 sq. ft.
Total Living: 1,178 sq. ft.
Price Tier: A

Main Ceiling: 8 ft.
Upper Ceiling: 8 ft.
Bedrooms: 2
Baths: 2
Foundation: Crawl, Slab, Opt. Basement, Opt. Daylight Basement

Mom and Dad waved from the front porch as the children splashed in the water. It was always so wonderful coming up to their vacation spot on the River Bend. The mornings were composed of gathering flowers that sprang up along the banks of the river and important trout fishing lessons from Dad. Afternoons consisted of picnics on the riverbank and long walks in the woods. Evenings were spent beside the fireplace where each family member shared stories of the day's adventures. This was the view of life that they enjoyed...the one that took place at River View.

BLUFF'S EDGE

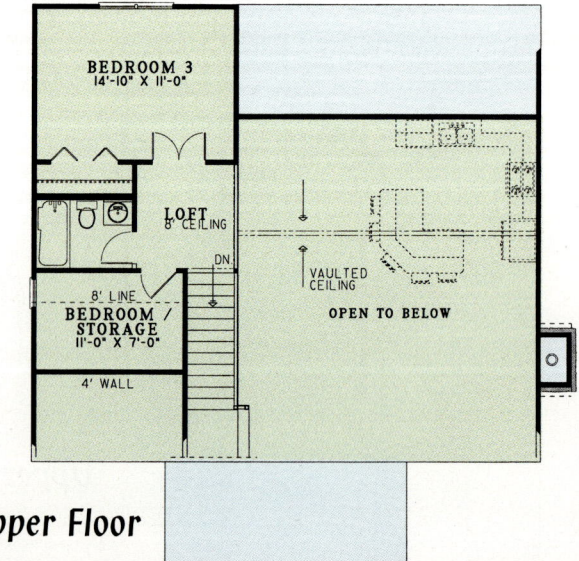

Main Floor

Upper Floor

Width:	40' 4"
Depth:	41' 6"
Main Floor:	1,070 sq. ft.
Upper Floor:	304 sq. ft.
Total Living:	1,374 sq. ft.
Price Tier:	A
Main Ceiling:	8 ft.
Upper Ceiling:	8 ft.
Bedrooms:	4
Baths:	2
Foundation:	Crawl, Slab, Opt. Basement, Opt. Daylight Basement

They reveled in the beauty of the forests' foliage as they hiked from the top of the mountain. Evergreens extended their arms to be touched by the sun's rays. Animals scampered about the ground and the trees. The family hiked from the cabin many times, but the views never ceased to take their breath away. The cabin sat on the edge of a bluff overlooking River Bend. The family vacations at Bluff's Edge were always a much anticipated time for family and friends.

PEBBLE CREEK

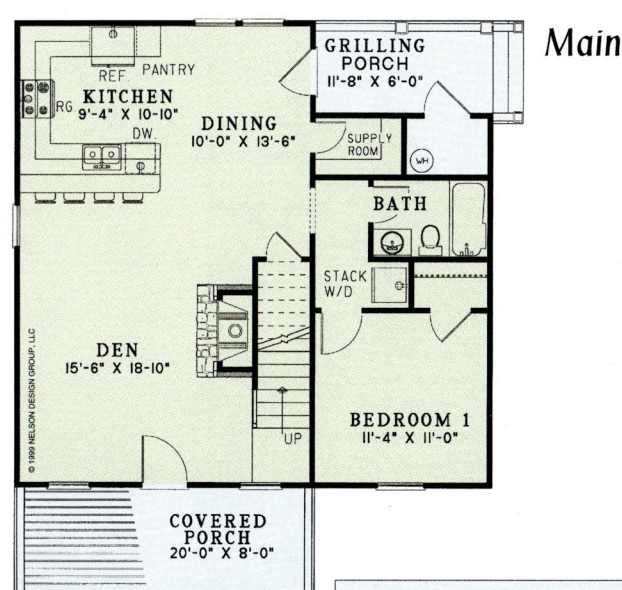

Main Floor

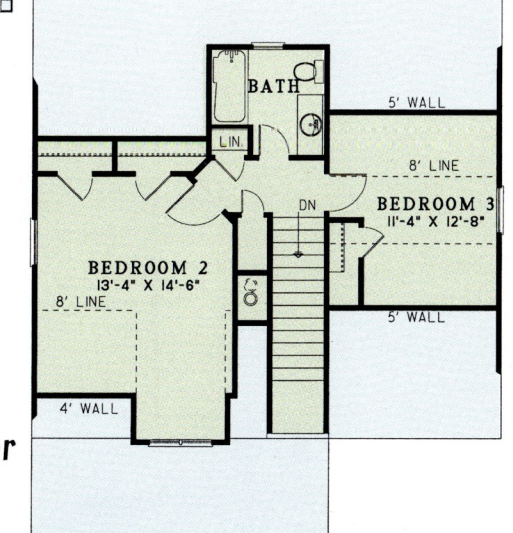

Upper Floor

Width:	31' 8"	Main Ceiling:	8 ft.
Depth:	38' 4"	Upper Ceiling:	8 ft.
Main Floor:	890 sq. ft.	Bedrooms:	3
Upper Floor:	507 sq. ft.	Baths:	2
Total Living:	1,397 sq. ft.	Foundation:	Crawl, Slab, Opt. Basement, Opt. Daylight Basement
Price Tier:	A		

*A*s the smooth stones skipped across the clear water, the children giggled with delight. Both remembered how Mom and Dad had taught them how to skip rocks - it was all in the wrist. There were many smooth, flat stones perfect for skipping that lined River Bend. At night, everyone would sit along the side of the river and talk about the adventures of the day. Adventures were always abundant...at Pebble Creek.

Hunter's Den

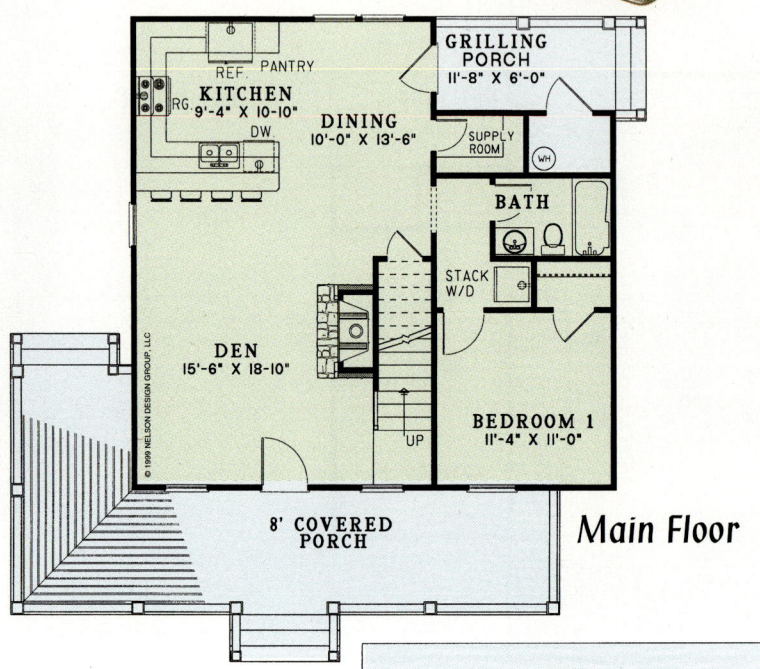

Main Floor

Upper Floor

Width: 39' 8"
Depth: 38' 4"
Main Floor: 890 sq. ft.
Upper Floor: 507 sq. ft.
Total Living: 1,397 sq. ft.
Price Tier: A

Main Ceiling: 8 ft.
Upper Ceiling: 8 ft.
Bedrooms: 3
Baths: 2
Foundation: Crawl, Slab, Opt. Basement, Opt. Daylight Basement

After a brisk fall day, hunters gather here to reminisce over the day's events. Each brother has his own rendition of how big the deer, that they encountered, really was. The days at Hunter's Den are like the leaves on a breeze, floating by with such peacefulness. As the men exchange stories on the front porch, their minds recall a time of when their parents had first built their getaway. Each brother remembered the hikes in the woods and exciting hunting trips with dad that all began here...at Hunter's Den.

Table Rock

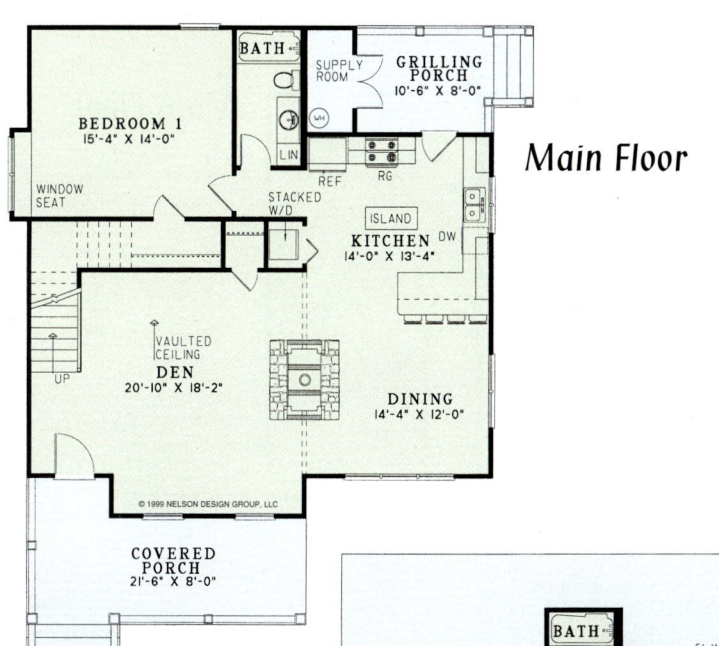

Main Floor

Upper Floor

Width: 37' 2"
Depth: 45'
Main Floor: 1,159 sq. ft.
Upper Floor: 383 sq. ft.
Total Living: 1,542 sq. ft.
Price Tier: B

Main Ceiling: 8 ft.
Upper Ceiling: 8 ft.
Bedrooms: 2
Baths: 2
Foundation: Crawl, Slab, Opt. Basement, Opt. Daylight Basement

*T*hey giggled with delight as the fish began to nibble on their toes as they dipped their feet into the water. The children always loved the lazy summers at Grandma's and Grandpa's cabin. They loved the early morning swims in River Bend's cool waters and the lemonade that Grandma served in the afternoons. What they especially enjoyed, was laying on the large flat rock that allowed the rivers water to gently splash over its surface providing cool relief from the summer's heat. The days here at Table Rock would always be home to their fondest memories.

Stone Brook

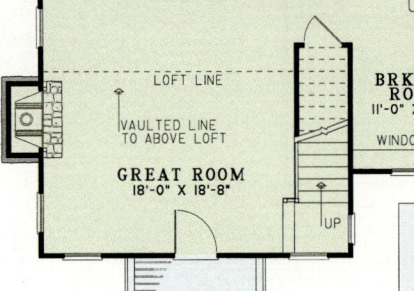

Main Floor

Upper Floor

Width: 36' 2"
Depth: 48'
Main Floor: 1,016 sq. ft.
Upper Floor: 409 sq. ft.
Total Living: 1,425 sq. ft.
Price Tier: A

Main Ceiling: 8 ft.
Upper Ceiling: 8 ft.
Bedrooms: 2
Baths: 2
Foundation: Crawl, Slab, Opt.
Basement, Opt.
Daylight Basement

As she walked down the stairs from the loft, she could see the sun rising like a fire. Across the horizon, when she sat on the window seat and stared out into the dawning of a new day, she could see the water rippling onto the shore to greet the stones for the first time that day. Catching a glimpse of movement, her eyes focused on her husband displaying a stringer of fish caught that morning in River Bend. This would be the first of many memorable weekends and vacations...at Stone Brook.

Canoe Point

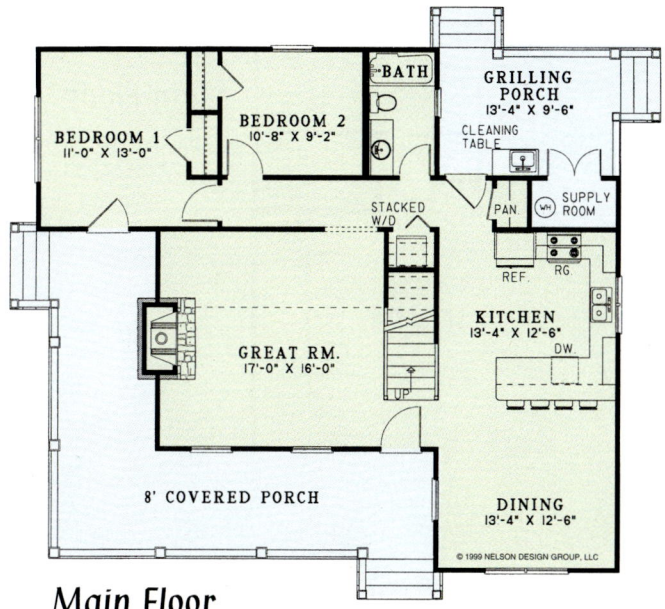

Main Floor

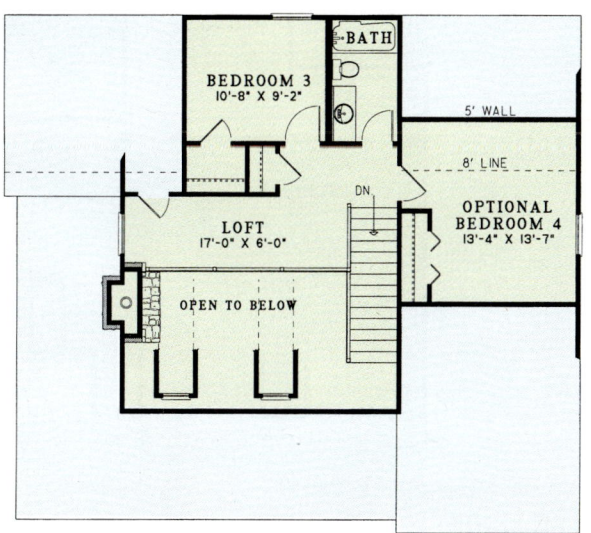

Upper Floor

Width: 44' 2"
Depth: 39'
Main Floor: 1,140 sq. ft.
Upper Floor: 332 sq. ft.
Total Living: 1,472 sq. ft.*
*Bonus: 199 sq. ft.
Price Tier: A

Main Ceiling: 8 ft.
Upper Ceiling: 8 ft.
Bedrooms: 4
Baths: 2
Foundation: Crawl, Slab, Opt. Basement, Opt. Daylight Basement

*T*hey sat on the front porch and watched as the canoes floated by. People always enjoyed canoeing at this point of River Bend because of its thrilling rapids. Watching the canoes was a family event because of the variety of expressions on the canoeists faces and the screams of excitement as they battled the rapids. Mom would make scorecards for everyone to hold up to rate the thrill-seekers on their skills. Canoe Point was a memorable place that was familiar to all.

To view similar plans visit www.84lumber.com/ndgplans - 800.359.8484

Piney Creek

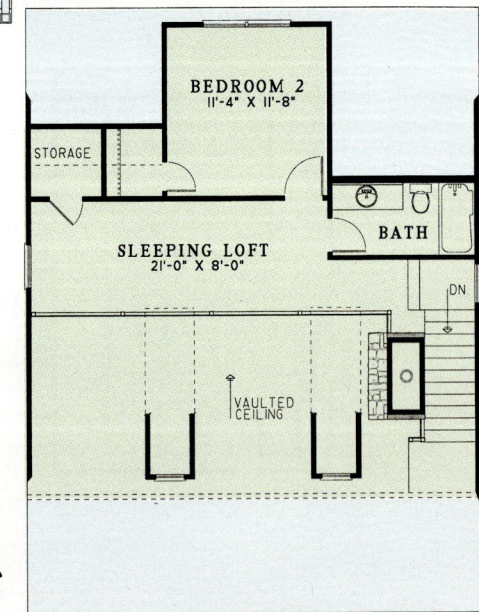

Main Floor

Upper Floor

Width: 32'
Depth: 42'
Main Floor: 948 sq. ft.
Upper Floor: 452 sq. ft.
Total Living: 1,400 sq. ft.
Price Tier: A

Main Ceiling: 8 ft.
Upper Ceiling: 8 ft.
Bedrooms: 2
Baths: 2
Foundation: Crawl, Slab, Opt. Basement, Opt. Daylight Basement

*A*s he helped her up to the steps of the cabin, the couple began reminiscing about the many summers they had spent there. The summer afternoons when their children and grandchildren came to visit were undeniably the most treasured. Watching as they caught their first fish, floated on intertubes and picked flowers in the field always brought a smile to their faces. As they looked out across River Bend, they imagined many generations of their family spending their summers here...at Piney Creek.

Creek Side

Main Floor

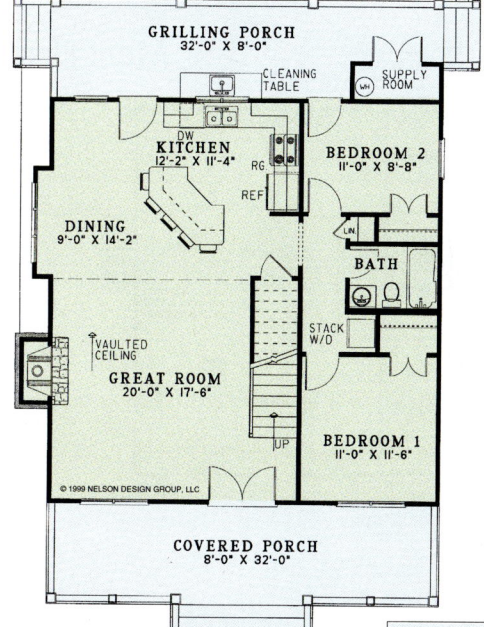

Upper Floor

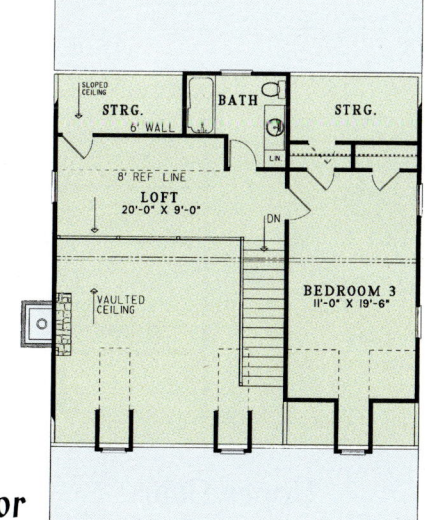

Width: 34' 4"
Depth: 48' 4"
Main Floor: 1,031 sq. ft.
Upper Floor: 513 sq. ft.
Total Living: 1,544 sq. ft.
Price Tier: B

Main Ceiling: 8 ft.
Upper Ceiling: 8 ft.
Bedrooms: 3
Baths: 2
Foundation: Crawl, Slab, Opt. Basement, Opt. Daylight Basement

*H*e began thinking where he was as he casts the fly rod upstream. A dream world. Not just any ole' dream world, but his dream world. Everything was as he had always imagined and hoped for. The cold, crisp waters of River Bend tickled his legs with its voice. Across the river, a trout leaped to an unknown destination. The porch of the cabin beckoned him to come and relax in the cool shade. The sun showered it's rays onto the water causing him to catch a glimpse of his own reflection. He was always a happy man when he was at his dream getaway called Creek Side.

LAKE SIDE

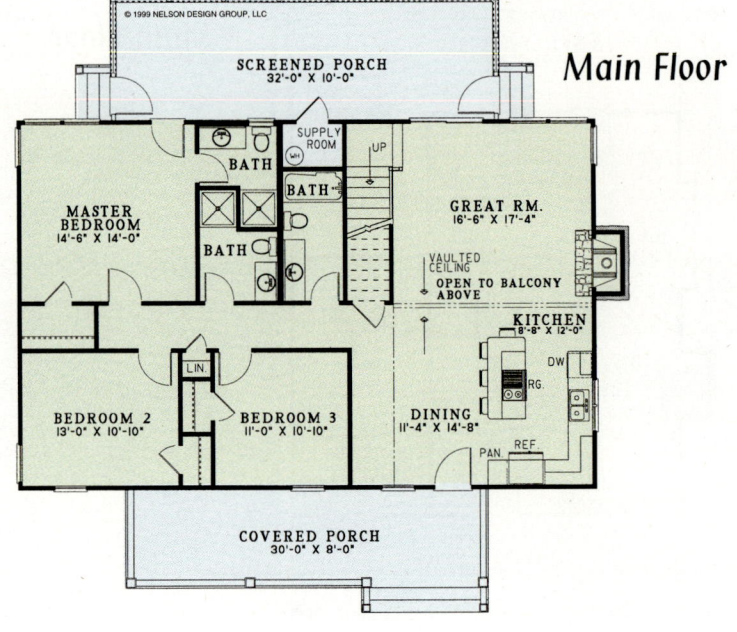

Main Floor

Upper Floor

Width: 50' 4"
Depth: 48'
Main Floor: 1,440 sq. ft.
Upper Floor: 530 sq. ft.
Total Living: 1,970
Price Tier: B

Main Ceiling: 8 ft.
Upper Ceiling: 8 ft.
Bedrooms: 4
Baths: 4
Foundation: Crawl, Slab, Opt. Basement, Opt. Daylight Basement

*T*hey woke up early that summer morning to watch the sun rise over the mountains. As they sat on the porch drinking coffee, they began talking about the future. This was only the first of many vacations at their new retreat. They began dreaming of the fishing lessons with their children and the nighttime storytelling beside the fireplace. This was a place in which to build traditions. Traditions that would last throughout the generations. Traditions that would begin here...at Lake Side.

To view similar plans visit www.84lumber.com/ndgplans - 800.359.8484

Stock Plans

For more than 15 years, Nelson Design Group, LLC has been designing *superior* homes for builders and custom plans for clients throughout the country. As a certified member of the American Institute of Building Designers (AIBD), we are nationally known and have been recognized and *highlighted* in publications such as *HomeStyles Publishing, Home Design Alternatives, Builder Magazine* (the official publication of the National Association of Home Builders), *Home Planners, Garlinghouse, Good Housekeeping, Old House Journal, House Beautiful, Southern Living, Better Homes and Gardens*, and others.

A successful and *innovative* company is created by providing the best possible product with creative and knowledgeable people to carry each project to completion. Nelson Design Group, LLC Residential Planners-Designers is one such success.

Our staff of designers offers the qualities a consumer searching for a home desires — experience, creativity and efficiency. We offer *unique* and diversified designs, as well as Southern Traditionals, Lake Houses, Country Styles and Modern Classics. We can modify any of our plans to suit your needs — saving time and guaranteeing customer *satisfaction*.

The next pages will reflect stock plans from our portfolio. Visit our web site at www.nelsondesigngroup.com for additional plans.

500 Maple Street

Main Floor

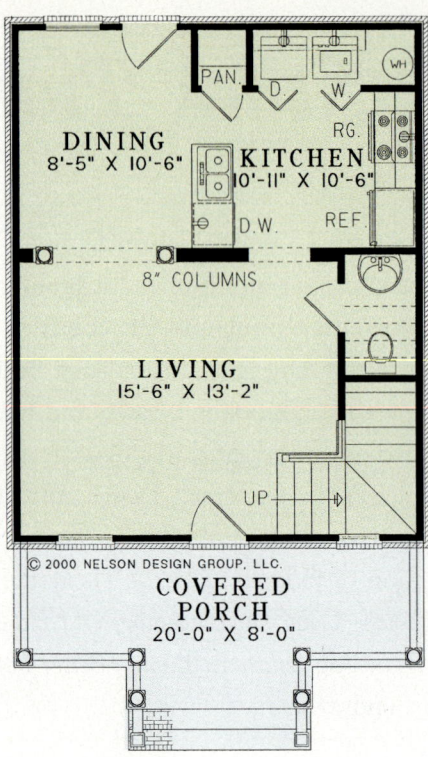

Upper Floor

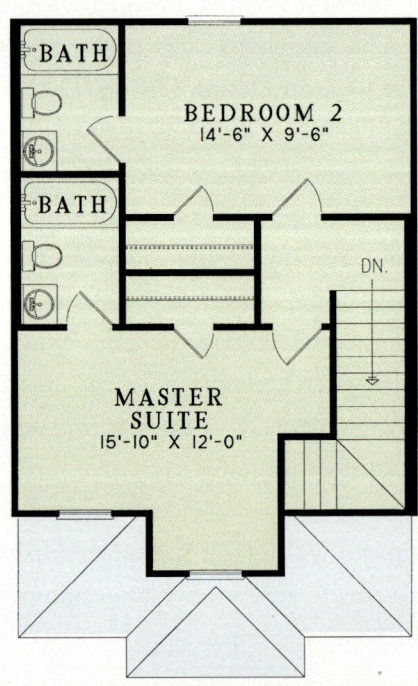

Quiet afternoons will find you rocking away on the covered front porch of this Nelson Design Group home. Imagine hosting family gatherings and entertaining in the spacious living room of this Traditional design. Serving your guests will be a breeze with the convenient kitchen open to the formal dining room, which is accented with elegant eight inch round columns. After the guests leave, you may retreat to the bedrooms upstairs, each with their own full bath and ample closet space. This design offers all the amenities you've come to expect in a home.

Width: 20' 0"
Depth: 33' 0"
Main Floor: 500 sq. ft.
Upper Floor: 480 sq. ft.
Total Living: 980 sq. ft.

Main Ceiling: 8 ft.
Upper Ceiling: 8 ft.
Bedrooms: 2
Baths: 2 1/2
Foundation: Crawl, Slab

Price Tier: A

130 Maple Street

This Southern Traditional Nelson Design Group home is packed with amenities that are sure to please you. An impressive tiled entry carries you into a spacious great room, which has an optional fireplace. Family traditions will be cherished in the adorable breakfast room and convenient kitchen with access to the rear patio. This design features two equally spacious bedrooms, divided by a full bath complete with 'his and her' vanities. The rear entry garage has ample storage space and gives much needed privacy.

Width: 27' 0"
Depth: 65' 2"
Total Living: 985 sq. ft.

Main Ceiling: 9 ft.
Bedrooms: 2
Baths: 1
Foundation: Crawl, Slab, Basement, Daylight Basement

Price Tier: A

To view similar plans visit www.84lumber.com/ndgplans - 800.359.8484

207 Maple Street

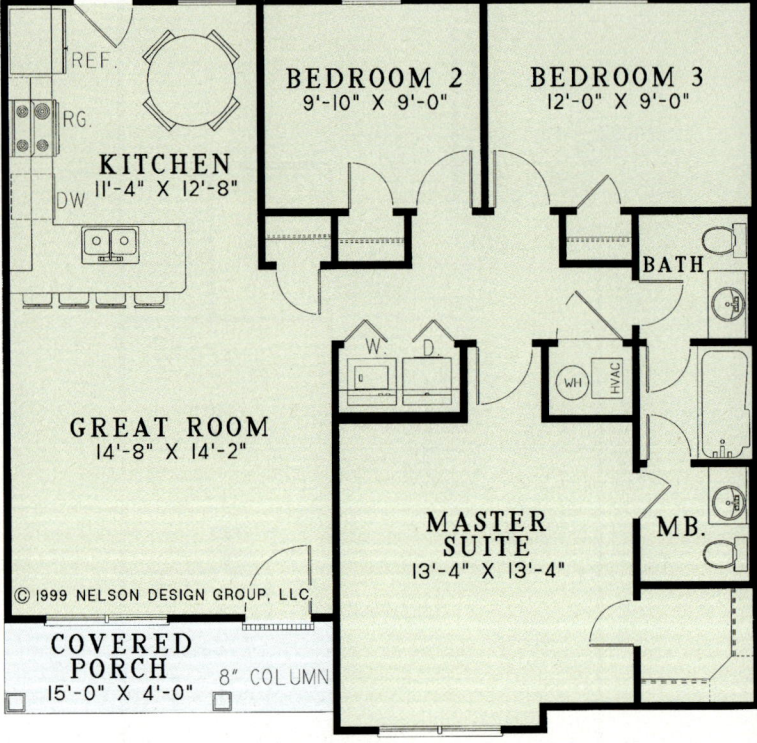

Check This Plan Mike

This charming Nelson Design Group country home is the perfect starter plan. Visit with neighbors on your front porch as the children ride their bikes. Upon entering, you'll feel all the comforts of home in your spacious great room which provides a comfortable atmosphere with an open view to the kitchen. Your master suite features a walk-in closet with a private access to the bath. Listening for that newborn baby is made easier with the nursery close by.

Width: 34' 6"
Depth: 32' 6"
Total Living: 1,029 sq. ft.

Main Ceiling: 8 ft.
Bedrooms: 3
Baths: 1 1/2
Foundation: Crawl, Slab

Price Tier: A

To view similar plans visit www.84lumber.com/ndgplans - 800.359.8484

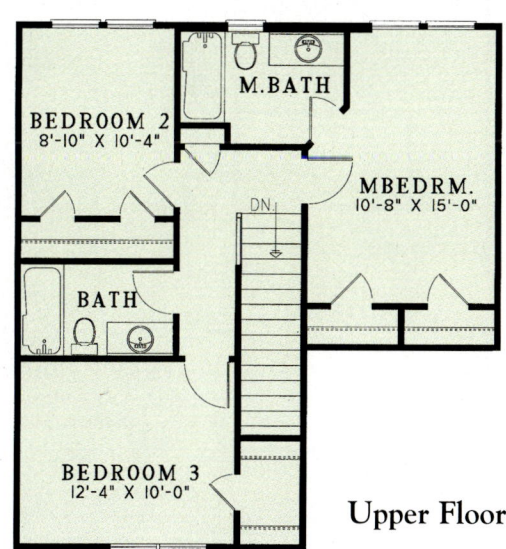

Main Floor

Upper Floor

188 Maple Street

This Nelson Design Group home offers cozy comfort, economical construction and plenty of space for formal entertainment and family living. An optional fireplace provides just the right touch for relaxation and casual conversation. The grilling porch is the perfect stage for the family outdoor chef. Eat at the breakfast bar for casual dining or enjoy the atmosphere of the spacious formal dining room. The sleeping quarters are located upstairs for additional privacy or when you need a quiet room to work away from family activity.

Width: 27' 0"
Depth: 45' 0"
Main Floor: 609 sq. ft.
Upper Floor: 642 sq. ft.
Total Living: 1,251 sq. ft.

Main Ceiling: 8 ft.
Upper Ceiling: 8 ft.
Bedrooms: 3
Baths: 2 1/2
Foundation: Crawl, Slab, Basement, Daylight Basement

Price Tier: A

To view similar plans visit www.84lumber.com/ndgplans - 800.359.8484

133 Maple Street

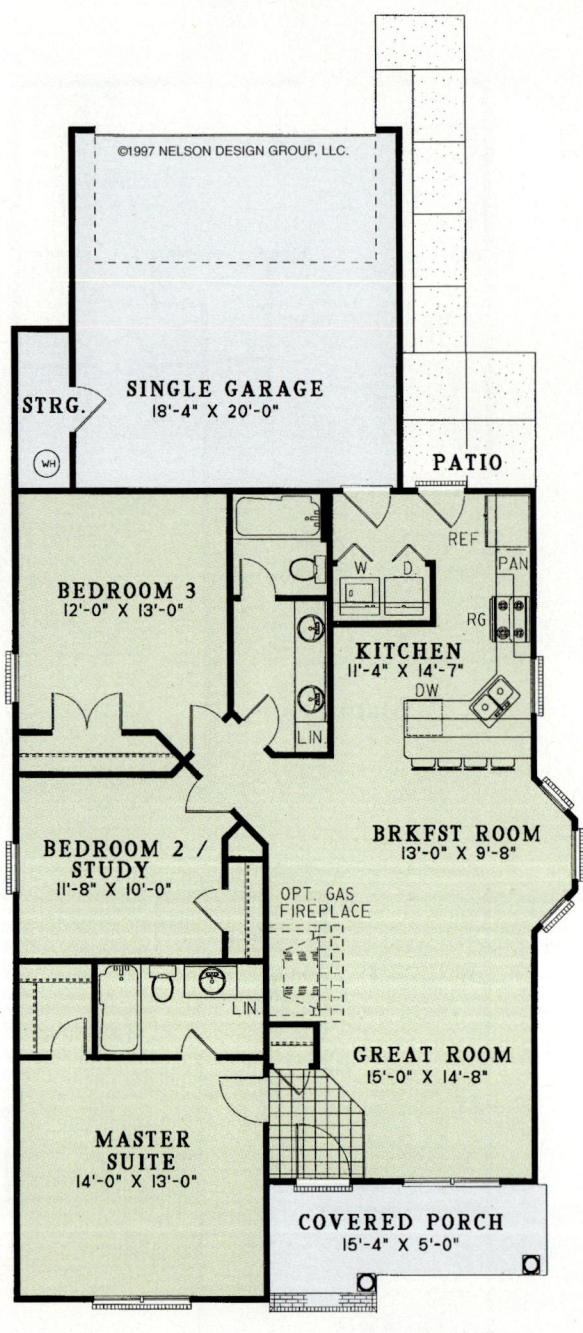

This charming Nelson Design Group country home has an adorable covered front porch to welcome your family and friends. The tiled entry opens to the great room with optional fireplace to remove the chill from winter evenings. Breakfast traditions begin in the kitchen with a bright bay window for those sunny mornings. The master suite has a walk-in closet and private bath. One bedroom can serve as an optional office for a family member who telecommutes or works out of the home.

Width: 32' 4"
Depth: 65' 0"
Total Living: 1,265 sq. ft.

Main Ceiling: 9 ft.
Bedrooms: 3
Baths: 2
Foundation: Crawl, Slab

Price Tier: A

To view similar plans visit www.84lumber.com/ndgplans - 800.359.8484

471 Spruce Street

Nelson Design Group gave this home a traditional design that focuses on today's active lifestyles. The plan is designed around a centralized great room that provides easy access to all sections of the home, including living and bedroom areas. A breakfast room more practical for quick family meals replaces the formal dining room for those occasions when time is at a premium. A secondary bedroom features a vaulted ceiling and a large, arched window.

Width: 45' 0"
Depth: 56' 0"
Total Living: 1,344 sq. ft.

Price Tier: A

Main Ceiling: 8 ft.
Bedrooms: 3
Baths: 2
Foundation: Crawl, Slab, Opt. Basement, Opt. Daylight Basement

200 Spruce Street

Elevation A

Elevation B

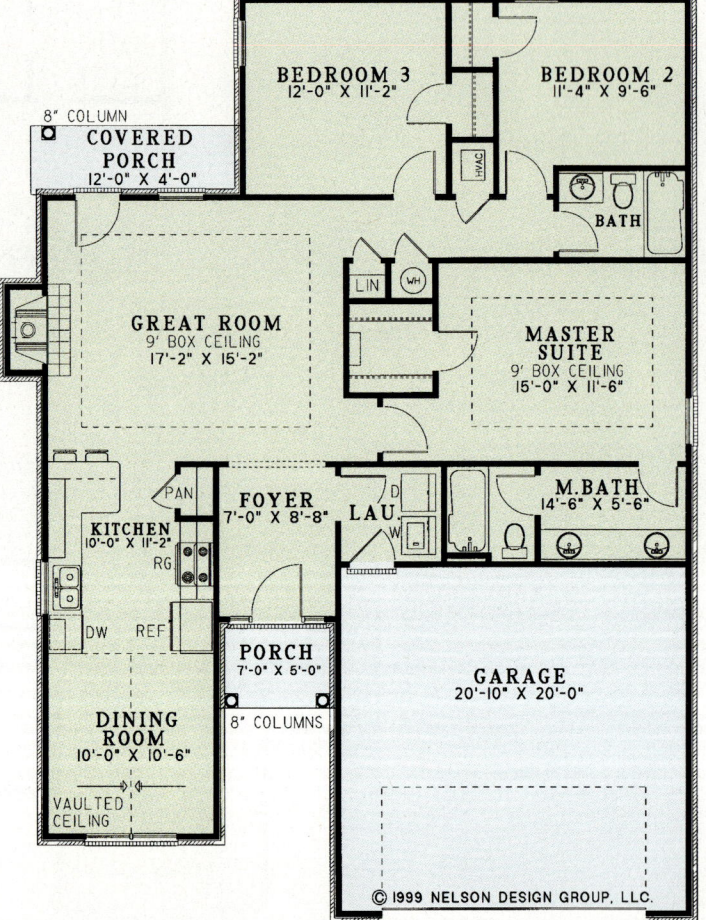

Entertaining will be easy in this Nelson Design Group home. The vaulted ceiling in the dining room creates a feeling of grandeur for your dinner party guests. Afterwards, lead your guests into the spacious great room and around the fire for dessert, coffee and conversation. Preparation of dinner is easy in your open kitchen with fluid access to the dining room. After your guests leave, retire for the evening to your master suite, enhanced by a nine foot boxed ceiling. But don't worry about the children, they will be nestled in their own bedrooms with plenty of space.

Width: 39' 2"
Depth: 53' 6"
Total Living: 1,355 sq. ft.

Price Tier: A

Main Ceiling: 8 ft.
Bedrooms: 3
Baths: 2
Foundation: Crawl, Slab, Opt. Basement, Opt. Daylight Basement

To view similar plans visit www.84lumber.com/ndgplans - 800.359.8484

382 Spruce Street

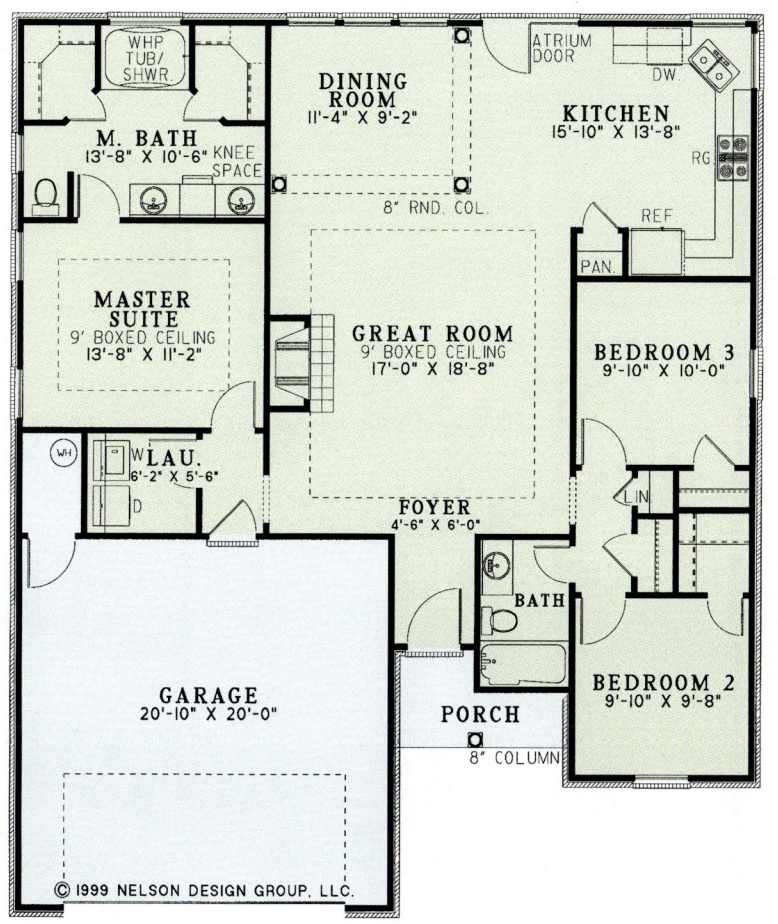

T his Nelson Design Group home allows you to picture life in perfection. Welcome friends and family into the comfortable great room, complete with gas fireplace. Beautiful columns define the dining room, which allow for a perfect evening dinner for two. An atrium door in the kitchen allows you to enjoy the back yard with ease. After a full day of activity, retreat to your master suite. You'll find the master bath most inviting with 'his and her' walk-in closets on either side of the whirlpool tub.

Width: 41' 10"
Depth: 48' 10"
Total Living: 1,382 sq. ft.

Price Tier: A

Main Ceiling: 8 ft.
Bedrooms: 3
Baths: 2
Foundation: Crawl, Slab, Opt. Basement, Opt. Daylight Basement

To view similar plans visit www.84lumber.com/ndgplans - 800.359.8484

102-2 Spruce Street

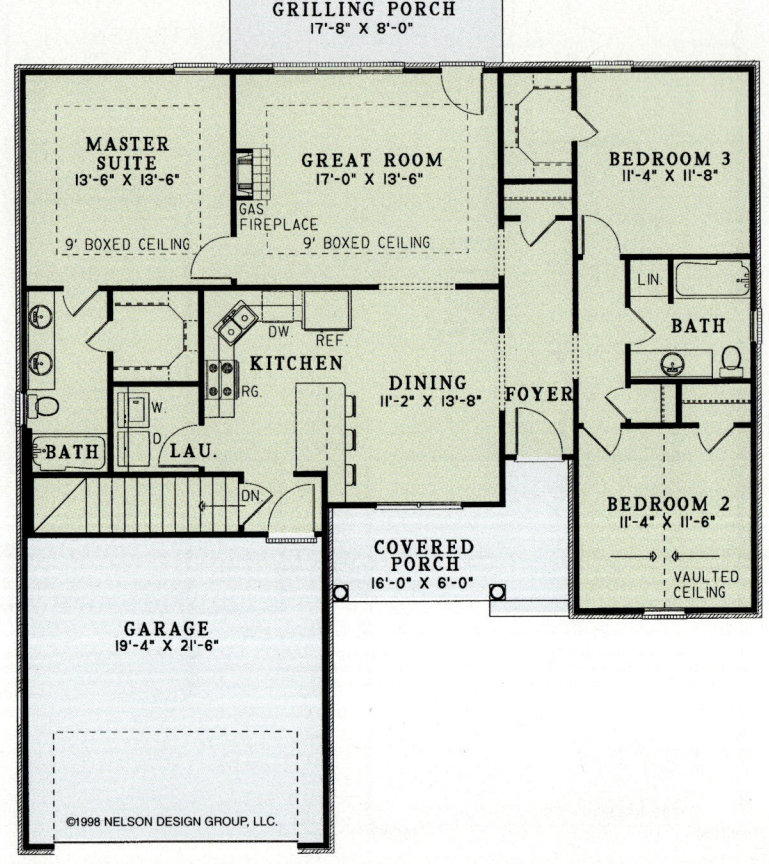

This adorable Nelson Design Group home is perfect for family gatherings. The comfortable great room, with fireplace and boxed ceiling, accommodates everyone and your spacious kitchen will be most convenient when preparing those last minute details. An eat-at bar counter can double as a buffet for your large dining room. One bedroom offers a spacious walk-in closet and the other features a vaulted ceiling. The master suite provides distance from the children for retreat and relaxation when things get too hectic.

Width: 48' 0"
Depth: 50' 0"
Total Living: 1,401 sq. ft.
Price Tier: A

Main Ceiling: 8 ft.
Bedrooms: 3
Baths: 2
Foundation: Basement, Daylight Basement

To view similar plans visit www.84lumber.com/ndgplans - 800.359.8484

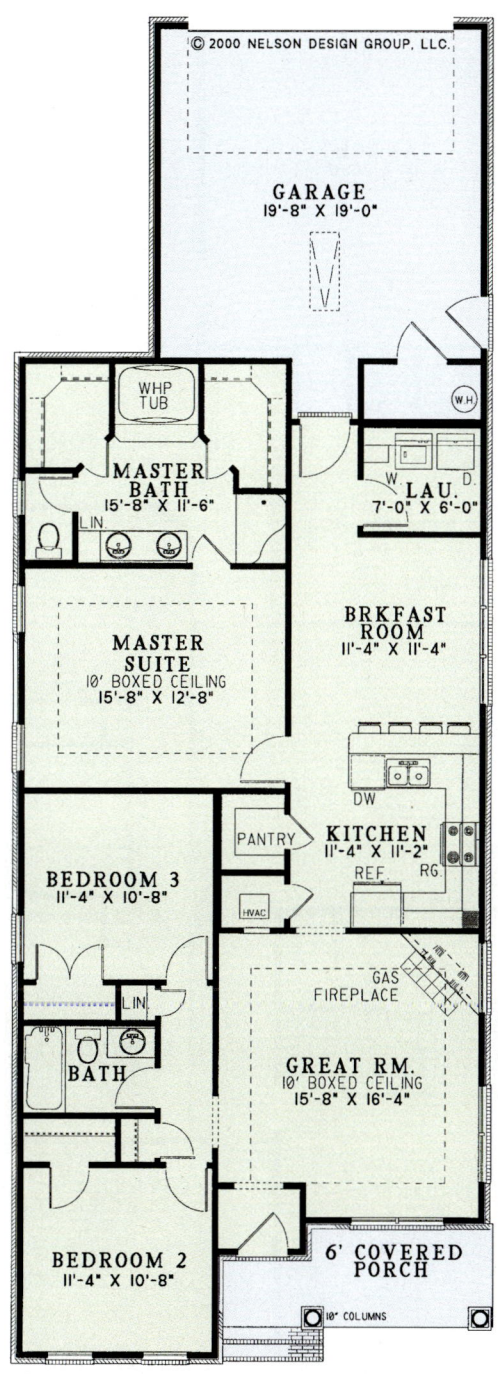

446 Maple Street

O n those cold winter nights, enjoy family time in your great room enhanced by an angled fireplace and a ten foot boxed ceiling. This Southern Traditional Nelson Design Group home kitchen features an eat at bar as well as a large breakfast room, making starting the day with your family a treat for all. The children will enjoy having their own section of the house with a full bath separating bedrooms two and three. As for you and your significant other, you'll find peace and luxury in the master bedroom adorned with ten foot ceilings and a large master bath complete with whirlpool tub, and 'his and her' vanities as well as spacious walk-in closets.

Width: 28' 0"
Depth: 77' 0"
Total Living: 1,445 sq. ft.

Main Ceiling: 9 ft.
Bedrooms: 3
Baths: 2
Foundation: Crawl, Slab

Price Tier: A

447 Maple Street

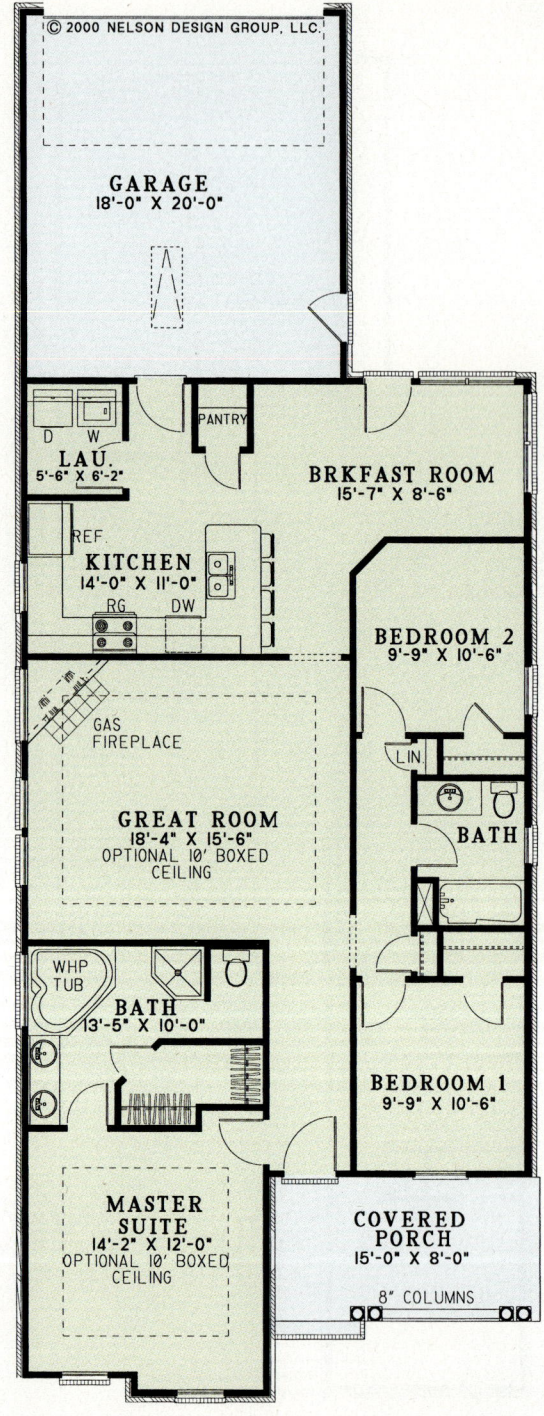

Luxurious living spaces in a narrow-lot design highlight this Nelson Design Group home. A covered front porch and simple layout strengthen this plan's charming appeal. A large breakfast room joins the kitchen, allowing you to take advantage of the convenient serving bar. An incredible master bath features a dual-sink vanity and a separate whirlpool tub and shower. Two nicely sized bedrooms share a full bath on the opposite side of the house.

Width: 29' 2"	Main Ceiling: 9 ft.
Depth: 76' 10"	Bedrooms: 3
Total Living: 1,449 sq. ft.	Baths: 2
	Foundation: Crawl, Slab

Price Tier: A

To view similar plans visit www.84lumber.com/ndgplans - 800.359.8484

146 Spruce Street

Elevation A

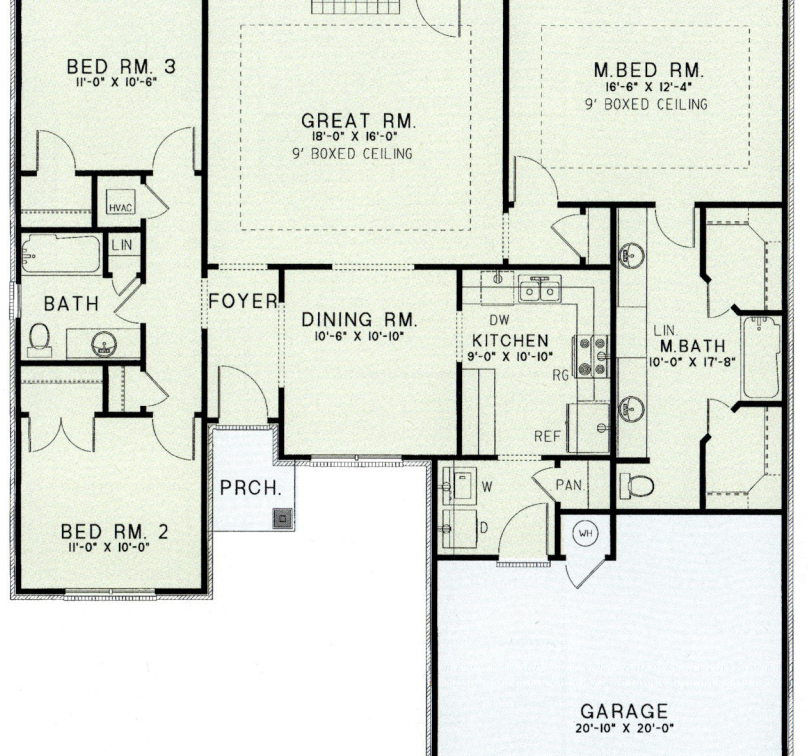

Elevation B

Turn your fantasy into reality with this split bedroom Nelson Design Group home. Lead your friends through the foyer into the spacious great room with convenient fireplace for drinks and conversation before moving into the dining room for the elegant cuisine you've prepared. Easy access from the dining room to the kitchen makes serving your guests a breeze. The children's bedrooms have spacious closets that will be ideal for toys. The other side of the home includes your private master suite featuring a secluded master bath with 'his and her' walk-in closets and double vanities.

Width: 46' 10"
Depth: 56' 4"
Total Living: 1,474 sq. ft.

Price Tier: A

Main Ceiling: 8 ft.
Bedrooms: 3
Baths: 2
Foundation: Crawl, Slab, Opt. Basement, Opt. Daylight Basement

To view similar plans visit www.84lumber.com/ndgplans - 800.359.8484

131 Maple Street

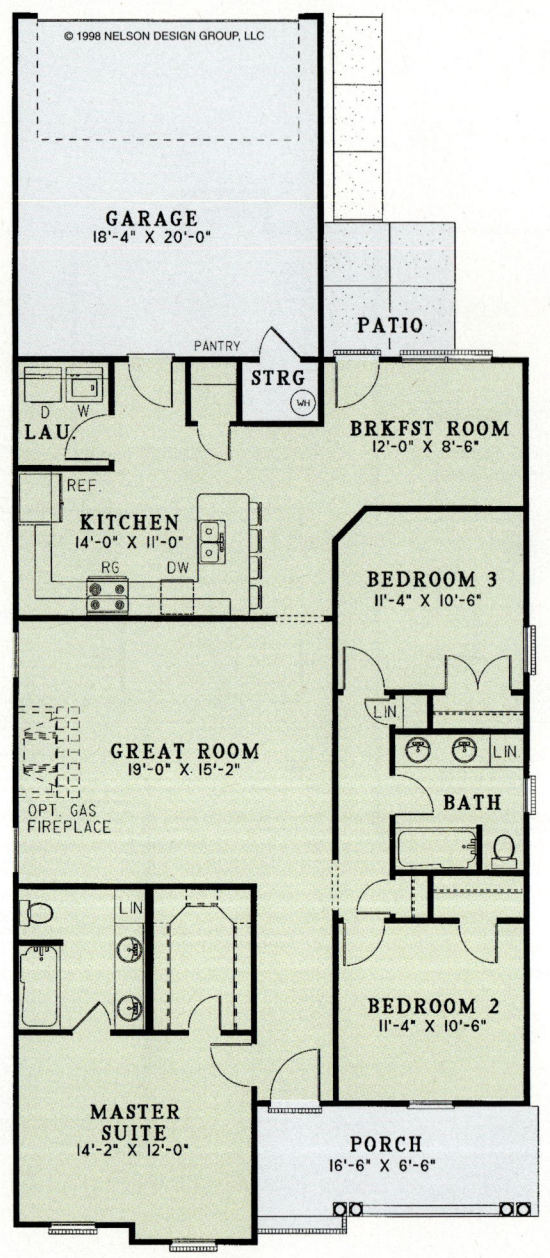

Charming columns welcome you onto the front porch of this Nelson Design Group home. Preparing morning breakfast will be easy in your open kitchen with fluid access to the breakfast room. Entertain family and friends in your spacious great room that comes complete with a gas fireplace for evenings that grow cooler. You will appreciate your master suite with ample storage in the convenient walk-in closest. Stay at home moms may utilize one of the bedrooms as an office or nursery.

Width: 31' 6"
Depth: 72' 10"
Total Living: 1,490 sq. ft.

Price Tier: A

Main Ceiling: 9 ft.
Bedrooms: 3
Baths: 2
Foundation: Crawl, Slab

To view similar plans visit www.84lumber.com/ndgplans - 800.359.8484

115 Spruce Street

Picture yourself in this Nelson Design Group home. Walking through the foyer, you'll enter the spacious great room with fireplace. A convenient bar located in the kitchen makes snack time a breeze. If you're hosting a dinner party, the open dining room with fluid access to the kitchen makes entertaining your guests easy. When night falls, retire to your master suite bathroom, which comes complete with double vanities, whirlpool tub and glass shower. Bedrooms two and three feature individual walk-in closets.

Width: 48' 6"
Depth: 48' 4"
Total Living: 1,500 sq. ft.

Price Tier: B

Main Ceiling: 8 ft.
Bedrooms: 3
Baths: 2
Foundation: Crawl, Slab, Basement, Daylight Basement

To view similar plans visit www.84lumber.com/ndgplans - 800.359.8484

113-1 Chestnut Lane

Front Elevation

Rear Elevation

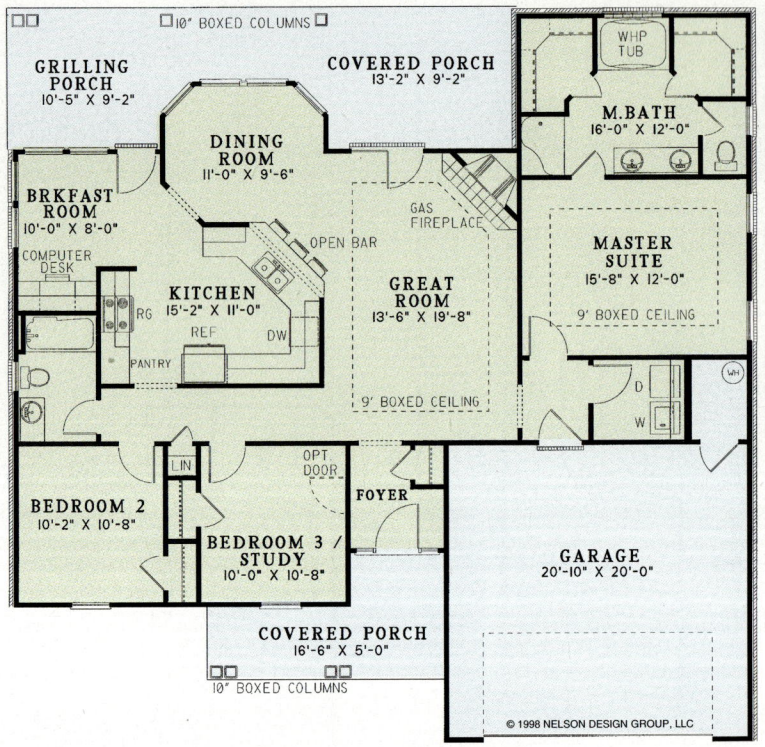

Numerous amenities within this Nelson Design Group traditional home create an attractive design. The great room, complete with fireplace, is the central entertaining area of your home. In your spacious kitchen you will be able to prepare anything your guests desire. Complete with french door access to the great room, you'll find a rear grilling porch - just right for summer barbeques. A convenient computer nook just off the kitchen allows you to monitor the children's activity. You may choose to spend a day lounging in your private master suite complete with whirlpool tub, separate shower and 'his and her' walk-in closets

Width: 51' 6"
Depth: 49' 10"
Total Living: 1,525 sq. ft.

Price Tier: B

Main Ceiling: 8 ft.
Bedrooms: 3
Baths: 2
Foundation: Crawl, Slab, Basement, Daylight Basement

To view similar plans visit www.84lumber.com/ndgplans - 800.359.8484

148 Spruce Street

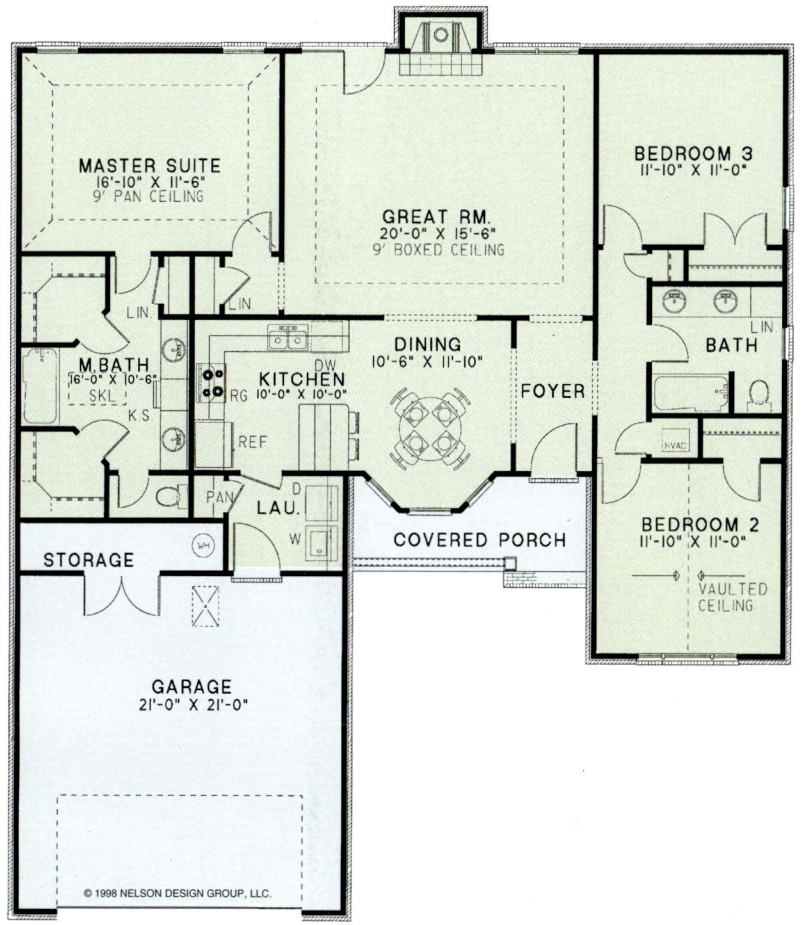

Welcome your friends and neighbors on the cozy front porch of this Nelson Design Group home. Leading your guests through the foyer, you'll enter the spacious great room which will prove to be a convenient gathering place with its inviting fireplace. Preparing meals is easy with the ample counter space in the open kitchen with view to the dining room. As evening approaches and your guests depart, retreat to your master bath, complete with whirlpool tub, skylights, and 'his and her' walk-in closets. But don't worry about the children, they have their own bedrooms with shared bath.

Width: 50' 0"
Depth: 56' 0"
Total Living: 1,538 sq. ft.

Price Tier: B

Main Ceiling: 8 ft.
Bedrooms: 3
Baths: 2
Foundation: Crawl, Slab, Basement, Daylight Basement

To view similar plans visit www.84lumber.com/ndgplans - 800.359.8484

132 Cottonwood Drive

Main Floor

Check This Plan Mike

Upper Floor

An elegant covered porch, decorative columns and dormers accent the simple yet stylish exterior on this Nelson Design Group home. A sunny site for casual dining awaits you in the breakfast bay. The elegant master suite includes his and her walk-in closets, a dual sink vanity and a whirlpool tub with a boxed window for ample lighting. Two bedrooms on opposite sides of the upper floor provide privacy while allowing access for all to a handy computer center.

Width: 34' 8"
Depth: 61' 10"
Main Floor: 990 sq. ft.
Upper Floor: 551 sq. ft.
Total Living: 1,541 sq. ft.

Main Ceiling: 9 ft.
Upper Ceiling: 8 ft.
Bedrooms: 3
Baths: 2
Foundation: Crawl, Slab, Basement, Daylight Basement

Price Tier: B

To view similar plans visit www.84lumber.com/ndgplans - 800.359.8484

437 Elm Street

Extending less than 28 feet wide, this Nelson Design Group home is perfect for narrow or zero lot developments. The vast great room is perfect for holiday entertainment as it offers a handsome fireplace and flows into separate sitting and dining areas. The walk-through kitchen features an island that also serves as an eat-at bar and blends with a breakfast nook. Lots of windows adorn the house, providing loads of natural lighting.

Width: 27' 8"
Depth: 76' 4"
Total Living: 1,574 sq. ft.

Main Ceiling: 9 ft.
Bedrooms: 3
Baths: 2
Foundation: Crawl, Slab

Price Tier: B

451 Aspen Heights

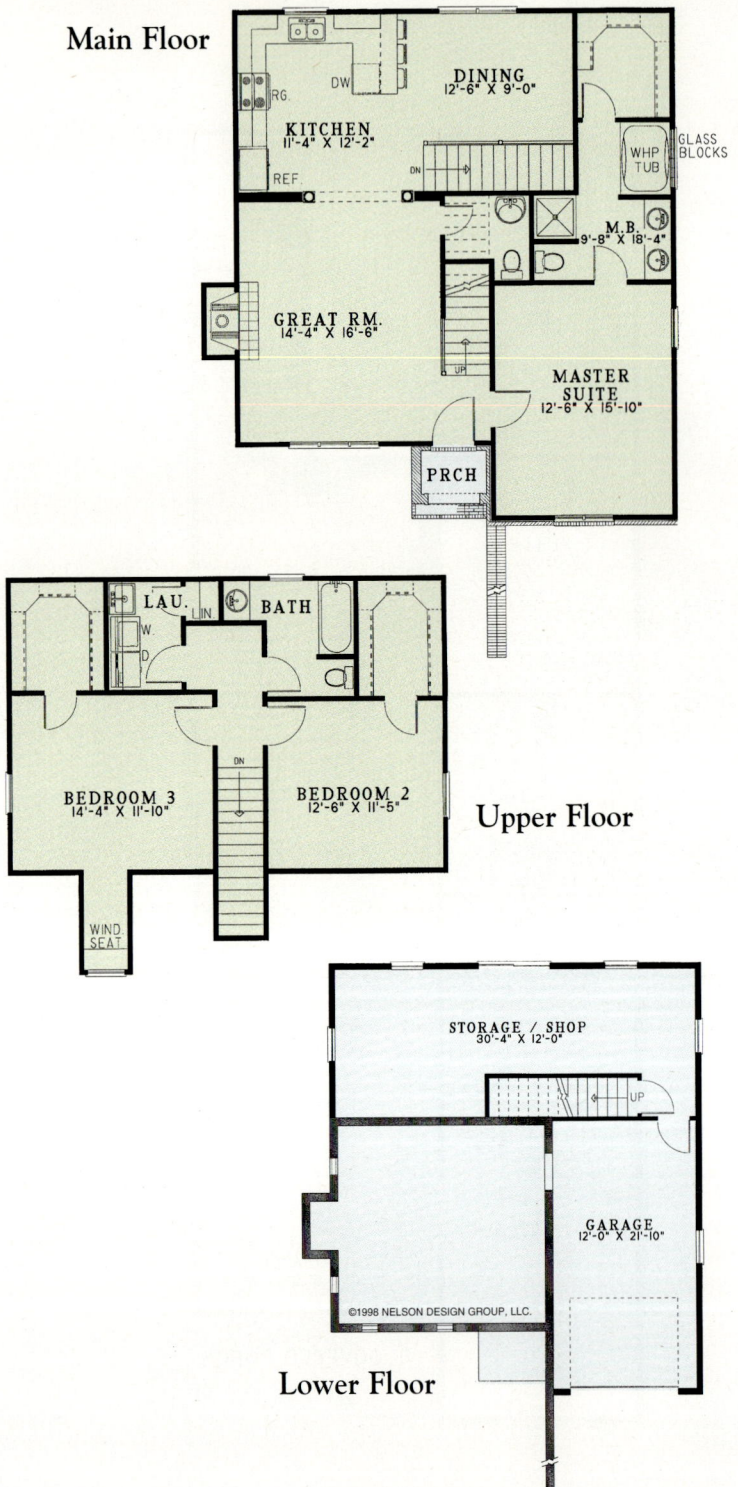

Main Floor

Upper Floor

Lower Floor

This split level plan has all the amenities you'll need to call it home. As you enter this Nelson Design Group home, a spacious great room with fireplace and column lined entry to the kitchen give an elegant flair to this traditional plan. Dinner parties as sure to be successful with the convenience of the kitchen open to the dining room. A set of stairs lead you to a full bathroom, laundry room with sink, and two bedrooms with large walk-in closets. One room features a lovely window seat allowing for natural light. The Master Suite is sure to capture your heart with its large bedroom and master bath.

Width: 33' 8"
Depth: 35' 2"
Main Floor: 1,008 sq. ft.
Upper Floor: 637 sq. ft.
Total Living: 1,645 sq. ft.

Main Ceiling: 9 ft.
Upper Ceiling: 9 ft.
Bedrooms: 3
Baths: 2 1/2
Foundation: Basement, Daylight Basement

Price Tier: B

To view similar plans visit www.84lumber.com/ndgplans - 800.359.8484

Check This Plan Mike

268 Walnut Lane

This Nelson Design Group home is wonderful for raising children. The gorgeous courtyard is certain to be a favorite for family cookouts and is viewed by several rooms. Your spacious kitchen, with fluid access to the dining room, makes preparing meals a breeze. The open great room, complete with fireplace, allows get-togethers and family time all the more simple. If you're concerned about room for the kids, don't worry. They'll have abundant space in the two extra bedrooms - one with walk-in closet. Your master suite includes a corner whirlpool bath, a separate shower and double vanities.

Width: 33' 10"	Main Ceiling: 9 ft.
Depth: 69' 6"	Bedrooms: 3
Total Living: 1,660 sq. ft.	Baths: 2
	Foundation: Crawl, Slab

Price Tier: B

To view similar plans visit www.84lumber.com/ndgplans - 800.359.8484

145-2 Spruce Street

Elevation A

Elevation B

Your dinner parties are certain to be successful in this Nelson Design Group split bedroom home. The expansive great room with gorgeous brick fireplace aids in creating the perfect ambiance for an evening of entertaining. The vaulted ceiling heightens the majestic feeling transformed in the dining room and kitchen area. When your guests leave, retreat to your master suite bathroom complete with corner whirlpool tub and glass shower, or enjoy private access to your covered porch. The children or guests will enjoy their own privacy with bedrooms on the other side of the home.

Width: 51' 6"
Depth: 52' 4"
Total Living: 1,680 sq. ft.

Price Tier: B

Main Ceiling: 8 ft.
Bedrooms: 3
Baths: 2
Foundation: Crawl, Slab, Basement, Daylight Basement

To view similar plans visit www.84lumber.com/ndgplans - 800.359.8484

349 Walnut Lane

Main Floor

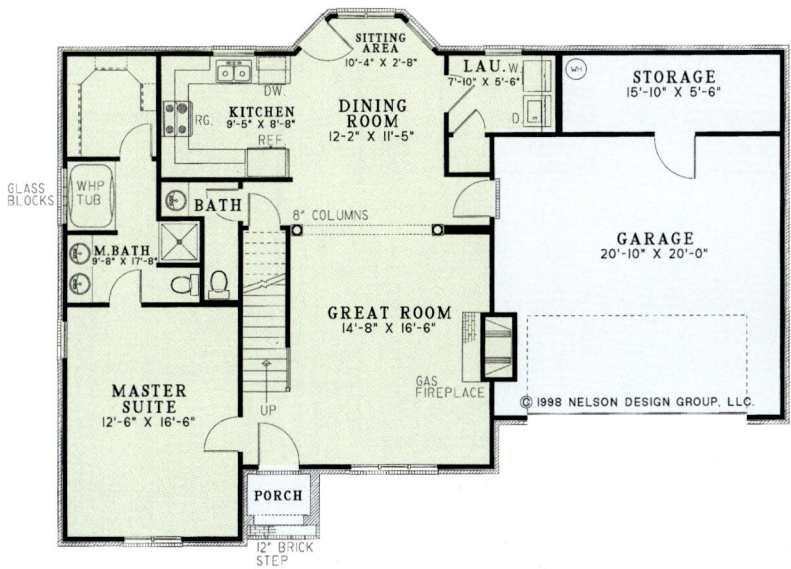

Upper Floor

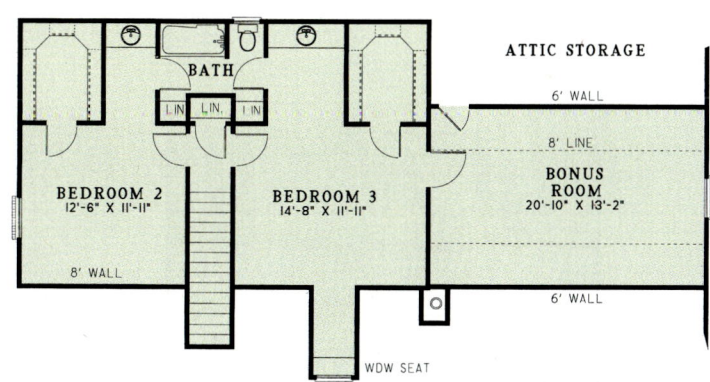

Elevation A

Elevation B

Enjoy all the comforts of home in this Nelson Design Group split bedroom plan. Step into the spacious great room and you'll find gorgeous columns framing the entry into a brilliant dining room. Serenity is uncovered in your secluded master suite and luxurious master bath with luminous glass blocks behind the whirlpool bath. Traveling upstairs, the children have ample bedroom space available in addition to walk-in closets and shared bath access. The bonus room can be utilized as a convenient play room or game room for children of all ages.

Width: 52' 10"
Depth: 37' 10"
Main Floor: 1,048 sq. ft
Upper Floor: 649 sq. ft.
Total Living: 1,697 sq. ft.*
*Optional Bonus: 275 sq. ft.

Main Ceiling: 9 ft.
Upper Ceiling: 8 ft.
Bedrooms: 3
Baths: 2 1/2
Foundation: Crawl, Slab, Basement, Daylight Basement

Price Tier: B

196 Walnut Lane

Main Floor

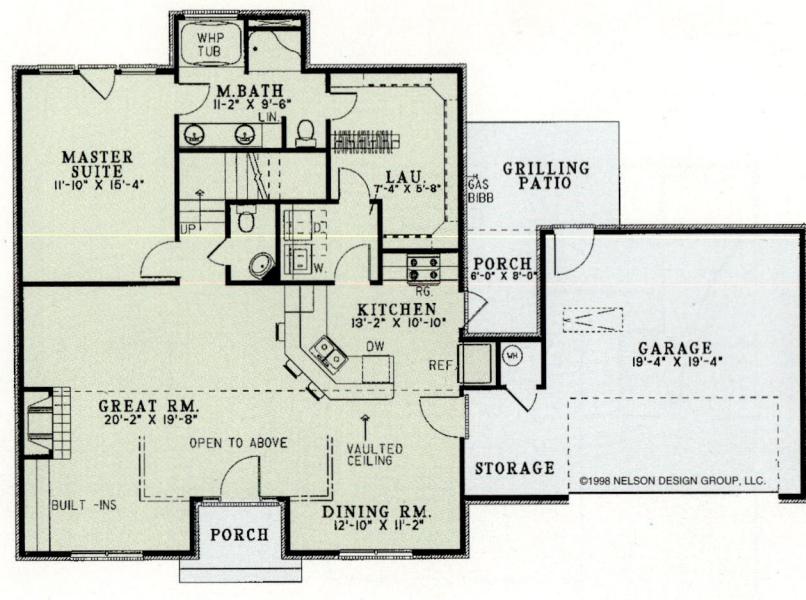

Upper Floor

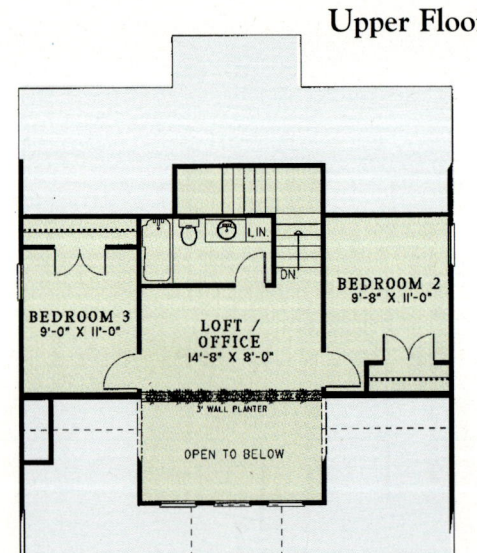

Enjoy the feel of a house in the country while maintaining all of the modern amenities in the Nelson Design Group home. The great room, entry and dining room flow into one expansive area to allow for family fun or more formal entertaining. An angled bar allows easy access from kitchen to the dining area and also serves as a breakfast bar. The master suite encompasses the rear of the main floor and includes a cavernous closet that also opens into the laundry area.

Width: 60' 0"
Depth: 40' 0"
Main Floor: 1,247 sq. ft.
Upper Floor: 466 sq. ft.
Total Living: 1,713 sq. ft.

Main Ceiling: 8 ft.
Upper Ceiling: 8 ft.
Bedrooms: 3
Baths: 2 1/2
Foundation: Crawl, Slab, Opt. Basement, Opt. Daylight Basement

Price Tier: B

To view similar plans visit www.84lumber.com/ndgplans - 800.359.8484

Main Floor

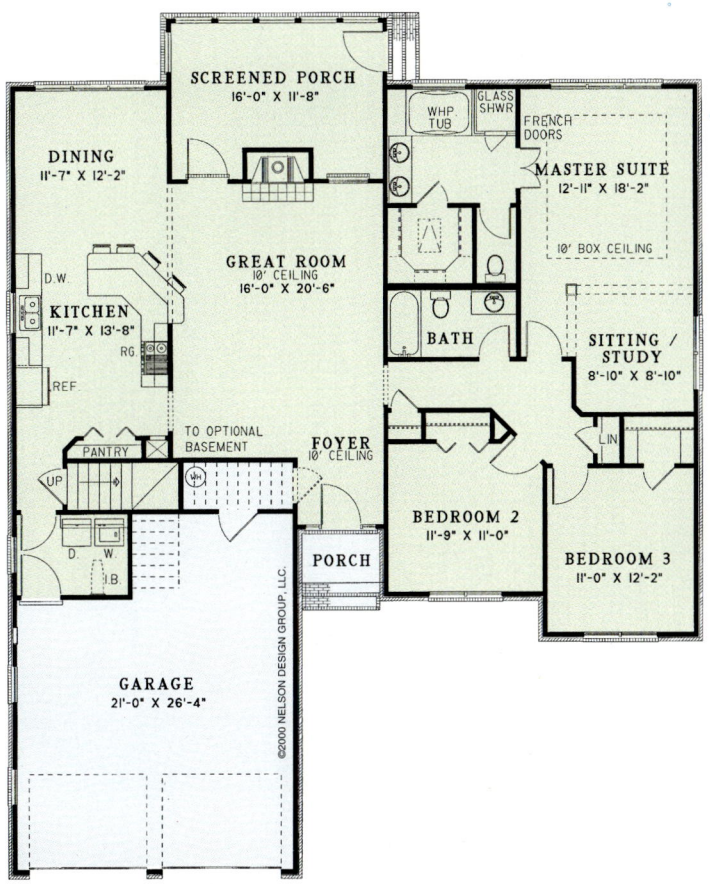

Upper Floor

507 Chestnut Lane

F orm and function combine in this Nelson Design Group home. A covered porch protects visitors from the elements. Walking into the foyer, they are greeted with a stunning view of the great room that includes a ten-foot ceiling, inviting fireplace, entry to the screened porch and a smooth transition into the dining room and kitchen. A sitting room adjoins the master suite for late-night reading after a relaxing bath in the whirlpool tub.

Width: 52' 0"
Depth: 63' 10"
Total Living: 1,732 sq. ft.*
*Optional Bonus: 243 sq. ft.

Price Tier: B

Main Ceiling: 9 ft.
Bedrooms: 3
Baths: 2
Foundation: Crawl, Slab, Opt. Basement, Opt. Daylight Basement

313 Chestnut Lane

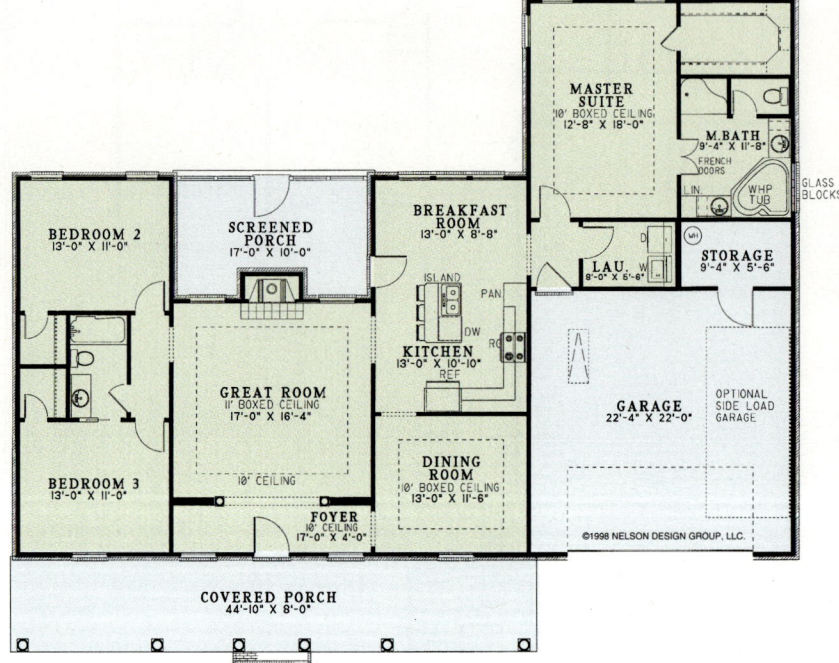

Beautiful columns on the front porch of this Nelson Design Group home create an ideal ambiance of days gone by. Enter the grand foyer with impressive columns wrapping around your comfortable and spacious great room. The convenient island in the kitchen makes preparing meals easier. The charming rear screened porch is the ideal retreat for coffee and the paper. Alluring French doors welcome you to your private master suite, complete with double vanities and luxurious corner whirlpool bath.

Width: 67' 0"
Depth: 54' 10"
Total Living: 1,746 sq. ft.

Price Tier: B

Main Ceiling: 9 ft.
Bedrooms: 3
Baths: 2
Foundation: Crawl, Slab, Opt. Basement, Opt. Daylight Basement

Check This Plan Mike

101-1 Brighton Court

Passersby will marvel at the lavish window accents and gabled roofline of this Nelson Design Group home. Walking through the foyer affords a stunning view of an immense open plan that begs to entertain. The vast great room merges with all living areas providing instant access and convenience. The walk-through kitchen features an angled bar and entry to the utility room and garage. Isolated at the rear of the house is the master suite with a 10' boxed ceiling and corner whirlpool tub with a glass block wall for natural lighting.

Width: 39' 0"
Depth: 72' 4"
Total Living: 1,750 sq. ft.

Price Tier: B

Main Ceiling: 9 ft.
Bedrooms: 3
Baths: 2
Foundation: Crawl, Slab, Basement, Daylight Basement

To view similar plans visit www.84lumber.com/ndgplans - 800.359.8484

480 Aspen Heights

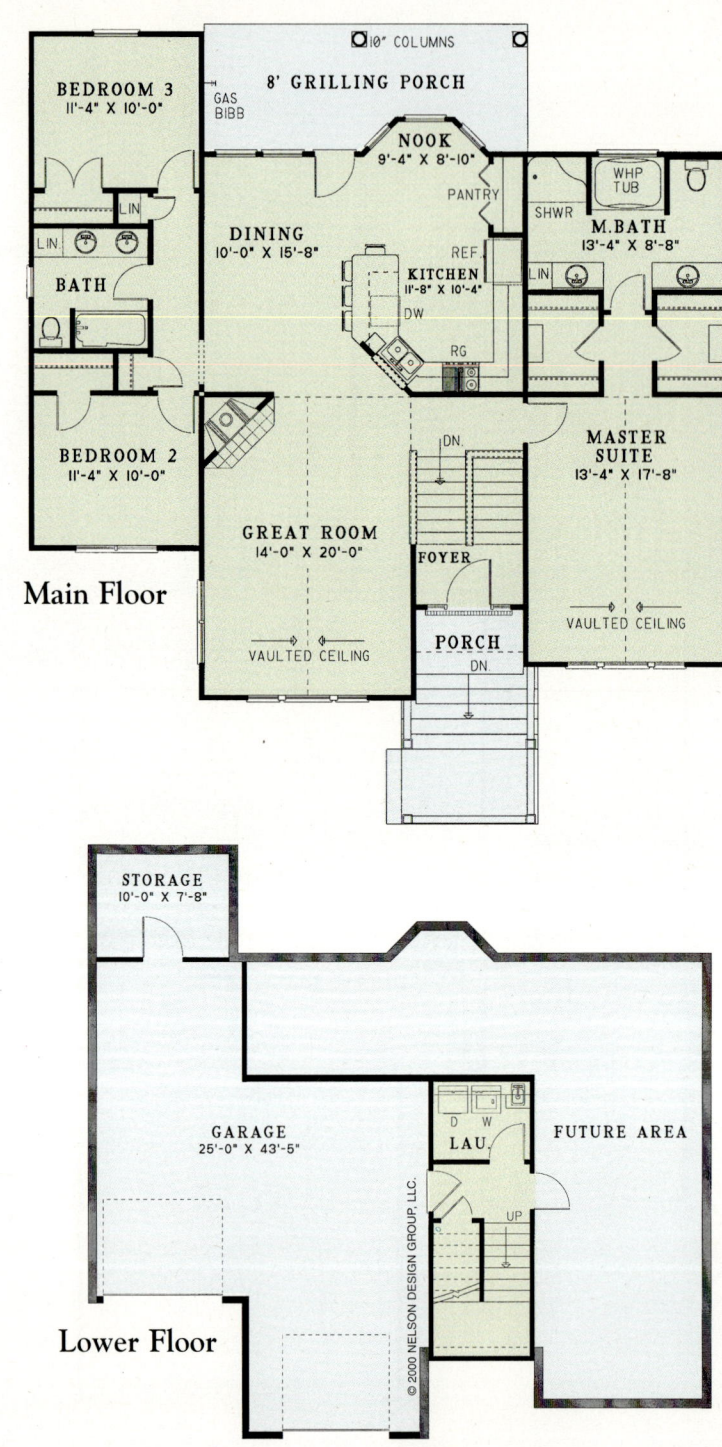

Main Floor

Lower Floor

A life of leisure awaits you in this stylish, split bedroom Nelson Design Group home. A romantic corner fireplace and vaulted ceiling welcome you to an impressive great room. The U-shaped kitchen serves the nearby breakfast bay and dining room. A large grilling porch adorned with decorative columns is ideal for enjoying the outdoors while entertaining friends and family. A lavish master suite showcases a vaulted ceiling, his and her walk-in closets, separate sink vanities and a whirlpool tub. The bonus area downstairs offers plenty of options for future expansion.

Width: 47' 8"
Depth: 44' 10"
Main Floor: 1,661 sq. ft.
Lower Floor: 103 sq. ft.
Total Living: 1,764 sq. ft.

Main Ceiling: 9 ft.
Lower Ceiling: 8 ft.
Bedrooms: 3
Baths: 2
Foundation: Basement, Daylight Basement

Price Tier: B

389 Quail Drive

Main Floor

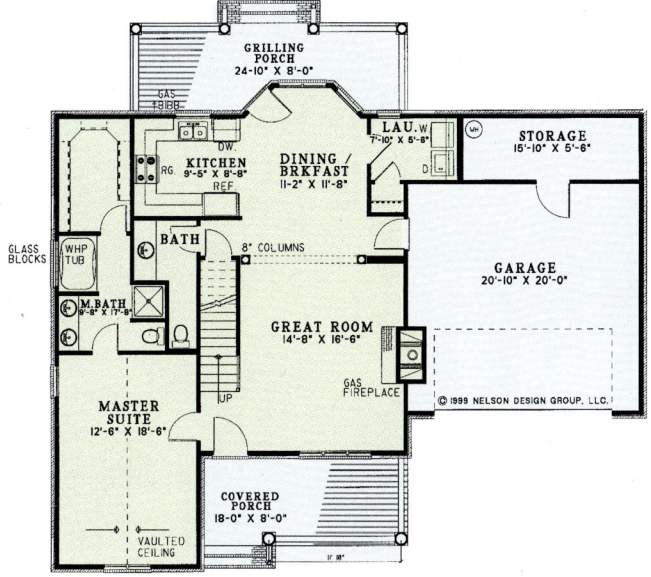

Upper Floor

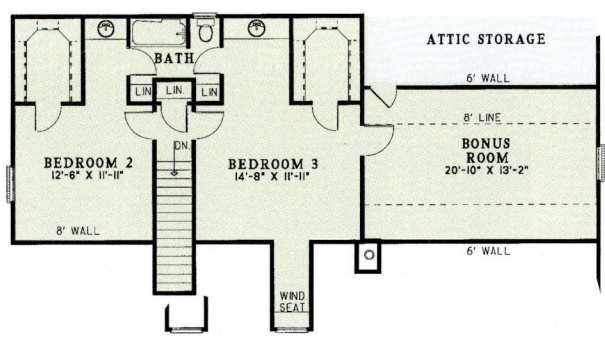

Elevation A

Elevation B

Two exterior options and a practical floor plan make this Nelson Design Group home a great choice. You'll enjoy hours of family fun in the large great room with cozy gas fireplace. The centralized dining area shows off a beautiful bay window with instant access to the kitchen, friendly grilling porch, utility room and garage. Upstairs the kids' bedrooms each have walk-in closets and their own vanity sinks to minimize bathroom disputes.

Width: 52' 10"
Depth: 48' 0"
Main Floor: 1,142 sq. ft.
Upper Floor: 635 sq. ft.
Total Living: 1,777 sq. ft.
*Optional Bonus: 293 sq. ft.
Price Tier: B

Main Ceiling: 9 ft.
Upper Ceiling: 8 ft.
Bedrooms: 3
Baths: 2 1/2
Foundation: Crawl, Slab, Opt. Basement, Opt. Daylight Basement

142 Olive Street

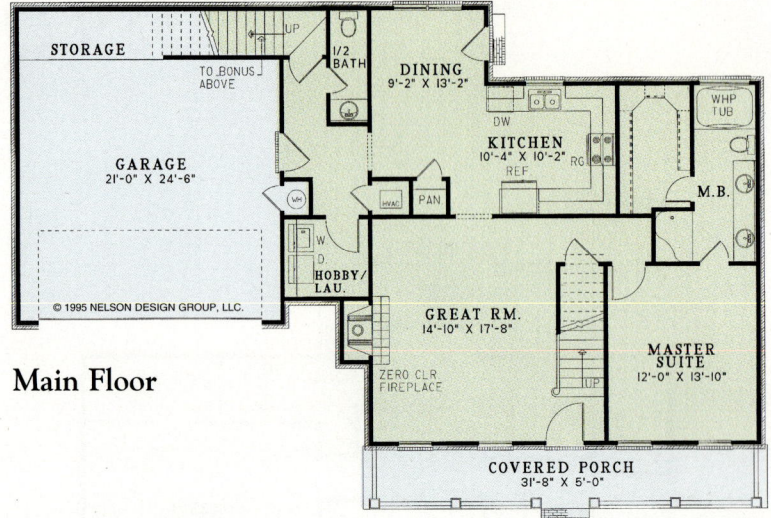

Main Floor

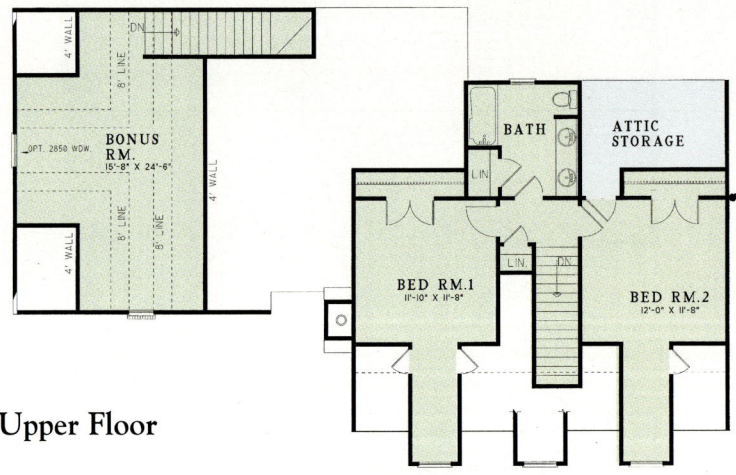

Upper Floor

A rocking chair on the front porch of this Nelson Design Group home awaits you. Entering this home, you'll encounter the spacious great room with a romantic fireplace for special occasions or everyday winter enjoyment. Preparing meals for the family will be easy with fluid access to the open kitchen. At the end of the day, relax in your master bath with soothing whirlpool tub. On the upper floor, the children will discover innovative ways to utilize the nook created by their windows. Maximize the bonus area over the garage as a future game room or home office.

Width: 60' 2"
Depth: 39' 10"
Main Floor: 1,124 sq. ft.
Upper Floor: 659 sq. ft.
Total Living: 1,783 sq. ft.*
*Optional Bonus: 324 sq. ft.

Main Ceiling: 8 ft.
Upper Ceiling: 8 ft.
Bedrooms: 3
Baths: 2 1/2
Foundation: Crawl, Slab, Basement, Daylight Basement

Price Tier: B

To view similar plans visit www.84lumber.com/ndgplans - 800.359.8484

496 Quail Drive

Glorious, soaring columns and an inviting covered porch welcome guests to this Nelson Design Group home. Walking through the open foyer reveals 12' ceilings in the foyer and dining room. Continuing through the great room you can't help but notice the friendly atmosphere afforded by the fireplace, smooth transition to the kitchen and breakfast room as well as the entryway to the grilling porch. The wide-open spaces continue with a 10' boxed ceiling and enormous walk-in closet in the master suite.

Width: 54' 2"
Depth: 57' 4"
Total Living: 1,786 sq. ft.*
*Optional Bonus: 343 sq. ft.

Main Ceiling: 9 ft.
Bedrooms: 3
Baths: 2
Foundation: Crawl, Slab, Opt. Basement, Opt. Daylight Basement

Price Tier: B

206-2 Anna Circle

An open floor plan, decorative columns and inviting fireplace make this Nelson Design Group offering a true home for the holidays. A centralized great room is ideal for family gathering and fun. Guests can then stroll into the beautiful formal dining room accented by a 10' ceiling and boxed columns. The walk-through kitchen provides smooth service for entrees in the dining room, hors d'oeuvres in the great room or brunch in the open breakfast room. French doors and a 9' boxed ceiling highlight the master suite.

Width: 54' 2"
Depth: 56' 4"
Total Living: 1,798 sq. ft.

Price Tier: B

Main Ceiling: 8 ft.
Bedrooms: 3
Baths: 2
Foundation: Crawl, Slab, Basement, Daylight Basement

To view similar plans visit www.84lumber.com/ndgplans - 800.359.8484

Check This Plan Mike

379 Spruce Street

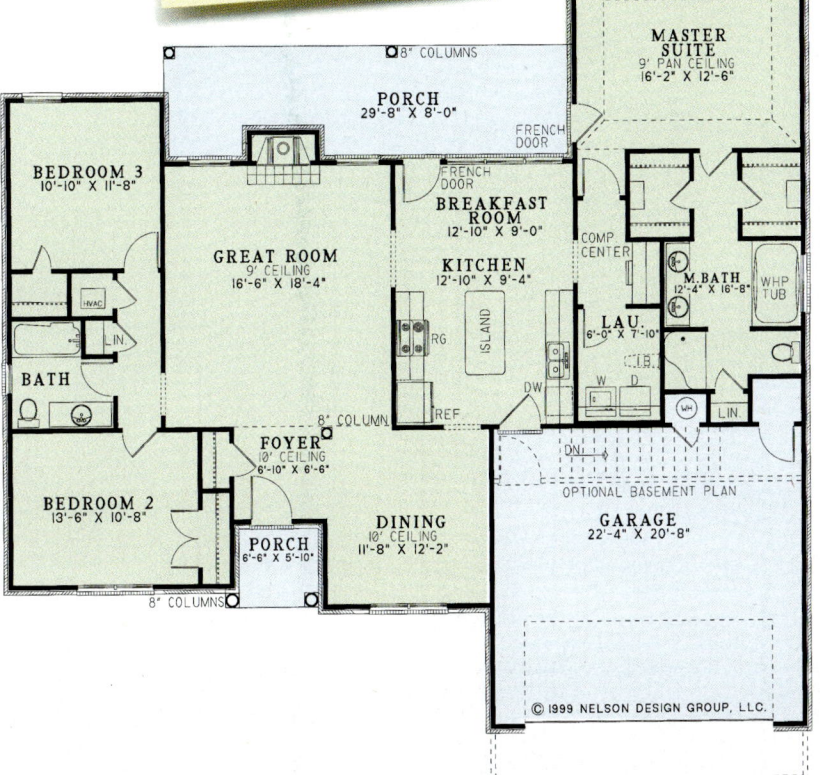

Elevation A

Elevation B

An open feeling is created in this Nelson Design Group home by use of high ceilings in several rooms. Preparing meals for your family is easy with your spacious kitchen, complete with center island. You may also entertain on your rear covered porch with french door access from the breakfast room as well as your master suite. Get lost in your expansive master bath, which includes double vanities, whirlpool tub and 'his and her' walk-in closets. You'll find the extra two bedrooms in this design just right for children, a home office or weekend guests.

Width: 58' 0"
Depth: 53' 6"
Total Living: 1,722 sq. ft.

Price Tier: B

Main Ceiling: 8 ft.
Bedrooms: 3
Baths: 2
Foundation: Crawl, Slab, Basement, Daylight Basement

To view similar plans visit www.84lumber.com/ndgplans - 800.359.8484

365 Spruce Street

Elevation A

Elevation B

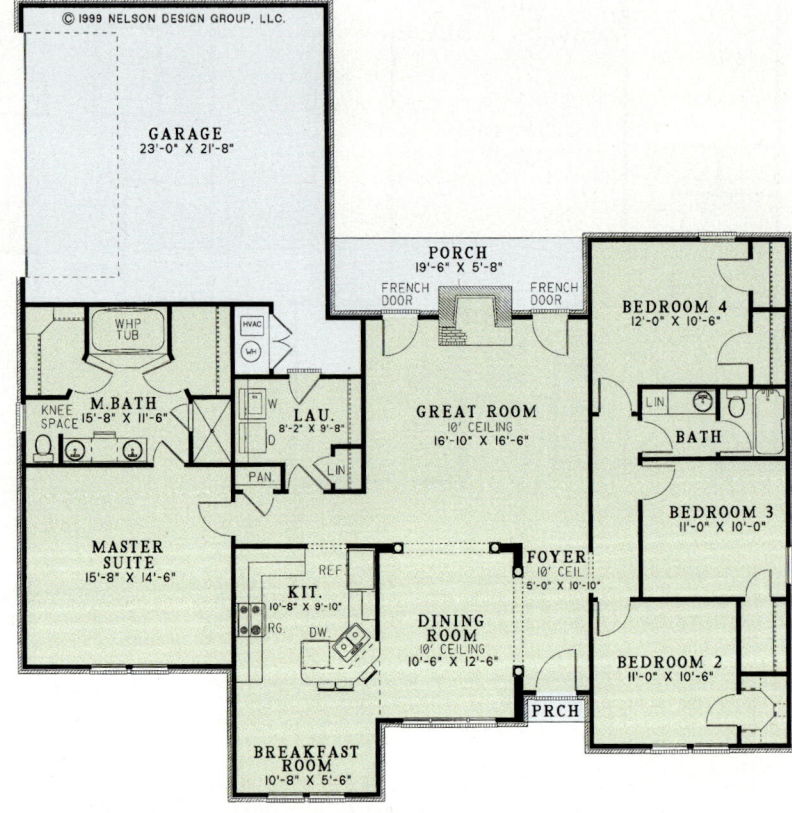

The entry of this split bedroom Nelson Design Group home shows off the sensational columns which frame the dining room. Romance the one you love by the fireplace in a comfortable great room with beautiful french doors accessing to the rear porch. Afterwards, retreat to your master suite and bath, complete with 'his and her' walk-in closets, double vanities and a wonderful whirlpool tub. Don't worry about the children, they will be having dreams of their own in the bedrooms located on the opposite side of this home.

Width: 58' 8"
Depth: 58' 6"
Total Living: 1,854 sq. ft.

Price Tier: B

Main Ceiling: 9 ft.
Bedrooms: 4
Baths: 2
Foundation: Crawl, Slab, Opt. Basement, Opt. Daylight Basement

To view similar plans visit www.nelsondesigngroup.com - 800.590.2423

Main Floor

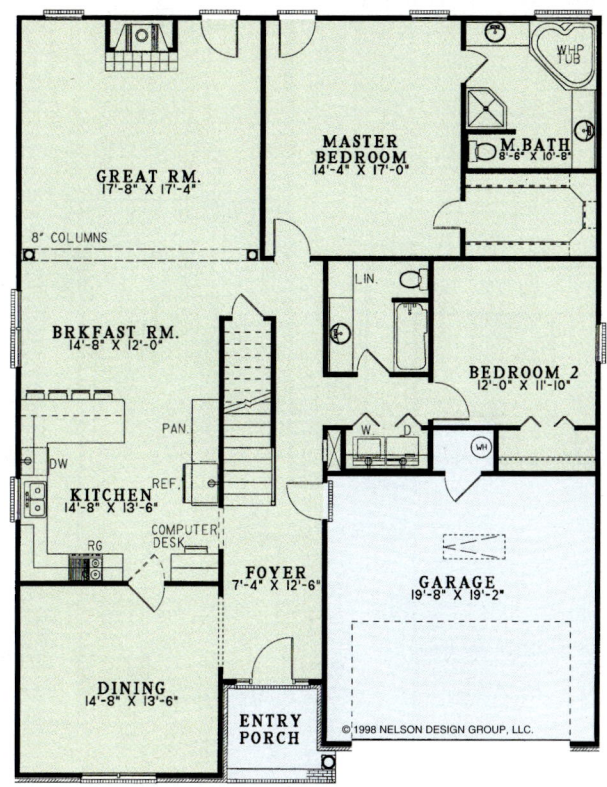

Upper Floor

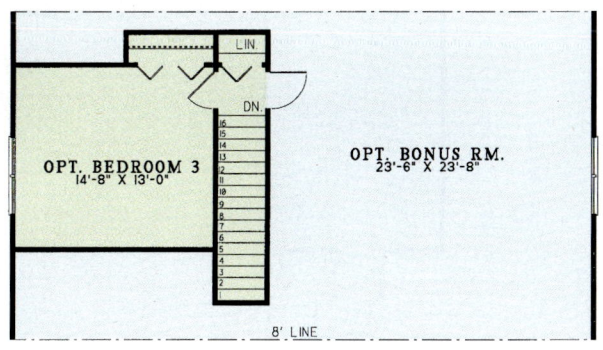

319 Maple Street

If you're just starting a family, or the children have left the nest, Nelson Design Group has created the ideal home for you. An impressive dining room has swinging door access to the spacious kitchen. Convenience of the computer center enables you to monitor the children while surfing the net. Handsome columns define a large great room that will attract the entire family. You will find your master bath perfect for relaxing with its soothing corner whirlpool tub. Upstairs, an optional bedroom and bonus area are available.

Width: 43' 0"	Main Ceiling: 9 ft.
Depth: 55' 0"	Upper Ceiling: 8 ft.
Total Living: 1,860 sq. ft.*	Bedrooms: 3
*Optional Bonus: 247 sq. ft.	Baths: 2
	Foundation: Crawl, Slab, Opt. Basement, Opt. Daylight Basement

Price Tier: B

To view similar plans visit www.nelsondesigngroup.com - 800.590.2423

543 Belmont Avenue

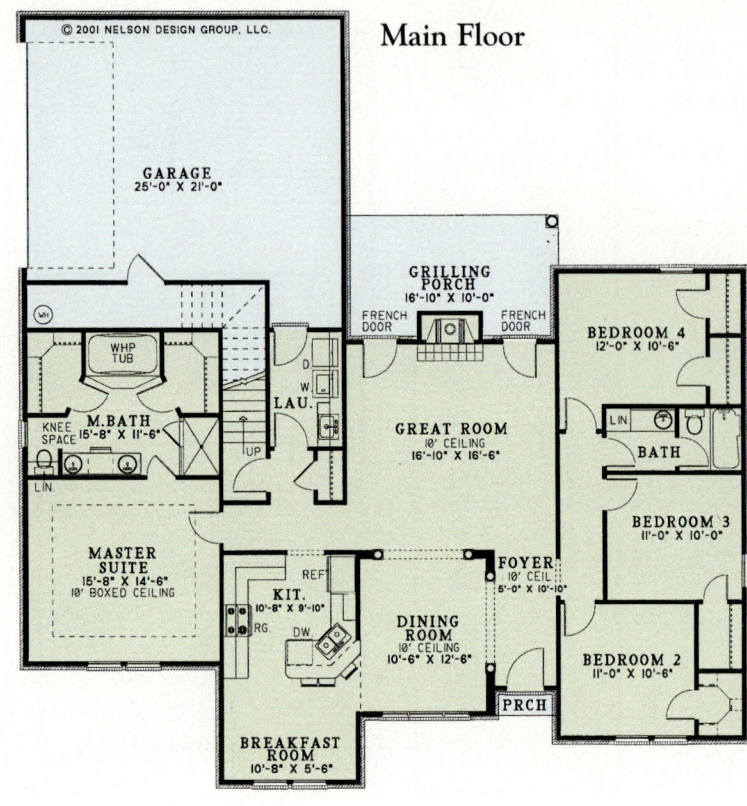

Main Floor

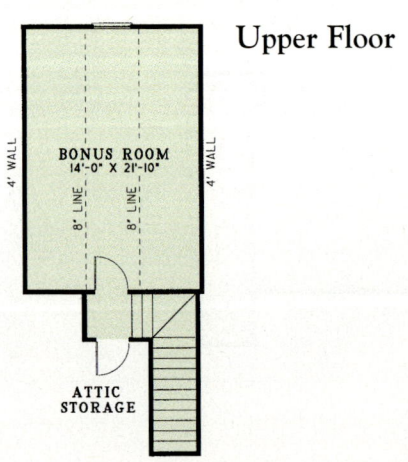

Upper Floor

This Nelson Design Group four-bedroom plan offers an elegant exterior and an interior ready for comfortable living. Enhanced by a 10' ceiling, the great room is anchored by a fireplace flanked by two stunning French doors offering access to a spacious grilling porch just made for back yard entertaining. His and her walk-in closets, a whirlpool tub and dual sink vanity compliment a magnificent master suite complete with a 10' boxed ceiling.

Width: 58' 8"
Depth: 61' 6"
Total Living: 1,863 sq. ft.*
*Optional Bonus: 365 sq. ft.

Main Ceiling: 9 ft.
Bedrooms: 4
Baths: 2
Foundation: Crawl, Slab

Price Tier: B

To view similar plans visit www.84lumber.com/ndgplans - 800.359.8484

Check This Plan Mike

483-1 Spruce Street

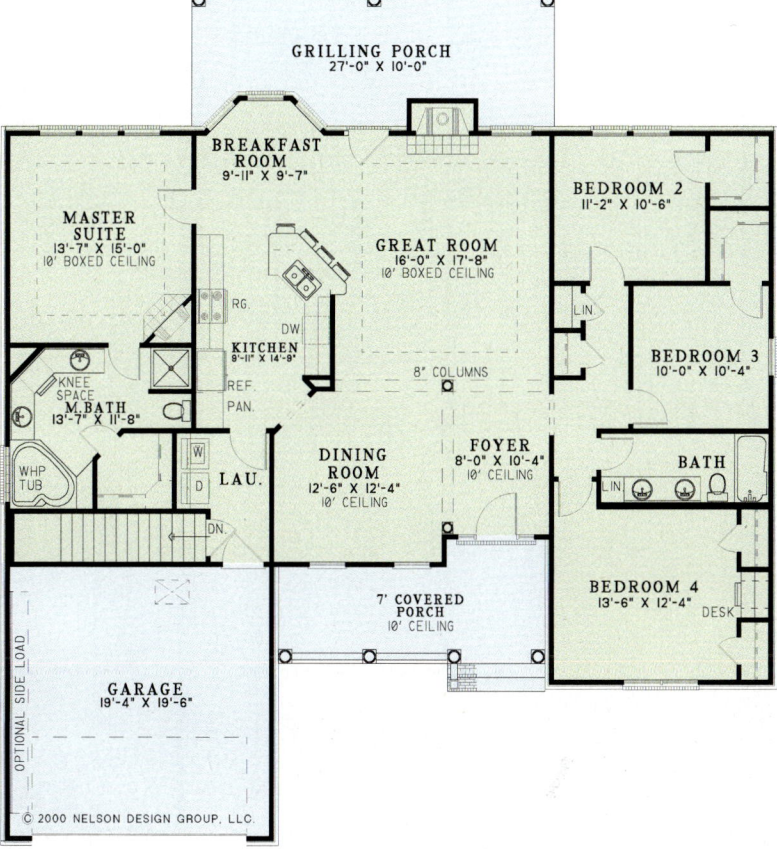

Multiple arches, alluring columns and a comfortable, covered porch welcome guests to this stylish Nelson Design Group home. The interior showcases an open, airy floor plan with smooth transitions and minimal wasted space. The large great room with 10' boxed ceiling flowing into the formal dining room provides ample space for extravagant parties or casual gatherings. The secluded master suite offers a soothing, relaxing atmosphere after a long and busy day.

Width: 57' 0"	Main Ceiling: 9 ft.
Depth: 61' 4"	Bedrooms: 4
Total Living: 1,880 sq. ft.	Baths: 2
	Foundation: Crawl, Slab, Basement, Daylight Basement

Price Tier: B

436 Mockingbird Lane

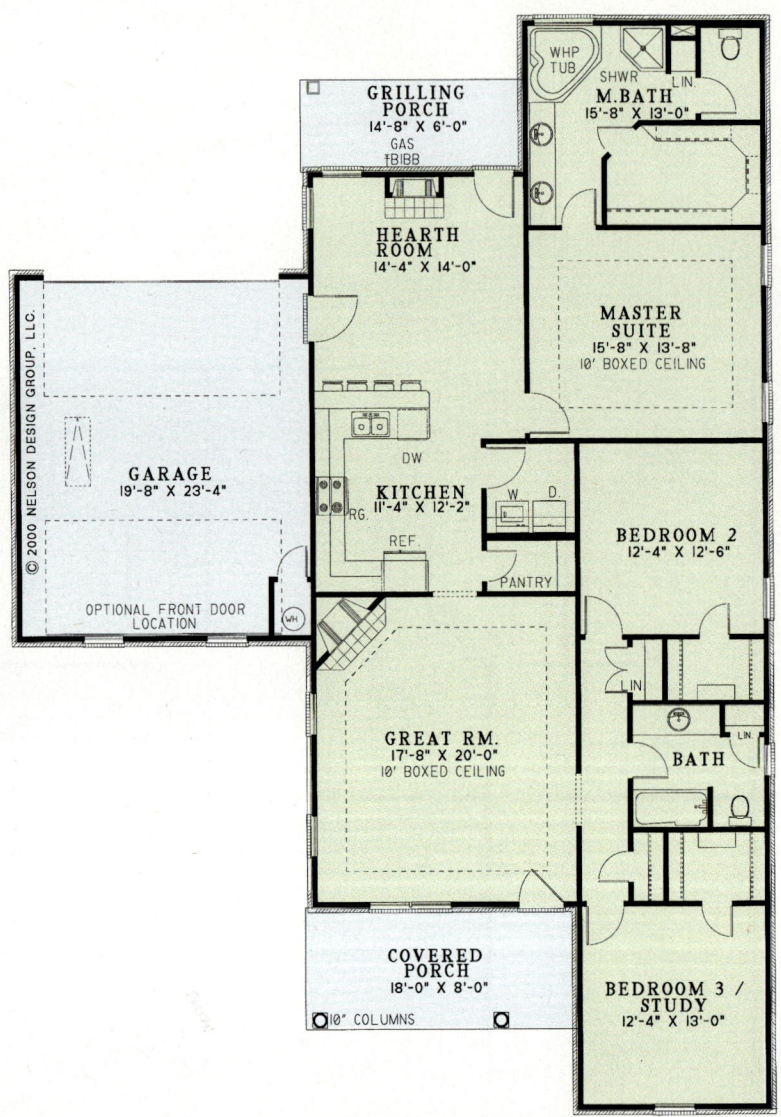

Large living spaces with quick and easy access to outdoor areas make this Nelson Design Group home a popular choice for those who entertain frequent guests. Lose yourself in the immense great room with a captivating fireplace and 10' boxed ceiling. The central kitchen allows quick and easy service to a breakfast bar, great room and magnificent hearth room. Holiday guests will be able to mingle in comfort with the spacious areas of this home.

Width: 51' 0"
Depth: 71' 4"
Total Living: 1,881 sq. ft.

Price Tier: B

Main Ceiling: 9 ft.
Bedrooms: 3
Baths: 2
Foundation: Crawl, Slab

To view similar plans visit www.nelsondesigngroup.com - 800.590.2423

509 Mockingbird Lane

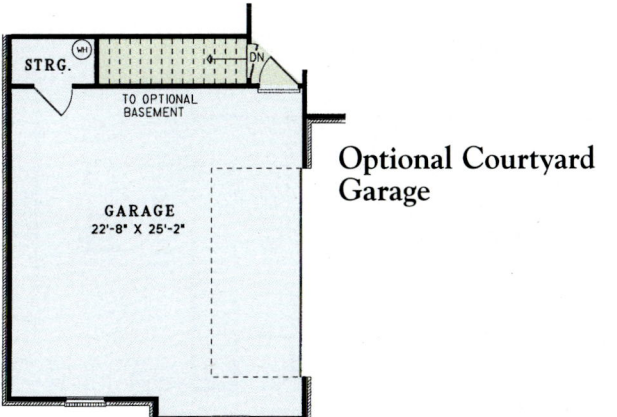

Optional Courtyard Garage

You'll enjoy entertaining in this elegant, open-space floor plan from Nelson Design Group. The dining room with column accents is ideal for formal dinner parties with coffee to follow in the spacious and comfortable great room where you'll find a cozy fireplace and easy access to the kitchen for snacks. When the guests have departed you can retire to your master suite for a relaxing soak in the large whirlpool tub or enjoy the privacy and comfort of the large, screened back porch.

Width: 56' 0"
Depth: 64' 4"
Total Living: 1,909 sq. ft.

Price Tier: B

Main Ceiling: 9 ft.
Bedrooms: 3
Baths: 2
Foundation: Crawl, Slab, Opt. Basement, Opt. Daylight Basement

To view similar plans visit www.nelsondesigngroup.com - 800.590.2423

178 Olive Street

Check This Plan Mike

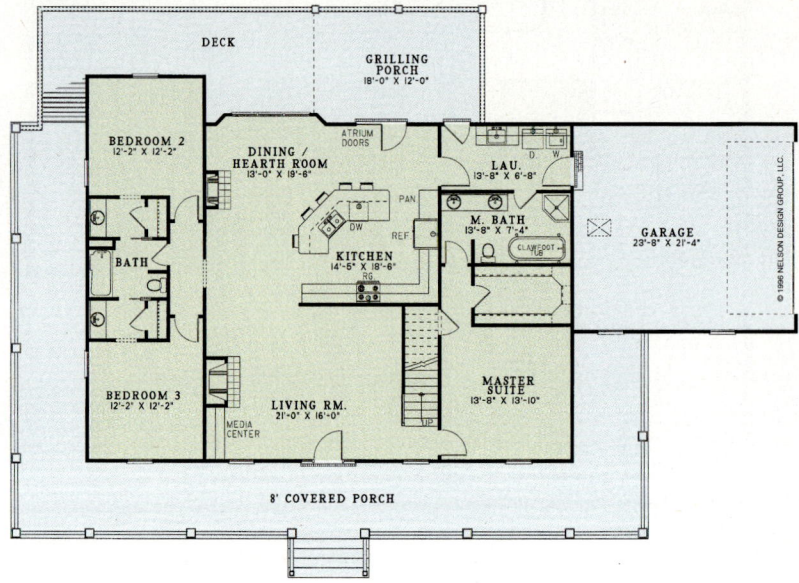
Main Floor

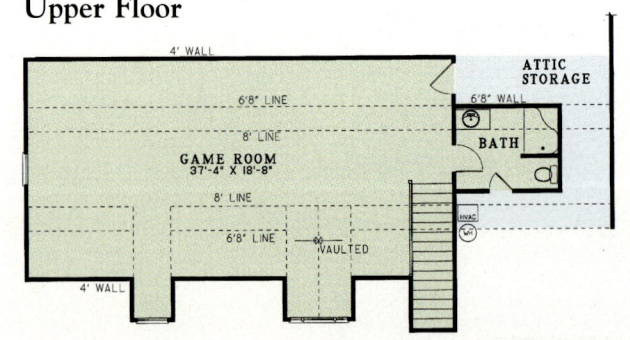
Upper Floor

This Nelson Design Group low country home has a wrap around porch that everyone will fall in love with. Upon entering, the beautiful fireplace and media center make for great entertaining. The hearth room's fireplace allows for more intimate gatherings. Notice the ample counter space in the kitchen as well as a convenient island bar. A large master suite provides plenty of storage space with your master bath sporting a magnificent claw-foot soaking bathtub. Two additional bedrooms share a walk-through bathroom. Upstairs, find a full bath and large gameroom.

Width: 84' 0"
Depth: 55' 6"
Total Living: 1,921 sq. ft.*
*Optional Bonus: 812 sq. ft.

Main Ceiling: 8 ft.
Upper Ceiling: 8 ft.
Bedrooms: 3
Baths: 3
Foundation: Crawl, Slab, Basement, Daylight Basement

Price Tier: B

435 Cottonwood Drive

Nelson Design Group presents a fabulous combination of practicality and elegance in this all brick, split-bedroom design. The covered front porch is an ideal place to relax and watch the kids. The great room serves as a central gathering point with its warming fireplace, 10' boxed ceiling and quick access to both family living and sleeping areas. There is room to roam in the expansive kitchen, making entertaining a breeze. At the end of the day, retire to the efficient master bath, where daily stress can disappear down the drain of your huge whirlpool tub.

Width: 36' 10"
Depth: 78' 10"
Total Living: 1,935 sq. ft.

Main Ceiling: 8 ft.
Bedrooms: 3
Baths: 2
Foundation: Crawl, Slab

Price Tier: B

205 Mockingbird Lane

Stately columns and a covered porch welcome you to this traditional Nelson Design Group four-bedroom home. The foyer ushers guests into your home with class and style. Built-in shelving in the boxed-ceiling great room takes advantage of the area next to the radiant fireplace for use as a media center or mini-library. The ample storage space provided by large walk-in closets throughout is sure to make organizing a snap. The luxuriously appointed master suite is located just off the breakfast room and features a 9' pan ceiling.

Width: 58' 0"
Depth: 54' 10"
Total Living: 1,940 sq. ft.

Price Tier: B

Main Ceiling: 8 ft.
Bedrooms: 4
Baths: 2
Foundation: Crawl, Slab, Basement, Daylight Basement

To view similar plans visit www.nelsondesigngroup.com - 800.590.2423

Check This Plan Mike

Main Floor

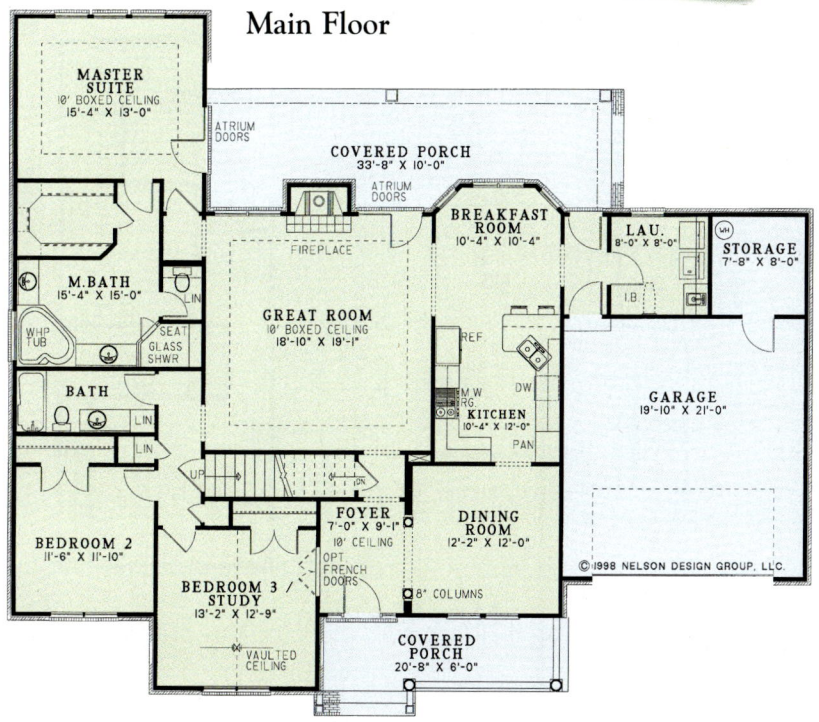

Upper Floor

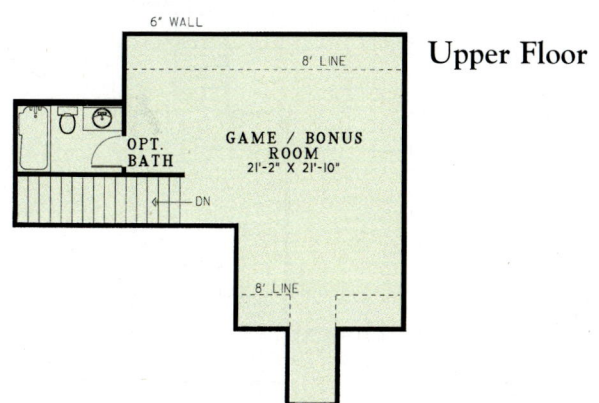

347 Maple Street

If you yearn for a functional yet beautiful home, Nelson Design Group has created such a home. Once inside, eight inch columns frame the dining room entry, allowing for elegant dining. A spacious great room provides ample room and atrium door access to the rear covered porch. The third bedroom has a vaulted ceiling and optional french doors for the ultimate study. Once guests leave, your master bath with all the amenities will be the most relaxing place in your home. Upstairs, find an optional bonus room and full bath.

Width: 66' 0"
Depth: 55' 0"
Total Living: 1,957 sq. ft.*
*Optional Bonus: 479 sq. ft.

Main Ceiling: 9 ft.
Upper Ceiling: 8 ft.
Bedrooms: 3
Baths: 2 plus (1 opt.)
Foundation: Crawl, Slab, Basement, Daylight Basement

Price Tier: B

To view similar plans visit www.nelsondesigngroup.com - 800.590.2423

544 Glendale Avenue

Elevation A

Elevation B

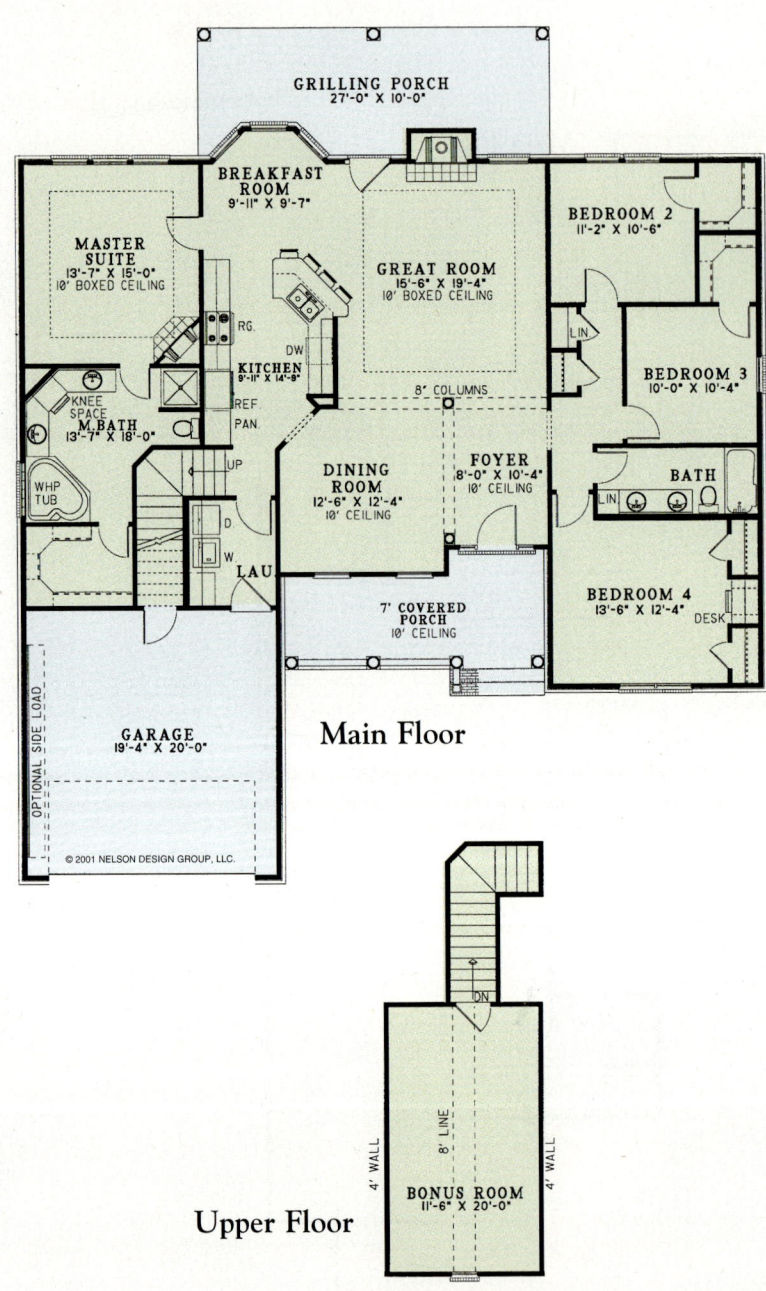

Main Floor

Upper Floor

Tall columns and 10' ceilings add elegance to an open floor plan in this split-bedroom Nelson Design Group home. The foyer flows effortlessly into the dining and great rooms. The bay-windowed breakfast room provides a sunny alternative to the formal dining room and affords a lively view of the back yard and grilling porch. With a large whirlpool tub, boxed ceiling and cozy corner fireplace, the master suite is truly a private sanctuary.

Width: 57' 0"
Depth: 64' 4"
Total Living: 1,965 sq. ft.*
*Optional Bonus: 251 sq. ft.

Price Tier: B

Main Ceiling: 9 ft.
Upper Ceiling: 8 ft.
Bedrooms: 4
Baths: 2
Foundation: Crawl, Slab, Opt. Basement, Opt. Daylight Basement

117 Glendale Avenue

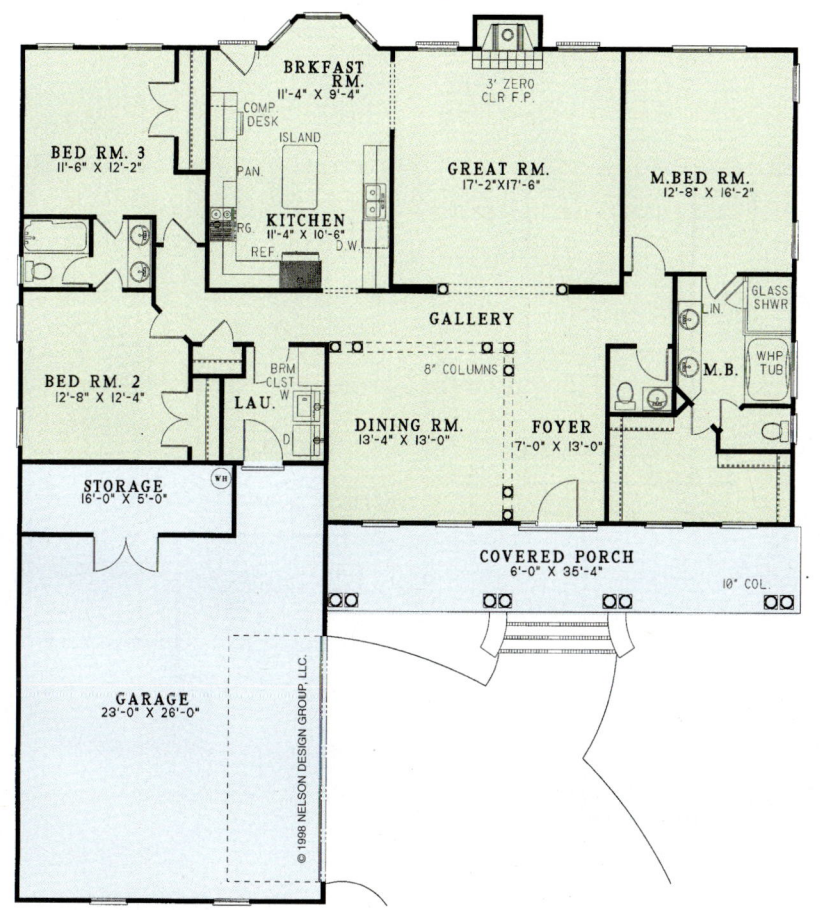

T his fashionable single level, split-bedroom Nelson Design Group home features deluxe amenities normally found in much larger plans. Columns offset the dining room as it blends with the foyer and gallery, which opens into the 17' square great room. The gourmet walk-through kitchen showcases a large island, computer desk and snappy access to the breakfast room. A zero-clearance fireplace draws the family together after dinner for enjoyable conversation and the occasional family game night.

Width: 59' 0"
Depth: 65' 4"
Total Living: 1,988 sq. ft.

Price Tier: B

Main Ceiling: 9 ft.
Bedrooms: 3
Baths: 2 1/2
Foundation: Crawl, Slab, Opt. Basement, Opt. Daylight Basement

378 Dogwood Avenue

Elevation A

Elevation B

Check This Plan Mike

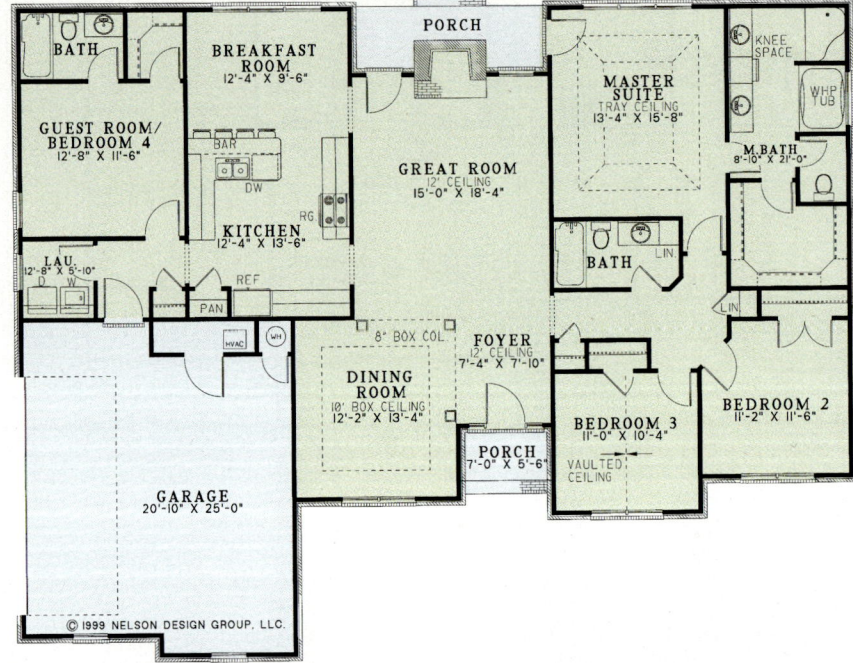

Beautiful boxed columns frame the regal dining room in this Nelson Design Group home. You will enjoy the openness of the great room with fireplace and access to the rear covered porch. When guests arrive, they will enjoy their own private suite with walk-in closet for ample storage. Mornings bring a new day and preparing breakfast will be enjoyable in your spacious kitchen with breakfast room. A beautiful tray ceiling adorns the master bedroom while the bathroom is complete with a huge walk-in closet, whirlpool tub and a corner glass shower.

Width: 64' 2"
Depth: 49' 0"
Total Living: 1,989 sq. ft.

Price Tier: B

Main Ceiling: 9 ft.
Bedrooms: 4
Baths: 3
Foundation: Crawl, Slab, Basement, Daylight Basement

To view similar plans visit www.nelsondesigngroup.com - 800.590.2423

381 Hickory Place

Enter the brick arched entry of this Nelson Design Group home and prepare for the perfect home. An inviting great room with romantic fireplace is a comfortable gathering room while a formal dining room allows for elegant entertaining.. The kitchen adjoins a large breakfast room with atrium door to the rear grilling porch. The master suite features a private office and has the ultimate master bathroom. A corner whirlpool tub is framed by columns and a large walk-in closet, shower and private toilet.

Width: 65' 2"
Depth: 63' 0"
Total Living: 1,994 sq. ft.

Price Tier: B

Main Ceiling: 8 ft.
Bedrooms: 3
Baths: 2
Foundation: Crawl, Slab, Basement, Daylight Basement

To view similar plans visit www.nelsondesigngroup.com - 800.590.2423

481 Aspen Heights

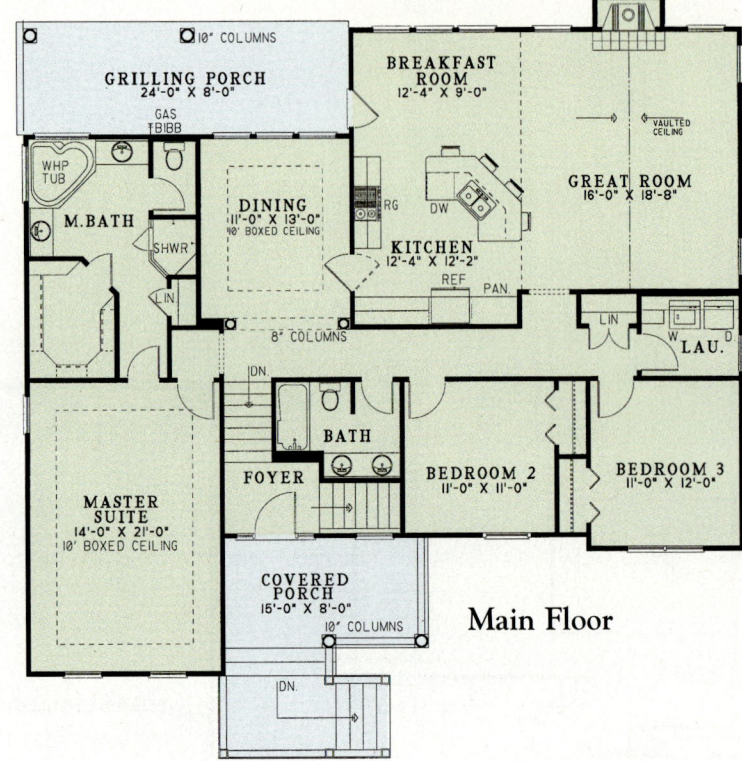

Main Floor

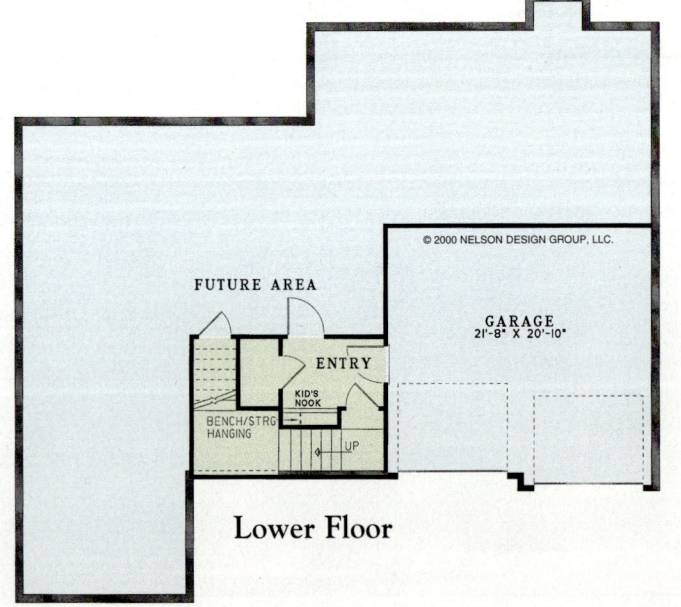

Lower Floor

This versatile offering from Nelson Design Group is as comfortable in the city as it is in the country. The down home great room feels even larger with the vaulted ceiling and barrier-free entry into the kitchen and breakfast room. The urban, open design kitchen features an island that serves double duty as a snack bar. The breakfast room is bright and sunny with access to a significant grilling porch where guests can mingle and converse. The lower floor holds endless expansion possibilities as family needs evolve.

Width: 53' 0"
Depth: 49' 4"
Main Floor: 1,935 sq. ft.
Lower Floor: 75 sq. ft.
Total Living: 2,010 sq. ft.

Price Tier: C

Main Ceiling: 9 ft.
Lower Ceiling: 8 ft.
Bedrooms: 3
Baths: 2
Foundation: Basement, Daylight Basement

To view similar plans visit www.84lumber.com/ndgplans - 800.359.8484

510 Quail Drive

This traditional one story plan from Nelson Design Group highlights a grand master suite located separately from the secondary bedrooms. Bask in the pure elegance of an arched entry, visitors can't help but feel at home in the marvelous great room with recessed fireplace and spacious entry to the formal dining room. The walk-through kitchen is a hub of activity as it allows access to the secondary bedrooms, breakfast room, dining room and utility room. Outdoor living is enhanced by the large screened porch and the optional courtyard garage.

Width: 59' 0"
Depth: 62' 10"
Total Living: 2,014 sq. ft.

Price Tier: C

Main Ceiling: 9 ft.
Bedrooms: 3
Baths: 2
Foundation: Crawl, Slab, Opt. Basement, Opt. Daylight Basement

To view similar plans visit www.84lumber.com/ndgplans - 800.359.8484

472-1 Mockingbird Lane

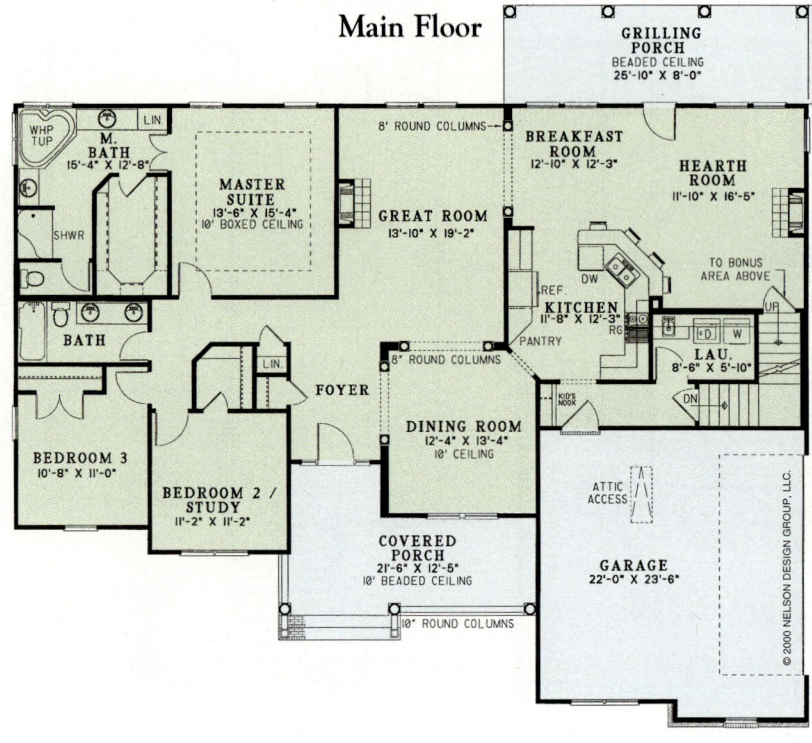

Main Floor

Upper Floor

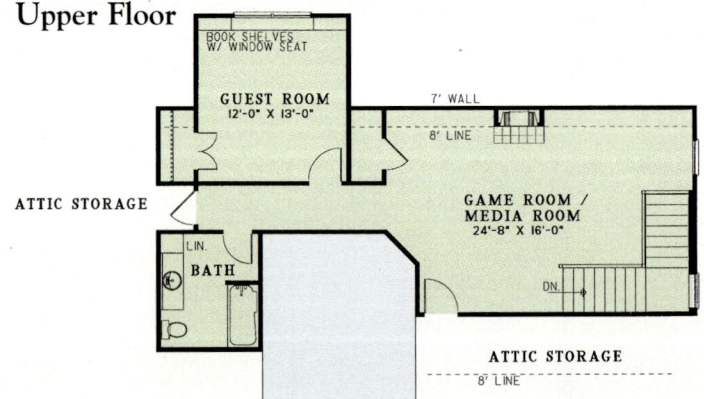

You'll enjoy entertaining family during those frigid winter months as holiday visitors gather around one of the three inviting fireplaces in this stunning Nelson Design Group two-story country home. The open floor plan allows everyone plenty of room to roam and the expansive kitchen allows for effortless service to all living areas. Overnight guests will enjoy the view from their window seat snuggled within an entire wall of built-in bookshelves. The luxurious master suite features a corner whirlpool tub with ample natural lighting and a 10' boxed ceiling.

Width: 66' 4"
Depth: 58' 7"
Total Living: 2,029 sq. ft.*
*Optional Bonus: 754 sq. ft.

Price Tier: C

Main Ceiling: 9 ft.
Upper Ceiling: 8 ft.
Bedrooms: 4
Baths: 3
Foundation: Crawl, Slab, Basement, Daylight Basement

To view similar plans visit www.84lumber.com/ndgplans - 800.359.8484

154 Chestnut Lane

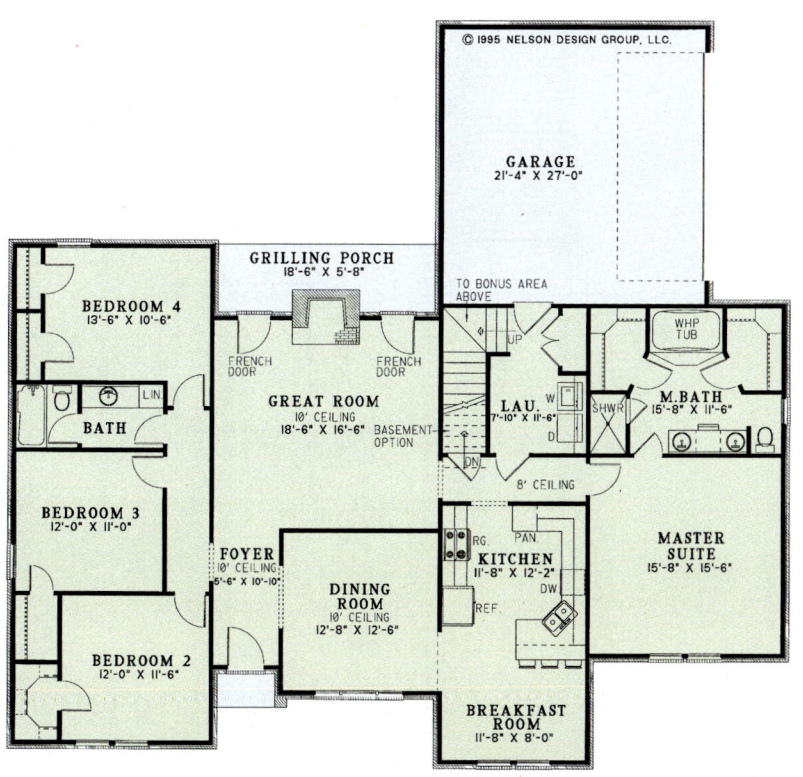

This Nelson Design Group home is a dream come true for the growing family. The spacious great room will serve as a gathering place for friends and family and has two beautiful French doors with easy access to the rear grilling porch for those weekend barbeques. The children will delight in the amount of closet space available in their rooms. Your secluded master suite allows you the privacy you need for today's lifestyle. The luxurious master bath with whirlpool bath will enable you to unwind after a long day at work.

Width: 63' 4"
Depth: 58' 6"
Total Living: 2,034 sq. ft.

Price Tier: C

Main Ceiling: 9 ft.
Bedrooms: 4
Baths: 2
Foundation: Crawl, Slab, Opt. Basement, Opt. Daylight Basement

To view similar plans visit www.84lumber.com/ndgplans - 800.359.8484

320 Olive Street

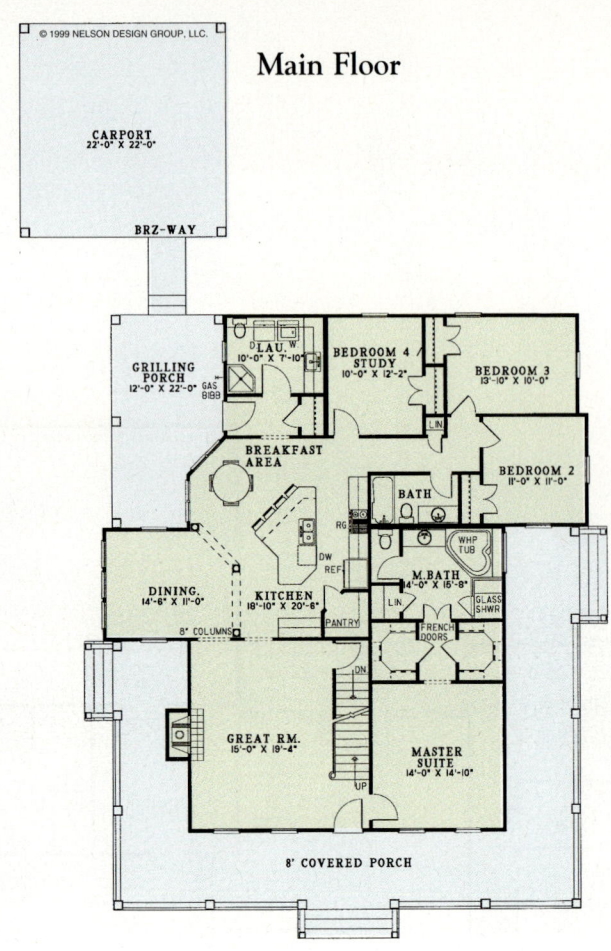

Main Floor

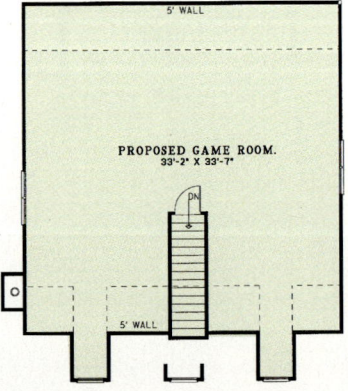

Upper Floor

This Nelson Design Group plan showcases a deep, wraparound front porch for summer shade, panoramic views and more than enough space for comfortable outside entertaining. When the weather turns cool everyone can warm their toes in front of the great room's zero-clearance fireplace while hot chocolate is being prepared in the nearby walk-through kitchen. The snack bar, breakfast room and formal dining room offer several mealtime options. His and her walk-in closets surround elegant French doors in the master suite leading to the well-appointed, sizable bath.

Width: 60' 6"
Depth: 91' 4"
Total Living: 2,039 sq. ft.*
*Optional Bonus: 1,155 sq. ft.

Price Tier: C

Main Ceiling: 9 ft.
Bonus Ceiling: 8 ft.
Bedrooms: 4
Baths: 3
Foundation: Crawl, Slab, Opt. Basement, Opt. Daylight Basement

Main Floor

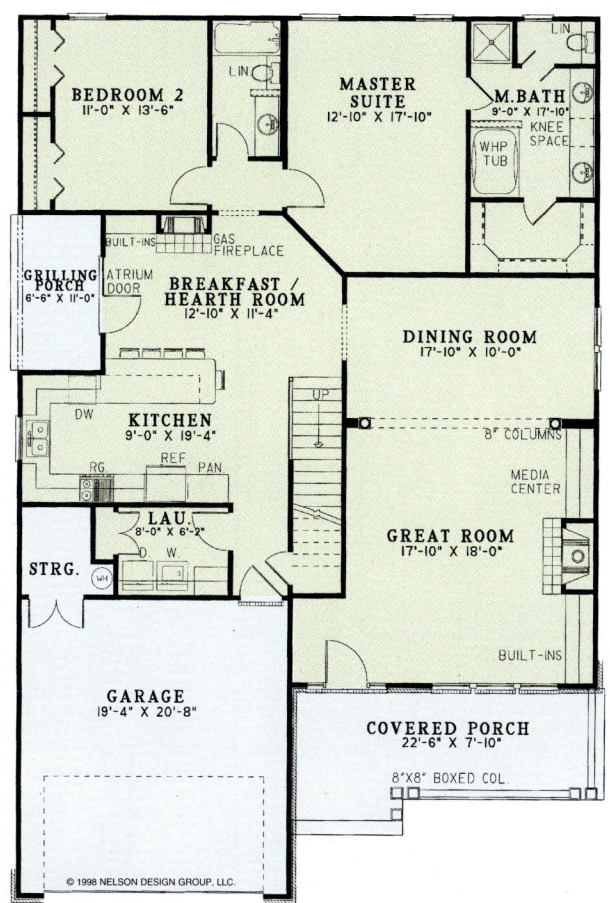

Upper Floor

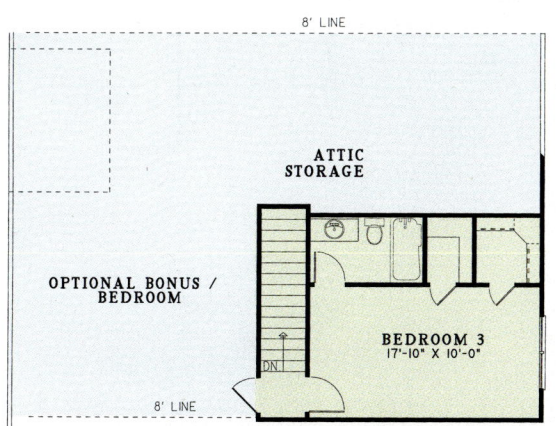

252 Maple Street

Imagine springtime afternoons on the porch swing of this Nelson Design Group home. Friends and family can mingle in the spacious great room before dinner is served in the dining room. Tradition can begin on Sunday mornings in your kitchen with easy access to the hearth room. The master suite of your home comes complete with corner glass shower, walk-in closet, double vanities and whirlpool tub. The optional upstairs area includes a bedroom, and a large bonus room that can serve as a play room for children of all ages.

Width: 42' 0"
Depth: 62' 4"
Main Floor: 1,768 sq. ft.
Upper Floor: 310 sq. ft.
Total Living: 2,078 sq. ft.

Main Ceiling: 9 ft.
Upper Ceiling: 8 ft.
Bedrooms: 3
Baths: 3
Foundation: Crawl, Slab, Opt. Basement, Opt. Daylight Basement

Price Tier: C

255 Cherry Street

Elevation A

Elevation B

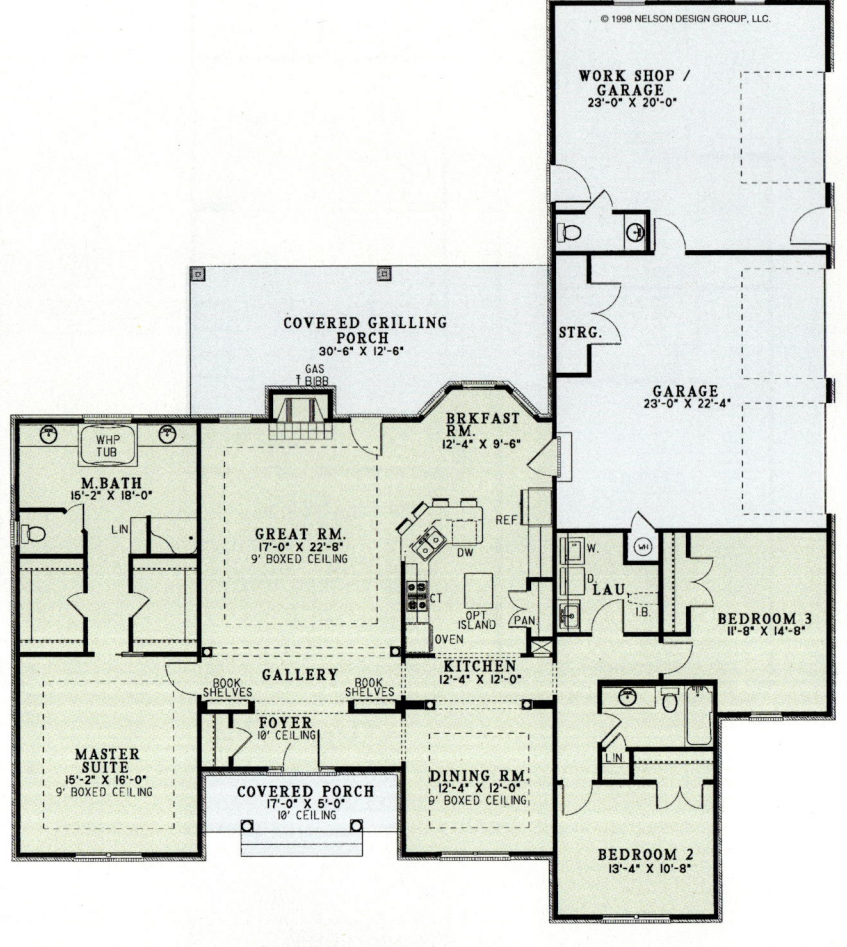

Imagine the compliments you'll receive while hosting a dinner party in this exquisite home from Nelson Design Group. Guests will marvel at the gallery lined with built-in bookshelves and the massive great room with elegant fireplace and high ceilings throughout. A stylish French door allows the dinner party to transition outside to the vast covered grilling porch. When the party is over, you can relax in the beautiful breakfast bay before retiring to the master suite enhanced by his and her walk-in closets and oversized whirlpool tub.

Width: 69' 2"
Depth: 74' 10"
Total Living: 2,096 sq. ft.

Price Tier: C

Main Ceiling: 8 ft.
Bedrooms: 3
Baths: 2 1/2
Foundation: Crawl, Slab, Opt. Basement, Opt. Daylight Basement

To view similar plans visit www.84lumber.com/ndgplans - 800.359.8484

Main Floor

508 Quail Drive

Upper Floor

The nostalgic front porch and magnificent columns welcome you to this charming Nelson Design Group Home. From the open foyer, guests can enter the study through stylish French doors, the formal dining room via the column-accented entry or the great room with a radiant corner fireplace. The family chef is sure to enjoy the large kitchen area with breakfast bar and swinging door access to the dining room. Elegant French doors and boxed ceiling highlight an impressive master suite.

Width: 61' 4"	Main Ceiling: 9 ft.
Depth: 68' 4"	Upper Ceiling: 8 ft.
Total Living: 2,100 sq. ft.	Bedrooms: 3
*Optional Bonus: 256 sq. ft.	Baths: 2
	Foundation: Crawl, Slab, Opt. Basement, Opt. Daylight Basement

Price Tier: C

190 Cherry Street

Elevation A

Check This Plan Mike

Elevation B

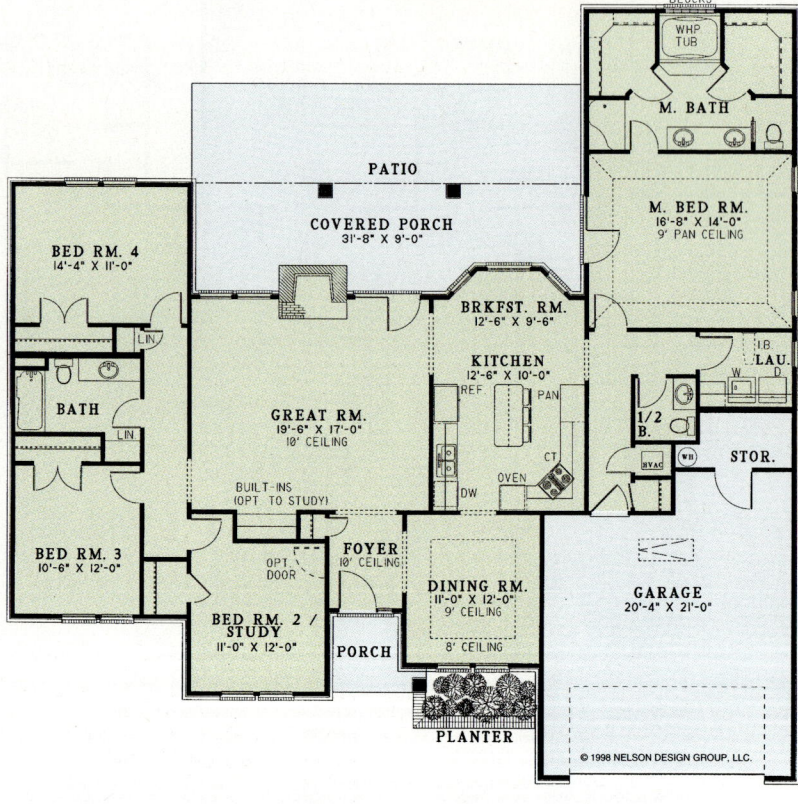

Imagine welcoming guests into this Nelson Design Group split bedroom home. The spacious dining room will be superb for your formal dinner parties followed by coffee in the comfortable great room. The morning sun rays shining through the bay window of the breakfast room is a beautiful beginning to each day. As night falls, your secluded master suite has a private access to the rear porch - perfect for watching the sun set. Rest and relaxation is found in your luxurious master bath with whirlpool tub and 'his and her' walk-in closets provide ample storage space.

Width: 64' 8"
Depth: 62' 1"
Total Living: 2,107 sq. ft.

Price Tier: C

Main Ceiling: 8 ft.
Bedrooms: 4
Baths: 2 1/2
Foundation: Crawl, Slab, Basement, Daylight Basement

200

To view similar plans visit www.84lumber.com/ndgplans - 800.359.8484

256 Olive Street

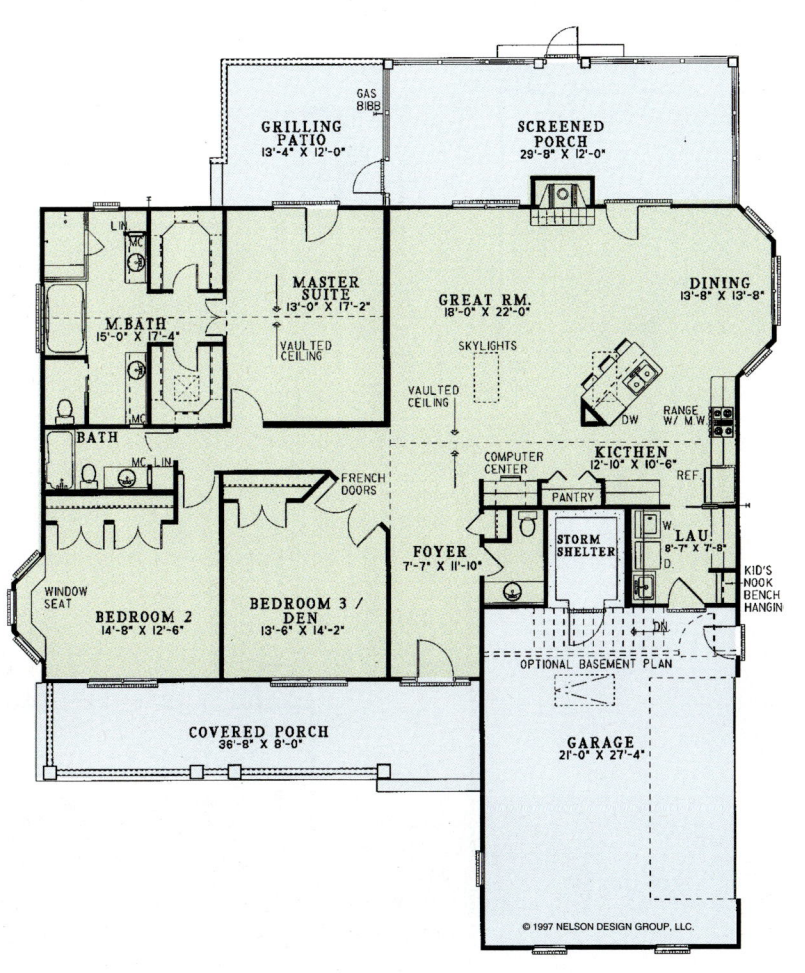

Fashion and function collaborate in this split-bedroom Nelson Design Group home tailor-made for your active lifestyle. Barrier-free transitions among the living areas create an ideal entertainment environment. Skylights bring natural lighting to the impressive great room and open, visitor-friendly kitchen that share a vaulted ceiling. The gorgeous master suite also features a vaulted ceiling, French doors leading to the bath, his and her walk-in closets and a large whirlpool tub. During harsh weather, the family can feel at ease in the built-in storm shelter.

Width: 63' 10"
Depth: 72' 2"
Total Living: 2,131 sq. ft.

Price Tier: C

Main Ceiling: 9 ft.
Bedrooms: 3
Baths: 2 1/2
Foundation: Crawl, Slab, Opt. Basement, Opt. Daylight Basement

469 Wingate Circle

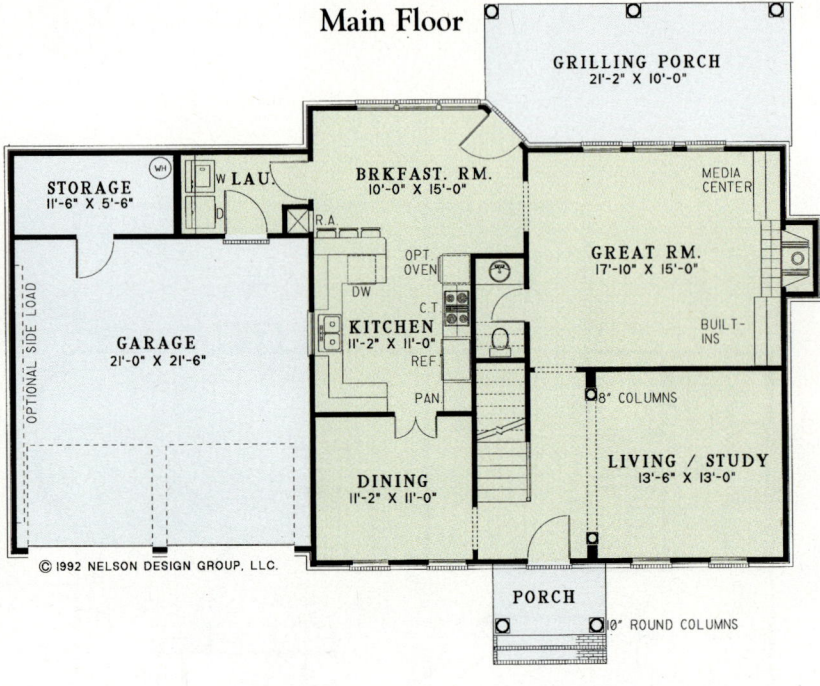

Main Floor

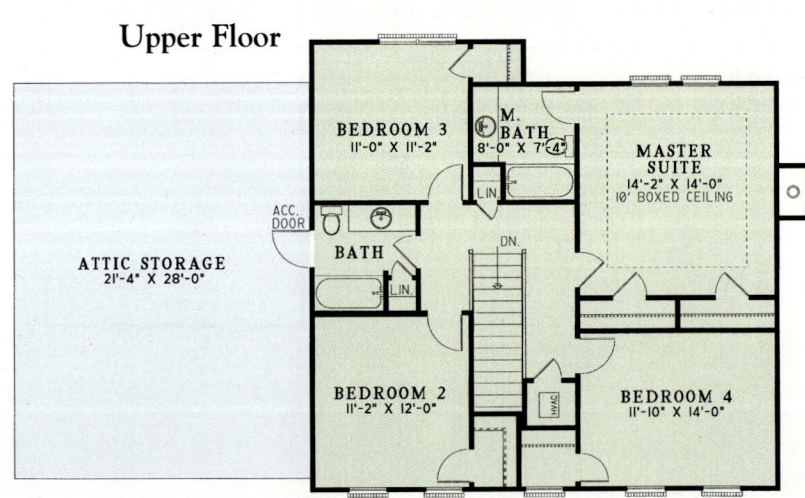

Upper Floor

Tall columns punctuate the elegant appearance of this four-bedroom Nelson Design Group Colonial-style home. The roomy entry connects the formal living and dining areas for those special occasions while the great room's fireplace, nestled among built-in media center and bookshelves, provides the ideal setting for gatherings both large and small. The central kitchen location makes it easy for one and all to retrieve that special dessert and afterwards, everyone can enjoy casual conversation on the spacious grilling porch.

Width: 55' 2"
Depth: 44' 0"
Main Floor: 1,113 sq. ft.
Upper Floor: 1,019 sq. ft.
Total Living: 2,132 sq. ft.

Main Ceiling: 8 ft.
Upper Ceiling: 8 ft.
Bedrooms: 4
Baths: 2 1/2
Foundation: Crawl, Slab

Price Tier: C

To view similar plans visit www.84lumber.com/ndgplans - 800.359.8484

194 Hickory Place

Life is but a dream in this Nelson Design Group home. An open floor plan with ten and eleven foot ceilings create a grand feeling. Admire the unique mirror image from the spacious great room and the comfortable hearth room with pass-through fireplace. The master suite is enhanced by a ten foot boxed ceiling and has a pocket door access to the master bath with a huge walk-in closet, whirlpool tub, separate shower and private toilet room.

Width: 58' 6"
Depth: 64' 6"
Total Living: 2,133 sq. ft.

Price Tier: C

Main Ceiling: 9 ft.
Bedrooms: 3
Baths: 2
Foundation: Crawl, Slab, Basement, Daylight Basement

169 Elm Street

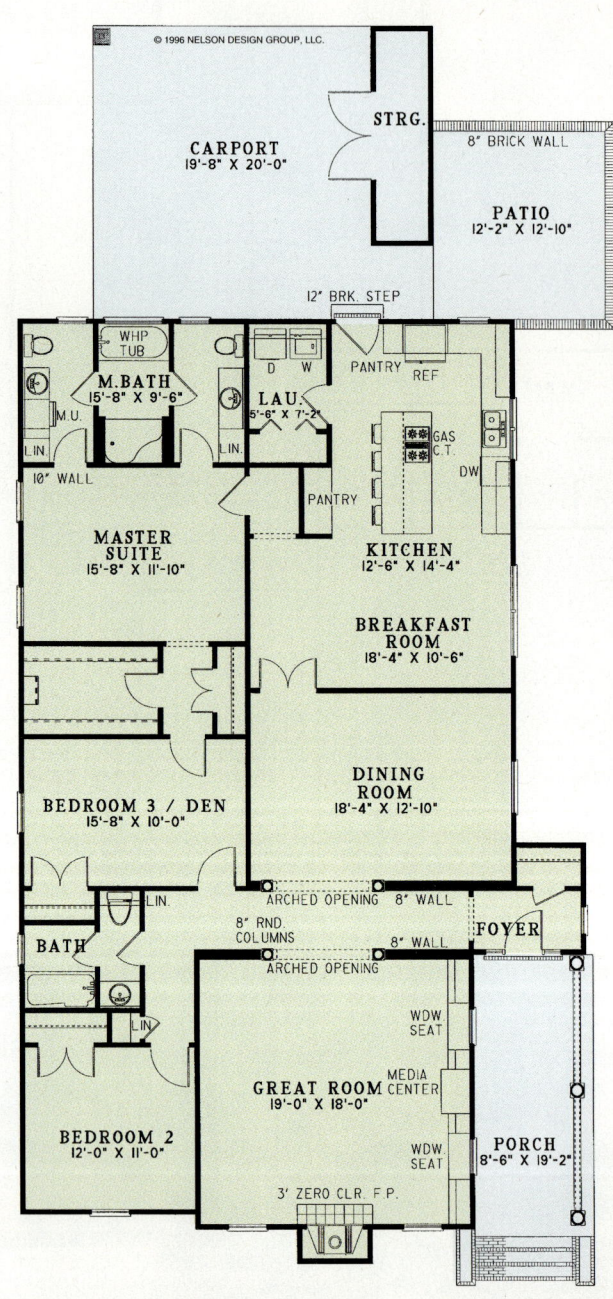

The charming front porch and comfortable interior help make this Nelson Design Group house a place you can call home. In the entry hall, twin arched openings beckon guests to the living and dining areas. The two window seats flanking the great room's built-in media center are ideal spots for the kids to anxiously await the return of Mom or Dad. A large island doubling as an eat-at bar separates the kitchen from the breakfast room.

Width: 40' 0"
Depth: 84' 4"
Total Living: 2,140 sq. ft.

Price Tier: C

Main Ceiling: 9 ft.
Bedrooms: 3
Baths: 2
Foundation: Crawl, Slab, Opt. Basement, Opt. Daylight Basement

To view similar plans visit www.84lumber.com/ndgplans - 800.359.8484

201 Poplar Avenue

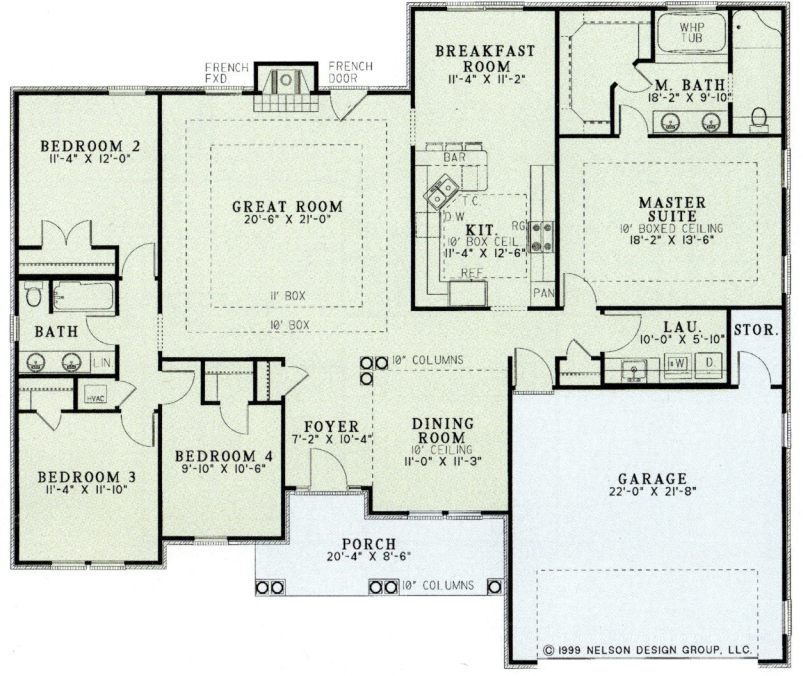

Memories are in the making in this Nelson Design Group home. Entertain with grand birthday parties in your elegant dining room. Or plan those family Christmas' at your home in your spacious great room with room for everyone. When all your guests leave and the children are tucked away in their own bedrooms, you'll find solace in your private master suite and bath. You'll find your master bath complete with double vanities, corner glass shower and whirlpool bath.

Width: 63' 0"
Depth: 52' 8"
Total Living: 2,148 sq. ft.

Price Tier: C

Main Ceiling: 9 ft.
Bedrooms: 4
Baths: 2
Foundation: Crawl, Slab, Opt. Basement, Opt. Daylight Basement

340 Olive Street

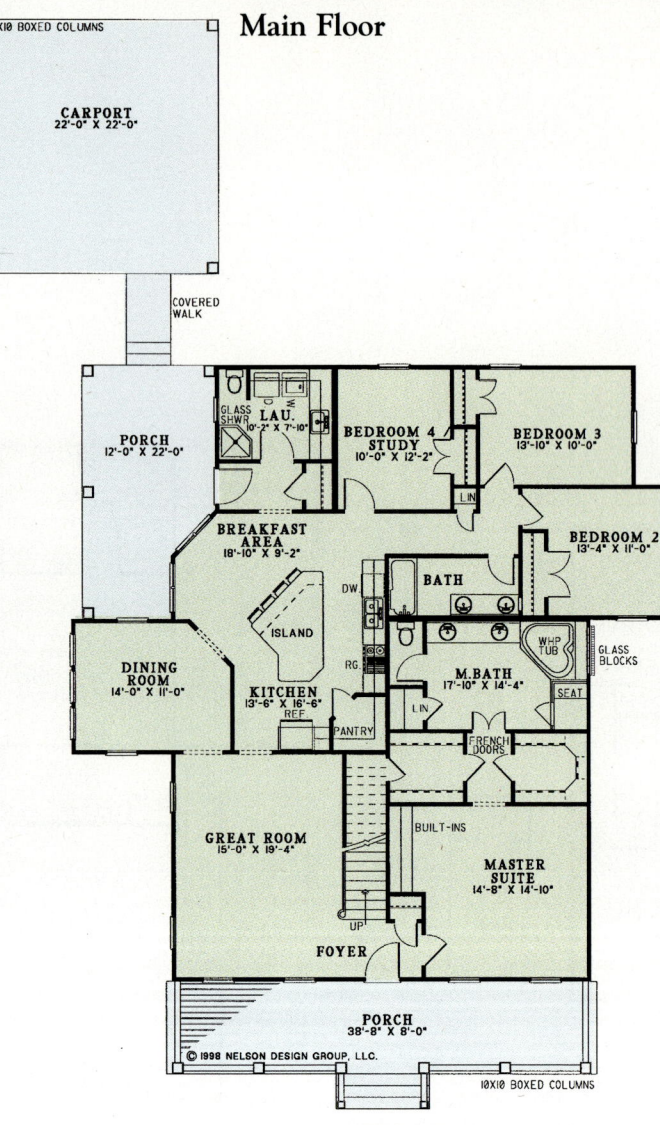

Main Floor

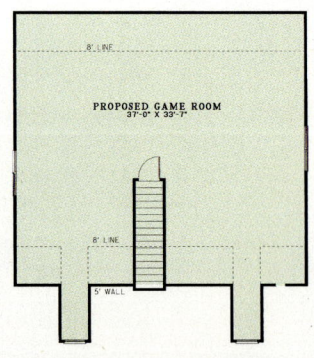

Upper Floor

Mom will be so proud as she visits you in this delightful Nelson Design Group home. She'll marvel at the amount of space available throughout the design and find the unique island in the kitchen a clever idea. A convenient shower in the laundry room is ideal when the children stampede in covered with mud. After the kids are tucked away into bed for the evening, you can finally retreat to your master suite for your own relaxation. Solitude within the confines of the luxurious corner whirlpool bath is a wonderful way to unwind when mother leaves.

Width: 62' 10"
Depth: 91' 4"
Total Living: 2,186 sq. ft.*
*Optional Bonus: 1,283 sq. ft.

Price Tier: C

Main Ceiling: 9 ft.
Upper Ceiling: 8 ft.
Bedrooms: 4
Baths: 3
Foundation: Crawl, Slab, Basement, Daylight Basement

515 Richmond Drive

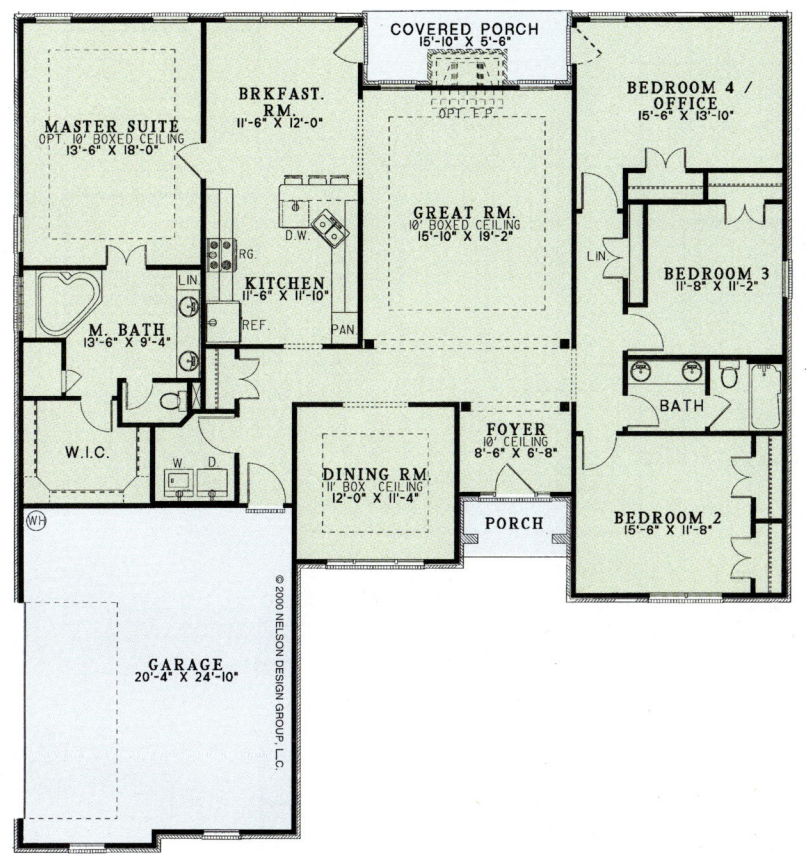

The handsome styling of this traditional Nelson Design Group home will keep the accolades coming your way for years to come. Boxed ceilings are scattered throughout for an added touch of elegance and class. All dining possibilites are covered between the formal dining room, the more casual breakfast room and the zap it and grab it eat-at bar. Weekend visitors will enjoy the secluded fourth bedroom with its private entrance to the rear porch. The luxury of the elaborate master suite is exemplified in the stylish French doors, giving way to a lavish bath area.

Width: 58' 0"
Depth: 66' 6"
Total Living: 2,187 sq. ft.

Price Tier: C

Main Ceiling: 9 ft.
Bedrooms: 4
Baths: 2
Foundation: Crawl, Slab, Opt. Basement, Opt. Daylight Basement

526 Olive Street

Elevation A

Elevation B

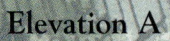

Main Floor

Upper Floor

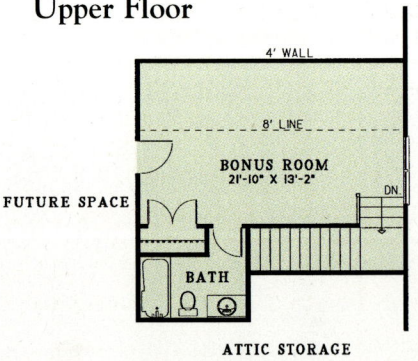

This extraordinary four-bedroom Nelson Design Group home showcases a master suite so elegant it demands its own wing. You'll have a tough time deciding where to entertain with two impressive covered porches and a delightful great room offering the comfort of a cozy fireplace. The center foyer opens to a boxed ceiling dining room and optional study with bookshelves. The master bedroom adorns a 9 foot ceiling and has a bathroom including 'his and her' walk-in closets centering a whirlpool tub. A bonus room is available upstairs for future needs.

Width: 66' 0"
Depth: 65' 2"
Total Living: 2,261 sq. ft.*
*Optional Bonus: 367 sq. ft.

Price Tier: C

Main Ceiling: 9 ft.
Upper Ceiling: 8 ft.
Bedrooms: 4
Baths: 3 1/2
Foundation: Crawl, Slab, Opt. Basement, Opt. Daylight Basement

To view similar plans visit www.84lumber.com/ndgplans - 800.359.8484

202 Glendale Avenue

This combination of a functional floor plan and two exterior options make this Nelson Design Group home a popular and versatile choice. The covered front porch opens to a high-ceiling foyer with column accents. Extravagant French doors off the gallery reveal a prominent window-lit formal dining room with a 13' ceiling sure to impress visitors. The split bedroom design allows parents and kids alike to bask in some quiet time after a day of family activities.

Width: 58' 0"
Depth: 69' 6"
Total Living: 2,189 sq. ft.

Price Tier: C

Main Ceiling: 9 ft.
Bedrooms: 4
Baths: 2
Foundation: Crawl, Slab, Opt. Basement, Opt. Daylight Basement

467 Kensington Cove

The exquisite exterior of this Nelson Design Group split-bedroom offering hints at the stylish features waiting to be found inside. Meticulous living spaces evolve from the foyer and all share 10' ceilings. Enjoy an appetizer by the fireplace or step outside and lounge on the festive patio until mealtime. The breakfast room merges with the kitchen allowing conversation during clean up. The master suite is accented by a stepped, boxed ceiling, his and her walk-in closets and a marvelous step-up whirlpool tub.

Width: 65' 2"
Depth: 63' 8"
Total Living: 2,210 sq. ft.

Price Tier: C

Main Ceiling: 8 ft.
Bedrooms: 4
Baths: 2 1/2
Foundation: Crawl, Slab

195 Richmond Drive

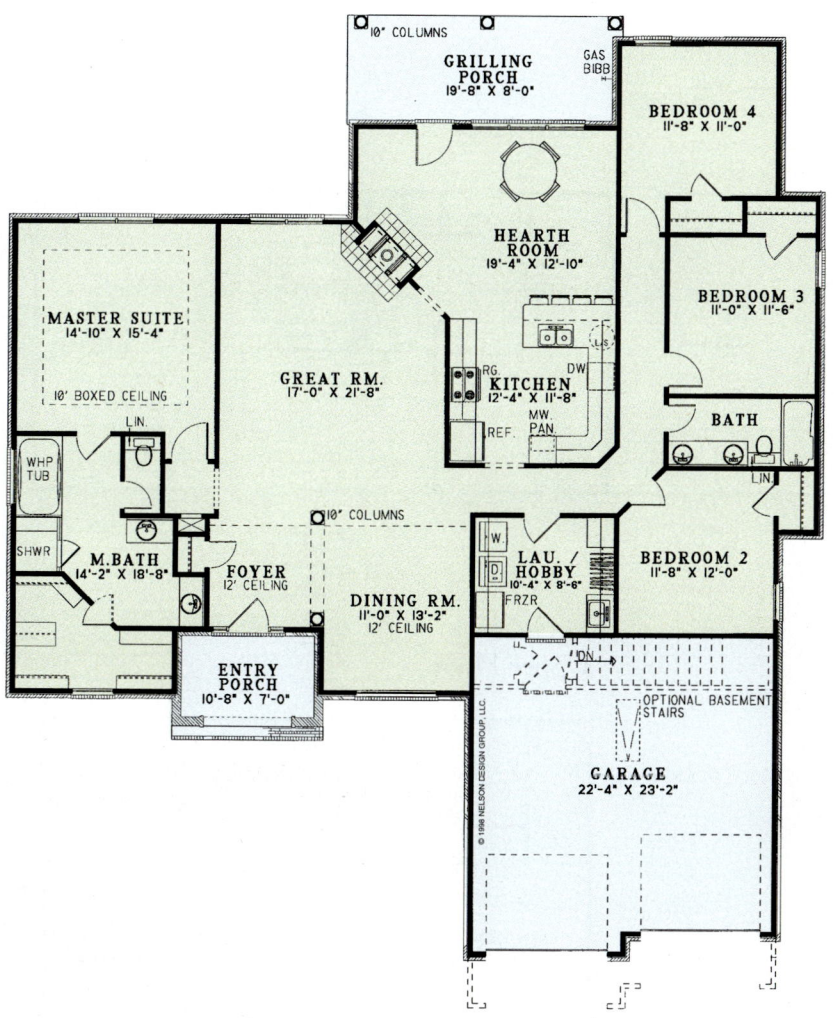

Whoever said it's the little details that count the most must have lived in this amazing Nelson Design Group home. The brick façade with multiple-gabled, hip roofline and stunning half-round transoms is sure to capture attention. Friends and family alike will marvel at the free-flowing living areas punctuated with a corner pass-through fireplace. The hearth room provides an alternate gathering place when the kids take over the great room. The user-friendly kitchen offers plenty of room to maneuver and an eat-at bar for quickie meals. The master suite's immense walk-in closet can handle even the most dedicated pack rat and then some.

Width: 60' 6"
Depth: 69' 2"
Total Living: 2,238 sq. ft.

Price Tier: C

Main Ceiling: 9 ft.
Bedrooms: 4
Baths: 2
Foundation: Crawl, Slab, Opt. Basement, Opt. Daylight Basement

275 Olive Street

Main Floor

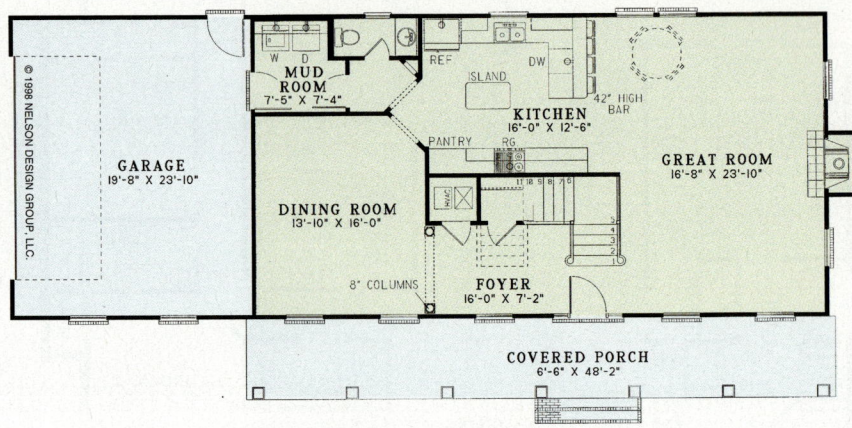

Upper Floor

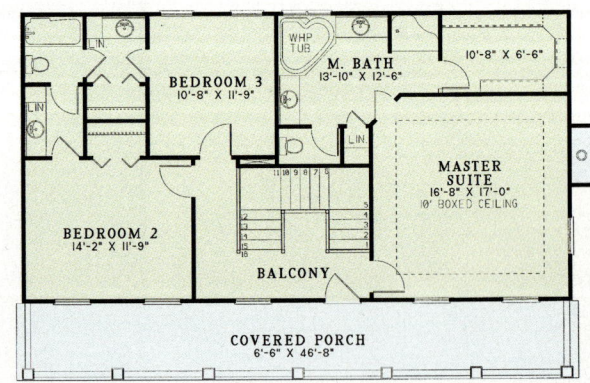

This is definately the life. A gorgeous Southern Traditional Nelson Design Group home offers almost everything. Family can gather around a cozy fireplace in the great room or enjoy the roomy kitchen/dining area. Magnificent columns welcome your guests into the grand dining room with fluid access to the kitchen for ease and preparation. A mud room with half bath is located at the garage entry. The children have the benefit of shared access to their bathroom upstairs with you close by in your master suite. A corner whirlpool tub will become a favorite haven for your relaxation, with a spacious walk-in closet conveniently located.

Width: 67' 2"
Depth: 31' 0"
Main Floor: 1,154 sq. ft.
Upper Floor: 1,093 sq. ft.
Total Living: 2,247 sq. ft.

Price Tier: C

Main Ceiling: 9 ft.
Upper Ceiling: 9 ft.
Bedrooms: 3
Baths: 2 1/2
Foundation: Crawl, Slab, Basement, Daylight Basement

To view similar plans visit www.84lumber.com/ndgplans - 800.359.8484

367 Walnut Lane

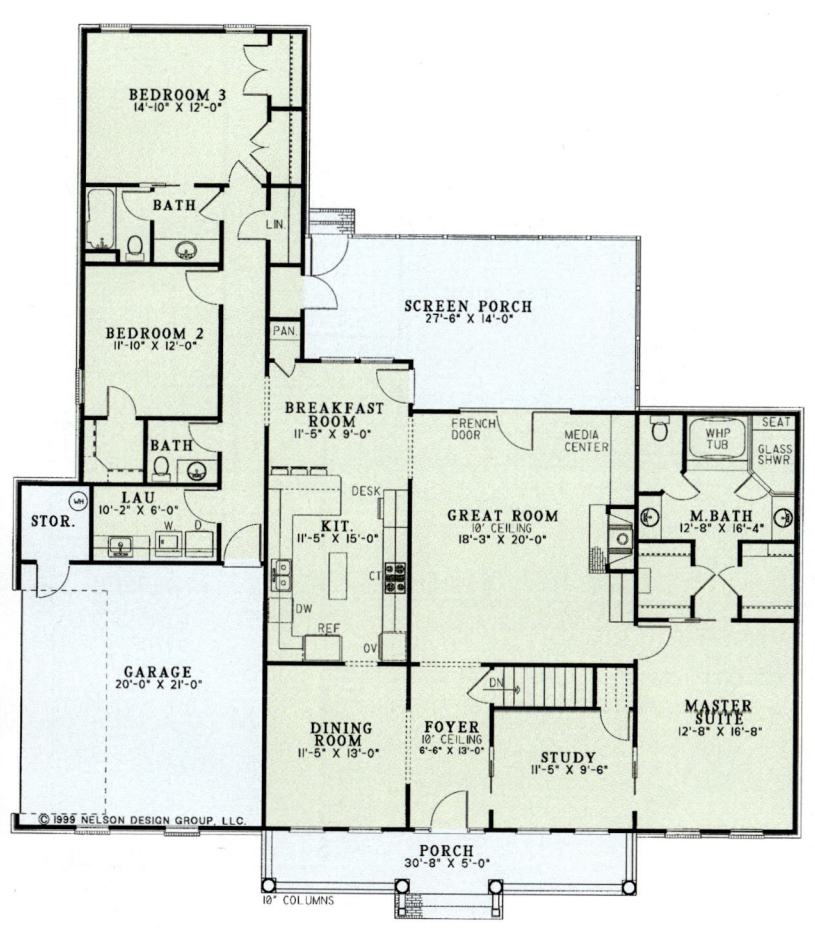

Life is but a dream in this Nelson Design Group split bedroom home. Rock the afternoon away in your rocking chair on the spacious front porch. As you enter the home, lead your guests into the dining room for the dinner you are preparing with easy access from the kitchen. After dinner, your guests can move to the great room for coffee and conversation. Finally, when your guest leave, you will find relaxation in your private master suite. The master bath comes complete with corner glass shower, double vanities, whirlpool bath and 'his and her' walk-in closets.

Width: 64' 0"
Depth: 69' 4"
Total Living: 2,263 sq. ft.

Price Tier: C

Main Ceiling: 9 ft.
Bedrooms: 3
Baths: 2 1/2
Foundation: Crawl, Slab, Opt. Basement, Opt. Daylight Basement

To view similar plans visit www.84lumber.com/ndgplans - 800.359.8484

463 Spruce Street

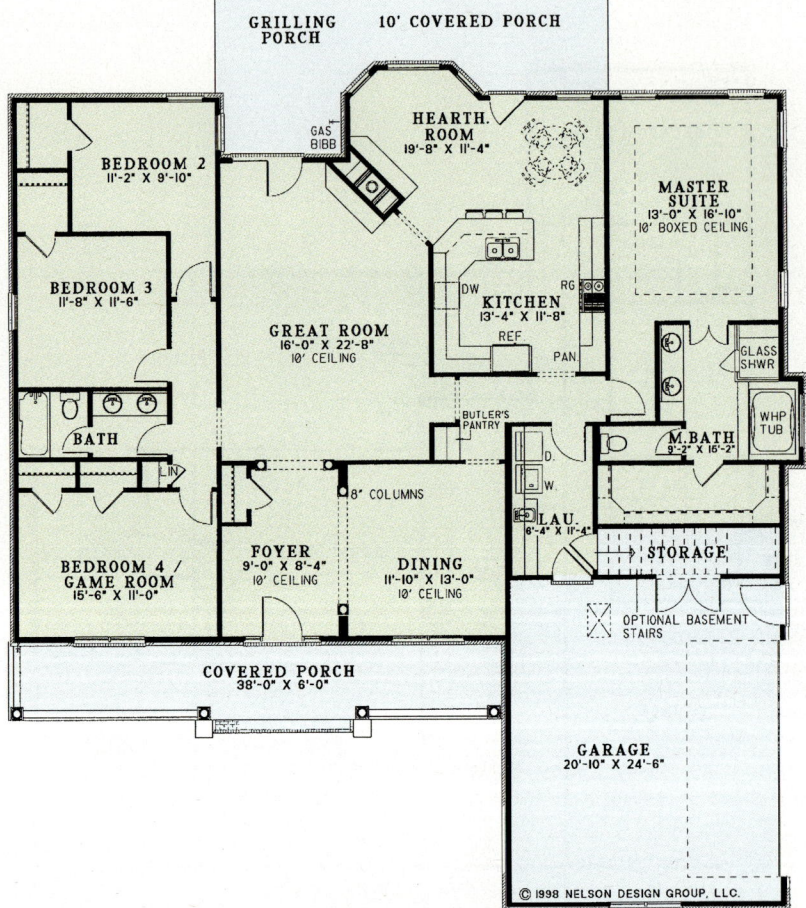

Exciting columns and ten foot ceilings add elegance to a comfortable, open floor plan, while secluded bedrooms are pleasant retreats in this Nelson Design Group home. A formal dining room features easy access to the kitchen which makes hosting dinner parties much easier. After dinner, lead your guests into the spacious great room for conversation or gather in the hearth room for coffee by the pass-through fireplace. Once the evening has ended, retreat to your master suite which is highlighted by a ten foot boxed ceiling and a spacious bath with a whirlpool bath.

Width: 61' 0"
Depth: 71' 8"
Total Living: 2,286 sq. ft.

Price Tier: C

Main Ceiling: 9 ft.
Bedrooms: 4
Baths: 2
Foundation: Crawl, Slab, Opt. Basement, Opt. Daylight Basement

Main Floor

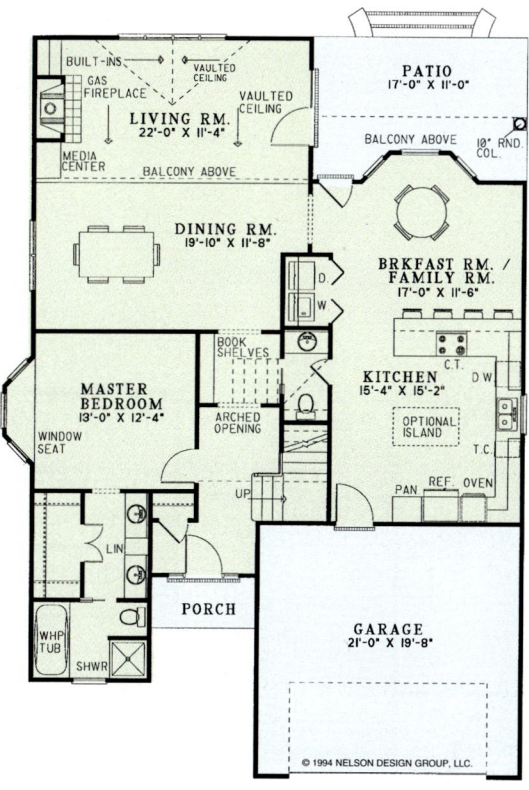

Upper Floor

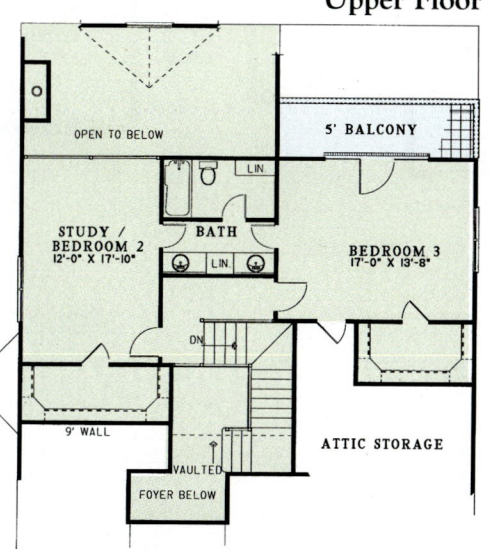

122 Brighton Court

The multi-storied foyer and living room provide an even larger feel to this already formidable home from Nelson Design Group. Arched openings escort you to the marvelous formal dining room that blends barrier-free into a captivating living room. There you'll find the gas fireplace, snuggled among built-ins and media center, gains prominence from the vaulted ceiling and balcony above. An enormous kitchen seats several at the eat-at bar where conversation flows effortlessly to the adjoining bay-windowed breakfast room. Upstairs features large, lovely Jack-and-Jill bedrooms that share a common bath.

Width: 42' 4"	Main Ceiling: 9 ft.
Depth: 58' 10"	Upper Ceiling: 9 ft.
Main Floor: 1,542 sq. ft.	Bedrooms: 3
Upper Floor: 745 sq. ft.	Baths: 2 1/2
Total Living: 2,287 sq. ft.	Foundation: Crawl, Slab

Price Tier: C

140 Richmond Drive

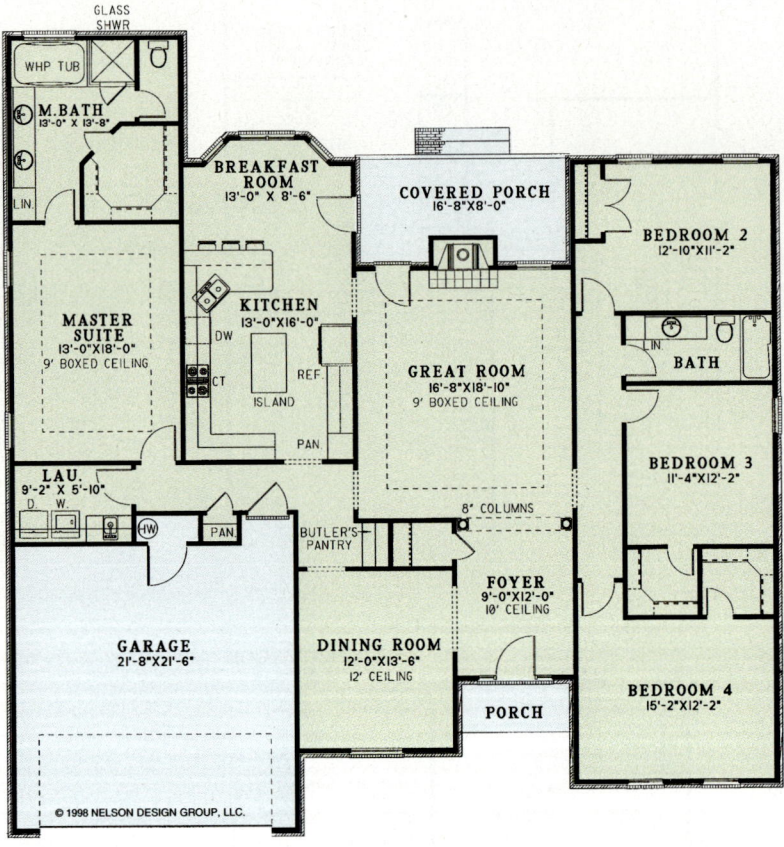

Among the eye-catching features of this Nelson Design Group four-bedroom plan are decorative quoins, tall hip roofline, and a huge arched window. Inside you will delight in the relaxing atmosphere of the great room featuring a grand fireplace and 9' boxed ceiling. The spacious kitchen allows for casual dining options at the functional snack bar or in the adjoining bay-windowed breakfast room. An elaborate master suite located away from the secondary bedrooms allows you to relax in comfort and privacy.

Width: 59' 6"
Depth: 60' 8"
Total Living: 2,319 sq. ft.

Price Tier: C

Main Ceiling: 8 ft.
Bedrooms: 4
Baths: 2
Foundation: Crawl, Slab, Opt. Basement, Opt. Daylight Basement

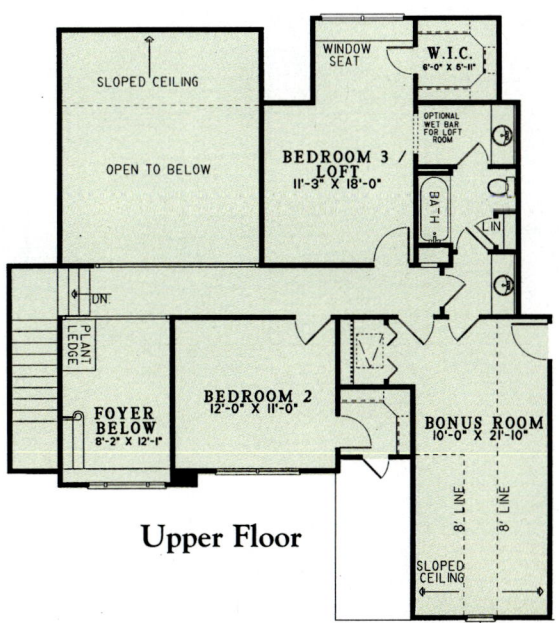

Main Floor

Upper Floor

511 Magnolia Drive

Neighbors will surely envy the elegant exterior of this charming Nelson Design Group home with its welcoming porch and gabled roofline. Inside, the two-story foyer blends wonderfully with the column-accented formal dining room and opens into the vast great room anchored by a stately fireplace. Enjoy casual meals by the fireplace as the hearth room flows barrier-free into the breakfast area and kitchen. Upstairs the loft bedroom steals the show with its extra-wide window seat, walk-in closet and private entrance to the upstairs bath.

Width: 56' 8"	Main Ceiling: 9 ft.
Depth: 57' 4"	Upper Ceiling: 8 ft.
Main Floor: 1,776 sq. ft.	Bedrooms: 3
Upper Floor: 584 sq. ft.	Baths: 2 1/2
Total Living: 2,360 sq. ft.	Foundation: Crawl, Slab, Opt. Basement,
*Optional Bonus: 262 sq. ft.	Opt. Daylight Basement

Price Tier: C

To view similar plans visit www.84lumber.com/ndgplans - 800.359.8484

368 Olive Street

Picture raising your family in this Southern Traditional Nelson Design Group home. Visit with the neighbors on the spacious covered porch with lemonade and conversation. Upon entering the foyer, lead your guests into the great room, complete with fireplace, built-ins and atrium door access to the rear covered porch. A bedroom near the master suite can function as a nursery for the baby or private study. You'll notice numerous amenities in your master suite and bathroom, including whirlpool tub, glass shower, 'his and her' walk-in closets and a private toilet. The amenities are endless in this classic plan

Width: 68' 0"
Depth: 74' 0"
Total Living: 2,388 sq. ft.
Price Tier: C

Main Ceiling: 9 ft.
Bedrooms: 4
Baths: 2 1/2
Foundation: Crawl, Slab, Opt. Basement, Opt. Daylight Basement

218 To view similar plans visit www.84lumber.com/ndgplans - 800.359.8484

149 Kensington Cove

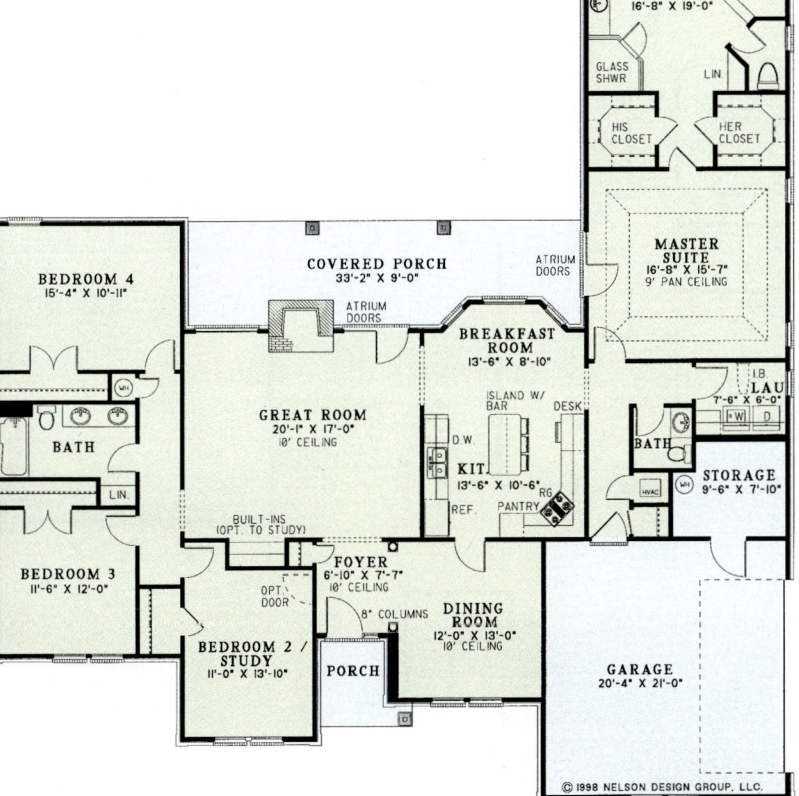

A sleek roofline and sheltered entry accent the stately elegance of this sprawling four-bedroom Nelson Design Group home. Once inside you will immediately notice the decorative columns leading to the formal dining room. The comforting great room fireplace serves as a central gathering point before heading through the atrium doors to the large covered porch. The family chef can entertain at the island bar while preparing the evening's feast in the spacious kitchen. The deluxe master suite features his and her walk-in closets, private entrance to the porch, and a raised corner whirlpool tub.

Width: 67' 2"
Depth: 71' 8"
Total Living: 2,392 sq. ft.

Price Tier: C

Main Ceiling: 8 ft.
Bedrooms: 4
Baths: 2 1/2
Foundation: Crawl, Slab, Basement, Daylight Basement

To view similar plans visit www.84lumber.com/ndgplans - 800.359.8484

514 Kensington Cove

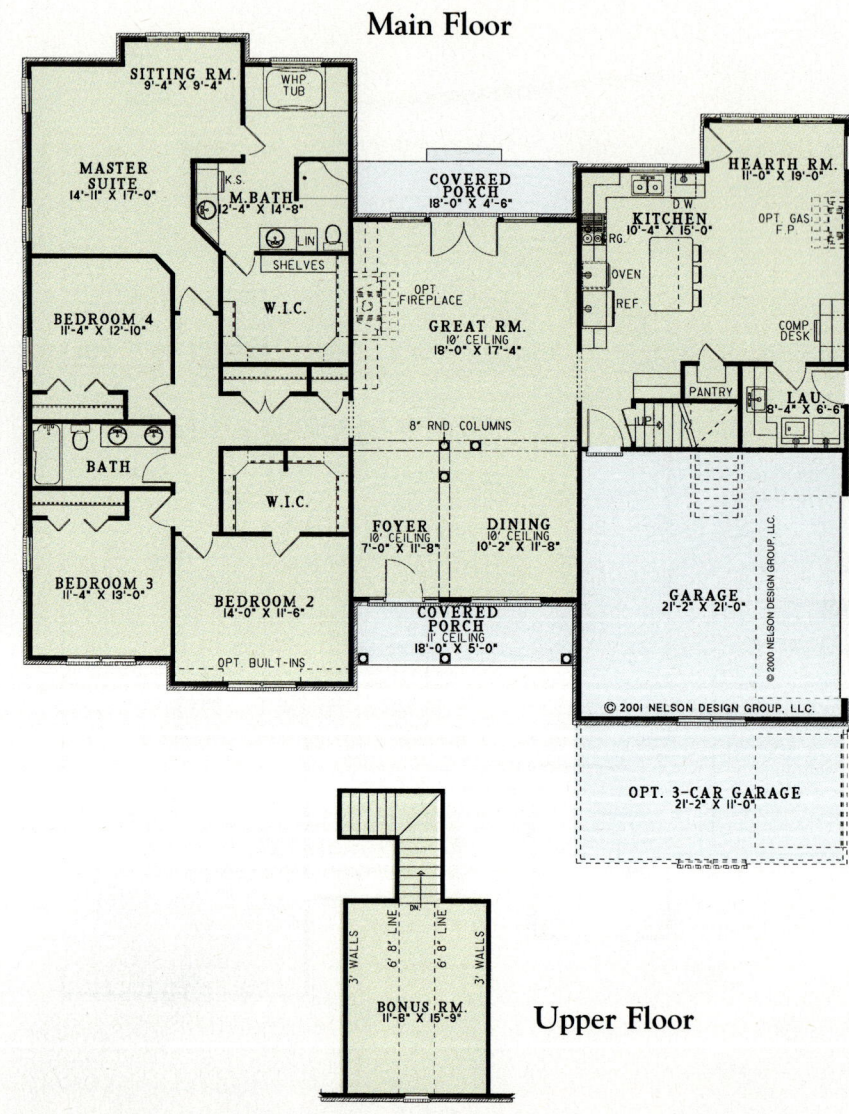

Main Floor

Upper Floor

The vast areas of this wide-open floor plan from Nelson Design Group provide the perfect atmosphere to host both formal and casual gatherings. Decorative columns adorn the transition from the extended foyer to the open areas of the formal dining and great rooms. Comfort abounds in the open kitchen area with its island bar, combined with the sunny breakfast room and built-in computer station. Optional gas fireplaces and built-ins provide just the right finishing touches to customize and personalize this astonishing home.

Width: 66' 4"
Depth: 54' 2"
Total Living: 2,394 sq. ft.*
*Optional Bonus: 202 sq. ft.

Price Tier: C

Main Ceiling: 9 ft.
Bedrooms: 4
Baths: 2
Foundation: Crawl, Slab, Opt. Basement, Opt. Daylight Basement

563 Country Club Drive

Main Floor

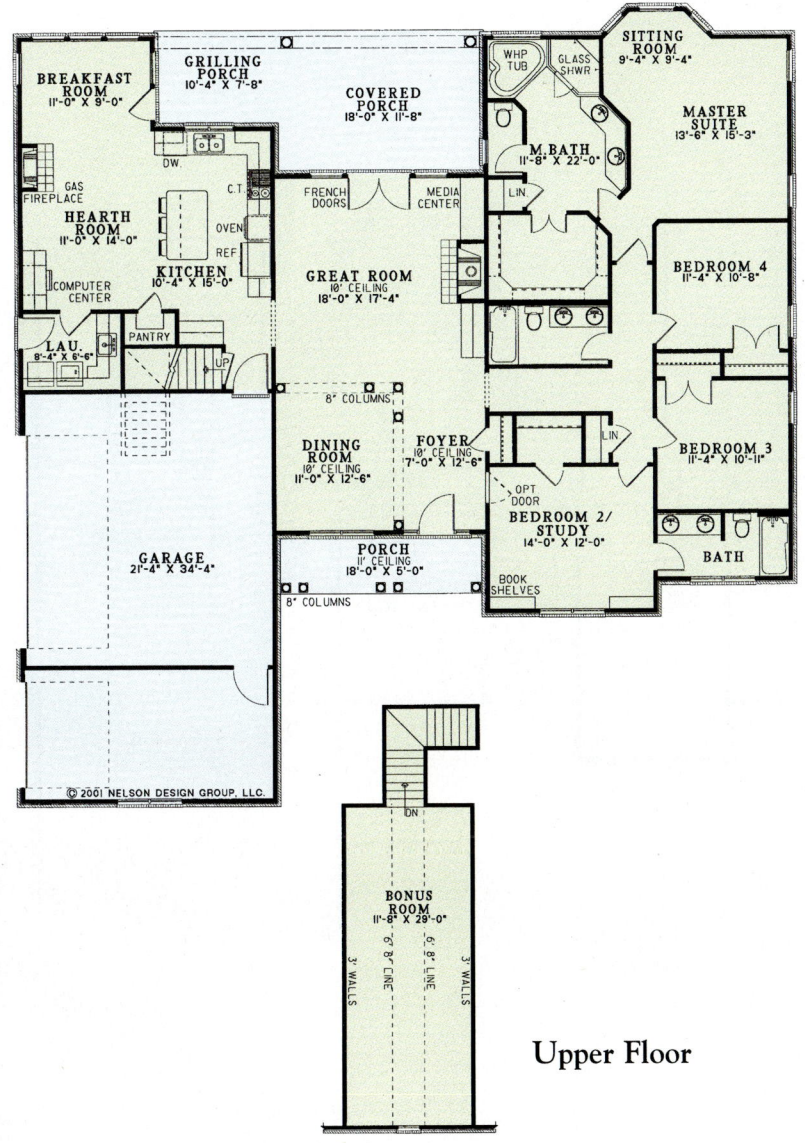

Upper Floor

Tradition begins in this Nelson Design Group home. As you enter through the foyer, you'll notice the elegant columns that define the dining room - perfect for elegant dinner parties. Your great room, complete with media center and fireplace has beautiful French door access to the rear porch for entertaining guests during the warm seasons. A cozy hearth room will become the favorite gathering room for the family with a computer center nearby. Upstairs, you'll discover a bonus room that can be converted into a playroom for the kids when company drops by.

Width: 66' 4"
Depth: 67' 2"
Total Living: 2,405 sq. ft.*
*Optional Bonus: 358 sq. ft.

Price Tier: C

Main Ceiling: 9 ft.
Upper Ceiling: 8 ft.
Bedrooms: 4
Baths: 3
Foundation: Crawl, Slab, Opt. Basement, Opt. Daylight Basement

To view similar plans visit www.84lumber.com/ndgplans - 800.359.8484

204 Richmond Drive

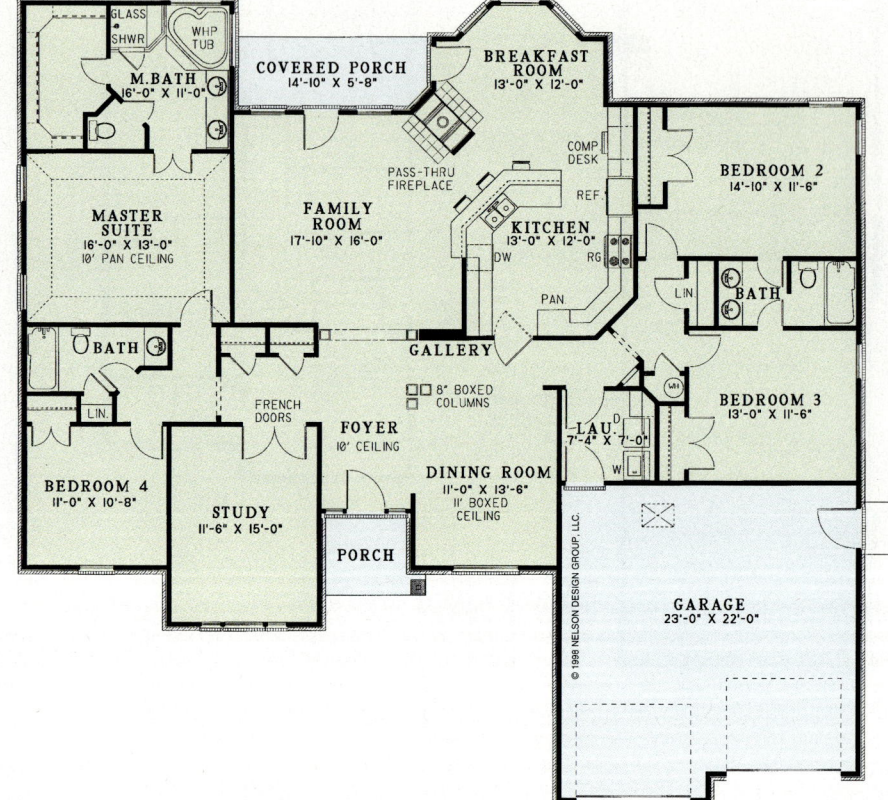

Casual sensibility intertwined with exciting angles defines this dazzling four-bedroom Nelson Design Group home. The impressive gallery demands attention with its French door entry into the large study and boxed columns detailing the formal dining room and family room. The openness of the pass-through fireplace merging with the spacious kitchen and sunny breakfast room promotes a cozy and casual atmosphere ideal for family fun and entertainment. A large master suite includes wonderful amenities.

Width: 65' 8"
Depth: 61' 7"
Total Living: 2,439 sq. ft.

Price Tier: C

Main Ceiling: 9 ft.
Bedrooms: 4
Baths: 3
Foundation: Crawl, Slab, Basement, Daylight Basement

128 Cherry Street

Capture the true essence of tradition in this Nelson Design Group home. Entering the home, you'll notice the attractive French doors opening to the study with an inviting private patio that is the perfect niche to finish that novel. While preparing dinner in your spacious kitchen, you can keep a close eye on the kids completing their homework in the convenient computer center. Dads will enjoy the rear covered porch accessible from several rooms. After the kids are tucked away, escape to your master suite with whirlpool bath.

Width: 67' 0"
Depth: 66' 0"
Total Living: 2,444 sq. ft.

Price Tier: C

Main Ceiling: 9 ft.
Bedrooms: 3
Baths: 2 1/2
Foundation: Crawl, Slab, Basement, Daylight Basement

To view similar plans visit www.84lumber.com/ndgplans - 800.359.8484

152 Richmond Drive

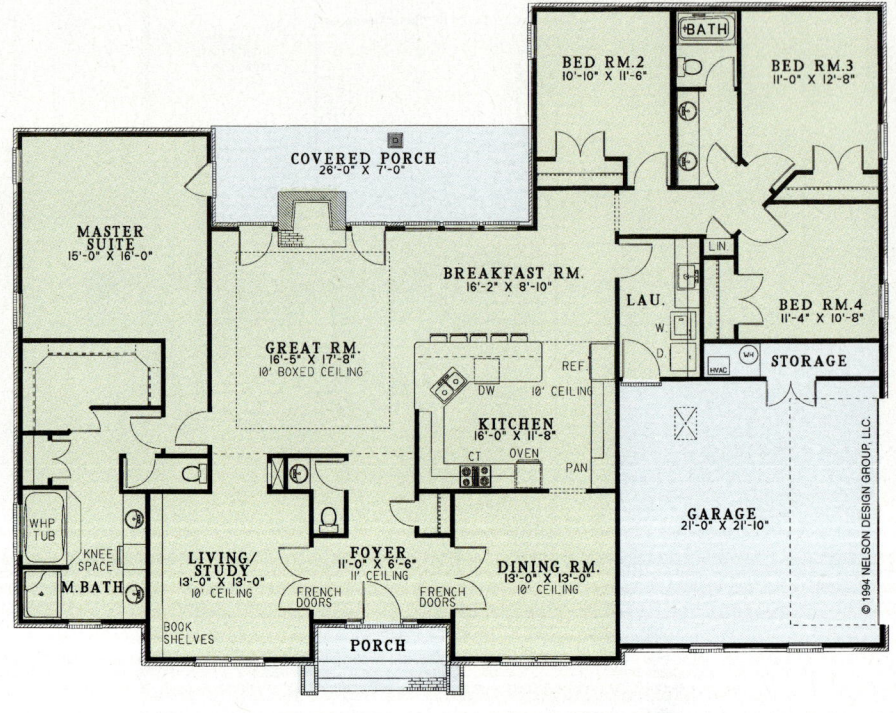

Nelson Design Group set the standard for homes to follow with the neo-traditional look of this all brick, four-bedroom design. Dramatic French doors flank the foyer leading to the formal dining and living rooms. With a wall of built-in bookshelves, the living room could easily serve as a study or library. The magnificent great room harbors a stunning fireplace nestled between twin doors leading to a sprawling covered porch. A superb breakfast room is the perfect accent to the spacious kitchen with its functional eat-at bar.

Width: 70' 0"
Depth: 51' 10"
Total Living: 2,444 sq. ft.

Price Tier: C

Main Ceiling: 9 ft.
Bedrooms: 4
Baths: 2 1/2
Foundation: Crawl, Slab, Opt. Basement, Opt. Daylight Basement

To view similar plans visit www.84lumber.com/ndgplans - 800.359.8484

Main Floor

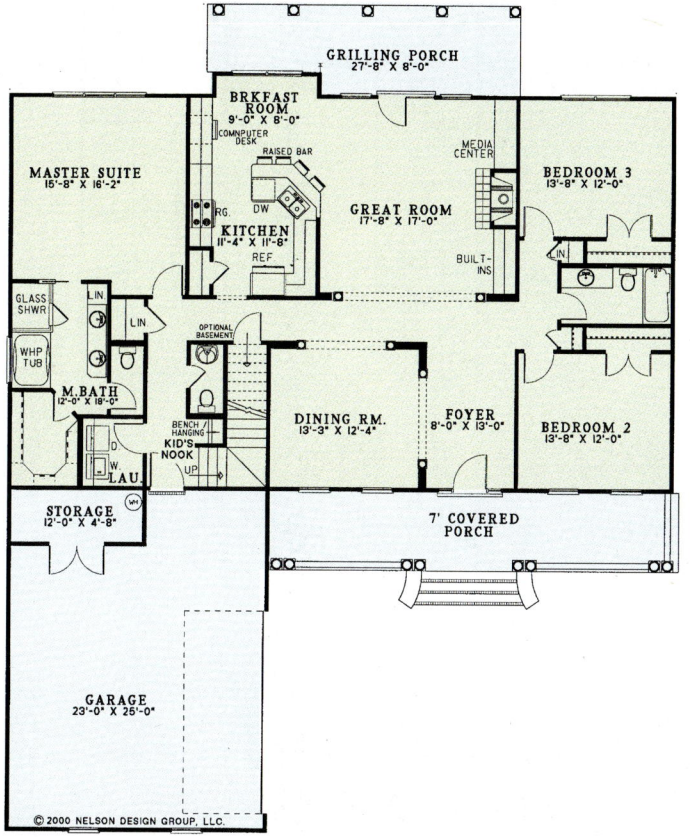

Upper Floor

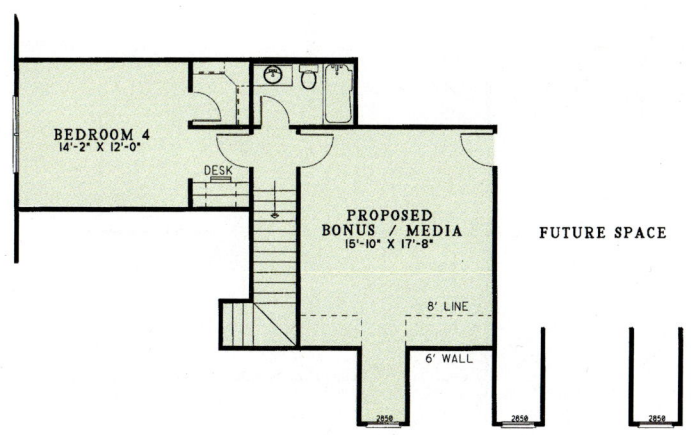

542 Glendale Avenue

Graceful country charm is highlighted in this Nelson Design Group home with its twin-columns, wonderful front porch and triple dormers. The children will be able to find their stuff with the handy kid's nook that provides bench and bin storage along with overhead hooks for coats and backpacks. The great room is sure to be the center of attention with a nifty fireplace nestled among the built-in media center and bookshelves. The functional raised bar distinguishes the kitchen from the adjoining breakfast room.

Width: 60' 0"
Depth: 73' 6"
Main Floor: 2,129 sq. ft.
Upper Floor: 316 sq. ft.
Total Living: 2,445 sq. ft.*
*Optional Bonus: 330 sq. ft.

Main Ceiling: 9 ft.
Upper Ceiling: 8 ft.
Bedrooms: 4
Baths: 3 1/2
Foundation: Crawl, Slab, Opt. Basement, Opt. Daylight Basement

Price Tier: C

To view similar plans visit www.84lumber.com/ndgplans - 800.359.8484

123 Canal Pointe

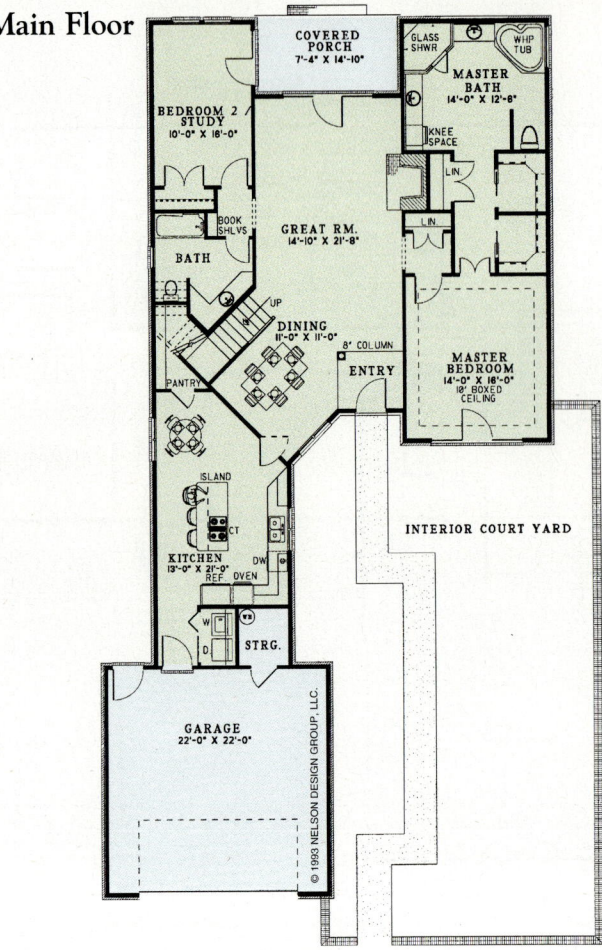

Main Floor

Upper Floor

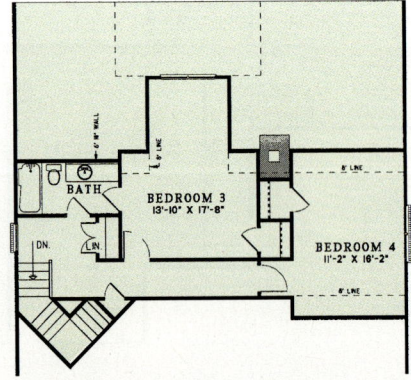

Nelson Design Group showcases a private courtyard and exciting floor plan in this one-of-a-kind design. The lavish courtyard holds endless options for the landscape enthusiast of the family. Inside, everyone can gather around the great room's central fireplace before heading to the angled dining room. The walk-through kitchen's exciting angles makes use of all available space and features a functional eat-at island. The spectacular master suite includes a window-laden private entrance to the courtyard, matching walk-in closets and a corner whirlpool tub.

Width: 50' 0"
Depth: 91' 6"
Main Floor: 1,820 sq. ft.
Upper Floor: 649 sq. ft.
Total Living: 2,469 sq. ft.

Main Ceiling: 9 ft.
Upper Ceiling: 8 ft.
Bedrooms: 4
Baths: 3
Foundation: Crawl, Slab

Price Tier: C

To view similar plans visit www.84lumber.com/ndgplans - 800.359.8484

546 Willow Lane

Main Floor

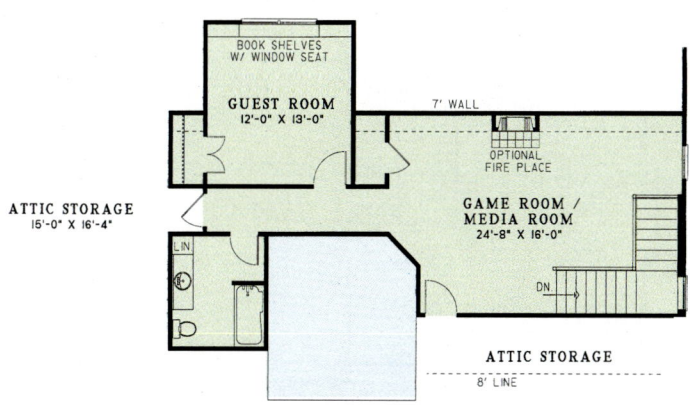

Upper Floor

This cozy Nelson Design Group home creates a warm invitation throughout starting with a lovely covered porch with columns, railing and a ten-foot ceiling. Upon entering the foyer, you can enter either the great room or luxurious column-lined dining room. The master suite and bedrooms are located on one side of the home apart from the living areas for privacy. One bedroom is located at the rear of the home as a secluded guest or teenager's room. A cozy hearth room adjoins the open kitchen and breakfast room with access to the rear-grilling porch, making for great entertaining options. Nearby stairs lead up to an additional guest room or home office, a game/media room with fireplace and a full bathroom.

Width: 66' 10"
Depth: 73' 4"
Total Living: 2,379 sq. ft.*
*Optional Bonus: 754 sq. ft.

Main Ceiling: 9 ft.
Upper Ceiling: 8 ft.
Bedrooms: 5
Baths: 4
Foundation: Crawl, Slab, Opt. Basement, Opt. Daylight Basement

Price Tier: C

To view similar plans visit www.84lumber.com/ndgplans - 800.359.8484

479 Willow Lane

Main Floor

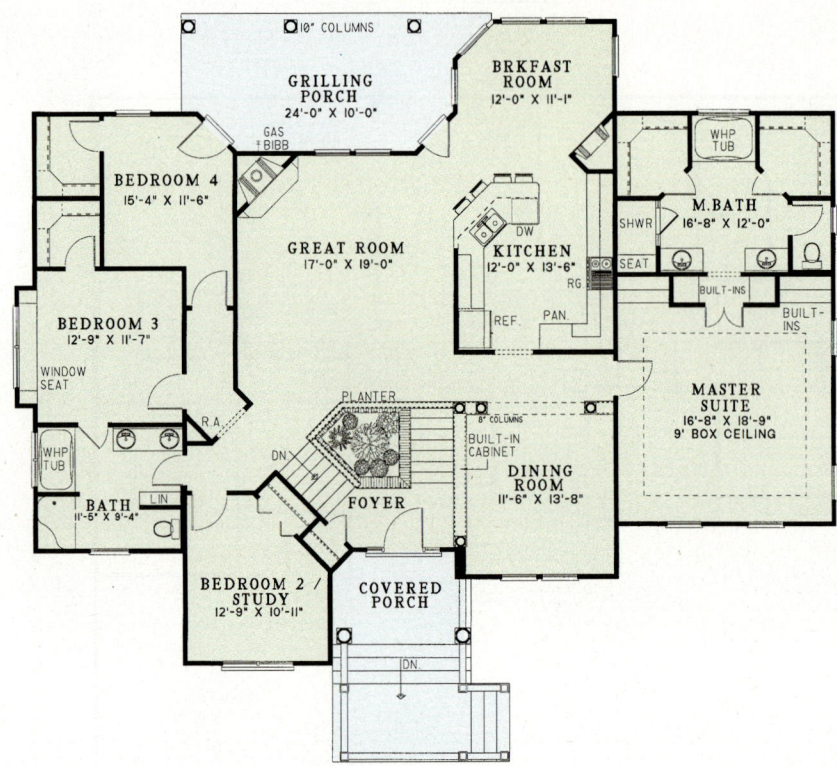

Lower Floor

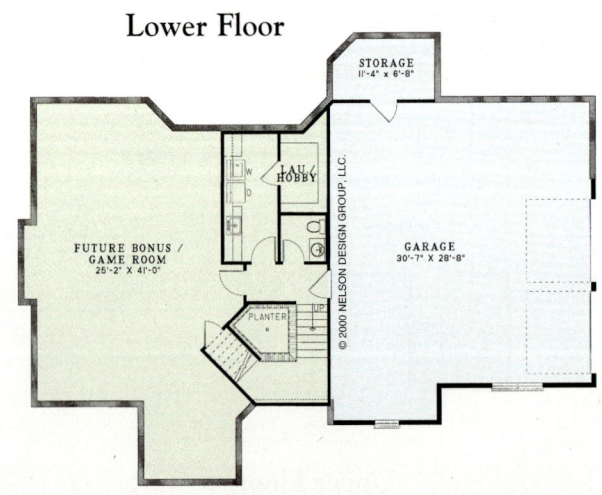

This trendy Nelson Design Group home with its mutiple-material exterior is equally suited for formal business entertaining or the casual excitement of a family get together. Greeted by the lovely planter, one can't help but notice the warm, comfortable feeling generated by the corner fireplace and how the great room flows effortlessly into the breakfast room and kitchen. Any overnight guests will enjoy bedroom details such as an extended window seat, walk-in closets and a bath rivaling many master baths. A glorious master suite includes an entire wall of built-ins surrounding elegant French door entry into the deluxe bath.

Width: 64' 0"
Depth: 49' 4"
Main Floor: 2,249 sq. ft.
Lower Floor: 246 sq. ft.
Total Living: 2,495 sq. ft.

Main Ceiling: 9 ft.
Lower Ceiling: 8 ft.
Bedrooms: 4
Baths: 2 1/2
Foundation: Daylight Basement

Price Tier: C

To view similar plans visit www.84lumber.com/ndgplans - 800.359.8484

118-1 Country Club Drive

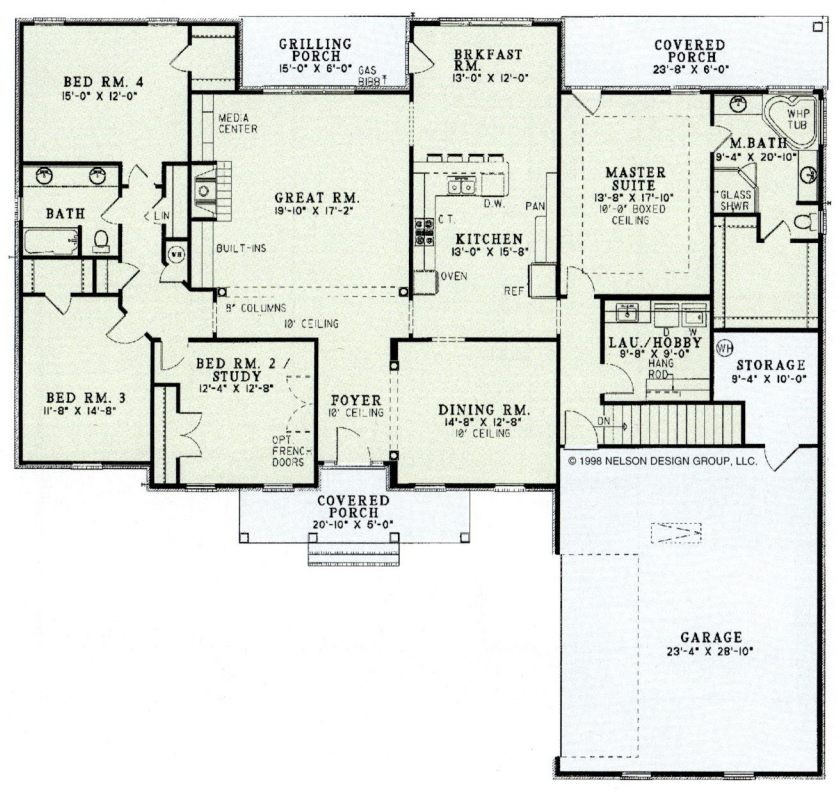

The dignified exterior of this Nelson Design Group home conceals an exciting floor plan and surprising detail that waits inside. The extended foyer opens into a sprawling great room with a fireplace anchoring a wall filled with built-in bookshelves and media center. The cozy breakfast room allows casual dining as well as swift access to the grilling porch and adjoining kitchen for seconds. Settling in for the night is a breeze with your own private covered porch and extraordinary corner whirlpool tub.

Width: 72' 10"
Depth: 67' 0"
Total Living: 2,502 sq. ft.

Price Tier: D

Main Ceiling: 9 ft.
Bedrooms: 4
Baths: 2
Foundation: Crawl, Slab, Basement, Daylight Basement

184 Kensington Cove

Substantial windows with half-round transoms flank a beautiful arched entry to this symmetrical plan from Nelson Design Group. Dividing the formal living and dining areas are exquisite columns and an extended foyer with a shared 12' ceiling. Through the oversized archway, a splendid, grandiose fireplace is centered between built-in media center and bookshelves. Where better to enjoy the splendid days of fall than the significant sun room adjacent to the great room. The second fireplace in the breakfast/hearth room will remove the chill while reading the morning paper.

Width: 63' 4"
Depth: 59' 10"
Total Living: 2,525 sq. ft.

Price Tier: D

Main Ceiling: 9 ft.
Bedrooms: 3
Baths: 2 1/2
Foundation: Crawl, Slab, Basement, Daylight Basement

Check This Plan Mike

371 Dogwood Avenue

Welcome your guests in the warm foyer of this Nelson Design Group home before leading them into the impressive dining room with magnificent columns framing the entry. After dinner, your guest will enjoy conversation in the spacious great room complete with fireplace and built-ins. Beautiful French doors open to the quiet study where you'll be able to concentrate on that work away from the office. The rear porch is attainable through the breakfast room and your secluded master suite. The children and guests can enjoy their own privacy with this split bedroom design.

Width: 70' 4"
Depth: 57' 2"
Total Living: 2,534 sq. ft.

Price Tier: D

Main Ceiling: 9 ft.
Bedrooms: 3
Baths: 2
Foundation: Crawl, Slab

To view similar plans visit www.84lumber.com/ndgplans - 800.359.8484

249-1 Kensington Cove

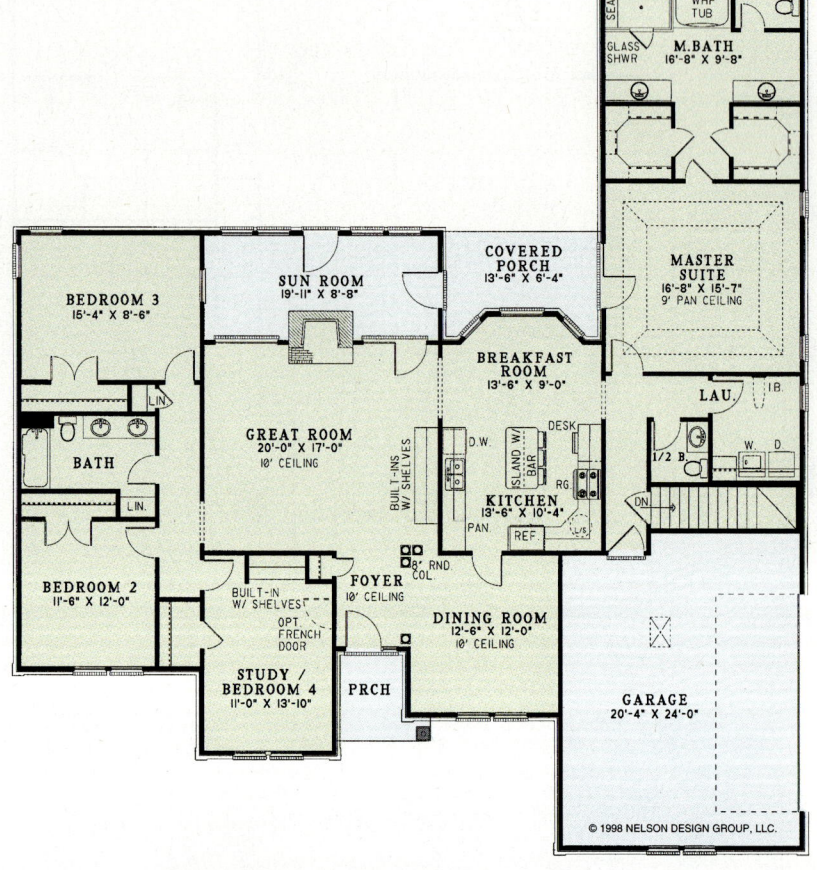

This enchanting Nelson Design Group home is well-suited for entertaining as well as relaxing. Guests are free to mingle in the voluminous great room warmed by the radiant fireplace. Afterwards they can continue out into the sun room via the French door as they comment on the exquisite detailing of the gourmet kitchen. Enjoy coffee while sitting by the bay-windowed breakfast room watching the sunrise. The master wing includes stylish detailing such as a private porch entrance, dual walk-in closets and a large bath with a large whirlpool tub and separate glass shower.

Width: 67' 2"
Depth: 71' 8"
Total Living: 2,537 sq. ft.

Price Tier: D

Main Ceiling: 9 ft.
Bedrooms: 4
Baths: 2 1/2
Foundation: Crawl, Slab, Basement, Daylight Basement

To view similar plans visit www.84lumber.com/ndgplans - 800.359.8484

366 Kensington Cove

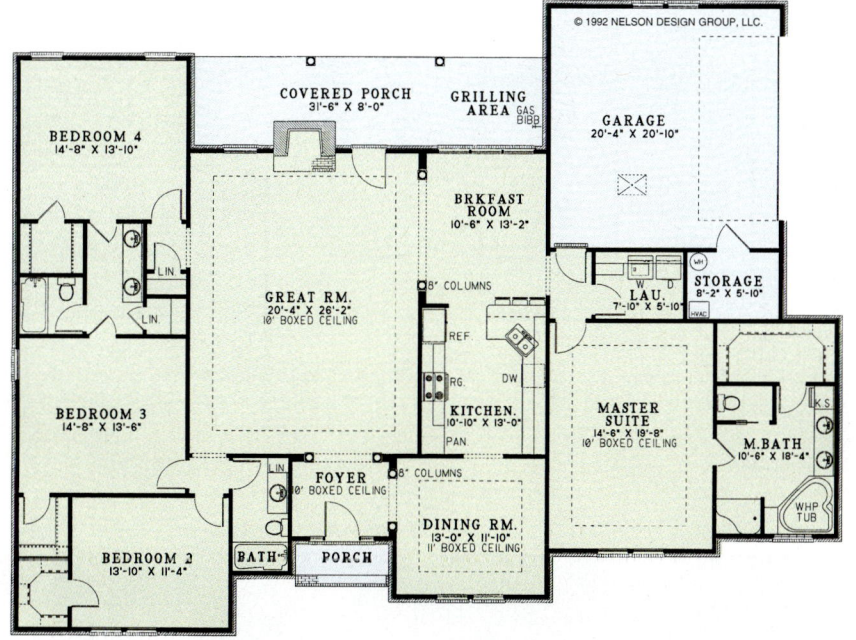

Decorative quoins and a smooth, hip roofline highlight the sleek exterior of this split-bedroom Nelson Design Group home. There is room for gatherings both large and small around the fireplace of the enormous great room or everyone can lounge on the expansive covered back porch. The sheltered grilling area allows outdoor grilling during inclimate weather. Storage will not pose any difficulty as all four bedrooms enjoy spacious walk-in closets.

Width: 72' 10"
Depth: 54' 8"
Total Living: 2,540 sq. ft.

Main Ceiling: 9 ft.
Bedrooms: 4
Baths: 3
Foundation: Crawl, Slab

Price Tier: D

To view similar plans visit www.84lumber.com/ndgplans - 800.359.8484

392 Country Club Drive

Elevation A

Elevation B

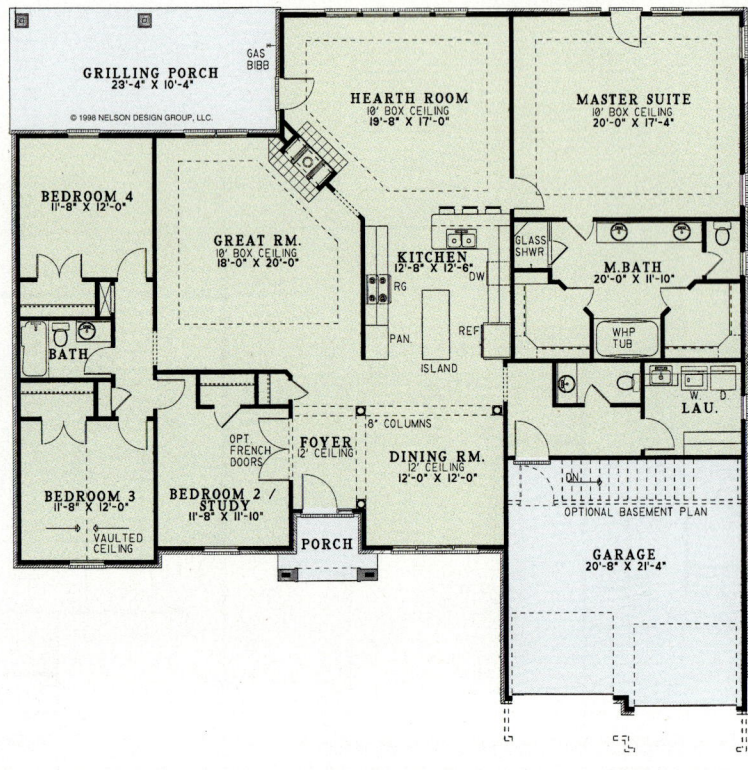

This four-bedroom Nelson Design Group home boasts a beautiful arched entry and choice of two exciting exteriors. Once inside, guests will appreciate the lavish columns offsetting the formal dining room and optional sleek French doors to the study. Boxed ceilings throughout enhance the open floor plan. A pass-through fireplace between the great room and hearth room extends class and elegance to this neo-traditional home. The large walk-through kitchen allows unimpeded access to all living areas of the house.

Width: 64' 0"
Depth: 60' 2"
Total Living: 2,554 sq. ft.

Price Tier: D

Main Ceiling: 9 ft.
Bedrooms: 4
Baths: 2 1/2
Foundation: Crawl, Slab, Opt. Basement, Opt. Daylight Basement

To view similar plans visit www.84lumber.com/ndgplans - 800.359.8484

465 Brandon Circle

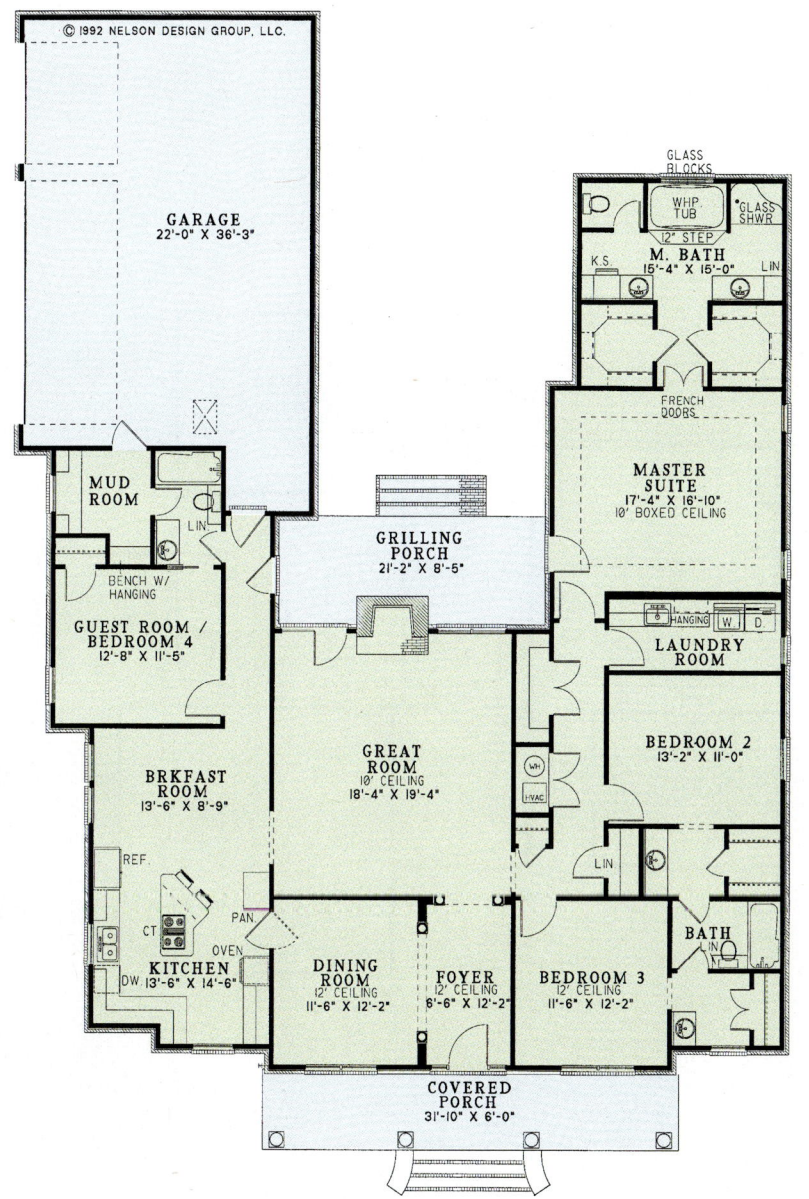

Steeped rooflines and a stately porch bid you welcome to this graceful Nelson Design Group home. Entertain by the richly appointed fireplace or relax on the grilling porch while final food preparations are made. Parents and kids alike will appreciate the much-needed private bath entrances in all four bedrooms provide. Open the door from the master suite to the grilling porch for a refreshing breeze while soaking in the raised whirlpool tub.

Width: 58' 10"
Depth: 77' 9"
Total Living: 2,555 sq. ft.

Price Tier: D

Main Ceiling: 9 ft.
Bedrooms: 4
Baths: 3
Foundation: Crawl, Slab, Opt. Basement, Opt. Daylight Basement

To view similar plans visit www.84lumber.com/ndgplans - 800.359.8484

235

156 Country Club Drive

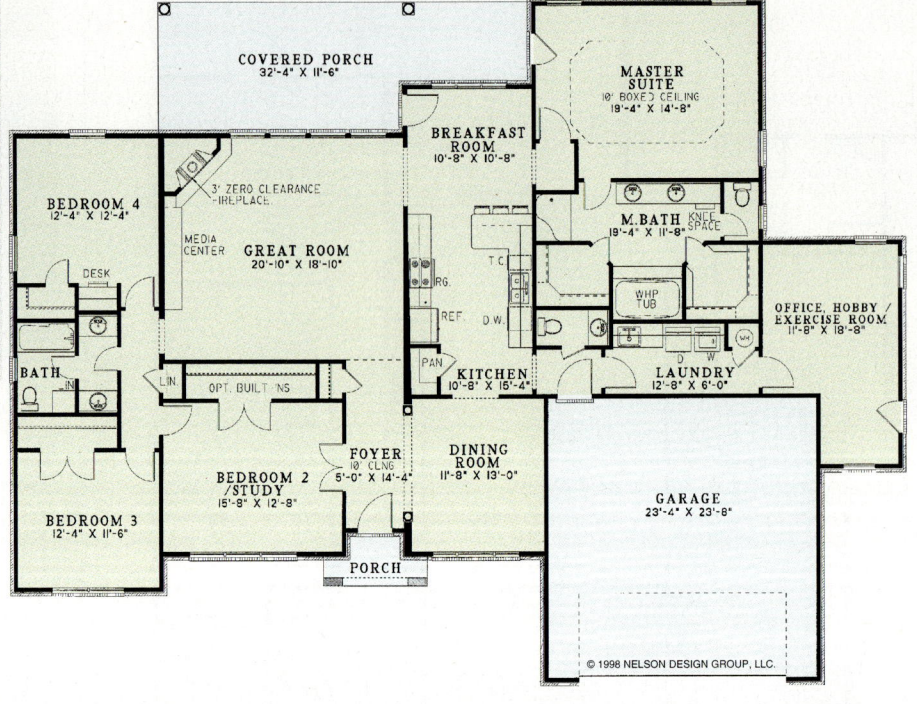

This magnificent home by Nelson Design Group has a split bedroom design with amenities galore. An arched entry welcomes you into a foyer with ten foot ceiling and through to a great room with built-in media center and corner fireplace. The master suite is enhanced by a ten foot boxed ceiling and accesses the covered porch. The master bathroom features a double vanity, separate shower and a whirlpool tub surrounded by his' and her' walk-in closets. The laundry room accesses either an exercise room or home office depending on your need. On the opposite side of the home are three additional bedrooms - one perfect for a study with optional built-in and French doors.

Width: 77' 0"
Depth: 57' 8"
Total Living: 2,582 sq. ft.

Price Tier: D

Main Ceiling: 9 ft.
Bedrooms: 4
Baths: 2 1/2
Foundation: Crawl, Slab, Opt. Basement, Opt. Daylight Basement

To view similar plans visit www.84lumber.com/ndgplans - 800.359.8484

Main Floor

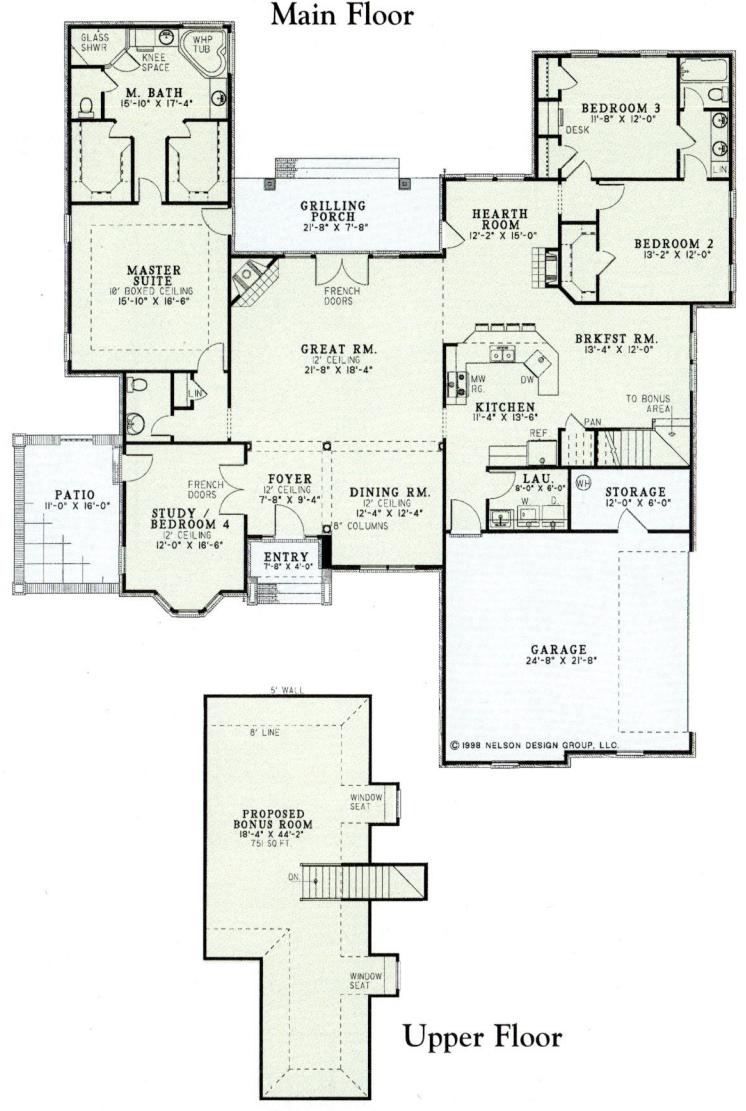

Upper Floor

380 Cherry Street

T his stately Nelson Design Group plan will be the talk of the neighborhood. The column lined foyer and dining room view an open great room with french door access to the rear grilling porch. This split bedroom floor plan allows two bedrooms both accessing a full bath off the hearth room - perfect for weekend guests. The kitchen/breakfast room can seat many and kids can enjoy the upstairs bonus area. A master suite full to the brim with amenities awaits the head of the house after working in the study on that special project.

Width: 67' 6"
Depth: 73' 10"
Total Living: 2,606 sq. ft.*
*Optional Bonus: 751 sq. ft.

Main Ceiling: 9 ft.
Upper Ceiling: 8 ft.
Bedrooms: 4
Baths: 2 1/2
Foundation: Crawl, Slab, Basement, Daylight Basement

Price Tier: D

502 Willow Lane

Main Floor

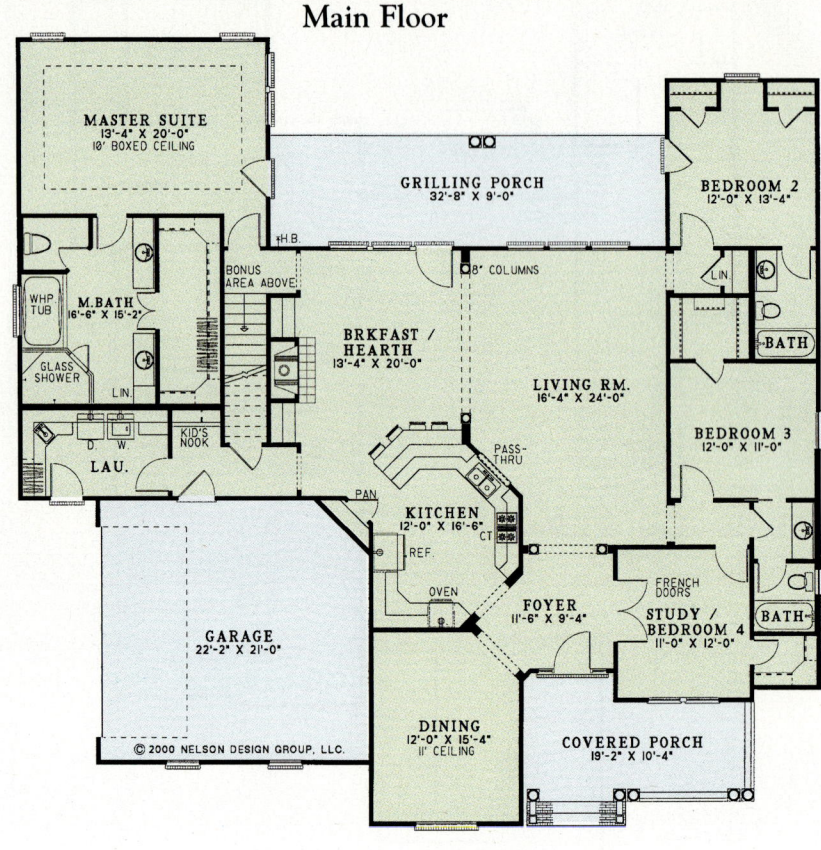

Upper Floor

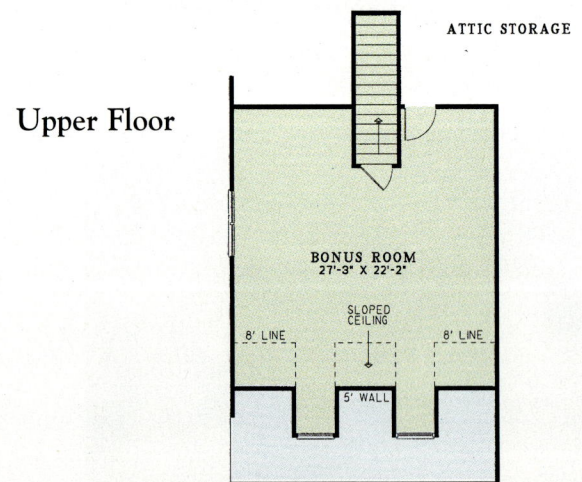

Don't be fooled by the traditional country appearance of this Nelson Design Group home. Inside you'll find exciting angles, a unique use of available space and enough open area to host the little league team dinner. Coming in from the garage, the kids have their very own nook to keep track of their stuff. The uniquely-designed kitchen is capable of serving any living area in the house, including the nearby grilling porch. The fireplace in the hearth room is centrally located so it also warms the living room. Walk-in closets accompany all four bedrooms while two of the three secondary bedrooms boast private bathroom entrances as well.

Width: 66' 4"
Depth: 64' 0"
Total Living: 2,624 sq. ft.*
*Optional Bonus: 561 sq. ft.

Price Tier: D

Main Ceiling: 9 ft.
Upper Ceiling: 8 ft.
Bedrooms: 4
Baths: 3
Foundation: Crawl, Slab, Opt. Basement, Opt. Daylight Basement

Main Floor

Upper Floor

Check This Plan Mike

111 Olive Street

L azy summer afternoons will find you in the rocking chair on the front porch of this Nelson Design Group home. The chef of the family will discover the usefulness of all the amenities available in the gourmet kitchen with a large walk-in pantry conveniently located for easy access. Your expansive master suite includes 'his and her' walk-in closets and a calming whirlpool bath to ease your worries away. The children will discover clever uses for their charming window seats and will also be able to see what is going on downstairs peaking over the balcony to below.

Width: 70' 2"	Main Ceiling: 9 ft.
Depth: 51' 4"	Upper Ceiling: 9 ft.
Main Floor: 1,813 sq. ft.	Bedrooms: 5
Upper Floor: 885 sq. ft.	Baths: 3
Total Living: 2,698 sq. ft.	Foundation: Crawl, Slab, Basement, Daylight Basement

Price Tier: D

To view similar plans visit www.84lumber.com/ndgplans - 800.359.8484

209 Olive Street

Main Floor

Check This Plan Mike

Memories will be cherished forever in this southern traditional Nelson Design Group home. Receive your dinner guests in the open foyer before seating them in the beautiful dining room. The children will enjoy the amenities in their rooms such as walk-in closets, built-in desks, and private baths that will alleviate morning chaos over equal bath time. You will enjoy amenities such as an atrium door to the rear porch for moonlight talks, 'his and her' walk-in closets, and a gorgeous whirlpool bath with glass blocks for enhanced lighting and privacy.

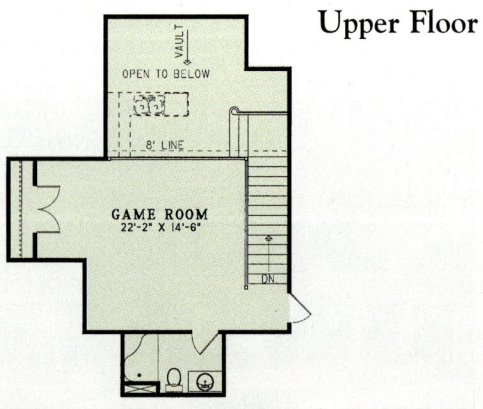

Upper Floor

Width: 69' 0"
Depth: 69' 10"
Main Floor: 2,352 sq. ft.
Upper Floor: 349 sq. ft.
Total Living: 2,701 sq. ft.

Main Ceiling: 9 ft.
Upper Ceiling: 8 ft.
Bedrooms: 3
Baths: 4 1/2
Foundation: Crawl, Slab, Basement, Daylight Basement

Price Tier: D

To view similar plans visit www.84lumber.com/ndgplans - 800.359.8484

327 Willow Lane

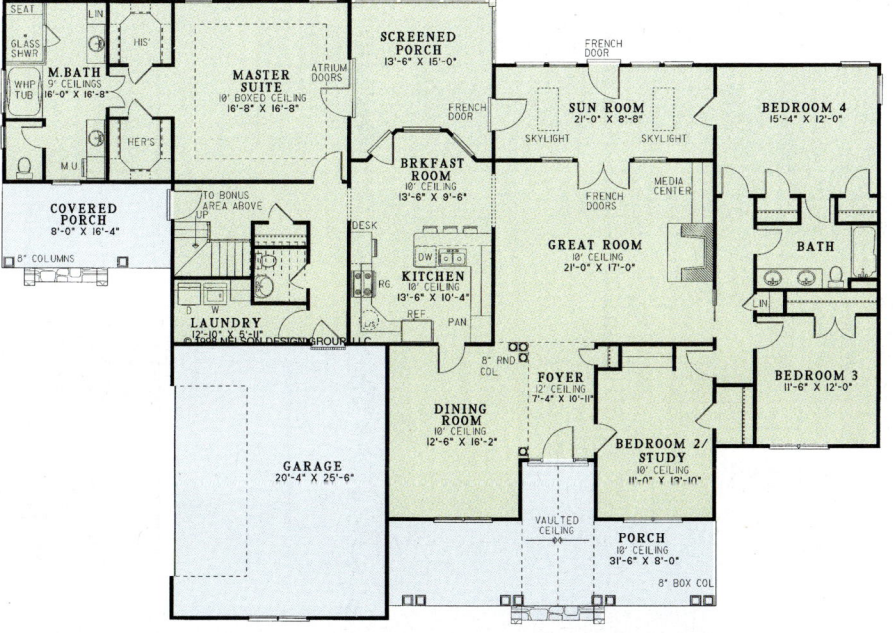

A splendid arched entry accented with elegant dual columns and flanked by charming dormers meshes cleanly with the smooth stucco and rock exterior of this Nelson Design Group offering. The sun room demands attention with its elegant French door entries, twin sky lights and quick access to three distinct areas of the home and the back yard. The screened porch is sure to be a hit with the beautiful atrium doors leading to the master suite and adjacent placement next to the kitchen.

Width: 84' 6"
Depth: 58' 6"
Total Living: 2,742 sq. ft.

Price Tier: D

Main Ceiling: 9 ft.
Bedrooms: 4
Baths: 2 1/2
Foundation: Crawl, Slab, Basement, Daylight Basement

372 Richmond Lane

Elevation A

Elevation B

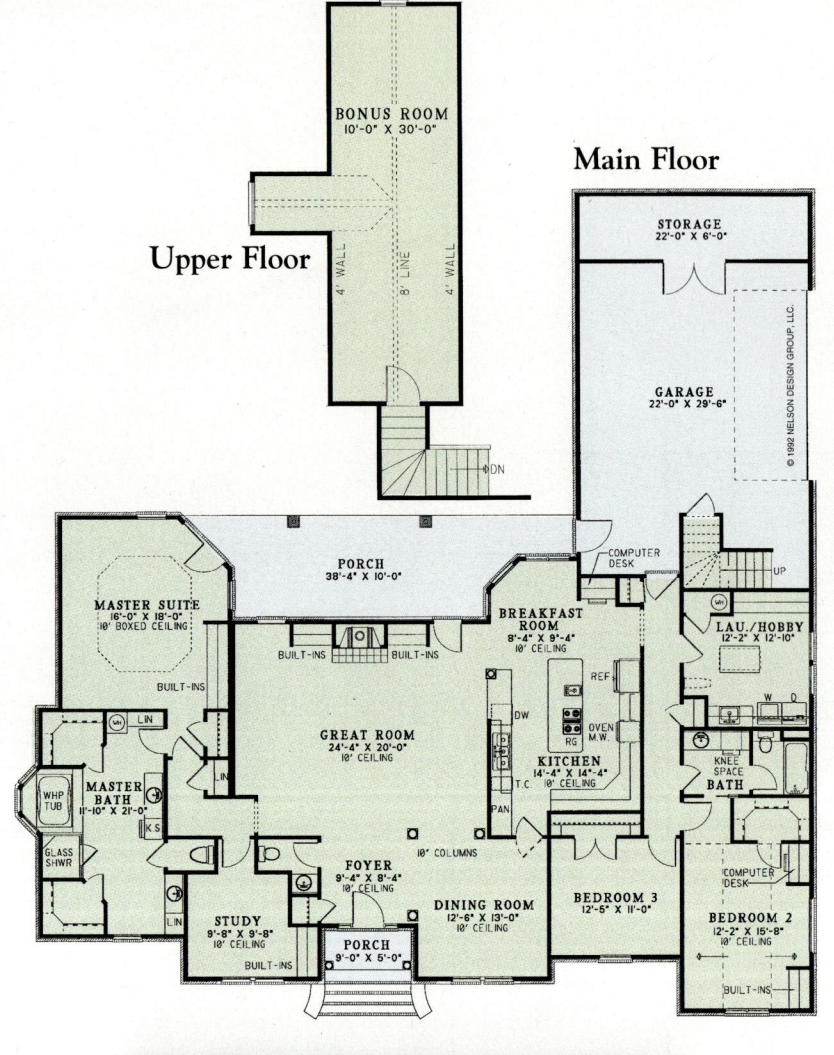

Upper Floor

Main Floor

Nelson Design Group created a home for the ages with the fine detailing of the master bedroom in this lavish home. The elaborate master suite presents an entire wall of built-ins along with an angled private entrance to the porch. A fireplace nicely settled between built-ins punctuates the enormous great room. The open styling beckons guests to roam and mingle. The oversized hobby room offers space galore for those do-it-yourself home projects.

Width: 76' 8"
Depth: 77' 7"
Total Living: 2,742 sq. ft.*
*Optional Bonus: 352 sq. ft.

Price Tier: D

Main Ceiling: 9 ft.
Upper Ceiling: 8 ft.
Bedrooms: 3
Baths: 2 1/2
Foundation: Crawl, Slab

To view similar plans visit www.84lumber.com/ndgplans - 800.359.8484

348 Willow Lane

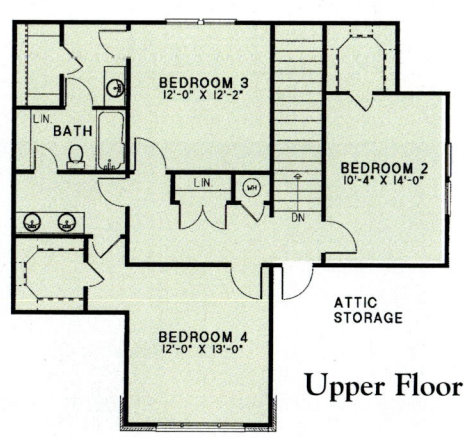

Main Floor

Upper Floor

The stately exterior of this Nelson Design Group home opens to a spacious and well-organized interior. The foyer, highlighted by graceful columns, separates the formal living and dining areas. Built-in bookshelves and media center surround the great room's elegant fireplace. Stylish Atrium doors provide access to the grilling porch where the family chef prepares the night's cuisine. Privacy is not an issue as all three secondary bedrooms offer walk-in closets and private bath entrances.

Width: 54' 2"
Depth: 73' 6"
Main Floor: 1,895 sq. ft.
Upper Floor: 889 sq. ft.
Total Living: 2,784 sq. ft.

Main Ceiling: 9 ft.
Upper Ceiling: 8 ft.
Bedrooms: 4
Baths: 2 1/2
Foundation: Crawl, Slab, Basement, Daylight Basement

Price Tier: D

129-3 Olive Street

Main Floor

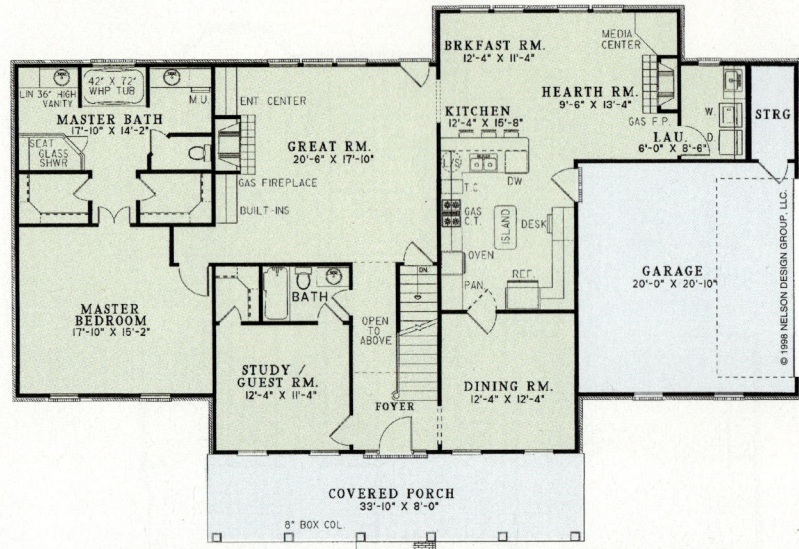

Upper Floor

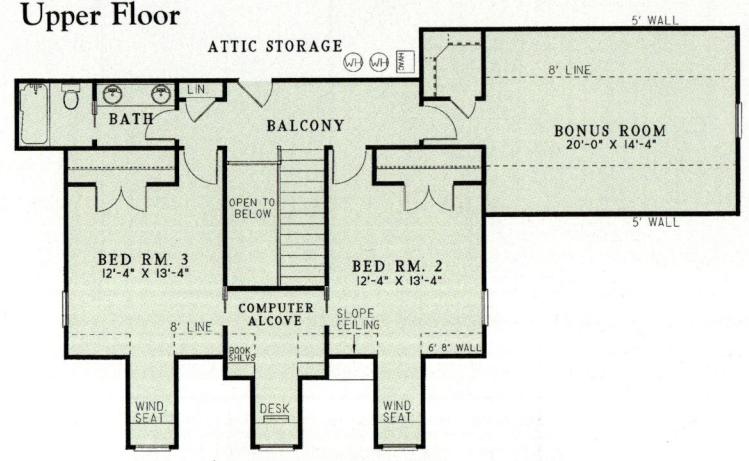

Picture yourself welcoming friends and family to Sunday dinner in this Nelson Design Group home. There will be plenty of room for buffet in your spacious kitchen with a hearth room and breakfast room. Afterwards, you can watch the ballgame in your great room with fireplace. Overnight guests will appreciate the convenient private bath available to them. Your secluded master bath includes marvelous 'his and her' walk-in closets and relaxing whirlpool bath. Upstairs, the unique computer alcove allows the children to finish their school projects with ease.

Width: 72' 4"
Depth: 48' 4"
Main Floor: 1,977 sq. ft.
Upper Floor: 812 sq. ft.
Total Living: 2,789 sq. ft.*
*Optional Bonus: 306 sq. ft.

Main Ceiling: 9 ft.
Upper Ceiling: 8 ft.
Bedrooms: 4
Baths: 3
Foundation: Crawl, Slab, Basement, Daylight Basement

Price Tier: D

To view similar plans visit www.84lumber.com/ndgplans - 800.359.8484

Main Floor

Upper Floor

434 Dogwood Avenue

Check This Plan Mike

The unmatched curb appeal of this spacious Nelson Design Group home showcases a covered, arched entry, beautiful bay window and multiple gables as part of an eye-catching exterior. Inside, the great room is located at the rear of the house, blending with the breakfast room and kitchen. A snack bar, fireplace, wide window seat and built-ins make this a special family gathering place. Also included are three elegant bedroom suites so there is no squabbling over shared bathroom time. Upstairs you'll find a centrally located computer center providing a great place for homework.

Width: 59' 0"	Main Ceiling: 9 ft.
Depth: 73' 0"	Upper Ceiling: 8 ft.
Main Floor: 2,126 sq. ft.	Bedrooms: 3
Upper Floor: 823 sq. ft.	Baths: 3 1/2
Total Living: 2,949 sq. ft.*	Foundation: Crawl, Slab, Opt. Basement,
*Optional Bonus: 442 sq. ft.	Opt. Daylight Basement

Price Tier: D

362 Cherry Street

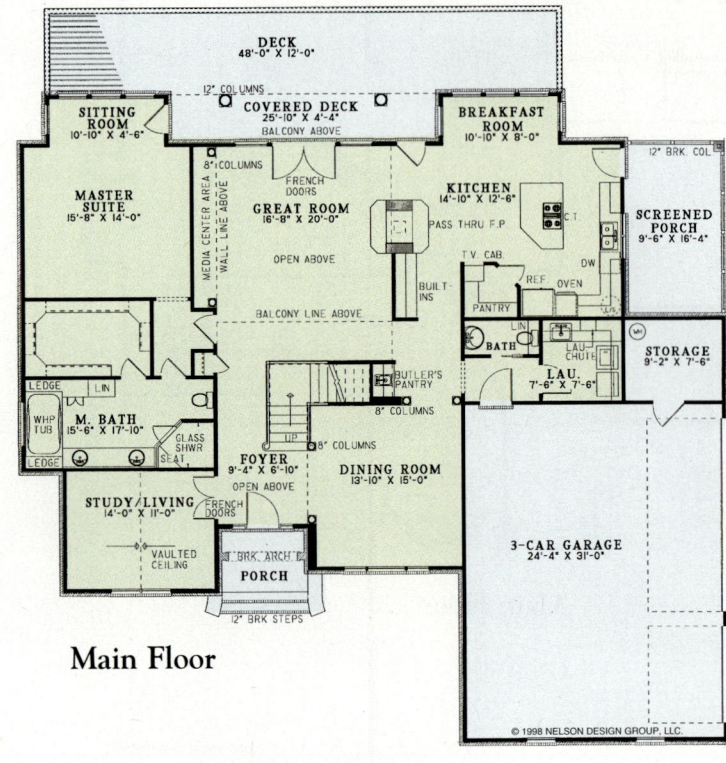

Main Floor

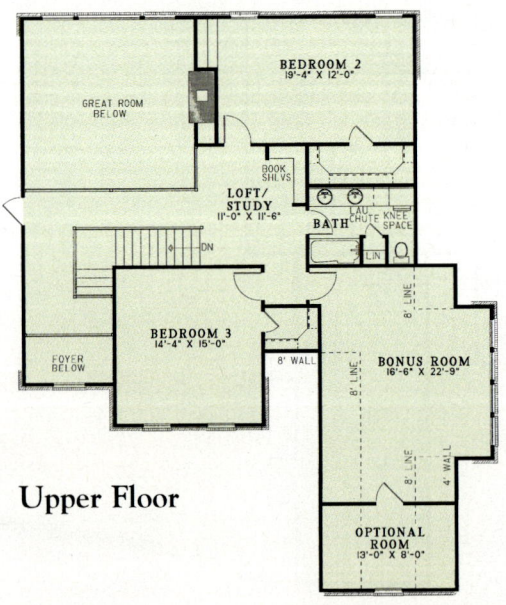

Upper Floor

Invite the family to your house for the holidays in this impressive Nelson Design Group split bedroom home. Enticing French doors open to your private study. A comfortable great room displays a distinctive fireplace that is shared with the kitchen. You can utilize the side screened porch as a convenient grilling porch. Slip off for the evening to your master suite with a sitting room that opens to the rear covered deck. On the upper floor, the childrens' rooms have spacious closets, and you have the opportunity for a home office and game room with the ample bonus and optional rooms available.

Width: 66' 8"
Depth: 60' 4"
Main Floor: 2,107 sq. ft.
Upper Floor: 1,001 sq. ft.
Total Living: 3,108 sq. ft.*
*Optional Bonus: 485 sq. ft.

Main Ceiling: 9 ft.
Upper Ceiling: 8 ft.
Bedrooms: 3
Baths: 2 1/2
Foundation: Crawl, Slab, Opt. Basement, Opt. Daylight Basement

Price Tier: E

To view similar plans visit www.84lumber.com/ndgplans - 800.359.8484

112 Sunset Drive

The double-door entry of this stylish Nelson Design Group home reveals sleek arches bordering the large formal dining room. The extensive grand room flows through the bay-windowed morning room into an elegant gathering room anchored by a majestic fireplace surrounded by built-in entertainment center and bookshelves. Interesting angles of the kitchen frame such fine accents as a double oven, built-in desk and functional island. Twin skylights provide a nice finishing touch to the extensive covered back porch. A finely detailed master suite includes a cozy sitting room, dual walk-in closets and an adjacent study.

Width: 70' 0"
Depth: 88' 2"
Total Living: 3,124 sq. ft.

Main Ceiling: 9 ft.
Bedrooms: 4
Baths: 3 1/2
Foundation: Crawl, Slab

Price Tier: E

375 Brandon Circle

Main Floor

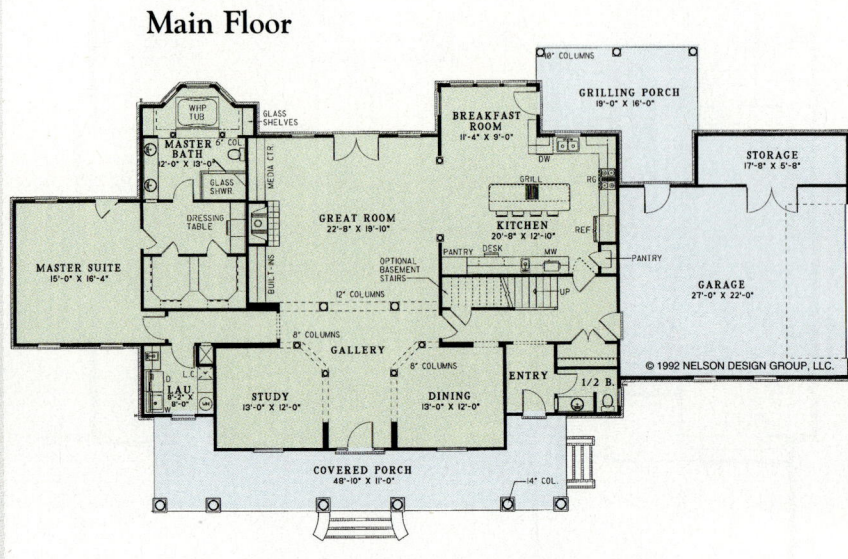

Upper Floor

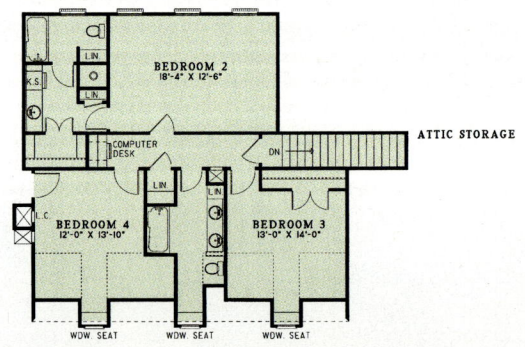

Nelson Design Group accented this traditional country-styled home by including stately interior columns throughout. The wide-open area of the main floor gives holiday guests room to maneuver. The great room features a built-in media center and bookshelves surrounding a radiant fireplace and blends nicely with a large kitchen and breakfast room combination. The utilitarian kitchen offers a desk, an island with a built-in grill, and swinging door access to the gallery. An elegant master bath includes a columned entrance to the whirlpool tub located in a beautiful bay window. Three window seats and a centrally located computer desk highlight the secondary bedrooms upstairs.

Width: 99' 4"
Depth: 53' 10"
Main Floor: 2,396 sq. ft.
Upper Floor: 799 sq. ft.
Total Living: 3,195 sq. ft.

Main Ceiling: 9 ft.
Upper Ceiling: 8 ft.
Bedrooms: 4
Baths: 3 1/2
Foundation: Crawl, Slab, Basement, Daylight Basement

Price Tier: E

376 Brandon Circle

Main Floor

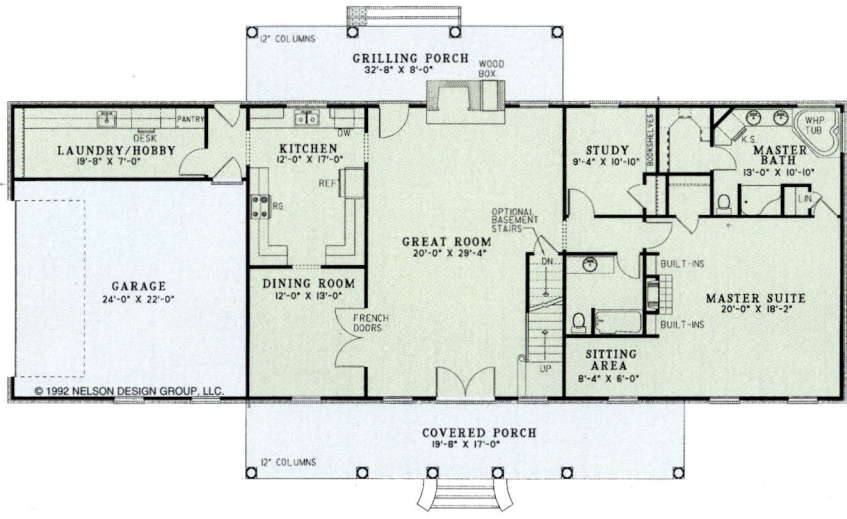

Upper Floor

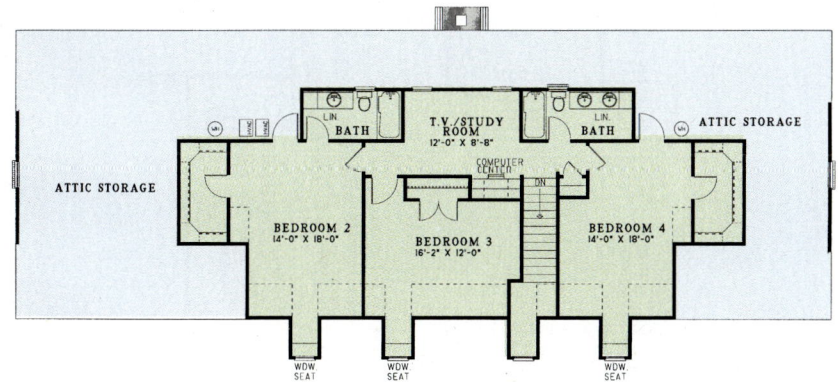

Elevation A

Elevation B

Fine detailing, such as French doors, multiple built-ins and a lavish fireplace in the master suite, fills this spacious Nelson Design Group home. The expansive great room centers around a wood-burning fireplace and access to the columned grilling porch. The extensive hobby room includes a desk and lots of storage space. The incredible master suite encompasses two baths, a fireplace, small sitting area and adjoining book-shelved study. Upstairs amenities feature three secondary bedrooms, a central study room with self-contained computer center and a massive amount of storage space.

Width: 86' 0"	Main Ceiling: 9 ft.
Depth: 46' 0"	Upper Ceiling: 8 ft.
Main Floor: 2,036 sq. ft.	Bedrooms: 4
Upper Floor: 1,181 sq. ft.	Baths: 4
Total Living: 3,217 sq. ft.	Foundation: Crawl, Slab, Opt. Basement, Opt. Daylight Basement

Price Tier: E

To view similar plans visit www.84lumber.com/ndgplans - 800.359.8484

151 Birchwood Lane

Main Floor

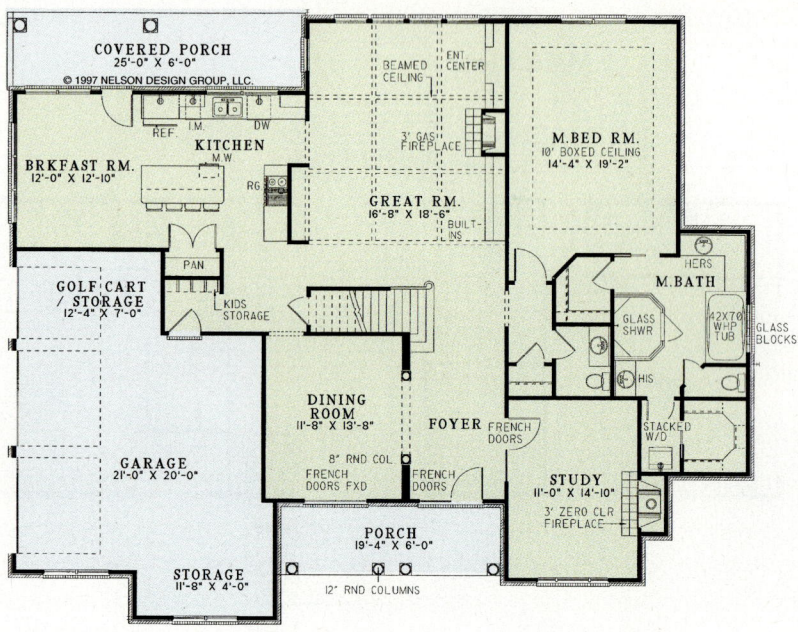

Upper Floor

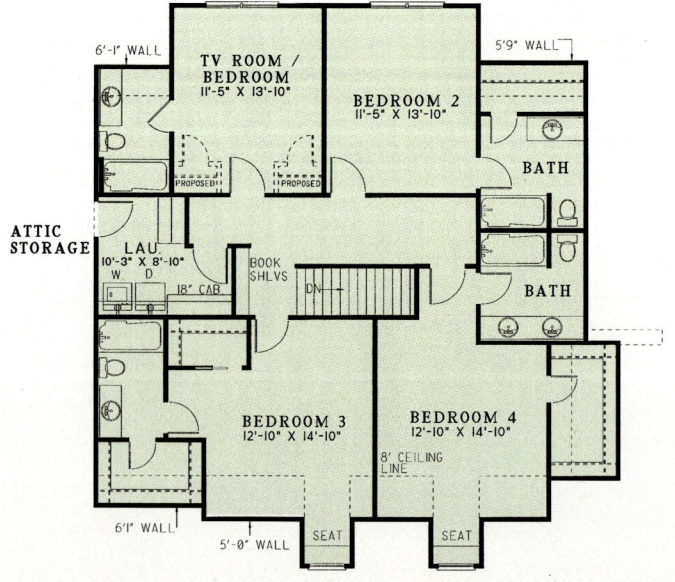

Amenities abound in this Nelson Design Group home. As you enter through the foyer, the dining room is set off by beautiful round columns and fixed French doors. The great room, a popular gathering place before any meal, has a fireplace and built-in media center. Preparing your cuisine is easy in the spacious kitchen with island bar and breakfast room with access to a convenient rear covered porch. You'll find your master bath complete with whirlpool tub, glass shower and 'his and her' walk-in closets. All of the upper bedrooms have their own private bathrooms.

Width: 63' 0"
Depth: 50' 4"
Main Floor: 1,974 sq. ft.
Upper Floor: 1,396 sq. ft.
Total Living: 3,370 sq. ft.

Main Ceiling: 9 ft.
Upper Ceiling: 8 ft.
Bedrooms: 5
Baths: 5 1/2
Foundation: Crawl, Slab, Basement, Daylight Basement

Price Tier: E

Main Floor

Upper Floor

222 Westwood Lane

Delight in the extravagant brick archways of this neo-traditional offering from Nelson Design group. The remarkable great room is brightly lit from the bank of windows on the far wall, highlighting the fireplace between the built-in media center and bookshelves. The breakfast room provides access to the covered porch and offers a smooth transition to the roomy kitchen featuring a large eat-at island. The master suite features a boxed ceiling with a romantic fireplace. Upstairs, an icemaker and refrigerator make entertaining in the game room a snap.

Width: 75' 2"	Main Ceiling: 9 ft.
Depth: 89' 6"	Upper Ceiling: 8 ft.
Main Floor: 2,633 sq. ft.	Bedrooms: 4
Upper Floor: 752 sq. ft.	Baths: 4
Total Living: 3,385 sq. ft.	Foundation: Crawl, Slab

Price Tier: E

147 Olive Street

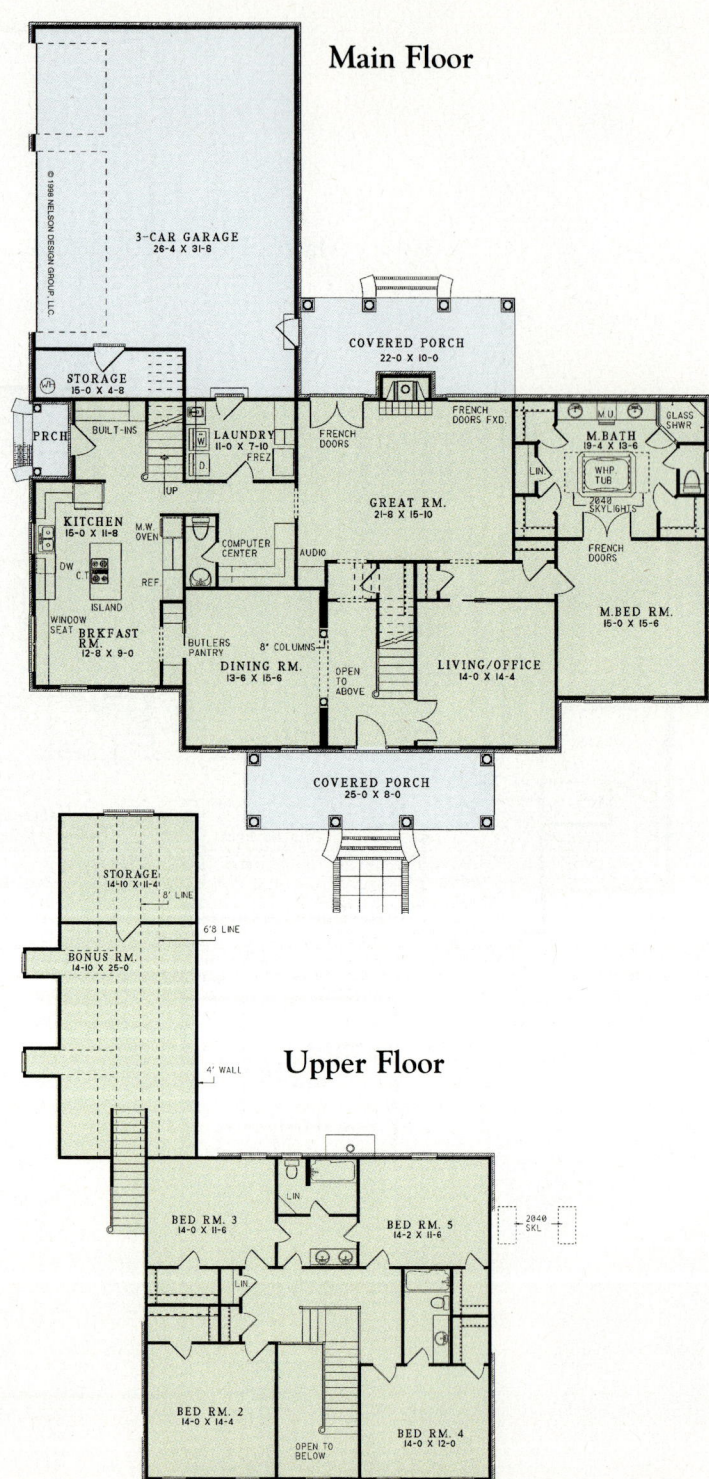

This majestic looking Nelson Design Group home is designed for the larger family. A beautiful built-in window seat aids in accommodating breakfast for everyone. You'll enjoy the convenient computer center which is arranged for optimum usage by the entire family. Enjoy the privacy of your master suite and bath with skylights above, increasing the amount of natural light. Upstairs, you'll have ample room for the children and all their belongings with four additional bedrooms and walk-in closet. Space is available for an optional bonus area that can serve as the family's game room.

Width: 68' 8"
Depth: 80' 0"
Main Floor: 2,202 sq. ft.
Upper Floor: 1,192 sq. ft.
Total Living: 3,394 sq. ft.*
*Optional Bonus: 396 sq. ft.

Main Ceiling: 9 ft.
Upper Ceiling: 8 ft.
Bedrooms: 5
Baths: 3 1/2
Foundation: Crawl, Slab, Basement, Daylight Basement

Price Tier: E

To view similar plans visit www.84lumber.com/ndgplans - 800.359.8484

540 Brandon Circle

Main Floor

Upper Floor

Nelson Design Group integrated three complete suites in this magnificent five-bedroom home. Walk-in closets and built-ins are utilized extensively throughout the secondary downstairs bedrooms with the second bedroom enjoying a complete computer center. A lovely corner fireplace graces the master suite while sleek French doors lead into the master bath. The large kitchen flows into a spectacular hearth room featuring a fireplace and access to the vast covered porch. Two secondary bedrooms upstairs flank the shared bonus room with an overhead view of the open kitchen below.

Width: 72' 10"	Main Ceiling: 9 ft.
Depth: 69' 10"	Upper Ceiling: 9 ft.
Main Floor: 2,607 sq. ft.	Bedrooms: 5
Upper Floor: 812 sq. ft.	Baths: 5
Total Living: 3,419 sq. ft.	Foundation: Crawl, Slab, Opt. Basement, Opt. Daylight Basement

Price Tier: E

100 Cherry Street

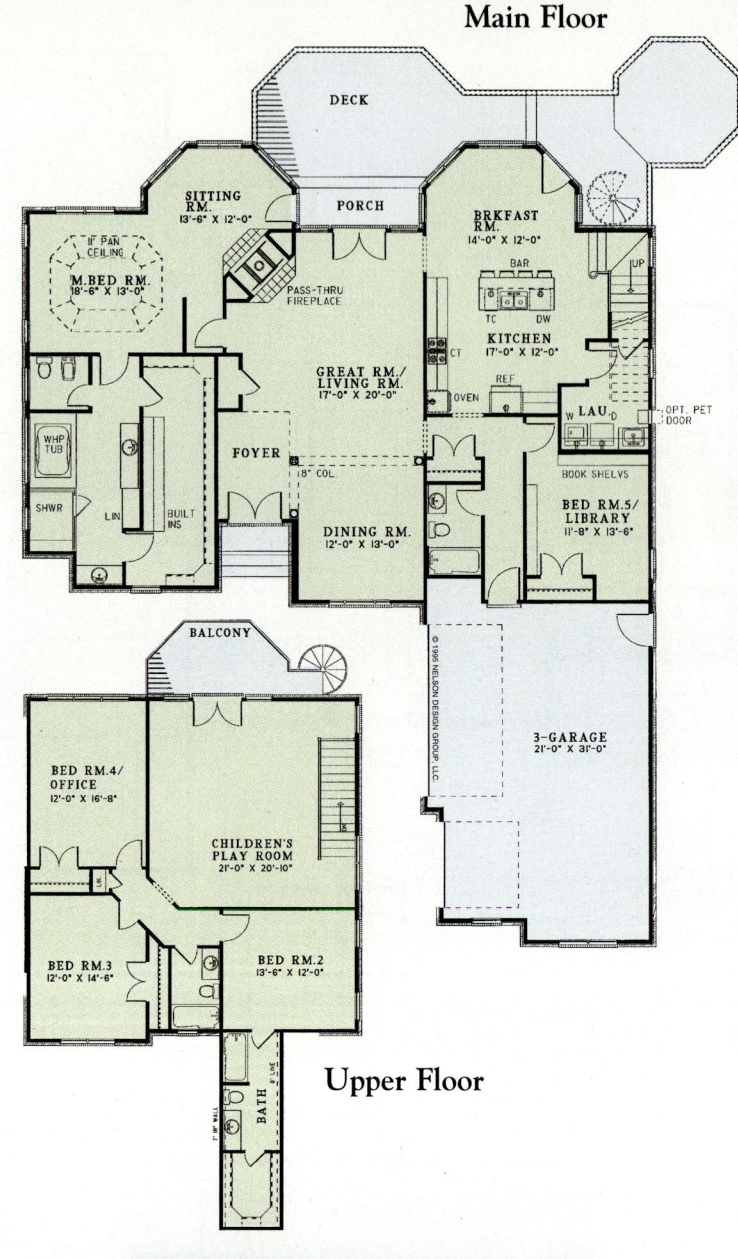

Main Floor

Upper Floor

An impressive split bedroom design makes this Nelson Design Group home a dream come true. You'll enjoy the pass-thru fireplace from the sitting room in your secluded master suite. A luxurious master bath has an enormous walk-in closet, which is every woman's fantasy. The kids will enjoy doing their research projects in the library conveniently located nearby. Entertaining with family and friends becomes a ritual in the spacious great room with fireplace to add warmth. Traveling upstairs, the children will find all the room they need with three bedrooms and a large playroom.

Width: 59' 6"
Depth: 74' 4"
Main Floor: 2,184 sq. ft.
Upper Floor: 1,253 sq. ft.
Total Living: 3,437 sq. ft.

Main Ceiling: 10 ft.
Upper Ceiling: 9 ft.
Bedrooms: 5
Baths: 4
Foundation: Crawl, Slab, Opt. Basement, Opt. Daylight Basement

Price Tier: E

To view similar plans visit www.84lumber.com/ndgplans - 800.359.8484

385 Brandon Circle

Main Floor

Upper Floor

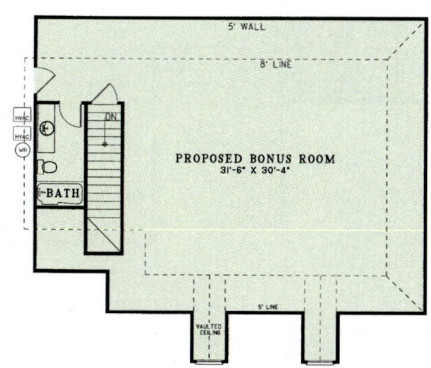

Elevation A

Elevation B

You're sure to enjoy the large great room featuring a built-in media center and fireplace in this Nelson Design Group home. A spacious kitchen holds a magnificent island and large, eat-at bar that easily serves the adjacent breakfast room. Relax in style on the spacious lanai and connecting terrace. The master suite accommodates a private terrace entrance, and raised whirlpool tub backed by sleek glass blocks. Upstairs, a mammoth bonus area with a full bath is capable of handling a variety of household activities.

Width: 89' 0"
Depth: 86' 4"
Total Living: 3,474 sq. ft.*
*Optional Bonus: 1,371 sq. ft.

Price Tier: E

Main Ceiling: 9 ft.
Upper Ceiling: 8 ft.
Bedrooms: 4
Baths: 5
Foundation: Crawl, Slab, Opt. Basement, Opt. Daylight Basement

To view similar plans visit www.84lumber.com/ndgplans - 800.359.8484

276 Birchwood Court

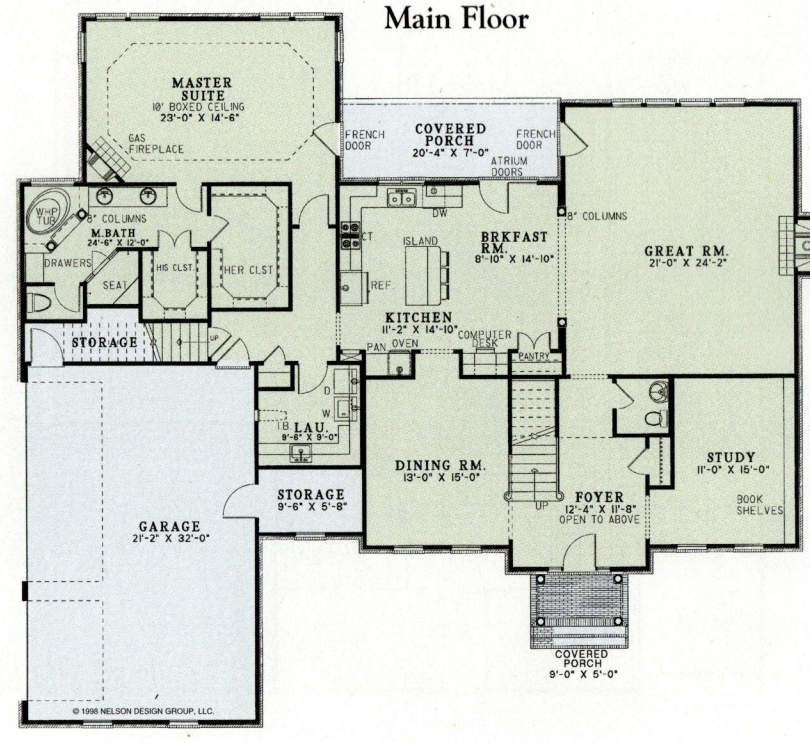

Main Floor

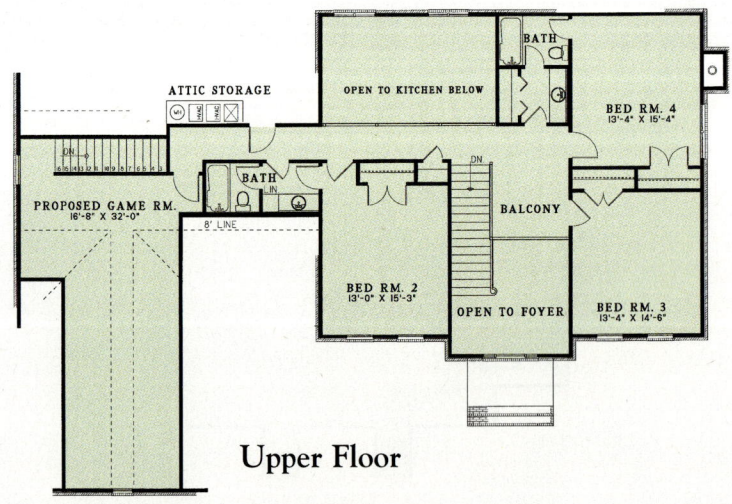

Upper Floor

From the central two-story foyer of this Nelson Design Group home you can easily access a shelf-lined study, elegant formal dining room or the spectacular great room punctuated by a fireplace and wide column-flanked entry. The breakfast room boasts an extra-large pantry, computer center and sleek atrium doors leading to the covered porch. The brilliant master suite employs interesting angles with a romantic corner fireplace, raised whirlpool tub with columned-entry, and huge dual walk-in closets. Two staircases lead to the game room and three secondary bedrooms located upstairs.

Width: 73' 10"
Depth: 63' 8"
Main Floor: 2,394 sq. ft.
Upper Floor: 1,094 sq. ft.
Total Living: 3,488 sq. ft.*
*Optional Bonus: 489 sq. ft.

Main Ceiling: 9 ft.
Upper Ceiling: 9 ft.
Bedrooms: 4
Baths: 3 1/2
Foundation: Crawl, Slab, Basement, Daylight Basement

Price Tier: E

To view similar plans visit www.84lumber.com/ndgplans - 800.359.8484

230 Main Street

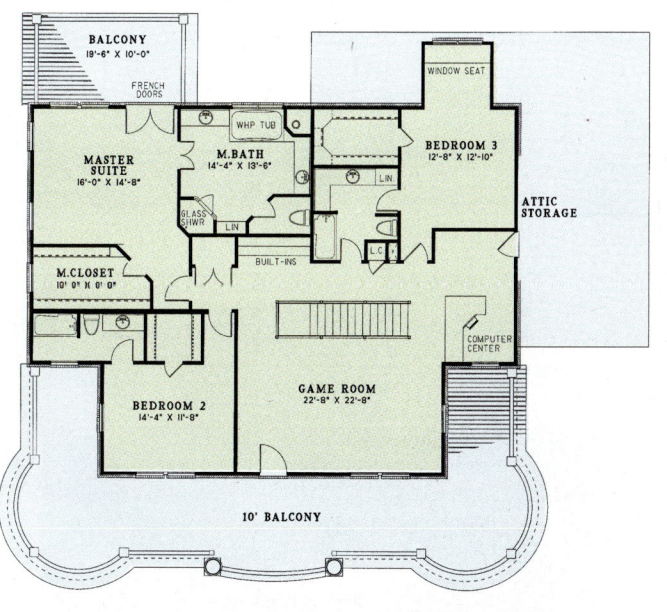

Main Floor

Upper Floor

Imagine coming home to this magnificent Nelson Design Group home with historical architectural details throughout the homes' interior and exterior. You'll be able to greet guests on the elegant front porch before leading them inside to gather in the spacious great room with corner fireplace. French doors access the rear covered porch allowing you to watch children at play. Upstairs, you'll discover the large game room with a computer center. All bedrooms are designed with ample closet space and individual baths. Experience your own private balcony in the master suite and proudly reminisce about one of history's finest eras.

Width: 68' 2"
Depth: 61' 0"
Main Floor: 1,583 sq. ft.
Upper Floor: 1,973 sq. ft.
Total Living: 3,556 sq. ft.

Main Ceiling: 10 ft.
Upper Ceiling: 9 ft.
Bedrooms: 3
Baths: 3 1/2
Foundation: Crawl, Slab, Basement, Daylight Basement

Price Tier: F

335 Birchwood Court

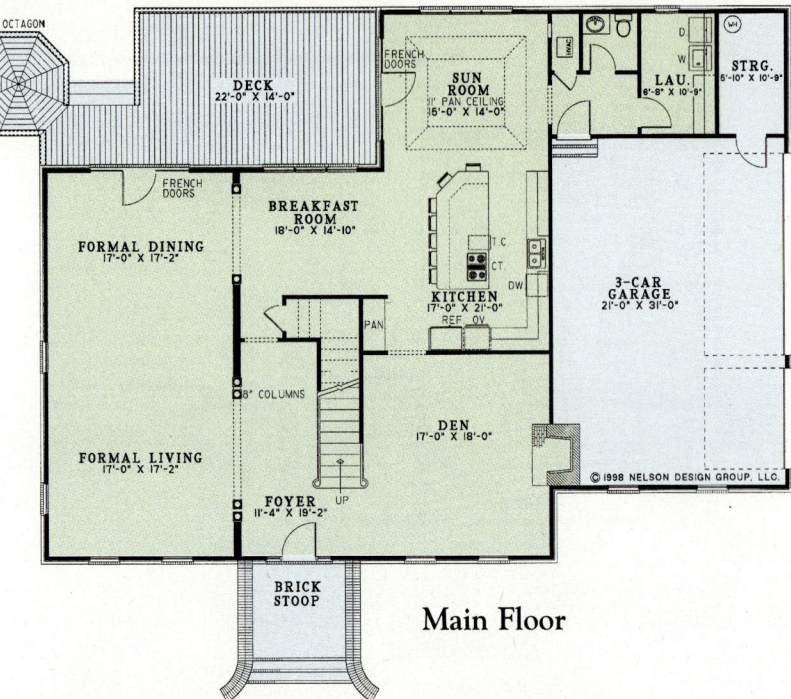

Main Floor

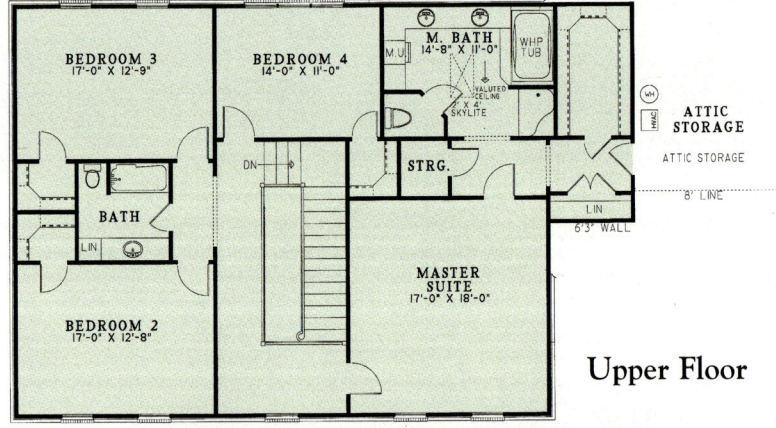

Upper Floor

Open, flowing living areas distinguish this Nelson Design Group home's sensible style and unique environment. The barrier-free integration of the formal living and dining rooms ensure smooth transitions while entertaining. An immense kitchen accommodates a functional island that seats seven. The spacious sun room boasts an 11' pan ceiling and one of two French door entries to the casual deck with its unique octagonal layout. In the master suite, located upstairs with the three secondary bedrooms, you'll find a vaulted ceiling, sky-lit bath with separate whirlpool tub and large walk-in closet.

Width: 67' 8"
Depth: 49' 0"
Main Floor: 2,018 sq. ft.
Upper Floor: 1,643 sq. ft.
Total Living: 3,661 sq. ft.

Main Ceiling: 10 ft.
Upper Ceiling: 9 ft.
Bedrooms: 4
Baths: 2 1/2
Foundation: Crawl, Slab, Opt. Basement, Opt. Daylight Basement

Price Tier: F

To view similar plans visit www.84lumber.com/ndgplans - 800.359.8484

Main Floor

Upper Floor

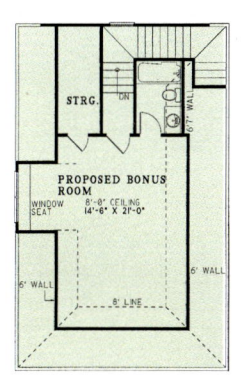
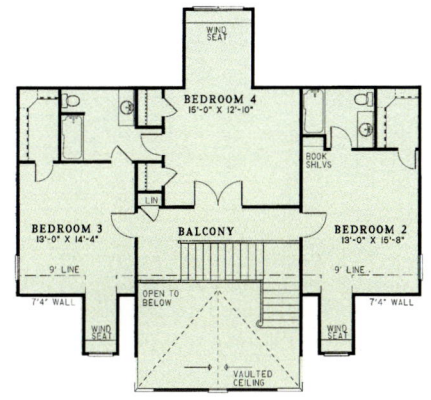

143 Olive Street

Holidays will be remembered when celebrating in this Nelson Design Group home. Upon entering the open foyer, your guests will enjoy the private sitting room to reminisce the days gone by. Your guests will enjoy the hearth room with coffee and conversation over a roaring fire. Entertain in the formal living area with handy wet bar. After your guests leave, retire to your spacious master suite with a fabulous corner whirlpool bath and corner glass shower. Upstairs, you'll find the children playing in their bedrooms with their own private window seats. A proposed bonus room offers numerous possibilities.

Width: 92' 5"	Main Ceiling: 10 ft.
Depth: 64' 0"	Upper Ceiling: 9 ft.
Main Floor: 2,651 sq. ft.	Bedrooms: 4
Upper Floor: 1,089 sq. ft.	Baths: 4 1/2
Total Living: 3,740 sq. ft.*	Foundation: Crawl, Slab, Opt. Basement, Opt. Daylight Basement
*Optional Bonus: 497 sq. ft.	

Price Tier: F

To view similar plans visit www.84lumber.com/ndgplans - 800.359.8484

486 Willow Lane

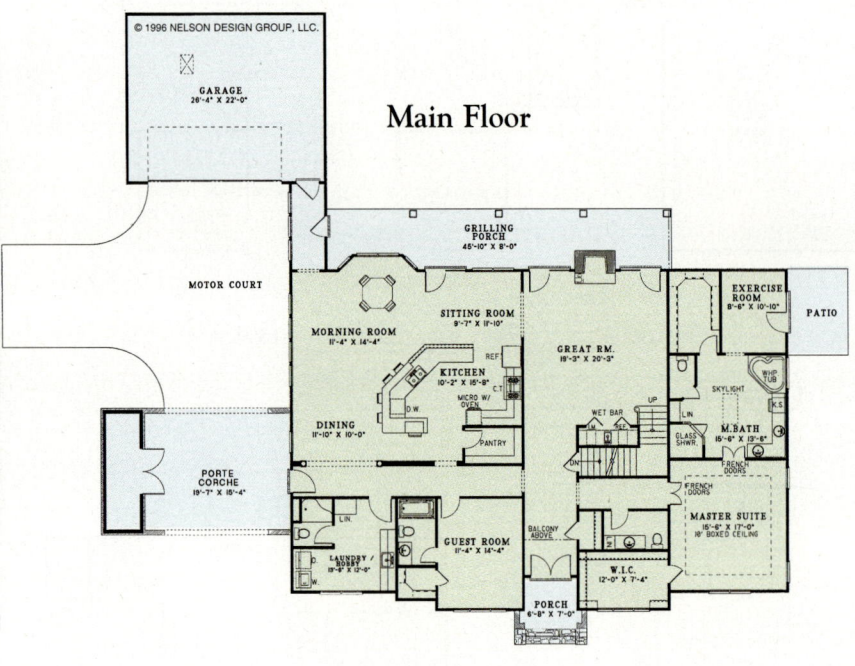

Main Floor

Upper Floor

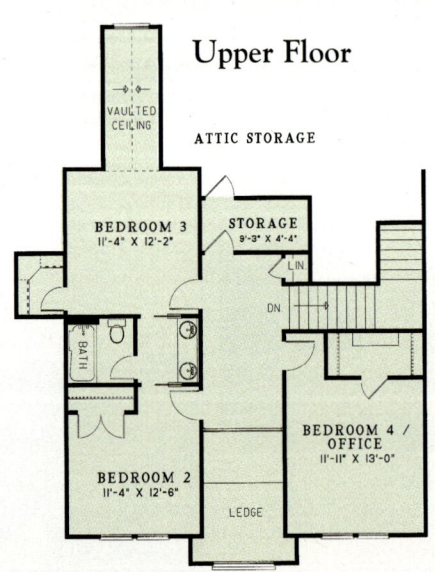

From the traditional porte corchere and motor court to the eloquent and modern master suite, no detail has been overlooked in this splendid offering from Nelson Design Group. The great room harbors a majestic fireplace tucked between two stylish entries to the expansive grilling porch. The functional kitchen features a large walk-in pantry and easily serves the adjoining sitting room, bright morning room with a beautiful bay window and formal dining room. Behind two lovely sets of French doors, the sky-lit master suite offers an exercise room and private patio in addition to the spacious bath.

Width: 92' 0"
Depth: 81' 4"
Main Floor: 2,967 sq. ft.
Upper Floor: 851 sq. ft.
Total Living: 3,818 sq. ft.

Main Ceiling: 9 ft.
Upper Ceiling: 8 ft.
Bedrooms: 4
Baths: 4 1/2
Foundation: Crawl, Slab, Opt. Basement, Opt. Daylight Basement

Price Tier: F

To view similar plans visit www.84lumber.com/ndgplans - 800.359.8484

Main Floor

Upper Floor

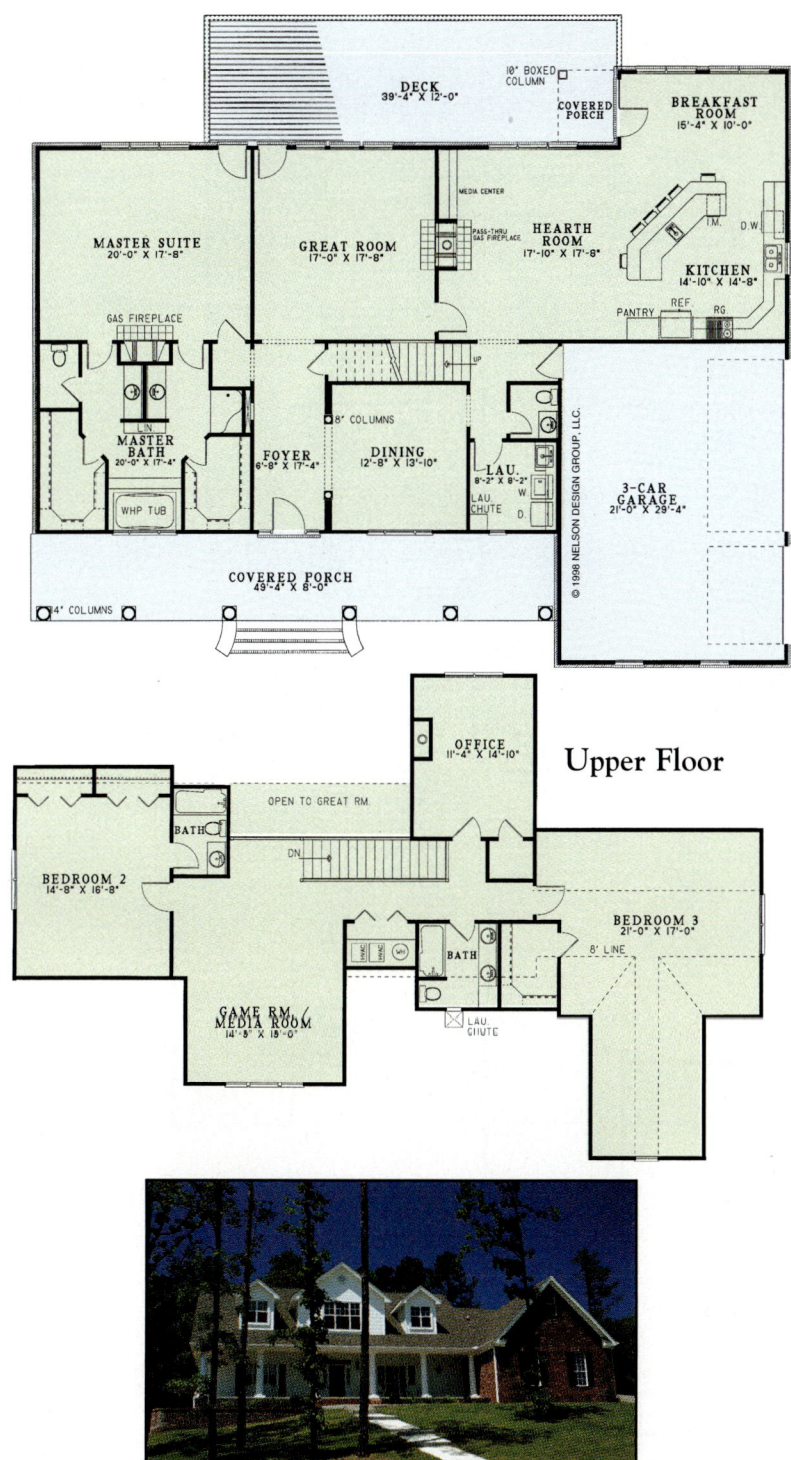

265 Walnut Lane

Visualize your family in this clever split bedroom Nelson Design Group home. Entering through the foyer, eight inch columns welcome you into the formal dining area. Enjoy family night in the great room with vaulted ceilings and a pass through fireplace that allows everyone the enjoyment of relaxing by the fire from either the great room or hearth room. Serve the kids breakfast at the island bar that is open to the breakfast room. End each day with dinner on your rear covered porch. The children will be nestled upstairs with plenty of space of their own after playing together in the game room.

Width: 71' 0"
Depth: 55' 0"
Main Floor: 2,291 sq. ft.
Upper Floor: 1,623 sq. ft.
Total Living: 3,914 sq. ft.

Main Ceiling: 9 ft.
Upper Ceiling: 8 ft.
Bedrooms: 3
Baths: 3 1/2
Foundation: Crawl, Slab, Opt. Basement, Opt. Daylight Basement

Price Tier: F

To view similar plans visit www.84lumber.com/ndgplans - 800.359.8484

403 Huntington Avenue

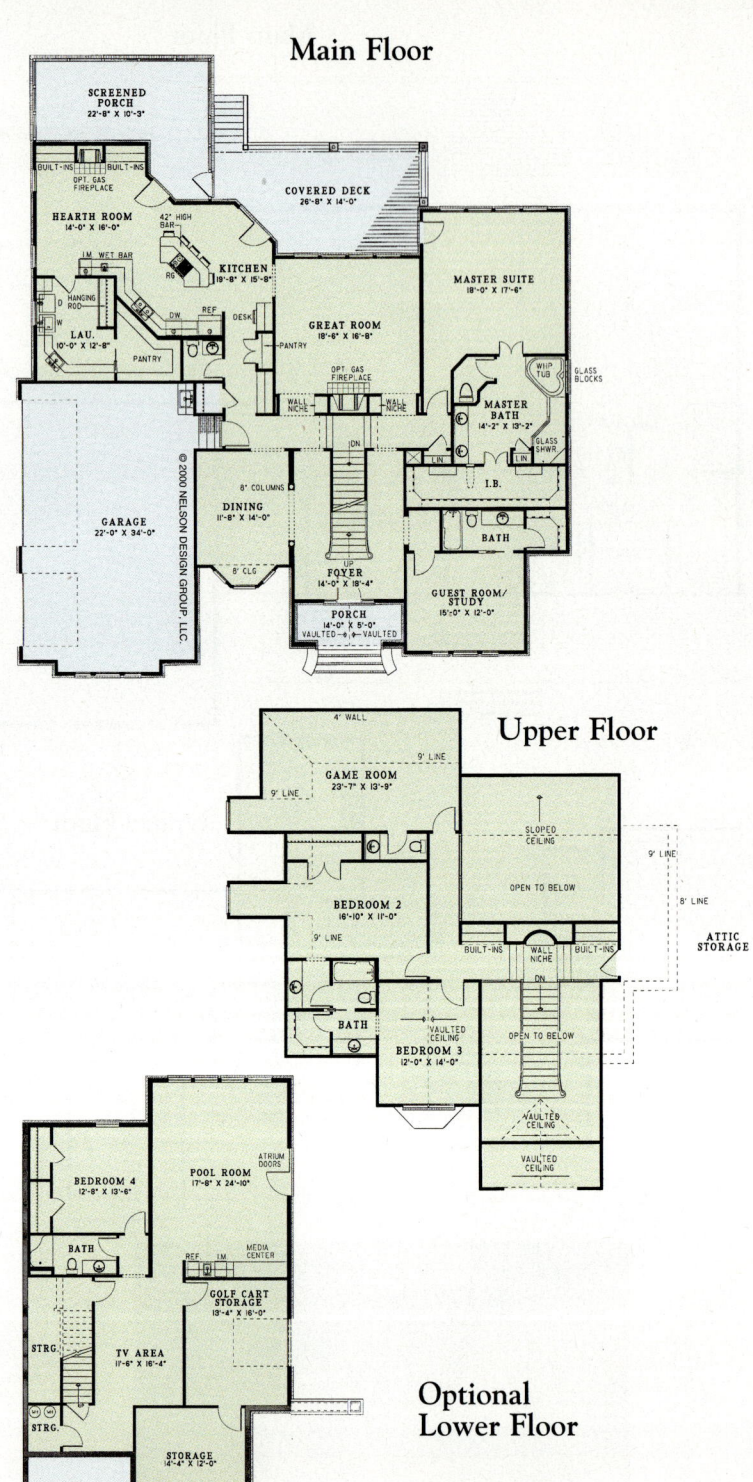

Main Floor

Upper Floor

Optional Lower Floor

Deceiving in its façade, this home from Nelson Design Group is both spacious and comfortable. A stunning stairway is centered in the two-story foyer, and beyond is the great room, also with a double-height ceiling, which overlooks a huge covered deck and separates living areas from sleeping quarters. The kitchen, laundry, pantry and hearth room are situated on the garage side of the house, while the master suite is located opposite. The upper floor hosts two bedrooms, a bath and a game room, and the lower level contains a fourth bedroom, bath and billiards room with kitchenette.

Width: 70' 0"
Depth: 75' 10"
Main Floor: 2,777 sq. ft.
Upper Floor: 1,170 sq. ft.
Optional Lower Floor: 1,616 sq. ft.
Total Living: 3,947 sq. ft.

Main Ceiling: 10 ft.
Upper Ceiling: 9 ft.
Lower Ceiling: 9 ft.
Bedrooms: 4
Baths: 4, 2-1/2
Foundation: Opt. Crawl, Opt. Slab, Daylight Basement

Price Tier: F

Main Floor

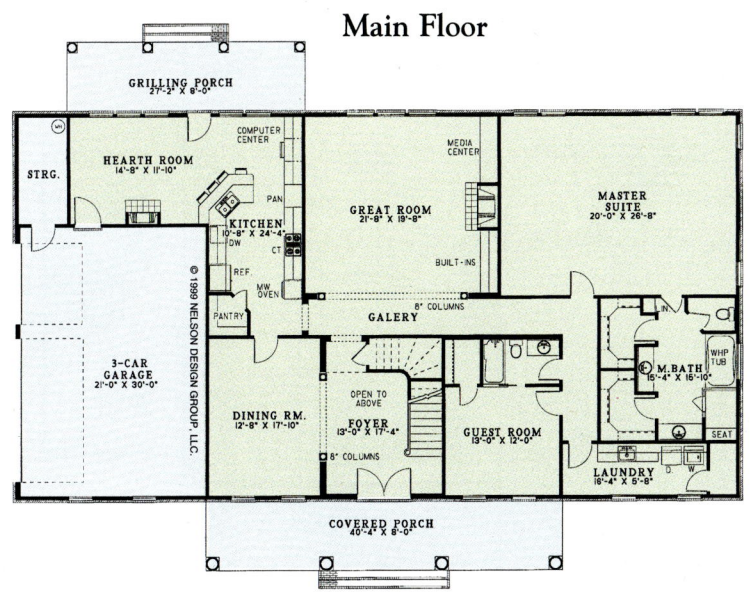

Upper Floor

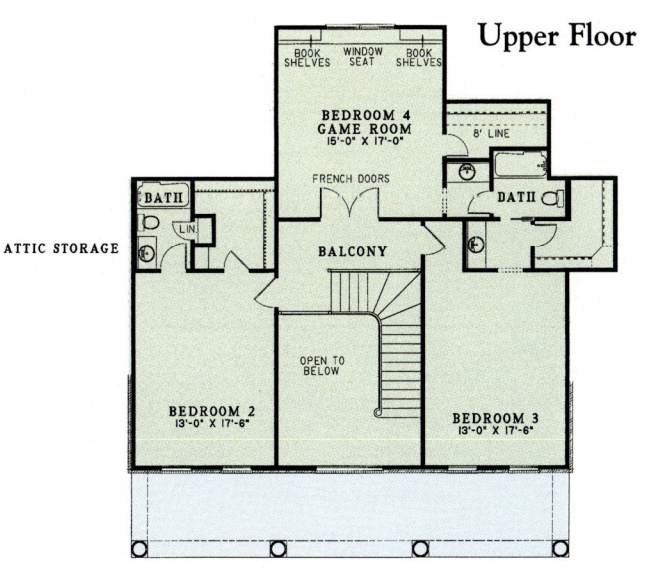

404 Huntington Avenue

The scale of the imposing portico and fanlight front entry is carried on inside this spectacular Nelson Design Group showcase home. A graceful stairway rises from the two-story center foyer to three large bedrooms upstairs. The dining room is spacious enough for elaborate sit-down affairs, the great room ample for entertaining and the master suite is simply enormous, with its twin closets, separate vanities and whirlpool tub. The kitchen wing includes walk-in pantry, computer center, snack bar and cozy hearth room with grilling porch access.

Width: 82' 0"	Main Ceiling: 10 ft.
Depth: 58' 10"	Upper Ceiling: 8 ft.
Main Floor: 2,782 sq. ft.	Bedrooms: 5
Upper Floor: 1,173 sq. ft.	Baths: 4
Total Living: 3,955 sq. ft.	Foundation: Crawl, Slab, Opt. Basement, Opt. Daylight Basement

Price Tier: F

223 Hickory Place

Main Floor

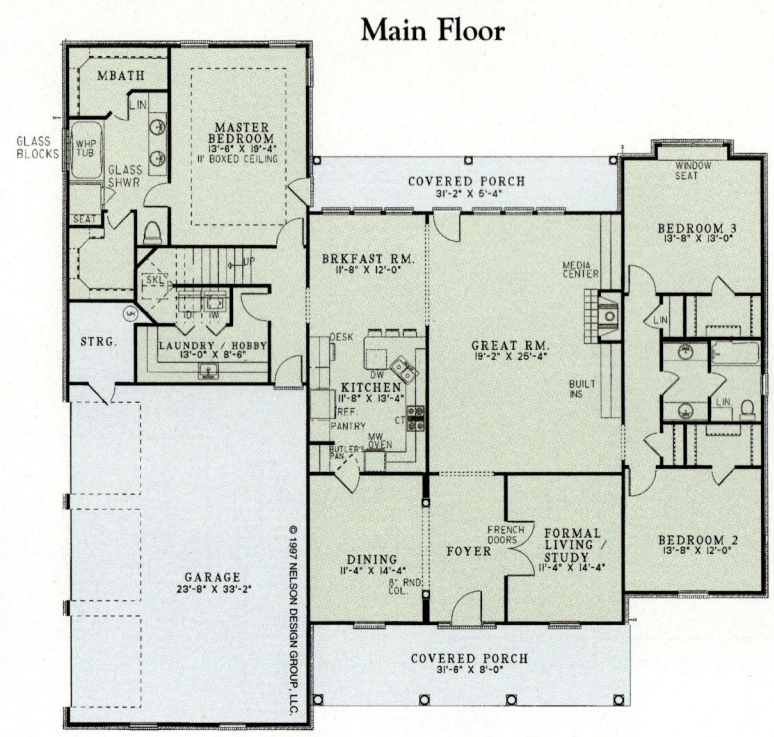

Upper Floor

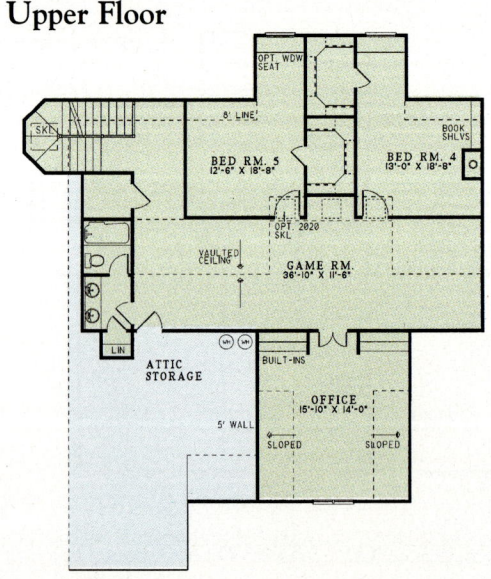

In the summer, welcome friends and family on the front porch of this Nelson Design Group home with lemonade and conversation. As you enter through the foyer, your guests will be amazed at the spacious dining room for easy entertaining. The expansive great room with gas fireplace will be the center of attention for warming those cold hands and sipping hot chocolate in the winter. Retire to your master suite and bath with whirlpool tub and 'his and her' walk-in closets. Traveling upstairs, you'll find ample bedroom space, plus game room for those sports buffs.

Width: 69' 10"
Depth: 67' 0"
Main Floor: 2,663 sq. ft.
Upper Floor: 1,431 sq. ft.
Total Living: 4,094 sq. ft.

Main Ceiling: 10 ft.
Upper Ceiling: 8 ft.
Bedrooms: 5
Baths: 3
Foundation: Crawl, Slab, Opt. Basement, Opt. Daylight Basement

Price Tier: G

Main Floor

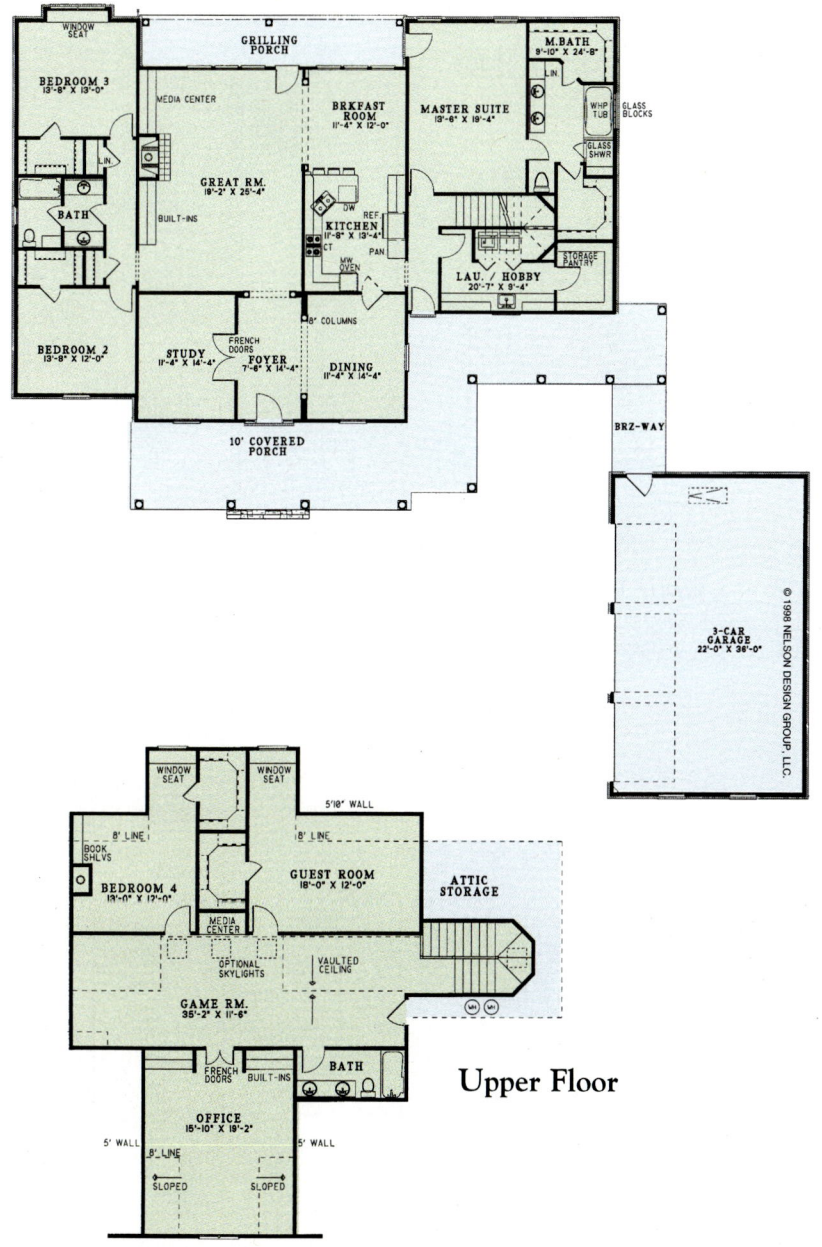

Upper Floor

396 Hickory Place

Strong natural elements securely anchor this Nelson Design Group home to its surroundings, while well-planned living spaces give it a modern freshness inside. The center foyer divides the dining room with its graceful columns from the study behind French doors. The great room with fireplace and built-ins splits the two downstairs bedrooms and bath from the master suite. Upstairs are two more bedrooms, another bath, a large office and a very large game room with media center. A breezeway connects the three-car garage to the main house.

Width: 92' 2"
Depth: 88' 7"
Main Floor: 2,719 sq. ft.
Upper Floor: 1,412 sq. ft.
Total Living: 4,131 sq. ft.

Price Tier: G

Main Ceiling: 10 ft.
Upper Ceiling: 8 ft.
Bedrooms: 5
Baths: 3
Foundation: Crawl, Slab, Opt. Basement, Opt. Daylight Basement

484 Huntington Avenue

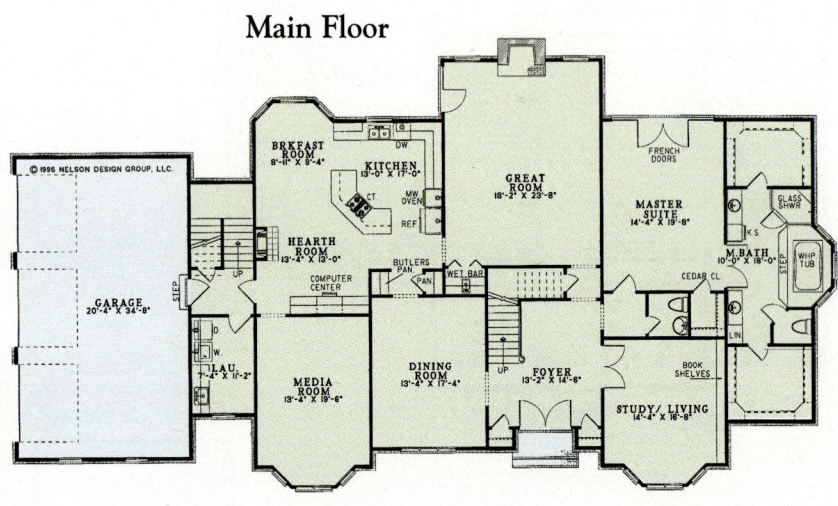

Main Floor

Upper Floor

Pick and choose your favorite elements in this Nelson Design Group manor: the grand stairway in the two-story foyer; the timeless combination of tall windows and tall bookshelves in the two studies (downstairs and up); the cast stone quoins, keystones and window bays; the integrated computer center outside the large media room. From the palatial master suite, complete with raised whirlpool tub and room-sized closets, to the butler's pantry near the large formal dining room, to the three bedrooms with private baths on the second floor, no detail of fine living has been overlooked.

Width: 96' 10"
Depth: 52' 0"
Main Floor: 2,958 sq. ft.
Upper Floor: 1,326 sq. ft.
Total Living: 4,284 sq. ft.

Main Ceiling: 9 ft.
Upper Ceiling: 9 ft.
Bedrooms: 4
Baths: 3 1/2
Foundation: Crawl, Slab, Basement, Daylight Basement

Price Tier: G

To view similar plans visit www.84lumber.com/ndgplans - 800.359.8484

Main Floor

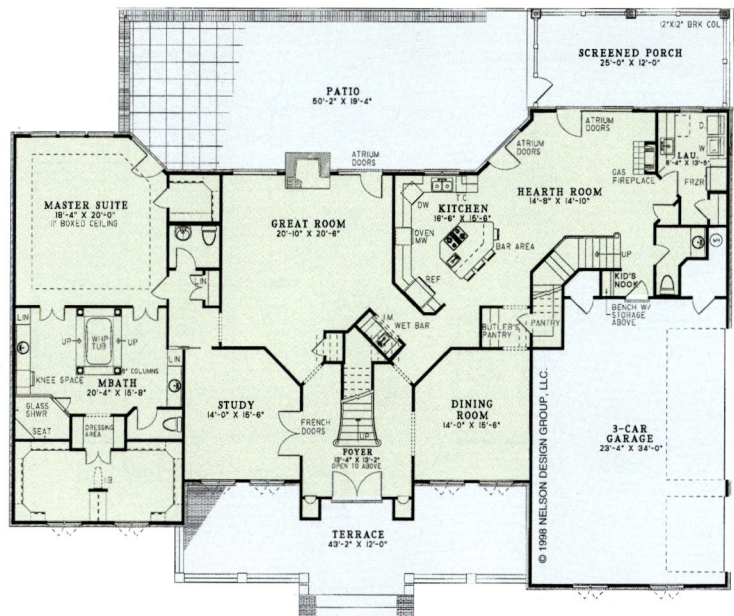

253 Birchwood Lane

Upper Floor

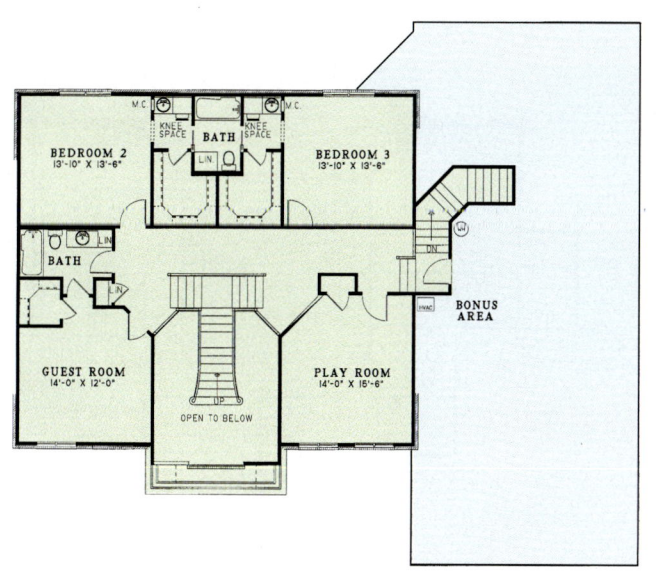

A unique split bedroom design and all the amenities you would expect are offered in this Nelson Design Group home. A marvelous terrace leads to the impressive French door entrance. Mornings will begin in the hearth room with quiet time or settle in your chair on the screened porch for that first cup of coffee. Entertaining is easy with a wet bar tucked away when those unexpected friends drop by. Enjoy an evening alone as you indulge yourself in your luxurious whirlpool bath. As for the kids, they'll be fine upstairs with bedrooms and generous play room for toys and activities.

Width: 87' 0"	Main Ceiling: 10 ft.
Depth: 70' 0"	Upper Ceiling: 9 ft.
Main Floor: 3,086 sq. ft.	Bedrooms: 4
Upper Floor: 1,386 sq. ft.	Baths: 3, 2-1/2
Total Living: 4,472 sq. ft.	Foundation: Crawl, Slab, Opt. Basement, Opt. Daylight Basement

Price Tier: G

273 Dogwood Avenue

Main Floor

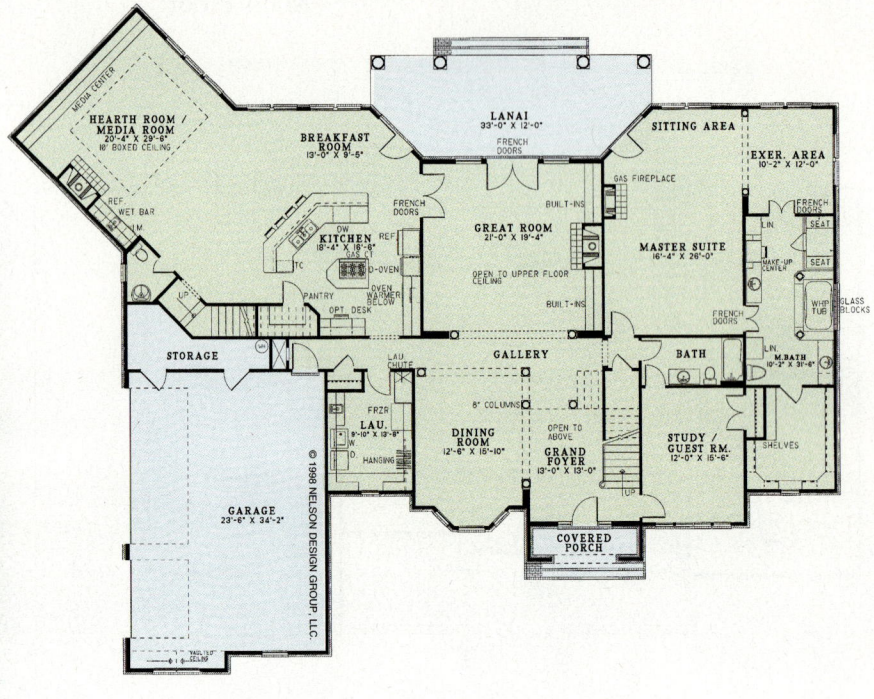

Upper Floor

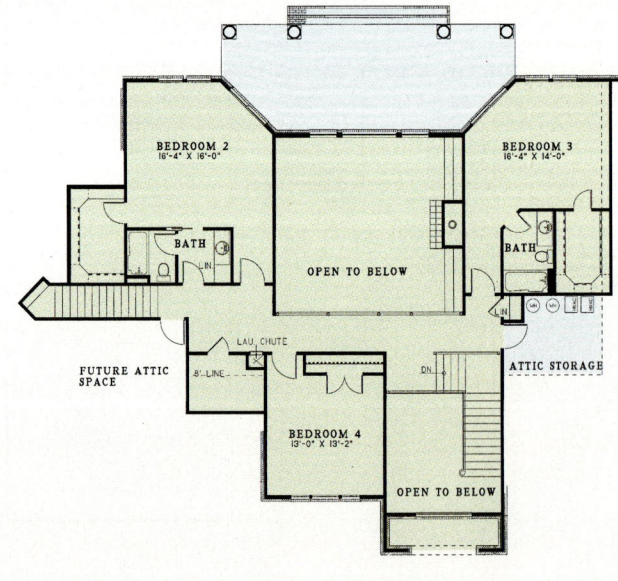

Imagine entertaining and the wonderful family gatherings that can be enjoyed in this Nelson Design Group home. Wonderful columns surround the spacious dining room as well as welcome you into the vast great room. Exquisite French doors lead to both the lanai and hearth room. Retire for the evening to your private master suite, complete with sitting and personal exercise areas. Then relax in the fabulous whirlpool bath with beautiful glass blocks that allow soothing natural sunlight. Upstairs, you'll have plenty of open space the kids or visitors can call their own.

Width: 96' 10"
Depth: 76' 6"
Main Floor: 3,526 sq. ft.
Upper Floor: 1,347 sq. ft.
Total Living: 4,873 sq. ft.

Main Ceiling: 9 ft.
Upper Ceiling: 8 ft.
Bedrooms: 5
Baths: 4 1/2
Foundation: Crawl, Slab, Basement, Daylight Basement

Price Tier: G

To view similar plans visit www.84lumber.com/ndgplans - 800.359.8484

Check This Plan Mike

478 Carolina Drive

Main Floor

Upper Floor

Lower Floor

The familiar exterior of this Nelson Design Group plan leaves you completely unprepared for the totally unpredictable interior. No fewer than three stairways connect the main floor with the two supplemental levels. The master suite has a private stairway to the enormous office overhead, and a convenient kitchen stairway ascends the nearly 40-foot game room that completes the second floor. The expandable lower level contains a huge garage, storage area, bath and storm shelter. The three secondary bedrooms are clustered on the main floor, with two baths.

Width: 64' 0"	Main Ceiling: 9 ft.
Depth: 88' 0"	Upper Ceiling: 8 ft.
Main Floor: 2,944 sq. ft.	Lower Ceiling: 10 ft.
Upper Floor: 1,847 sq. ft.	Bedrooms: 4
Lower Floor: 187 sq. ft.	Baths: 5 1/2
Total Living: 4,978 sq. ft.	Foundation: Basement, Daylight Basement

Price Tier: G

493 Main Street

Main Floor

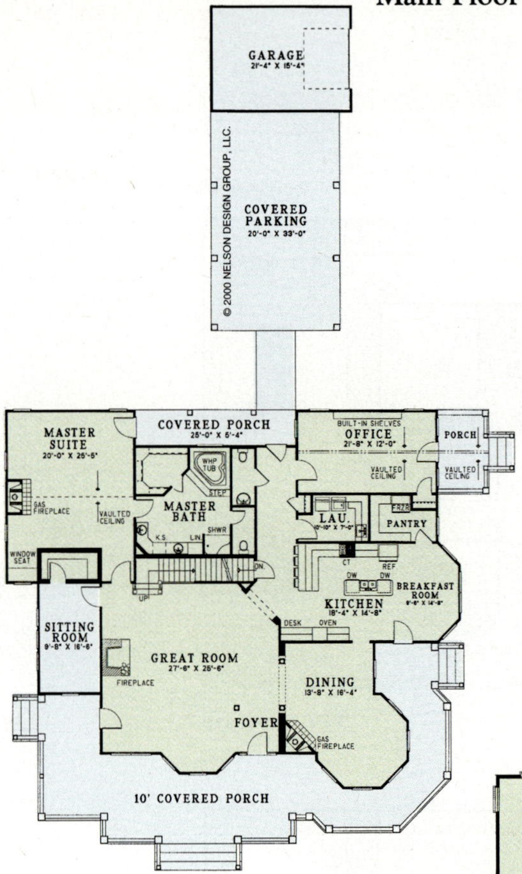

Upper Floor

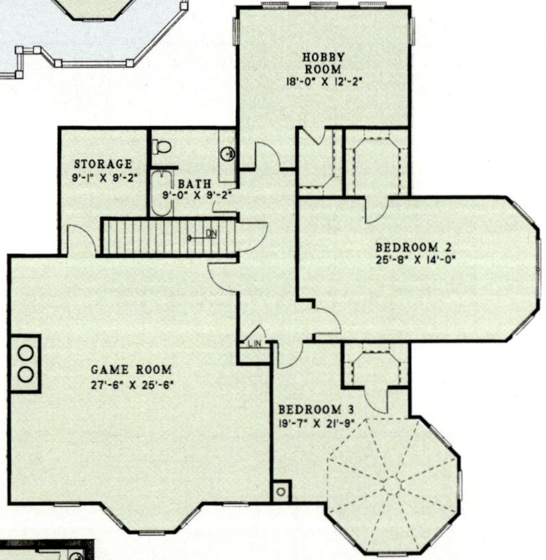

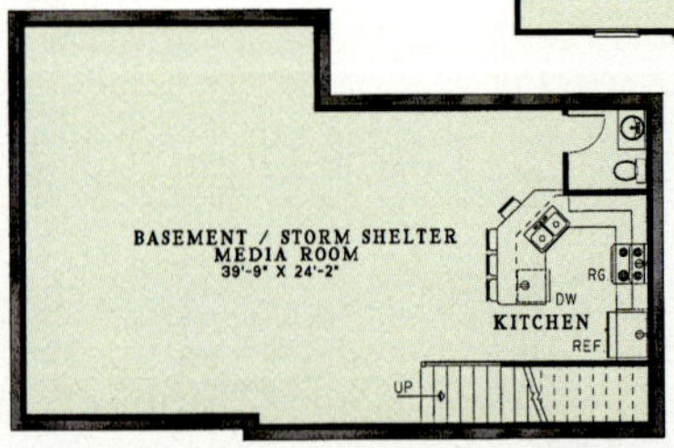

Lower Floor

This Nelson Design Group home is literally "back to the future," with traditional clapboard siding, deep wraparound porch, tall windows and historic turret on the outside, and modern amenities galore on the inside. Designed for living, the 3-bedroom home includes six 20-foot rooms, including large great room with fireplace, huge game room and unique basement media room, which doubles as a well-equipped-with kitchen and bath-storm shelter. The octagonal turret enhances the formal dining room as well as the third bedroom.

Width: 75' 10"
Depth: 126' 6"
Main Floor: 3,173 sq. ft.
Upper Floor: 2,120 sq. ft.
Lower Floor: 946 sq. ft.
Total Living: 6,239 sq. ft.

Main Ceiling: 10 ft.
Upper Ceiling: 9 ft.
Lower Ceiling: 9 ft.
Bedrooms: 3
Baths: 2, 2-1/2
Foundation: Basement, Daylight Basement

Price Tier: G

To view similar plans visit www.84lumber.com/ndgplans - 800.359.8484

138 Cherry Street

Upper Floor

Main Floor

Picture raising your children and grandchildren in this traditional Nelson Design Group home. Begin each day in your own private exercise room, then on to a hearty breakfast in the breakfast room. After the children return from school, they can begin their homework in the private study or convenient computer room. End your day in your elegant and secluded master suite. Upstairs, you will find ample room for children and visiting relatives. Of course, everyone will enjoy home movies with popcorn and soda in the wonderful home theater.

Width: 81' 6"
Depth: 93' 2"
Main Floor: 3,276 sq. ft.
Upper Floor: 2,272 sq. ft.
Total Living: 5,548 sq. ft.

Main Ceiling: 9 ft.
Upper Ceiling: 9 ft.
Bedrooms: 5
Baths: 4 1/2
Foundation: Crawl, Slab, Opt. Basement, Opt. Daylight Basement

Price Tier: G

To view similar plans visit www.84lumber.com/ndgplans - 800.359.8484

342 Dogwood Avenue

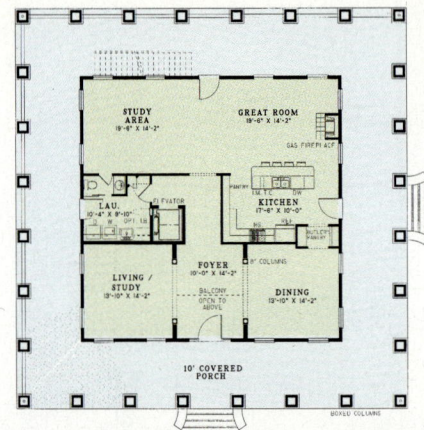

Main Floor

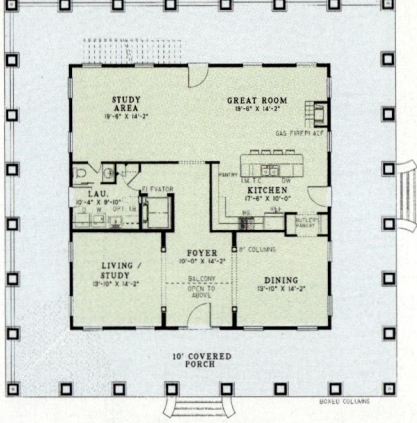

Upper Floor A

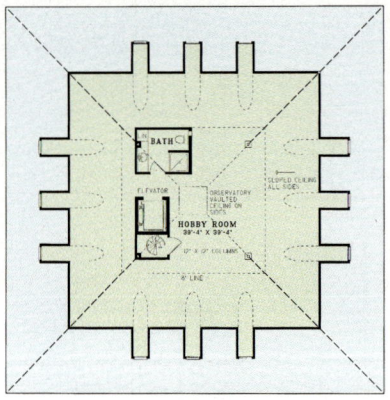

Upper Floor B

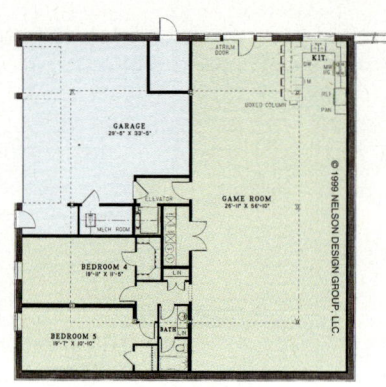

Lower Floor

Nelson Design Group has created a Southern plantation style home that emulates tradition at its finest. Wrap around porches with boxed columns will welcome family and friends with the opportunity for sipping lemonade while engaging in outdoor conversation. Bedrooms on the upper floor enable close monitoring of the younger children while the older children find themselves on the lower level with a massive game room and kitchen area. Access all floors of this home by the elevator or beautiful spiral staircase to the expansive hobby room and observatory.

Width: 60' 2"
Depth: 60' 2"
Main Floor: 1,600 sq. ft.
Upper Floor A: 1,530 sq. ft.
Upper Floor B: 1,744 sq. ft.
Lower Floor: 2,559 sq. ft.
Total Living: 7,433 sq. ft.

Main Ceiling: 9 ft.
Upper Ceiling A: 9 ft.
Upper Ceiling B: 8 ft.
Lower Ceiling: 9 ft.
Bedrooms: 5
Baths: 5 1/2
Foundation: Basement, Daylight Basement

Price Tier: G

To view similar plans visit www.84lumber.com/ndgplans - 800.359.8484

(A) Home Plan Books, (B) Feature Sheets, (C) Collection Portfolios, (D) Web Support, (E) Identity Packages, (F) Framed Prints, (G) Backlit Duratran Posters, (H) Gold Framed Print, (I) Virtual Tours

Marketing

Nelson Design Group offers a wide variety of marketing tools that will assist you in selling your homes. Because we cater daily to a diverse marketplace with a broad mix of consumers, real estate professionals and home builders, we know what buyers want, how builders build and how to design and market homes that sell quickly.

NDG offers a complete product line of marketing materials including full color feature sheets, framed and matted color renderings, street scapes and outdoor promotional signage allowing the builder/developer to have cost effective marketing materials on their homes and for their businesses.

Our in-house marketing and design staff provides you with everything you need to develop a turn-key marketing program and they can answer any questions you or your staff may have. We provide valued expertise throughout all phases of development from site selection to layout and final marketing strategies.

Mike,

I just want to thank you for all of your company's hard work during the design and marketing process of my latest development. This was my first experience with your firm and I'm so pleased to have found someone that can carry me through the entire process of planning, design and marketing... the added benefit of your Tru-Cost estimating for keeping up with my building budget... It was a refreshing change and a pleasure working with your firm.
Thanks,

Chris Kellner

Kellner
CUSTOM BUILDERS

That Works

Home Plan Books
Nelson Design Group wants to ensure that our customers have the most current and helpful designs available to choose from. We have published a set of plan books complete with renderings, floorplans, and specs of more than 400 homes.

Feature Sheets
These customized color renderings portray the specifications and sales copy describing each home plan. Each full color 8 1/2" x 11" sheet is customized with your logo and design features.

Collection Portfolios
You will find individual designs and also several different groups of plans such as our new Wellington and Renaissance Collections. Our designs have complementary themes that work together to build a single home, a neighborhood, or a full-scale development.

Framed Prints
Greet your clients with an attractive display perfect for hanging in your office lobby or in the show home itself. Each 16" x 20" framed and matted print includes design highlights and contact information for your company.

See Page 286 for more Marketing Prices

Identity Packages

Nelson Design Group's in-house design department can develop a professional image for your firm including company logos, brochures and home marketing programs.

Indoor/Outdoor Posters

These 24" x 36" full color posters are perfect for displaying at the Open House, Grand Opening, Sales Office or the Model Home. The posters can be used for backlit duratran signs or laminated for outdoor use.

Multi-Media Support

NDG's website provides a builder an opportunity to promote their website and also link to our home plan search. We also produce video, computer and virtual tours that will assist in the marketing of your firm and/or projects..

Professional Services

Save valuable time and money by utilizing NDG's advertising services. We have an in-house staff of experienced marketing specialists to assist you in every phase of your project...from beginning to end.

These following services are available:

Home Development Consultation
Custom Design
Home Marketing Analysis
Job Site Consultation
News Releases
Ad, Logo and Brochure Design

See Page 286 for more Marketing Prices

Tru-Cost
ESTIMATING

Tru-Cost Estimating is a valuable tool for use in planning and construction of your new home. Tru-Cost is available for each of NDG's plans.

We provide a complete estimate, similar to a bid, that will act as a checklist for all items you will need to select or coordinate during your building process. Tru-Cost will provide you a direct comparison to track your cost and help you stay within budget.

Tru-Cost has options that allow you to customize your estimate, to include labor rates and material prices for your area and can be imported into Tru-Cost software. The key to a successful project is to have a realistic budget, Tru-Cost is the solution.

Estimating Your Home Cost...

Cut your construction estimating time in half!

Guaranteed

Missing time with your family?

With Tru-Cost Estimating Software, you will reduce the time being spent on estimating your new home construction. Tru-Cost is designed with the small builder in mind utilizing simple to use menus, standard construction divisions and a master database that contains hundreds of pre-defined materials that can be modified to your local building and material cost. The software is easily modified to fit the way you estimate and construct your homes.

Call today for more information, 1-800-590-2423.

Tru-Cost
ESTIMATING

Special Offer
Purchase Tru-Cost Software for $299 (reg. $595) and receive 3 stock estimates FREE (value $375) with the purchase of 3 stock plans.

Tru-Cost Estimating

Tru-Cost is adaptable to a variety of estimating techniques and methods. By utilizing a ledger entry format, creating a bid is as simple as selecting items from the Master Database.

Tru-Cost Estimating provides a simplified method for calculating costs for equipment, labor, material, and sub contractors, thus creating more accurate bids and easier cost tracking. Tru-Cost has multiple reports that assist a variety of tasks, from ordering materials to negotiating price with clients. Tru-Cost can automatically update pricing on previous bids to meet current prices within the Master Database.

Ledger Entry Form

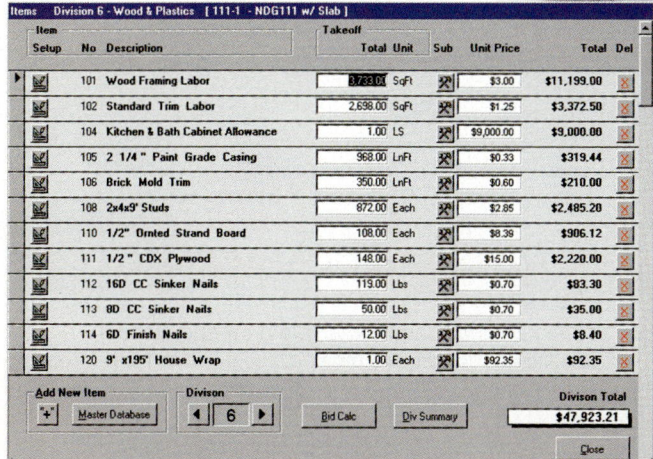

Itemized Listing

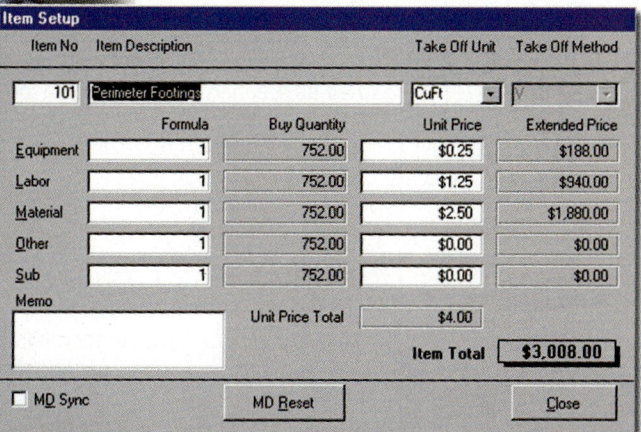

Advantages

- Quick startup
- Save time with material databases
- Import estimates from NDG
- Create a variety of reports
- Export reports to Excel or Palm Pilot
- Technical Support
- 16 Standard Construction Divisions

Bid Overview

Features

- Organize sub-contractor bids
- Itemize materials per catagory
- Easy to adjust material takeoff qty's
- Adjust overhead and profit margins
- Mark up individual category's; equip., labor, materials, etc.
- Step-by-step instructional and interactive tutorial

281

WHAT'S INCLUDED IN YOUR NELSON DESIGN GROUP BLUEPRINTS

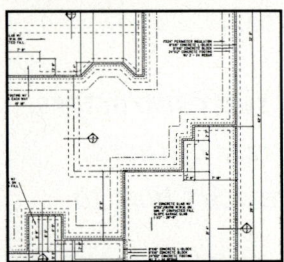

FOUNDATION PLANS
(1/4" or 1/2" = 1')
Most plans are available with a slab or crawl space foundation. Optional walkout style basement (three walls masonry with a wood framed side or rear wall) or full basement available if plan allows, at an additional cost. Please call for details.

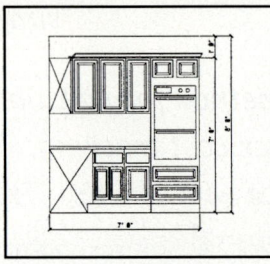

KITCHEN AND BATH ELEVATIONS
(1/2" = 1')
The kitchen and bath elevations show the arrangement and size of each cabinet and other fixtures in the room. These drawings give basic information that can be used to create customized layouts with a cabinet manufacturer.

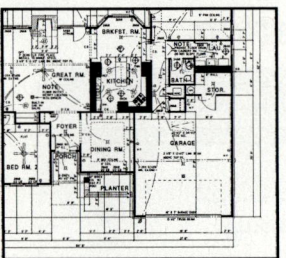

FLOOR PLANS
(1/4" = 1')
Each home plan includes the floor plan showing the dimensioned locations of walls, doors and windows as well as a schematic electrical layout.

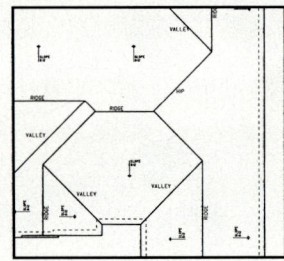

ROOF OVERVIEW PLAN
(1/4" = 1')
This is a "bird's eye" view showing the roof slopes, ridges, valleys and any saddles.

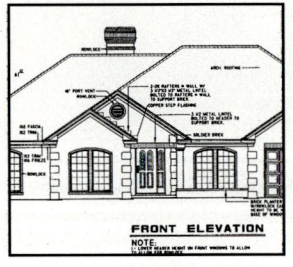

ELEVATION SETS
(1/4" = 1')
All plans include the exterior elevations (front, rear, right and left) that show and describe the finished material of the house.

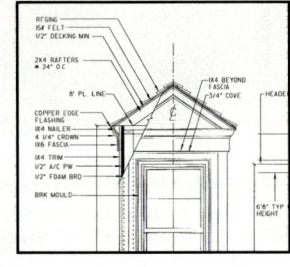

MISCELLANEOUS DETAILS
(3/4" = 1')
These are included for many interior and exterior conditions that require more specific information for their construction.

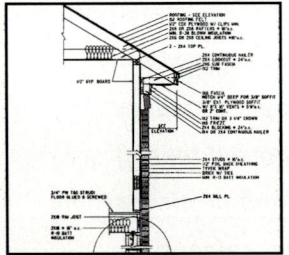

DETAIL SECTION(S)
(1/4" or 1/2" = 1')
The building sections are vertical cuts through the house showing floor, ceiling and roof height information.

Nelson Design Group, LLC Home Plans do not carry an architect/engineer stamp.

Code Compliance: Our plans are drawn to meet the 1995 CABO One & Two Family Dwelling Code and the 1994 Standard Building Code with the 1996 Georgia amendments. Many states and counties amend the codes in their area. Consult your local building officials to determine the plan, code and site requirements.

Heated and Cooled Square Footage calculations are made from outside the exterior frame wall and do not include decks, porches, garages, basements, attics, fireplaces, etc. We include two story and vaulted areas only once in the calculations of the first floor. Stairs are counted once. Balconies and open walkways in two-story and vaulted areas are included in square footage of the second floor.

ADDITIONAL PLAN SERVICES PROVIDED BY NELSON DESIGN GROUP

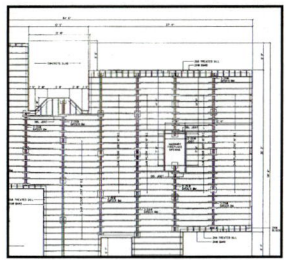

FLOOR FRAMING PLANS

(1/4" = 1'-0")
Each floor framing plan shows each floor joist indicating the size, spacing and length. All beams are labeled and sized.

$100.00 (includes one floor. Additional floors $50.00 each)

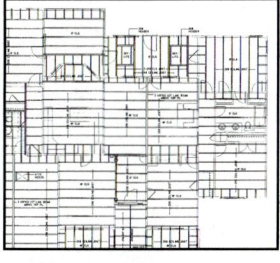

CEILING JOIST FRAMING PLAN

(1/4" = 1'-0")
The ceiling joist framing plan shows each ceiling joist indicating the size, spacing and length. All beams are labeled and sized.

$100.00

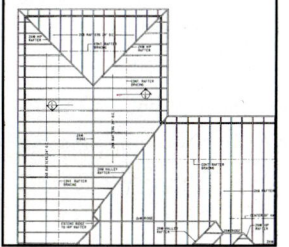

ROOF FRAMING PLAN

(1/4" = 1'-0")
The roof framing plan shows each rafter, valley, hip and ridge indicating the size, spacing and length. All beams are labeled and sized.

$100.00

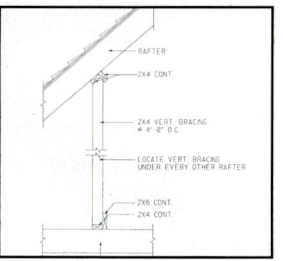

MISCELLANEOUS FRAMING DETAILS

Each framing plan sheet includes any framing details that are needed (boxed ceiling details, connection details, etc.) All of the framing is designed using conventional framing materials. Open web trusses are used in most one-and-a-half story and two-story plans.

RIGHT-READABLE REVERSED PLANS

Right-readable reversed plans are available should you wish to build your home reverse of the one shown in our book. The lettering and dimensions appear right reading. From the total number of sets ordered, all plans will be reversed. Check the appropriate area on the area form or let us know when ordering.

TRU-COST ESTIMATING

Nelson Design Group has developed the Tru-Cost Estimating system to be a valuable tool for builders to use in the planning and construction of new homes. We have combined a thorough database of items required for construction. We offer three different options for our customers by providing estimates for all of our Stock Plans, as well as Modified and Custom Plans. Our Custom Estimate is not only available for our plans, it's also offered for our customer's plans. The Custom Estimate service allows the customer to modify or change any of the pricing or materials they may wish to use.

Base NDG Plan Estimate	$125.00
Revised Estimate for NDG Stock Plan	$250.00
Custom Estimate starting at	$500.00
Estimating Software	$595.00

REPRODUCIBLES

With the purchase of a reproducible set (vellums), a license and copyright release are also provided. Similarly, the purchase of reproducible home plans carries the same copyright protection as mentioned in this book. It is generally allowed to make up to a maximum of 10 copies for the construction of a single dwelling only. To use any plans more than once, and to avoid any copyright licenses infringement, it is necessary to contact Nelson Design Group, LLC to receive a release and a license for any extended usage. Nelson Design Group, LLC will make special provisions for plan usage within developments when previous arrangements have been made directly with Nelson Design Group, LLC.

CAD DISKS

CAD Disks are available on all plans. Standard formats are DWG and DXF. See order form for pricing.

MODIFY YOUR NELSON DESIGN GROUP STOCK PLAN

Not only do we have numerous designs prepared for various sized homes, we encourage the modification of our stock plans to meet personal specifications. Nelson Design Group will help you fulfill your dreams with a customized computer area, media center, hearth room, privacy nooks or whatever your needs entail.

Modification work has a per plan set up charge and hourly fee or, is priced per total square footage under roof depending on the changes required or the complexity. To receive an estimated fee and completion time for modifications please call 1-800-590-2423 or fax us a copy of the floor plan, the changes you wish to make along with your daytime phone number.

A fee of the reproducible cost and the set up fee are required before revisions can be made, and the remaining fees are to be paid prior to shipping.

Any modifications made to the vellums by parties other than Nelson Design Group, LLC voids any warranties express or implied including the warranties of fitness for a particular purpose and merchantability. We recommend that an engineer in your area review your plans before actual construction begins due to local codes.

Foundation Alterations
Optional Basement Foundation - $250.00
Optional Daylight Basement Foundation - $250.00

Call our modification department for questions regarding custom foundation modifications.

Exterior Materials
Siding to Brick - $250.00
Brick to Siding - $250.00

Garage Alterations
Side Load to Front Entry - $250.00
Front Entry to Side Load - $250.00
Two Car to Three Car - $375.00

COPYRIGHT LAWS OF NELSON DESIGN GROUP

Reproduction of the illustration and working drawings of these home plans, either in whole or in part, including any form and/or preparation of derivative works thereof, for any reason without prior written permission is strictly prohibited. The purchase of a set of home plans in no way transfers any copyright or other ownership interest in it to the buyer except for a limited license to use that set of home plans for the construction of one, and only one, dwelling unit. The purchase of an additional set (s) of that home plan at a reduced price from the original set or as part of a multiple set package does not convey to the buyer a license to construct more than one dwelling. This is also the case with reproducible vellum, CAD disks or any multimedia.

Similarly, the purchase of reproducible vellum carries the same copyright protection as mentioned above. It is generally allowed to make up to a maximum of 10 copies for the construction of a single dwelling only. To use any plans more than once, and to avoid any copyright licenses infringement, it is necessary to contact the plan designer to receive a release and a license for any extended usage. Nelson Design Group, LLC will make special provisions for plan usage within developments when previous arrangements have been made directly with Nelson Design Group, LLC.

Whereas a purchaser of reproducible is granted license to make copies, it should be noted that as copyright material, making photocopies from blueprints is illegal.

Copyright and licensing of home plans for construction exist to protect all parties. It respects and supports the intellectual property of the original architect or designer. Copyright law has been reinforced over the past few years. Willful infringement could cause settlements for statutory damages up to $100,000.00 plus attorney fees, damages and loss of profits.

CUSTOMER INFORMATION

Name: _____

Company Name: _____

Address: _____

City: _____ State: _____ Zip: _____

Phone: _____ Fax: _____

E-mail Address: _____

Credit Card #: _____ Exp. Date: _____

☐ VISA ☐ MasterCard ☐ AmEx ☐ Discover

☐ Check/Money Order Enclosed (U.S. Funds)

BLUEPRINT PRICING

Price Tier	Square Feet	One Set	Four Sets	Eight Sets	Twelve Sets	Repro Sets	CAD Disk
A	0-1499	$400	$435	$475	$520	$585	$1,060
B	1500-1999	$440	$475	$515	$560	$630	$1,105
C	2000-2499	$480	$515	$555	$605	$670	$1,145
D	2500-2999	$550	$585	$635	$675	$755	$1,430
E	3000-3499	$610	$645	$685	$730	$805	$1,480
F	3500-3999	$650	$685	$730	$780	$855	$1,530
G	4000 and up	$700	$735	$775	$820	$900	$1,575

NUMBER OF SETS

☐ **ONE SET** (stamped "not for construction") Recommended for preview study

☐ **FOUR SETS** Recommended for bidding

☐ **EIGHT SETS** Recommended for construction

☐ **TWELVE SETS** Recommended for multiple bids

☐ **REPRODUCIBLE SETS** Recommended for construction/modifications

☐ **CAD Disks** DXF/DWG Files

Prices are subject to change. Special or grouped plans may vary in price.

SHIPPING AND HANDLING

	1-3 Sets	4-7 Sets	8 or more Sets	Repro Sets	CAD Disk
U.S. Regular (5-6 business days)	$17.50	$20.00	$25.00	$17.50	$15.00
U.S. Express (2-3 business days)	$35.00	$40.00	$45.00	$35.00	$30.00
Canada Regular (5-7 business days)	$40.00	$45.00	$50.00	$40.00	$35.00
Canada Express (2-4 business days)	$55.00	$60.00	$65.00	$55.00	$50.00
Overseas/Airmail (7-10 business days)	$70.00	$80.00	$90.00	$70.00	$60.00

Prices are subject to change.

	Plan # ___	Plan # ___	Plan # ___
Price Tier			
Number of Sets			
Blueprint Cost			
Additional Sets @ $40 each			
Right Readable-Reversed Sets @ $50			
Tru-Cost Estimating @ $125			
CAD Disk			
Reproducible Sets			
☐ Crawl			
☐ Slab			
☐ Basement			
☐ Basement (Opt.) @ $250.00			
☐ Daylight Basement			
☐ Daylight Basement (Opt.) @ $250.00			
Tru-Cost Software @ $595.00			
☐ Other			
Sub-Total			
Shipping & Handling			
TOTAL			

Additional Sets - Additional individual sets of plan ordered at point of sale are **$40** each.

Right Readable-Reversed Plans - A **$50** surcharge. From the total number of sets you order above, all plans will be reversed. You pay only **$50**. Note: All plans are produced using computers, and all text is reversed as well.

All Nelson Design Group, LLC sales are non-credit purchases. The total amount is due when your order is placed. Orders may not be returned or exchanged. All orders are final.

MAIL TO: **84 Homes**

84 Lumber Company

109 Route 519, Eighty-four, PA 15330

Phone: 800-359-8484 • Fax: 724-225-0462

www.84lumber.com/ndgplans

For Technical Assistance call:

800-590-2423

Big Image On A Small Budget?

Whether You Build One or 100 Homes A Year, Project The Professional Image of the Largest Builders!

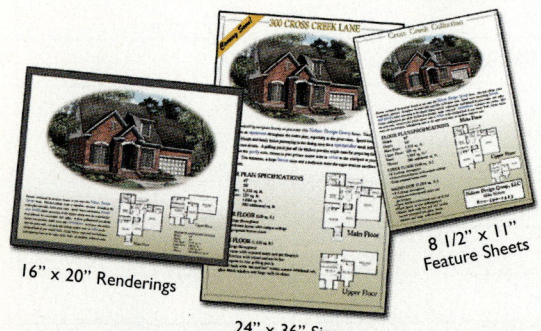

16" x 20" Renderings
8 1/2" x 11" Feature Sheets
24" x 36" Signs

Feature Sheets
8.5" x 11" customized color rendering with floor plan, your color logo and customized bullet points. **$50**
100 sheets/pack - 20% discount with 2 packs or more

Framed Prints
Professionally framed and matted 20" x 24" color renderings customized with your logo, floor plan and bullet points.
Black Metal. **$89**
Gold Wood. **$150**

Outdoor Signage
24" x 36", similar to above but in vertical format laminated and weatherproofed, customized and ready for display in front of your construction site.
Color Laminated. **$195**
Free blueprint of yard sign holder with sign purchase

Interior Signage
24" x 36", customized and ready for mounting on foamcore backing. Perfect for displaying on easels at Open Houses, Grand Openings, Sales Offices, Model Homes, etc.
Full Color. **$150**
call for details

Brochures
Have your own customized brochure introducing and promoting your company or development as well as your benefits with photos and logo display. . . . . **Call**

Logo and Artwork
Nelson Design Group's graphics and marketing team will develop a professional logo or other art design for your company, development, etc. . . . . From **$150**

Dura-trans
Special backlit 'Dura-tran' color images ready for display. Available in a variety of custom sizes. . . . . **$125** to **$195**

Various Printing
Nelson Design Group can handle most every requirement, i.e. business cards, letterhead, envelopes, presentation folders, thank-you cards - and more. **Call**

Video Presentations
We can produce a video presentation for you to play on VHS videotape and/or CD. Ask for the Nelson Design video as an example!. . . . . **Call**

3-D Virtual Reality Tours
Nelson Design Group provides this cutting edge service enabling the consumer to view the homes interior through 3-D visualization. . . . . **Call**

Promotion, Ad Placement, Public Relations And More!
Nelson Design Group has experienced professionals to assist you in every phase of your marketing program. . . . . **Call**

For under $250 per home, you can have the 'look' of a
BIG BUILDER!

A customized 24" x 36" Yard Sign and 100 - 8.5" x 11" Feature Sheets with your Localized Information, Logo, etc. is only $239!

Builders & Developers Look!
See Who We Are - What We Do
What We Offer...
Call for our 6 minute introductory presentation available on VHS video tape or CD-ROM

See your 84 Lumber Sales Associate, or contact:

Nelson Design Group LLC
RESIDENTIAL PLANNERS - DESIGNERS

Call 1-800-590-2423
or e-mail us at
info@nelsondesigngroup.com
Also, see our website:
http://nelsondesigngroup.com

Nelson Design Group LLC

RESIDENTIAL PLANNERS - DESIGNERS

Collections including Narrow Lot, Duplexes & Cottage Cabin Designs

Create Your Own Development!

We offer collections, **Windstone Collection I, II & III, Cross Creek Collection, and Sage Meadows Collection, The Village at Wellington, Renaissance Collection** and **Urban Collection** for narrow lot configurations in Traditional Neighborhood, French Country and European Traditional styles. Our **Duplex Collection I** features over 40 designs that represent actual homes.
The **Waterfront Collection** and **River Bend Collection** of lake homes and cottage cabins are perfect for weekend or second residences.
The **Florida Collection** feature 12 designs for coastal living.
All of our collections are provided in presesentation folders with floor plans and renderings ideal for Clients, Bankers, City Planners, etc.

Individual Preview Portfolio..$20
Any 5 Portfolios................(A savings of $25)...............$75

Kitchen and Bath CD

Nelson Design Group is pleased to introduce a revolutionary concept in Kitchen and Bath design. Our *innovative* interactive CD interfaces with most 2-D architecture programs and allows you to view *hundreds* of kitchen and bath designs, specifically suited for your particular space specifications. At the click of a mouse, import kitchen and bath plans directly into your existing plan for a world of options in DXF format.

Designer Kitchen and Bath CD-ROM......................................$49.95

Tru-Cost Estimating Software

Tru-Cost was developed as a valuable tool for your construction business; the software is easy to learn, and adapts to a variety of estimating methods and techniques. Nelson Design Group offers estimates on all of our home plans, which can be e-mailed and imported directly into the Tru-Cost software for editing and tracking costs during construction. We intently listen to our customers and incorporate the features they desire. Please take the time to evaluate the Tru-Cost Estimating 30-day trial version. Your response is greatly appreciated and your comments are always welcome. All of our updates are free of charge and if you need personal assistance, please call us at 1-800-590-2423.

Tru-Cost Estimating Software..$595

See page 280 for special offer!

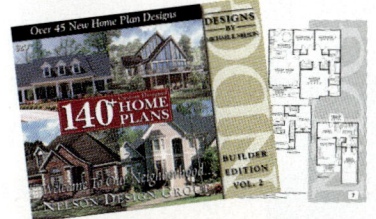

Home Plan Books

Nelson Design Group wants to ensure that our customers, whether consumers or builders, have the most current and helpful designs available. Hence, we have created a full color plan book complete with more than 135 renderings and floor plans. We also offer 2 black and white, 80-page books. Volume I features renderings and specs on more than 150 plans. Volume II includes over 140 home designs. Each book contains different floor plans.

"New Beginnings" Color Book..$15
Builder Edition - Volume I..$10
Builder Edition - Volume II...$10
All 3 Plan Books..$30

LiveSouth.com
The best source for choosing your place in the South

You'll find...
Top-rated Communities
Builder Information
in one convenient location...

LiveSouth.com

Order your complimentary subscription to Living Southern Style Magazine at LiveSouth.com